The History of Doing

The History of Doing

An Illustrated Account of Movements
for Women's Rights and Feminism in India 1800–1990

◆

RADHA KUMAR

V
VERSO
London · New York

First published by Kali for Women, New Delhi
and by Verso 1993
© Radha Kumar 1993
Photo research by Kali for Women
All rights reserved

Verso
UK: 6 Meard Street, London W1V 3HR
USA: 29 West 35th Street, New York, NY 10001–2291

Verso is the imprint of New Left Books

ISBN 0–86091–455–0
ISBN 0–86091–665–0 (pbk)

British Library Cataloguing in Publication Data
A catalogue record for this book is available from the British Library

Library of Congress Cataloging-in-Publication Data
A catalogue record for this book is available from the Library of Congress

Typesetting by IPP Catalog Publications Pvt. Ltd., New Delhi
Printed in India by Indraprastha Press (CBT), New Delhi

DEDICATION

This book is dedicated to the memory of Rana Sen, who exclaimed in tones of surprised gratification upon reading its very first draft 'good gracious, Radha, I believe you might produce a halfway decent book!'

My first meeting with Rana was one I never failed to remind him of, maliciously: I was invited, as a 'girlfriend', to a political discussion on the new phase of the Indian Workers' movement, in 1978. Rana was standing on a bed (which served as a podium), declaiming; when there came a lull, I asked 'but what part do women workers play in this new struggle, or are they undifferentiated?' Rana bowed, and said: 'There is always a place in our hearts for you.' I subsided.

Our friendship began then: he had already captured my imagination. As we grew to know each other better, I discovered a patriarch of an old and generous order; a man whose intellectual and emotional curiosity was such that what would begin as an often frivolous argument about feminism would be presented to me the next day as a feminist insight into human action. He helped me clarify my ideas; above all, by first rejecting and then absorbing my views, he gave me worth.

And so, to Rana, with a song in my heart.

ACKNOWLEDGEMENTS

My first thanks go to Kamaladevi Chattopadhyaya, who suggested to me, when I was working as her research assistant, that I might later use some of the data I collected for her to produce a book of my own, and who is sadly no longer alive to see the fruition of her suggestion. Thanks are also owed to the Centre for Informal Education and Developing Societies in Bangalore, who funded part of this research.

There are so many individuals who contributed to this book that I would like to apologise in advance to anyone I have inadvertently omitted, but special thanks are owed to Shiela Rowbotham, Edward and Dorothy Thompson, and Mary Kaldor for reading and commenting on drafts; to Madhu Sarin, for not only reading a part of the book, but cooking and keeping house while I wrote the introduction; to Shoba Sadagopan, who taught me how to look anew at many of my inherited ideologies; to Vibhuti Patel and Gail Omvedt, for sending me documents which I could not have otherwise laid hands upon; and to all the women in Stri Sangharsh, and Women and Politics, two groups which I not only love deeply, but owe great gratitude to for all I have learnt both politically and personally about feminism in India, and of course to my parents and grandparents for things too numerous to be named.

And last but not least, to use a popular Indian phrase, thanks to my publisher Urvashi Butalia, whose patience throughout this endeavour is legendary amongst those who know me well.

CONTENTS

1. Introduction

This book attempts a brief interpretative history of women's movements in India, from the beginning of the nineteenth century until the present day. Close on two hundred years of activity in a country the size of a continent cannot be adequately described in a volume of this kind, hence what is presented here is a selective survey of major campaigns, organizations and figures, concentrating on the terms in which issues were defined and fought for, the kinds of movements which developed, and the historical attitudes which they revealed.

One of the major problems of embarking on such a work has been the paucity of literature available as a source, and the unevenness of the sources which were traceable. For example, some information is available on notable women reformers in the late nineteenth century, or on nationalist leaders who were women, in the twentieth century. We find a number of biographies, autobiographies, memoirs, collections of speeches and writings throughout the first half of the twentieth century fairly readily—but these are largely about the lives and work of individual women. There is perhaps a bare handful of texts describing women's movements, and even here the bias is towards middle class and upper caste movements. Given that the late nineteenth and early twentieth centuries saw a growing and active feminist movement, it is somewhat surprising that debates about the nature, tactics and strategy of campaigns, which are an inevitable part of any movement, have not been detailed. Unfortunately, this book does not do much to fill in such lacunae, because of limitations of time and space, and because other debates were not fully recorded. Possibly, such issues did not assume the importance which they do now, and in fact when reading individual accounts one gets the feeling that the simple coming together of large numbers of women from different backgrounds, especially in the movement, was so exhilarating that it overshadowed other questions.

In contrast, the contemporary feminist movement in India has concentrated mainly on documenting women's movements, in particular those of landless labourers and the working class. Indeed, amongst large sections of the contemporary movement there is the feeling that singling out individual women not only leads to a biased and partial view of the movements they were or are engaged in, but also reaffirms hierarchical leadership structures and hides from history the majority which makes up any movement. Hence the reader will find a number of figures in the first part of this book, which deals with the pre-Independence period, and hardly any individual accounts, biographies, etc., in the second part, which deals with the contemporary period.

The division between pre and post-Independence feminisms in India is partly descriptive and partly convenient. The experience of colonial rule was one of the most important formative influences on the feminist movement of the early twentieth century, whereas an equivalent influence on contemporary feminism has been the experiment of democracy in post-Independence India. This does not mean that there is no continuity between pre and post-Independence women's movements: not only are our roots in the former, but distinctions between the two are made in the context of continuity.

The nineteenth century was a period in which the rights and wrongs of women became major issues: if early attempts at reforming the conditions under which Indian women lived were largely conducted by men, by the late nineteenth century their wives, sisters, daughters, protegees and others affected by campaigns, such as that for women's education, had themselves joined in movements. By the early twentieth century women's own autonomous organizations began to be formed, and within a couple of decades, by the thirties and forties, a special category of 'women's activism' was constructed. 'Equality between the sexes' was guaranteed by the Constitution of Independent India, and there was a comparative lull in feminist activities until the nineteen-seventies, when the Constitutional promise of equality was denounced as sham. A spate of new women's organizations was born and old ones revitalized by the nineteen-eighties. The special category of 'women's activism' was newly researched and expanded with a view to charting its specificities, as well as the 'logical' and organic links between feminism and Marxism, feminism and anti-communalism, feminism and anti-casteism, etc.

Throughout the period most campaigns for an amelioration of women's conditions were based on the liberal-democratic premise that it was both wrong and unfair that certain categories of human beings (defined by circumstances outside their control such as birth) should be treated as inferior to other categories. The relationship between this premise, however, and the matter of gender difference was always an ambiguous one. In the early years of movements for women's rights, for example, it was more or less taken for granted that the difference between the sexes was such that their roles, functions, aims and desires were different. And hence not only had they to be differently reared but differently treated in general. Over time this difference was itself adduced as a major reason for reforming women's conditions. While early nineteenth century reformers argued that women's difference from men was no reason for their subjection, later reformers argued that it was precisely this difference which made women socially useful (women as mothers), and hence proper care for their conditions of being was socially necessary. As women themselves joined campaigns, and also formed their own organizations, this point of difference, being as mother, was again stressed, but this time as an argument for women's rights, to speech, education and emancipation. The terms, however, in which this argument was advanced had changed: from earlier functionalist emphases on rationalizing the family to the creation of an archetypal mother figure, evoking deep, often atavistic, images through the use of metaphor and symbol.

The first half of the twentieth century saw a symbolic use of the mother as a rallying device, from feminist assertions of women's power as mothers of the nation, to terrorist invocations of the protective and ravening mother goddess, to the Gandhian lauding of the spirit of endurance and suffering embodied in the mother. Here too we can trace a shift. Where in the early twentieth century the feminist assertion of maternal power by such women as Madame Cama and Sarojini Naidu contained a darkling threat ('remember that the hand that rocks the cradle rules the world'), Gandhi's emphasis on the ennobling qualities of motherhood sought explicitly to curb or subdue the most fearsome aspects of femininity, which lie in erotic or tactile domains.

Because of his self-feminization and his feminization of politics, Gandhi was hailed as the parent of the 'Indian women's movement', and his depiction of women's innate qualities was eagerly received by many feminists as expanding and detailing many of their self-definitions. Despite this, his view of the relationship between the sexes was neither fully nor widely accepted by feminists: while to him the sexes were different and complementary, there was considerable ambivalence among the feminists on this question. When it came to the sphere of rights, for example, feminist demands for parity with men (in property rights, to suffrage and education), cut across the affirmation of gender-based

difference, for these said that in these spheres at any rate men and women were equal, or the same. To this extent pre-Independence feminists clung with one hand to gender-based definitions of themselves while reaching with the other for an existence based on equality and sameness rather than complementarity and difference.

In post-Independence India the contemporary feminist movement began by basing itself firmly on principles of equality and asserting that gender-based structures, such as the sexual division of labour, oppressed and subordinated women. The difference between men and women was held largely (and by implication 'merely') to be a biological one, which should not affect women's right to equality with men in both public and private spheres. The symbol of the mother was now only rarely used as a rallying or entitling device: instead, two self-images replaced it, the woman as daughter and the working woman. Both in a way turned attention away from the woman as mother or wife: the former focussed on the formation of a woman rather than her role; the latter looked at her productive rather than reproductive capacities. This marked a sharp turn from the pre-Independence movement, which was almost exclusively concerned with women in relation to men.

The use of a daughter symbol appears especially significant because it moved into a new kind of self-exploration, starting from childhood itself. In a series of exhibitions, plays and pamphlets, contemporary feminists have emphasized the pain and helplessness of being born a girl; the shock of puberty and the associated development of sexual fear; the terrible rejection of being 'sent away' at marriage; loneliness and loss of the self after marriage; and a repetition of the entire cycle of pain, fear and rejection through the birth of another daughter.

This cry of vulnerability and helplessness brought a new subjectivity into Indian feminism, expressing emotions which had not so far been expressed. At the same time, the focus on working women represented at one level a rejection of the wife-mother-power image, replacing it with the image of an economically independent woman, at another the development of class-consciousness accompanied by an interest in organizing and mobilizing women, and at a third a growing involvement of feminists with workplace politics. While pre-Independence feminists had largely accepted the sexual division of labour, in the nineteen-seventies feminists pointed out not only that it offered women unequal wages, relegated them to 'unskilled' spheres of work, and pushed them into the reserve army of labour, but also that it masked the whole area of domestic labour and reproduction of labour power, so that a kind of free service was offered to capital.

Feminist class-consciousness in the nineteen-seventies was accompanied by a heightened awareness of the innumerable inequalities in India, both between men and women and between women themselves, which stemmed from a series of different power structures, feeding into each other, based on caste, tribe, language, religion, region etc., as well as class. The complexity of such a situation confronted feminists with serious problems when it came to holistic overreaching campaigns for change. If 'equality for whom?' was an inevitable question which feminists now asked themselves, so was the allied question 'will demands for equality which are framed in the context of X structure of inequality inadvertently create new inequalities in Y structure?'

The concept of equality thus had to be widened to cover a whole range of inequalities in such a way that the space for feminine assertion which any one structure contained, would be preserved, while inequalities would be removed. At the same time, demands for equality with men grew slightly less important than before, as more and more demands for the right to control over one's own life began to be made. Economic independence began to be seen as at best a partial means to this end, which had to be complemented by a series of rights in other spheres, among which one of the most important was the woman's right to control over her own body. An interesting contrast here is between the late nineteenth to early twentieth century concern for women's bodies as sites of racial and national regeneration, and the late twentieth century feminist assertion that a woman's body must not be treated as the subject of social control. To put this in perspective, the terms in which this assertion was made were fairly modest: that the legal definition of crimes relating to the sexual invasion of women's bodies be widened to include family rape and the rape of prostitutes; and that the scientific invasion of women's bodies through experimental technologies to regulate biological reproduction—especially the use of poor women in the developing countries as guinea pigs for testing new contraceptive methods—be stopped.

So, from early nineteenth century definitions of the suffering of Indian women and the need for reform, by the early twentieth century the emphasis had shifted to stressing women's right to be treated as useful members of society, and by the late twentieth century to demanding that women should have the power to decide their own lives. Putting it another way, it can be argued that over the last one hundred and eighty years, the focus of campaigns for an improvement in women's lives has changed from needs to rights and within this from the restricted right to parity in selected areas to the larger right of self-determination.

What self-determination means has become the subject of increasingly wide debate in the Indian feminist movement. If equality with men in all legally conferred rights is an important part of it, implying that men and women should be regarded as the same, the issue of difference remains important in the feminist movement. The argument that feminist organizational structures and modes of functioning have to be different from conventional ones, for example, bases itself both on a critique of the latter as being hierarchical, power-based and male dominated, and on the premise that our forms of action must reflect the feminine values of gentleness and care. An affirmation of gender-based difference, moreover, has been more explicitly made in the nineteen-eighties, when a stream developed within the feminist movement, which celebrates femininity as being pagan, intuitive, anarchic, inventive and nurturing. As against early twentieth century definitions of masculinity and femininity being complementary, however, there is here a privileging of the feminine and a certain rejection of the masculine. (This has sometimes been construed as a rejection of the male sex).

In this book, therefore, a tension between the desire for equality which opposed sex-based differentiation, and the sex or gender-based celebrations of the feminine, is seen as characteristic of feminism in India (perhaps all over the world). At the same time, movements which do not appear to ostensibly display this tension have been included, for the following reasons: firstly, they have become the subject of study by contemporary feminists, and have become in a sense 'ours' under the rubric of women's activism, influencing campaigns, tactics and strategies. Secondly, they show how in practically all liberation movements in which women have been involved on a large-scale, anti-patriarchal issues inevitably surface (how they are dealt with is another matter). And thirdly, they counterpoint distinctions between the sex or gender-based attitudes of feminists and non-feminist supporters of women's rights.

Among the movements showing anti-patriarchal elements which have been covered here, a sub-division can be made between those which were women's movements, such as the communist-led food campaigns of the nineteen-forties, Chipko, the anti-alcohol and anti-price-rise movements of the nineteen-seventies; and those which were primarily dominated by men but in which large numbers of women were active, such as the nationalist, Tebhaga and Telangana movements. The former focussed on issues which are regarded mainly as 'women's concerns', because they were ancillary to the role of a housewife: water for the home, fuel for heating and cooking, food, money for food; while these issues did not always come up in the latter, problems of male-domination were generally brought up during their course just as they were in women's movements—especially important issues being alcoholism, wife-beating and male control over resources which were vital to the maintenance of the family. Moreover, in both, women learnt to confront capital and the state, to work together in groups or organizations, and to feel united as women.

While these movements challenged areas of male control or oppression, they did not demand parity or equality with men, nor did they struggle against sex-based definitions of the 'roles' of men and women, or the codification of biological difference in social practice. To this extent, they did not display the tension between sameness and difference we have defined as characteristic of feminism. In fact, most of them appeared to directly or indirectly affirm the principle of complementarity between the two distinct biologically defined areas of masculine and feminine, but opposed practices of privileging men over women. It is in this sense that they have been described as anti-patriarchal.

One of the most fascinating aspects of the movements described above is how many of them have used shame as a tactic to punish their opponents. Women in the food and anti-price rise campaigns offered bangles to male officials and politicians, to symbolize their emasculation; women in anti-alcohol, anti-wife beating and anti-dowry campaigns blackened the faces of male culprits to humiliate them before their communities (an example of the literal as symbolic, the blackened faces as face lost); women in the no-tax and no-rent campaigns during the nationalist movement camped outside, and on occasion inside, the houses of those who bought confiscated goods from the government to embarrass them into returning the goods; and in working-class agitations such as strikes, women were often put in the front ranks, so that blacklegs would feel that 'even women' had more courage than them.

While shame is one of the oldest means of punishment or humiliation, it is significant that it has surfaced as a major tactic in anti-patriarchal women's movements but not in feminist ones. One of the reasons for this might be that its tactical use is generally based on an acceptance of conventional definitions of masculinity and femininity, as described above. Another might be that the efficacy of such a method depends on its use within a reasonably well-knit community: if a man is to be shamed into acknowledging—and repenting—his transgression of the norms of his community, then such norms have to reflect values shared by both the punishers and the punished. Arguably, no such situation existed for feminists, as their values can only rarely have been shared by the targets of their attack. In which case, efforts to shame might well have failed: the nationalist tactic of shaming the police, by confronting them with women demonstrators, for example, worked only very briefly. To extend this argument a little further, as the power of shame is weakened by the development of a modern society, which allows anonymity and possibilities of escape from being known, and this itself means that it is no longer a particularly effective means of punishment or deterrence: not only are the police anonymous, the dowry-murderer, rapist and molester can all move to another area, literally taking themselves outside the purview of the punishment.

In this context, one of the first points to strike attention is the extent to which, over the last couple of centuries, legislation has been a dominant and continuing demand of movements against women's oppression. If this reflects a need to put state control in place of other modes of social regulation, it also shows how legislation has provided forms of escape and protection from existing social practices. The terrain of rights, for example, has been largely mapped through the law in the modern world. Yet doubts and fears about the nature of legislation and the role of the state have formed a kind of constant undercurrent to movements for women's rights, even while they have demanded this or that legislation. Without refining too much on the fact that this book begins and ends with campaigns for the outlawing of *sati*, parallels between the ways in which these problems have appeared in the two campaigns, one in the early nineteenth century and the other in the late twentieth century, are sufficiently close to be startling. Both Ram Mohan Roy and contemporary feminists voiced the unhappy feeling that they were being thrown back on demands for legislation at a time when violence against women, and the legitimization of such violence, were mounting. Similarly, both expressed fears that legislation was not only inadequate as a solution, but might actually lead to a conservative backlash. The orthodox response to both Ram Mohan Roy and contemporary feminists, in fact, was that neither represented the 'true' desires of Indian women or Indian society, being de-racinated westernists.

Parallels between methods used by pre and post-Independence activists can also be found, especially in dealing with problems arising out of the working of laws in practice. One such is the question of judicial interpretation. Discovering, for example, that the 1856 law allowing widow remarriage which he had campaigned for was open to misuse, Ishwar Chandra Vidyasagar turned to attempting its amendment. Similarly, discovering that the anti-rape law they had fought for in 1980 contained a regulation 'safety clause' which the Supreme Court used in 1990 to undermine the entire logic of the changes effected by their campaign, contemporary feminists have turned to demanding an amendment of the clause. In both cases the problem was one of judicial interpretation, and the solution sought was through legislatively restricting the scope for interpretation.

Several of the dangers of such a course have been pointed out by feminists in the nineteen-seventies and eighties, who have asked whether the state should be encouraged to practise its powers to curb judicial options in this way; and whether safety clauses which are not intended to provide for exceptions to the norm should be curtailed. Both these points have been especially stressed by Marxist-Leninists, whose experience in civil liberties and democratic rights movements has engendered close attention to the law. A third point, which is somewhat cynically acknowledged by contemporary feminists, but which has not perhaps been explicitly stated (insofar as it has not led to a change of course), is that experience has shown that the ingenuity of the judiciary in finding ways to exercise their freedom to interpret the law is rarely matched by any anticipatory checks in statute (take, for example, the unexpected aftermath of the Muslim Women's Bill, where legislation curbing the rights of Muslim women to maintenance resulted in a spate of judgements giving them higher awards of maintenance than before).

Literature of the period appears to indicate that these points have been raised mainly by the contemporary feminist movement, implying that they were not of such importance in the pre-Independence period. If this was natural enough for Vidyasagar's time when the law and its paraphernalia were in the process of codification and formation, a different set of reasons has to be found for the early twentieth century feminists. One reason might be that the main thrust of their energies was in the battle for state control through the ouster of the British; another could be that the ills of state-formation in colonial India were attributed largely to foreign rule, and it was assumed that these would disappear with Independence, rather than remain endemic.

Turning now to the issue of state implementation of the law, many of the experiences and responses were again similar in pre and post-Independence India. Laws were passed but not implemented, for a variety of reasons (ranging from fear of wounding religious sentiments to the simple fact of the culprit being in the category which is 'above the law'). This gave rise to outraged protest from reformers and feminists, but by and large did not result in the construction of mechanisms to ensure better implementation. As in the issue of judicial interpretation of the law, concern over implementation has consisted of much greater attention to detail in post-Independence India than was shown before Independence. Interestingly, this has taken the form of campaigning for reform in existing bodies for implementation (more women in the police force, separate cells for crimes against women, etc.), as well as in existing structures (that feminist groups be given some sort of locus to work with the police, to monitor and even replace them when they refuse to act).

Broadly speaking then, campaigns for legislation on women's rights have reflected common problems and concerns over the entire period, which are perhaps inherent in the development of this country, where attempts at homogeneity have often been made in the absence of a social consensus between the many heterogeneous groups which live here. This has been the source of one of the deepest sorrows of activists throughout: indeed, most discussions of legislation have explicitly acknowledged the terrible dilemmas of fighting for legal reforms which may never be embedded in social practice. At one extreme this has entailed the feeling that the law is the last and hopeless resort of the weak; at another the seemingly contradictory sense that the domain of legislative reform is open mainly to those with some power in the modern nation-state, upper-middle class urbanites.

Taking an overview of the preoccupation with law which has been described above, it can be said to show a trajectory of development, from a primary focus on codification in the early to mid-nineteenth century to a concern for implementation as well as codification by the early twentieth century, and an awareness of both the incipient dangers of many kinds of codification as well as the need for reformed state and voluntary mechanisms for implementation. From this it appears that over time the ramifications of administering society have become both clearer and more important in movements for women's rights.

One example of this is the way a debate over representation has developed. While the issue was rarely referred to until the early twentieth century, by the nineteen-twenties a feminist argument for representation went roughly as follows: granting that women's primary role might be as mothers, motherhood was socially useful, and by virtue of this women should be involved in structuring and organizing society; such an involvement would entail women's representation not only in Parliament but also in general movements and organizations—particularly in the nationalist struggle. If by the late twentieth century the state has appropriated the task of managing women's involvement in social administration to a certain extent, through, for example, identifying 'the household as a unit of society', contemporary feminist debates over representation mark a sharp diversion from pre-Independence ones. Not only is the issue more important now than literature shows it to have been then, there is today a deep ambivalence over whether the belief that there is an enormous common area of experience between women as a sex is to be given greater weight than the conviction that women do not form an undifferentiated category due to class, caste, and other distinctions, or vice versa. In terms of representation, this has meant the simultaneous acceptance of 'women's representation' in Parliament or lesser administrative bodies, and reiteration that bourgeois women cannot represent proletarian women, uppercaste women cannot represent dalit women, and so on.

It is a bleak irony for contemporary feminists that queries and self-doubts raised about representation should have come back to roost in recent times. The 'orthodox' response to—or attack upon—feminism in the last few years has been to marginalize them by affirming their lack of representativeness, in terms which seem to turn the cycle as far as Ram Mohan Roy. Interestingly, his period has been analysed as one of crisis engendered by the encounter with British coloni-alism. Could it be that the present reaction also represents a kind of crisis, perhaps within a society which is witnessing the spread of democratisation while remaining reft by inequalities?

2. The Nineteenth Century

An early (probably twentieth century) drawing of a sati. Artist unknown.

The nineteenth century could well be called an age of women, for all over the world their rights and wrongs, their 'nature', capacities and potential were the subjects of heated discussion. In Europe feminist consciousness began spreading during and after the French Revolution, and by the end of the century feminist ideas were being expressed by radicals in England, France and Germany. By the mid-nineteenth century the 'woman question' had become a central issue for Russian reformers and anarchists; while in India the wrongs of women began to be deplored by social reformers mainly in Bengal and Maharashtra. British relations with these two states had begun much earlier than in other parts of India; Bengal, in particular, had known the British through the East India Company from the early

eighteenth century. What began as a trading relationship expanded into domination and rule, and the intimacy this engendered between the British and the Indians brought their differences into sharp focus.

It is generally agreed that the Indian social reform movement of the nineteenth century grew out of this encounter. In the colonial economy with its new agrarian and industrial relations accompanied by a vast and expanding administrative structure, existing dominant groups (gentry, traders, scribes, rentiers, tax collectors, etc.) began to be forged into a middle-class, or bourgeoisie. As an Indian bourgeois society developed under Western domination, this class sought to reform itself, initiating campaigns against caste, polytheism, idolatry, animism, purdah, child-marriage, sati and more, seeing them as elements of a 'pre-modern' or primitive identity. Being part of a process of self-definition, the majority of these campaigns focussed on issues which were significant largely for the three upper-castes who constituted the bourgeoisie. Underlying these campaigns were redefinitions of the spheres of the public and private, the world and the home,[1] the male and female. As such, the social reform movement can be characterized as playing an important part in the formation of a new set of patriarchal gender-based relations, essential in the constitution of bourgeois society.

Recent research has added several important qualifications to this view. First of all, it has been pointed out that not all issues of social reform were engendered by the British encounter alone, though they were restructured by it. The eighteenth century was a period of flux for India, a time when the old order of the Mughal Empire and the independent princely states was crumbling, leaving spaces for new movements to develop. For example, the anti-caste movement which developed in nineteenth century Maharashtra had a long history of precedents, and grew partly out of the crumbling of Brahmanic hegemony with the disintegration of Peshwa rule around the turn of century, even though the Brahmans later re-formed as a dominant group under the British.[2] Similarly, the noted reformer, Ram Mohan Roy, was influenced by eighteenth century Sufi arguments for religious reform as much as by English rationalism.[3]

Secondly, it has been argued that much of what can be said of the social reform movement can be said of other, often opposing, movements of the period, such as revivalism and nationalism. Ashis Nandy, for example, has described how the revivalist and nationalist construction of an anti-imperialist hero reflected an internalization of colonial definitions of the ideal man, choosing for him the 'manly' qualities lauded by the Victorians rather than those which local traditions held in awe, because the latter were scorned as effeminate by the British.[4] The same can be said of definitions of the 'womanly woman', as Uma Chakravarti shows in her description of the ideal 'Aryan' woman, who was defined by reformers, revivalists and nationalists alike, using a mixture of Anglicism and Orientalism.[5]

Following from this, much of what has been said of revivalism and nationalism can also be said of social reform; for example, the revivalist nationalist search for a glorious, pre-colonial, caste-based 'tradition' was a project which reformers had also entered into, as Arundhati Mukhopadhyaya has shown.[6] In addition, the revivalist demonology of Islam and the Moslem 'invader' was one shared by reformers, who described Mughal rule as the period in which Hinduism 'declined' and was 'corrupted' citing the Hindu woman as a prime example of community degradation.

Yet if reformers, revivalists and nationalists all shared, and aided in creating a dominant discourse, they were also in conflict with each other, and with themselves. There was a rhetoric of equality within reform which the revivalists did not share. And the two defined themselves in opposition to each other.

The social reform movement, with which we open the period discussed here, cannot itself be described as a uniform one, for different campaigns and issues were taken up at different times in different regions. As has been said earlier, campaigns for reform first appeared in Bengal, where a shaken *bhadralok* aristocracy were being recast into a bourgeoisie which they had to share with members of their own community who had lost caste by entering forbidden professions, as well as with other upwardly mobile castes. Changes in land relations (the Permanent Settlement), which had been instituted by the British partly to secure the co-operation of the native elite by giving zamindars permanent proprietory rights, introduced a contractual system which undermined their traditional grounds for social dominance, inducing anomie. (As well, the settlement pauperized considerable sections of the peasantry, pushing them into landless labour). At the same time, the spread of British education, which was part of the policy of building a class which would be loyal to their new rulers, introduced the native elite to ideas which were creating ferment in Britain, especially rationalism, evolutionism, and utilitarianism. Calcutta became an exciting intellectual centre, and most of the early reform campaigns were launched here by an eagerly developing intelligentsia. Prominent among them were radical students, many taught by H. Derozio, a young Anglo-Indian who was fired by the concepts of liberty and equality in the French Revolution. Dubbed the Young Bengal Movement, these groups concentrated mainly on defying caste bans with such gestures as eating meat and drinking wine, and attempting to reform women. Arguing that the latter campaigns were fuelled by a crisis in the mother-worshipping culture of Bengal, Ashis Nandy has pointed out the connected issues of orality and mothering which underlay the two kinds of campaigns.[7]

Interestingly, of the various issues and campaigns concerning women which arose in the early nineteenth century, two of the earliest were initiated by the same people, but showed different trajectories of development. As far as we know, the importance of educating women was first discussed publicly in Bengal by the Atmiya Sabha, founded by Ram Mohan Roy in 1815; in the same year he wrote the first text attacking sati to be published in an Indian language (Bengali). Yet the campaign for the abolition of sati garnered mainly British support, and was short-lived, while the women's education movement was 'Indianized' over the course of the century.

Though Roy was one of the first Indians to campaign against sati U.S. and British missionaries had, from the turn of the eighteenth century, cited it as an example of Hindu barbarism, while British administrators had used it as a reason for ruling India (the civilizing mission). For some years, however, British Parliament refused to legislate against sati, on the grounds that this would constitute interference in the religious affairs of the Hindus. The tension between this position and their self-defined role as the bringers of enlightenment to India, led them to seek a series of compromise solutions in the early years of the nineteenth century, when they passed laws distinguishing between enforced and voluntary sati, much as the Mughals had done several centuries earlier. This distinction outraged many of the campaigners against sati, who felt, according to Edward Thompson, that it legitimized the act by saying that particular forms of it were legally acceptable.[8] The issue became a battle ground for English politicians, with the Tories supporting non-interference, and the Liberals campaigning for legislative action. The Liberals themselves were divided into Radicals and Evangelists: the latter were especially active in the construction of an image of the cruel and superstitious native who needed Christian salvation. The entry of Hindu social reformers into the campaign provided the Liberals with the one kind of support they had entirely lacked, that of members of the community which practised sati.

In 1817, Mrityunjaya Vidyalamkara, the Chief Pundit of the Supreme Court, announced that sati had no *shastric* sanction, and one year later, in 1818, the provincial governor of Bengal, William Bentinck, prohibited sati in his province. It took another eleven years for this prohibition to be extended to other parts of India, and the Sati Abolition Act was passed in 1829, when Bentinck had become Governor-General of India.[9] Its enactment was accompanied by fear of an upsurge of protest from the orthodoxy; Roy himself expressed doubts as to the wisdom of legislating against sati, especially by foreign rulers, fearing that a defensive reaction among the Hindus might well be engendered, which would exacerbate the problem. However, though there was some protest from the Hindu orthodoxy, it was considerably less than had been fearfully anticipated. A petition was got up and sent to the Governor-General and British Parliament; and, in 1830, orthodox Hindus in Calcutta formed the Dharma Sabha, to campaign against the abolition of sati.[10] (Partly as a result of their protests, an amendment was made in the Indian Penal Code some ten years later, which again distinguished between 'voluntary' and forcible sati, permitting the former).[11] The only areas where violence ensued over the issue were certain of the independent princely states, where the zeal of their British Residents led them to disregard the limits of their position and use British troops to forcibly stop incidents of sati.[12] Violence here was largely against the Residents' usurping of the powers of the prince.

Recent historical research suggests that the nineteenth century sati abolition movement might have created the myth of an existing practice where none existed. Not only was sati neither common nor widespread, it could never be either continuously, for its truth lay in being heroic or exceptional. The only example we appear to have of a widespread incidence of sati is in the early decades of the nineteenth century in Bengal, where there seemed to have been more than one incident of sati a day, even after Bentinck had outlawed it in that province. Some doubt has been cast on these figures, the bulk of which were collected at the height of the sati abolition movement, and in a province ruled by the chief British opponent of sati, William Bentinck. They do not specify, for example, what kinds of distinctions were made between suicide by widows and sati, and it is possible that a combination of ignorance and the desire to prove the gravity of sati as a problem might have led administrators to transpose from the former category into the latter. Anand Yang has shown, moreover, that a considerable proportion of the satis recorded for early nineteenth century Bengal were of women who killed themselves years after their husbands had died.[13] This could have been because their lives had become intolerable rather than because the *sat* had entered them.

In other words, the incidence of sati in early nineteenth century Bengal testified not so much to the widespread existence of a practice, as to its recreation by a community in crisis. Several points can be adduced in support of this view, not least of which is that the practice at this point was espoused largely by the urban nouveau riches, and was overwhelmingly found in and around Calcutta, which was probably of all Indian cities the one most intimate with the West. It appears, moreover, that there were some among the British themselves who suspected that the Bengali 'epidemic' of sati (to use Ashis Nandy's phrase) was an assertive-defensive reaction to colonial rule: no less a person than Warren Hastings said that it was largely due to the 'fanatic spirit roused by the divided state of feeling among the Hindus'.[14]

A further reason for the popularity of sati in early nineteenth century Bengal was adduced by campaigners for the abolition of the practice, who felt that it was at least partly due to the fact that Bengal was dominated by the *dayabhaga* form of inheritance, under which widows could inherit their husbands' property if the latter died without having a son, even if the family was undivided. At a time when Bengal was devastated by recurrent famines and epidemics, such a reason might have become important to groups which were also suffering from a breakdown of modes of caste authority.[15]

164. Sati: Regulation XVII, A.D. 1829 of the Bengal code (4 December 1929)

A regulation for declaring the practice of suttee, or of burning or burying alive the widows of Hindus, illegal, and punishable by the criminal courts. Passed by the governor-general in council on the 4th December 1829, corresponding with the 20th Aughun 1936 Bengal era; the 23rd Aughun 1237 Fasli; the 21st Aughun 1237 Vilayati; the 8th Aughun 1886 Samvat; and the 6th Jamadi-us-Sani 1245 Hegira.

1. The practice of suttee, or of burning or burying alive the widows of Hindus, is revolting to the feelings of human nature; it is nowhere enjoined by the religion of the Hindus as an imperative duty; on the contrary a life of purity and retirement on the part of the widow is more especially and preferably inculcated, and by a vast majority of that people throughout India the practice is not kept up, nor observed: in some extensive districts it does not exist; in those in which it has been most frequent it is notorious that in many instances acts of atrocity have been perpetrated which have been shocking to the Hindus themselves, and in their eyes unlawful and wicked. The measures hitherto adopted to discourage and prevent such acts have failed of success, and the governor-general in council is deeply impressed with the conviction that the abuses in question cannot be effectually put an end to without abolishing the practice altogether. Actuated by these considerations governor-general in council, without intending to depart from one of the first and most important principles of the system of British government in India, that all classes of the people be secure in the observance of their religious usages, so long as that system can be adhered to without violation of the paramount dictates of justice and humanity, has deemed it right to establish the following rules, which are hereby enacted to be in force from the time of their promulgation throughout the territories immediately subject to the presidency of Fort William.

2. The practice of suttee, or of burning or burying alive the widows of Hindus, is hereby declared illegal, and punishable by the criminal courts.

3. First. All zamindars, taluqdars, or other proprietors of land, whether malguzari or lakhiraj; all sadar farmers and under-renters of land of every description; all dependent taluqdars; all naibs and other local agents; all native officers employed in the collection of the revenue and rents of land on the part of government, or the court of wards; and all munduls or other head men of villages are hereby declared

especially accountable for the immediate communication to the officers of the nearest police station of any intended sacrifice of the nature described in the foregoing section; and any zamindar, or other description of persons above noticed, to whom such responsibility is declared to attach, who may be convicted of wilfully neglecting or delaying to furnish the information above required, shall be liable to be fined by the magistrate or joint magistrate in any sum not exceeding two hundred rupees, and in default of payment to be confined for any period of imprisonment not exceeding — months.

Secondly. Immediately on receiving intelligence that the sacrifice declared illegal by this regulation is likely to occur, the police darogha shall either repair in person to the spot, or depute his mohurrir or jamadar, accompanied by one or more burkundazes of the Hindu religion, and it shall be the duty of the police-officers to announce to the persons assembled for the performance of the ceremony, that it is illegal; and to endeavour to prevail on them to disperse, explaining to them that in the event of their persisting in it they will involve themselves in a crime, and become subject to punishment by the criminal courts. Should the parties assembled proceed in defiance of these remonstrances to carry the ceremony into effect, it shall be the duty of the police-officers to use all lawful means in their power to prevent the sacrifice from taking place, and to apprehend the principal persons aiding and abetting in the performance of it, and in the event of the police-officers being unable to apprehend them, they shall endeavour to ascertain their names and places of abode, and shall immediately communicate the whole of the particulars to the magistrate or joint magistrate for his orders.

Thirdly. Should intelligence of a sacrifice have been carried into effect before their arrival at the spot, they will nevertheless institute a full enquiry into the circumstances of the case, in like manner as on all other occasions of unnatural death, and report them for the information and orders of the magistrate or joint magistrate, to whom they may be subordinate.

4. First. On the receipt of the reports required to be made by the police daroghas, under the provisions of the foregoing section, the magistrate or joint magistrate of the jurisdiction in which the sacrifice may have taken place, shall enquire into the circumstances of the case, and shall adopt the necessary measures for bringing the parties concerned in promoting it to trial before the court of circuit.

Secondly. It is hereby declared, that after the promulgation of this regulation all persons convicted of aiding and abetting in the sacrifice of a Hindu widow, by burning or burying her alive, whether the sacrifice be voluntary on her part or not, shall be deemed guilty of culpable homicide, and shall be liable to punishment by fine or by both fine and imprisonment, at the discretion of the court of circuit, according to the nature and circumstances of the case, and the degree of guilt established against the offender; nor shall it be held to be any plea of justification that he or she was desired by the party sacrificed to assist in putting her to death.

Thirdly. Persons committed to take their trial before the court of circuit for the offence above mentioned shall be admitted to bail or not, at the discretion of the magistrate or joint magistrate, subject to the general rules in force in regard to the admission of bail.

5. It is further deemed necessary to declare, that nothing contained in this regulation shall be construed to preclude the court of nizamat adalat from passing sentence of death on persons convicted of using violence or compulsion, or of having assisted in burning or burying alive a Hindu widow while labouring under a state of intoxication, or stupefaction, or other cause impeding the exercise of free will, when, from the aggravated nature of the offence, proved against the prisoner, the court may see no circumstances to render him or her a proper object of mercy.

165. Bengal government to the court of directors on sati (4 December 1829)

6. Your honourable court will be gratified by perceiving the great preponderance of opinions of the most intelligent and experienced of the civil and military officers consulted by the governor-general, in favour of the abolition of suttees, and of the perfect safety with which in their judgment the practice may be suppressed.

7. A few indeed were of opinion that it would be preferable to effect the abolition by the indirect interference of the magistrates and other public offices with the tacit sanction alone on the part of government, but we think there are very strong grounds against the policy of that mode of proceeding, independently of the embarassing situation in which it would place the local officers, by allowing them to exercise a discretion in so delicate a matter. To use the words of the governor-general, we were 'decidedly in favour of an open avowed and general prohibition, resting altogether upon the moral goodness of the act, and our power to enforce it.'

8. Your honourable court will observe that the original draft of the regulation was considerably modified before its final enactment, and that it was deemed advisable, at the suggestion of the judges of the nizamat adalat, to omit the distinction originally made between misdemeanour and culpable homicide, in being accessory to a suttee, and also in the degree of interference to be exercised by the police-officers. Upon the fullest consideration of the objections taken by the court, we determined that it would be better to leave the apportionment of punishment to be regulated by the commissioners of circuit, according to the nature and circumstances of each case, and that separate special instructions should be issued to the police-officers, as well as to the European authorities, to ensure a moderate and lenient exercise of the powers vested in them respectively by the regulation.

9. Finally, also, we were induced by the advice of the nizamat adalat to leave out a provision that the Mahomedan law-officers should not take any part in trials in cases of suttee. We were disposed to think that the attendance of the law-officers might be liable to misconstruction, and afford an opening to objections which it was desirable as much as possible to avoid; at the same time the opinion of the court against excepting the offence in question from the ordinary course of trial, was doubtless entitled to much weight, and upon the whole we were willing to be guided by their judgement in omitting the section altogether.

10. We beg to refer your honourable court to the enclosures contained in the letter from the registrar of the nizamat adalat under date the 3d instant (No. 21), for the special instructions above noticed, which have been issued to the commissioners of circuit, the magistrate, and the police-officers for their guidance.

11. In conclusion we venture to express a confident expectation that under the blessing of divine providence the important measure which we have deemed it our duty to adopt will be efficacious in putting down the abhorrent practice of suttee, a consummation, we feel persuaded, not less anxiously desired by your honourable court than by every preceding government of India, although the state of the country was less favourable in former times than at present, for its full and complete execution. It would be too much to expect that the promulgation of the abolition will not excite some degree of clamour and dissatisfaction, but we are firmly persuaded that such feelings will be short-lived, and we trust that no apprehension need be entertained of its exciting any violent opposition or any evil consequences whatever.

The petition of the Hindus against the abolition of sati (19 December 1829)

We the undersigned beg leave respectfully to submit the following petition to your Lordship in council in consequence of having heard that certain persons taking upon themselves to represent the opinions and feelings of the Hindu inhabitants of Calcutta have misrepresented those opinions and feelings and that your Lordship in council is about to pass a resolution founded on such erroneous statements to put a stop to the practice of performing suttees, an interference with the religion and customs of the Hindus which we most earnestly deprecate and cannot view without the most serious alarm.

With the most profound respect for your Lordship in council we the undersigned Hindu inhabitants of the city of Calcutta beg leave to approach you in order to state such circumstances as appear to us necessary to draw the attention of government fully to the measure in contemplation and the light in which it will be regarded by the greater part of the more respectable Hindu population of the Company's territories who are earnest in the belief as well as in the profession of their religion.

From time immemorial the Hindu religion has been established and in proportion to its antiquity has been its influence over the minds of its followers. In no religion has apostasy been more rare and none has resisted more successfully the fierce spirit of proselytism which animated the first Mahomedan conquerors.

That the Hindu religion is founded like all religions on usage as well as precept and one when immemorial is held equally sacred with the other. Under the sanction of immemorial usage as well as precept Hindu widows perform of their own accord and pleasure and for the benefit of their husbands' souls and for their own the sacrifice of self immolation called suttee—which is not merely a sacred duty but a high privilege to her who sincerely believes in the doctrine of her religion—and we humbly submit that any interference with a persuasion of so high and self annihilating a nature is not only an unjust and intolerant dictation in matters of conscience but is likely wholly to fail in procuring the end proposed.

Even under the first Mussalman conquerors of Hindustan and certainly since this country came under the Mogul government, notwithstanding the fanaticism and intolerance of their religion no interference with the practice of suttee was ever attempted. Since that period and for nearly a century the power of the British government has been established in Bengal Bihar and Orissa and none of the governors-general or their councils have hitherto interfered in any manner to the prejudice of the Hindu religion or customs and we submit that by various acts of the parliament of Great Britain under the authority of which the honourable Company itself exists, our religion and laws, usages and customs such as they have existed from time immemorial are inviolably secured to us.

We learned with surprise and grief that while this is confessed on all hands the abolition of the practice of suttee is attempted to be defended on the ground that there is no positive law or precept enjoining it. A doctrine derived from a number of Hindus who have apostatized from the religion of their fore-fathers who have defiled themselves by eating and drinking forbidden things in the society of Europeans and are endeavouring to deceive your Lordship in council by assertions that there is no law regarding suttee practices and that all Hindus of intelligence and education are ready to assent to the abolition (of them) on the ground that the practice of suttee is not authorized by the laws fundamentally established and acknowledged by all Hindus as sacred. But we humbly submit, (on) a question so delicate as the interpretation of our sacred books and the authority of our religious usages none but pandits and brahmins and teachers of holy lives and known learning and authority ought to be consulted and we are satisfied and flatter ourselves with the hope that your Lordship in council will not regard the assertion of men who have neither any faith nor care for the memory of their ancestors or their religion: and that if your Lordship in council will assume to yourself the difficult and delicate task of regulating the conscience of a whole people and deciding what it ought to believe and what it ought to reject on the authority of its own sacred writers that such a task will be undertaken only after anxious and strict enquiry and patient consultation with men known and reverenced for their attachment to the Hindu religion, the authority of their lives and their knowledge of the sacred books which contain its doctrines. And if such a satisfactory examination should be made we are confident that your Lordship in council will find our statements to be correct and will learn that the measure will be regarded with horror and dismay throughout the Company's dominions as the signal of an universal attack upon all we revere.

We further beg leave to represent that the enquiry in question has been already made by some of the most learned and virtuous of the Company's servants whose memory is still reverenced by the nations who were under their rule and that Mr.Warren Hastings late governor-general at the request of Mr.Nathaniel Smith the then chairman of the court of directors (the former being well versed in many parts of the Hindu religion) having instituted the enquiry was satisfied as to the validity of the laws respecting suttees—that a further and similar enquiry was made by Mr. Wilkins who was deputed to and accordingly did proceed to Benares and remain there a considerable time in order to be acquainted with the religion and customs in question, that his opinion was similar to that of Mr.Warren Hastings and that this opinion was since confirmed by Mr.Jonathan Duncan whose zealous and excellent administration in Benares and other parts of Hindustan will long be remembered by the nations with gratitude.

In the time of Lord Cornwallis some of the Christian missionaries who then first appeared in this country secretly conveyed to the council some false and exaggerated accounts of the suttee practice and first advanced the assertion that it was not lawful. His Lordship in council after enquiry and by the assistance of Mr.Duncan was satisfied of its lawfulness and was contented to permit us to follow our customs as before.

In the time of Lord Moira and Amherst a number of European missionaries who came out to convert Hindus and others renewed their attack upon this custom and by clamour and falsely affirming that by compulsive measures Hindu women were thrown into the fire procured the notice of government and an order was issued requiring magistrates to take steps that suttees might perform their sacrifice at their pleasure and that no one should be allowed to persuade or use any compulsion. On the concurrent reports of various gentlemen then cognizant the widows went to the funeral pyres of their deceased husbands cheerfully, these governors-general were satisfied and no farther interference was attempted.

The ratified measure last adverted to did not answer the object proposed and it proved (as we humbly submit) the unpolicy of interference in any degree with matters of conscience.

The fact was that the number of suttees in Bengal considerably increased in consequence within a short time—and in order to ascertain the cause a reference was made to the sadar diwani adalat who could assign no satisfactory cause to account for it. Though it might perhaps have occurred to gentlemen of so much experience that the interference of government even to this extent with the practice was likely by drawing to it the attention of the native community in a greater degree than formerly to increase the number of votaries.

From a celebrated instance relating to suttees that we immediately hereafter beg leave to cite your Lordship in council will find that on the occasion alluded to no other good was obtained by an attempt to prevent the widow burning with her deceased husband than that religion was violated and to no purpose a suttee. In the time of Lord Clive his diwanraja, Nobkissen endeavoured to prevent a widow performing the sacrifice by making her believe that her husband had been already burnt and when she discovered that she had been deceived offering her any sum of money that might be required for her support as a recompense but nothing would satisfy her and she starved herself to death. His Lordship then gave orders that no one should be allowed to interfere with the Hindu religion or customs.

Independent of the foregoing statement your Lordship in council will see that your predecessors after long residences in India having a complete knowledge of the laws and customs of Hindus were satisfied as to such laws and never came to a resolution by which devout and conscientious Hindus must be placed in the most painful of all predicaments and either forego in some degree their loyalty to government and disobey its injunctions or violate the precepts of their religion.

Before we conclude we beg to request your impartial consideration of the various acts of parliament passed from time to time since the reign of his Majesty George the Third and which have ever since been strictly preserved. The substance and spirit of which may be thus summed up viz: that no one is to interfere in any shape in the religion or the customs of Hindu subjects. These acts conceived in the spirit of trust wisdom and toleration were passed by men as well acquainted at least as any now in existence with our laws. Our language our customs and our religion have never been infringed by the wisest of those who have here administered the powers of government and we trust will be preserved for the future as for the past inviolate as they are a most solemn pledge and charter from our rulers to ourselves, on the preservation of which depend rights more sacred in our eyes than those of property or life itself—and sure we are that when this most important subject has been well and maturely weighed by your Lordship in council the resolution will be abandoned and that we shall obtain a permanent security through your Lordship's wisdom against the renewal of similar attempts.

Further, changes in the property form due to the Permanent Settlement, and accompanying laws which were intended to develop a land-owning class similar to that in England, might also have undermined the claims of widows. The British themselves did not permit widows to succeed to their husbands' ancestral property; even the struggle for married women's property rights began in England in the mid-nineteenth century, and was won only after some twenty years.

Interestingly, Bentinck used the strategy of marshalling *shastric* texts to show that sati was not a required, or religiously sanctioned practice. The same strategy had been used by Ram Mohan Roy, in his *A Conference Between an Advocate for and an Opponent to the Practice of Burning Widows Alive.* This work was written in 1815, allegedly after Roy saw his sister-in-law forced onto his brother's funeral pyre, but translated into English only three years later, in 1818. In it Roy set out to prove that none of the ancient Hindu prescriptive texts laid down that a widow must commit sati; in effect, its incidence testified to the degeneration of the Hindu ethos. In response, a hundred and twenty-eight pundits published a 'manifesto' asserting that Roy's arguments were incorrect, and that he could not be said to be representative of Hindu opinion. In his reply to this manifesto, Roy again marshalled textual evidence, dwelling particularly on the *shastras*, to show that, according to them, sati was not obligatory, and was in fact the 'least virtuous act' a widow could perform, which had meaning only if it was voluntary.[16]

This view of the *shastras* as being analogous to the Bible or Koran in laying down ethical laws for the faithful was not common amongst Hindus, whose religious practices and beliefs were not contained in either one text or a set of texts alone. Yet it permeated British attitudes towards Hinduism, and they relied largely upon *shastric* texts in their later codification of Hindu personal law.

Significantly, Roy did not question the premise that suicide could be noble, as did the British supporters of the sati abolition movement. For Christians suicide was sinful and criminal; for Hindus several kinds of suicide could be holy. The orthodox Hindu argument was that sati allowed women, who were 'devoid of virtuous knowledge', to acquire such knowledge and gift it to their families; against this Roy argued that women clearly possessed virtuous knowledge, for their lives showed that they were 'infinitely more self-sacrificing than men'.[17] In stressing that heroism was part of women's daily lives, Roy attempted to deal with the heroic by transforming it from being exceptional to being everyday: if, to some extent, this de-heroized the heroic by rendering it commonplace, it also burdened Indian (Hindu) women by defining them as essentially and continuously self-sacrificing. In movements to follow this point became a kind of refrain in arguments on the nature and rights of

women in India; self-sacrifice was frequently cited as a quality distinguishing Indian women from 'Western' ones. This distinction was at least as important in the West as in India itself: If sati was cited as exemplifying the primitive barbarism of the Orient, it was also cited as exemplifying the wifely devotion and spiritual strength (including physical courage) of the Oriental woman.[18]

If the sati abolition movement provided one of the 'reasons' advanced in favour of reforming women's conditions, the women's education movement was to provide another.

The first schools for girls were started by English and American missionaries in the 1810s;[19] in 1819 the first text on women's education in an Indian language (Bengali) by an Indian, Gourmohan Vidyalamkara, was published by the Female Juvenile Society in Calcutta.[20] By 1827 there were twelve girls' schools run by missionaries in Hooghly district; one year later, the Ladies' Society for Native Female Education in Calcutta and its Vicinity opened schools which were run by a Miss Cook, and it seems that Muslim women in the poor areas where some of the schools were located were enthusiastic about them.[21]

By the mid-nineteenth century women's education had become an issue which was campaigned for by unorthodox Hindus, Brahmos[22] and radical students in Bengal, especially Calcutta. Fears of the evangelical intentions of missionary schools were aired at the same time as Brahmo and Hindu schools for girls were opened in Bengal, and were partly responsible for their opening. While the missionary schools of the early nineteenth century had been attended largely by girls from poor families,[23] these new schools catered to girls of the upper castes.[24] First forays into the *zenanas* (women's quarters), or *andarmahals* as they were known in Bengal, also began to be made at this time by campaigners for adult education for women. Known as the 'home education' movement, these forays too were initiated by English, Scottish and North American missionaries, who were, within some years, joined by Brahmos. Over time, the curricula were adopted by Brahmos to suit what they felt were Bengali requirements.[25]

The movement for women's education is generally described as having been formed by the need of a rising middle class to adapt its women to a Western milieu. With the growth of British education and new employment opportunities for men, the public private dichotomy grew into an opposition between the world and the home, rather than a complementarity of the two. To put it crudely, instead of being a sanctuary (or, indeed, even while remaining something of a sanctuary), the home began to represent the dead weight of traditions which were scorned as bigoted or barbaric. It had, therefore, to be reformed and brought into complementarity with the new world outside. Sumanta Banerjee has described how the traditions of the andarmahal were brought under critical scrutiny, especially insofar as they concerned entertainment through popular cultural forms such as songs and recitals (*kirtans, panchalis, kathakathas*). Under colonial influence, the *bhadralok* learnt to view these forms as low and 'obscene': from the late eighteenth to the end of the nineteenth century both missionary and administrative literature abounds with horrified descriptions of the abandonment which 'even' upper-class natives enjoyed both in religious ritual and entertainment. Nor is it surprising that the ribald humour of popular Bengali songs, in particular, drew disfavour from the Victorians, who condemned so much of their own literary heritage as being lewd. The *bhadralok* began to frown upon popular, traditional songs and recitals within the andarmahal as exposing women to wantonness and vulgarity: at the same time, women's enjoyment of such entertainment was described as indicating their 'natural' tendency towards depravity.[26] (This latter view is of course entrenched in traditional Hindu conceptions of feminine nature). Women's education, thus, was a way of both detaching upper-caste women from any contact with 'the vulgar masses', and of curing them of their latent vulgarity.

One of the effects of the women's education movement, therefore, was also to marginalize popular forms of women's entertainment, pushing their performers into seeking new avenues of employment. Traditional spaces for the expression of 'a woman's voice' were thus further curtailed.

The mid-nineteenth century also saw the growth of reform movements in Bombay Presidency, beginning with attacks on 'priestly obscurantism' and 'the institution of caste'.[27] As in Bengal, initial attacks came in the form of polemics against orthodox Hindu custom, followed by the spread of reform-based organizations and the founding of institutions such as schools and homes. Yet there were important differences in the social reforms of Bombay Presidency and Bengal: from its inception, social reform in Bombay was composed of two separate but often interconnected strands: the anti-caste movement launched by low-caste and 'untouchable' groups, and the high caste movement for reform. In contrast, social reform in Bengal was dominated by the upper-castes, and though there were spaces for reform issues in popular movements, as with the Vaishnavites, these were not incorporated into mainstream social reform campaigns, nor did they acquire the ideas of modernism and progress which can be held to characterize nineteenth-century social reform. Attacks on caste-hierarchies and caste-based power structures in Bombay did not, however, lead to the founding of a new religious body as they did in Bengal, nor even to major movements for religious reform.

In the 1830s a movement to bring converts back into the Hindu fold started in Bombay city. A Hindu Missionary Society was founded which performed ceremonies to admit Hindus who were converts to Christianity or Islam back into Hinduism; the Society also simplified the marriage ceremony (which took several days) and trained priests, not all of whom were Brahmans.[28]

By the 1840s radical Brahman students in both Poona and Bombay city espoused the reform of Hinduism; students in Poona modelled themselves on the Derozians in Calcutta and came to be known as the Young Poona group; in 1848, the Brahman aristocrat G.H. Deshmukh ('Lokahitwadi') began publishing attacks on the Hindu priesthood; and the dalit Jyotirao Phule (affectionately called Jyotiba) founded his first school for girls in Poona. One year later, the Paramahansa Mandali was founded in Bombay city, by both Brahmans and non-Brahmans; its members campaigned against caste-segregation, and held secret meetings at which they ate beef and drank wine together. In the same year, students of Elphinstone College in Bombay opened a school for girls and started a monthly magazine for women.[29] By 1852 Phule had opened three schools for girls, and one for 'untouchables'.[30]

Orthodox Hindu reactions to these developments were not slow to come, and were considerably stronger in Bombay than in Bengal, especially in Poona. One of the reasons for this was that Brahman power-structures were far stronger in Bombay presidency than in Bengal, and Poona was a centre of Brahmanic culture. On a few occasions, social reformers were even beaten up; Phule, who lived in Poona, faced enormous hostility from caste Hindus for his presumption in attempting to raise the status of 'untouchables', especially girls. Under pressure from conservative Brahmans, his father threw him out of his home, and he was ostracized by many members of his own community.[31]

By the 1850s orthodox Hindu reaction to social reform campaigns had also grown considerably stronger. This was partly a natural corollary of the growing strength of these campaigns, and partly a reaction to the kind of support the British were giving to them and the way they were used to fuel European contempt for 'natives'. When I.C. Vidyasagar launched a campaign to remove the ban on widow remarriage, in the early 1850s, he began, as other social reformers had done, with a tract in Bengali showing that widow remarriage was accepted by the *shastras*, and he debated the issue with Hindu pundits in Sanskrit. The debate was taken up by the vernacular press and soon songs were heard both praising and lambasting the campaign and its leader. Describing some of the songs of praise, Sumanta Banerjee has pointed out that many of them adopted the 'widow's voice', telling of her pleasure at the prospect of

VERNACULAR STANDARDS OF EXAMINATION FOR GIRLS' SCHOOLS AND ZENANAS

Note 1. — The text-books named in the table are recommended for the present. It will, however, be open to the managers of schools to substitute for those mentioned any other books of the same value, character, and standard of difficulty.

Note 2 — In Standards IV., VI., and VII. the departmental examinations for scholarships will be held in the text-books named.

Subject	LOWER PRIMARY STANDARDS				UPPER PRIMARY STANDARDS			MIDDLE STANDARD
	Standard I (A)	Standard I (B)	Standard II	Standard III	Standard IV	Standard V	Standard VI	Standard VII
Reading	To recognize and name the letters of the alphabet, vowels and consonants.	To have a correct knowledge of the sound and formation of the different vowel signs, from Part I., Barnaparichay.	To read with intelligence from any primer; to spell without mistake up to Part II., Barnaparichay.	Competent knowledge of spelling in Part II., Barnaparichay; Intelligent reading of Shikshasopan, Part III.; reciting ten lines of poetry from Padyapath I.	Bodhoday with explanation; Padyapatha I committed to memory, with explanation.	Questions out of the first half of Bastubichar; reading and explanation from Charupath II., and Padyapath II., committing to memory of Padyapath II.	Questions from Bastubichar; reading and explanation from Akhyan Manjari II.; Kabitasangraha I., committed to memory, with explanation and paraphrasing.	Sitarbanabas, Padyapath III., Prabandha Kusum by Rajani Kanta Gupta.
Writing	To write the letters legibly.	Writing easy words from dictation.	Dictation from the primer used in the class.	Dictation from the reading book.	Dictation from Bodhoday, each passage slowly read out twice. Reading from manuscript.	Dictation from Charupath II., each passage read slowly twice. Writing in simple Bengali the purport of lessons; reading from manuscript.	Short essays on subjects treated in the text-books of the class.	Short essays on familiar subjects.
Arithmetic	To count up to 50, and be able to state of what two digits each number is composed. Easy mental arithmetic.	Writing down numbers of two digits; addition of numbers not exceeding two digits.	Numeration and addition of numbers up to four digits.	Numeration in five figures; addition; subtraction; tables up to 3 x 10.	Numeration in six figures; simple addition, subtraction, multiplication and division; tables up to 20 x 10; country tables to gandakia.	The four simple and two compound rules; tables up to 12 x 12; easy money reductions; mankasa, serkasa.	Four simple and compound rules; bazaar weights and measures, mankasa, serkasa, bighakali, katakali, mashmahina.	Add to Standard VI., simple proportion and simple fractions.
Grammar	…	…	…	Classification of letters vowels, and consonants.	Easy sandhi of vowels from the reader.	Sandhi of vowels and consonants; easy samas.	Sandhi, karak, stritva, samas.	Questions arising out of the text-books.
Geography	…	…	…	…	Definitions, illustrated by the map, general knowledge of India.	Definitions, general knowledge of Asia, knowledge of the district of Bengal.	Knowledge of map of the world, and of India in detail.	Add to Standard VI., general knowledge of the four quarters.
History	…	…	…	…	…	History of Bengal for Beginners, by Raj Krishna Mukerjea.	History of Bengal for Beginners, by Raj Krishna Mukerjea.	History of India by Ramgati, Nyayaratna. (Hindu and Mohammedan periods.)
Domestic Economy	…	…	…	…	Garhasthya Swasthyabidbi, by Chandranath Bose.	Garhasthya Path, by Chandranath Bose.	Garhasthya Path.	The Way to Health.
Needlework	…	Hemming; or, Arithmetic to Standard II.	Top sewing or seaming; or, Arithmetic to Standard IV.	Running and felling; or, Arithmetic to Standard V.	Marking, stitches all crossed the same way and making a koorta; or, Arithmetic to Standard VI.	Cutting out a koorta, sewing on buttons and strings, and making buttonholes; or, Arithmetic to Standard VII.	Gathering and sewing on a band, darning, and herringboning; or, Prani Brittanta.	Cutting out and making a piran; and fancy-work; or, Padartha Bidya.
Optional subject. **English Language**	…	…	…	Step by step.	Royal Reader I.; dictation; nouns and verbs.	Royal Reader II.; dictation; parts of speech.	Royal Reader III.; letter writing; easy parsing.	Royal Reader IV.; letter writing; parsing.

CALCUTTA,
The 22nd of May, 1893.

C.A. MARTIN,
Offtg. Director of Public Instruction.

escaping from widowhood into remarriage.[32] Even the weavers of Santipur took their looms into the fray, and verses about the campaign appeared on their cloth. Vidyasagar then translated his tract into English, and gave copies of it to British officials. With their advice, he submitted a petition to the Governor-General in 1855, asking for a law to be passed recognizing widow remarriage. In the same year a draft Bill was introduced in the legislative Council by J.P. Grant, which was based on Vidyasagar's petition. Yet, of the arguments advanced by Vidyasagar in his petition only one was focussed on by Grant. The petition argued that there were many Hindus who practised widow remarriage but who were now unable to do so as the courts run by the East-India Company and the British government had declared this illegal; moreover, the ban on widow remarriage 'tends generally to depravation of morals'. Several historians have pointed out that the British codification of Hindu law tended to impose Brahmanic ritual on all Hindus; according to Vidyasagar's petition, this had happened with the ban on widow remarriage. The Bill, therefore, could as well have been seen as a repeal of the British law against widow remarriage. Yet the situation was complicated in two ways: for the Brahman-dominated Hindu orthodoxy the argument that many Hindu communities allowed widows to remarry was a challenge to their

Drawing by Herbert Johnson in Mary Frances Billington: *Women in India*, rpt. Delhi, Amarko Book Agency, 1973.

A BILL TO
Remove all legal obstacles to the marriage of Hindoo Widows

Preamble

Whereas it is known that, by the law as administered in the Civil Courts established in the territories in the possession and under the Government of the East India Company, Hindoo Widows, with certain exception, are held to be, by reason of their having been once married, incapable of contracting a second valid marriage, and the offspring of such Widows by any second marriage are held to be illegitimate, and incapable of inheriting propertys and whereas many Hindoos believe that this imputed legal incapacity, although it is in accordance with established custom, is not an accordance with a true interpretation of the precepts of their religion, and desire that the Civil law administered by the Courts of Justice shall no longer prevent those Hindoos who may be so minded from adopting a different custom, in accordance with the dictates of their own consciences: and whereas it is just to relieve all such Hindoos from this legal incapacity of which they complain; and the removal of all legal obstacles to the marriage of Hindoo Widows will tend to the promotion of good morals and to the public welfare—It is enacted as follows:—

Marriage of Hindoo Widows legalized

1. No marriage contracted between Hindoos shall be invalid, and the issue of no such marriage shall be illegitimate, by reason of the woman having been previously married or betrothed to another person who was dead at the time of such marriage, any custom and any interpretation of Hindoo law to the contrary notwithstanding.

Rights of widow in deceased husband's property, to cease on her re-marriage

II. All rights and interests which any Widow may have in her deceased husband's property by way of maintenance, or by inheritance to her husband or to his lineal successors, or by virtue of any will or testamentary disposition conferring upon her, without express permission to remarry, only a limited interest in such property, with no power of alienating the same, shall, upon her re-marriage, cease and determine as if she had then died; and the next heirs of her deceased husband, or other persons entitled to the property on her death, shall thereupon succeed to the same.

III. On the re-marriage of the Hindoo Widow, if neither the Widow nor any other person has been expressly constituted by the will or testamentary disposition of the deceased husband, the guardian of his children, the father or paternal grandfather, or the mother or paternal grandmother, of the deceased husband, or any male relative of the deceased husband, may petition the highest Court having original jurisdiction in Civil cases in the place where the deceased husband was domiciled at the time of his death, for the appointment of some proper person to be guardian of the said children, and thereupon it shall be lawful for the said Court, if it shall think fit, to appoint such guardian, who, when appointed, shall be entitled to have the care and custody of the said children, or any of them, during their minority, in the place of their mother; and in making such appointment the Court shall be guided, so far as may be, by the laws and rules in force touching the guardianship of children who have neither father nor mother. Provided that, when the said children have not property of their own sufficient for their support and proper education whilst minors, no such appointment shall be made otherwise than with the consent of the mother, unless the proposed guardian shall have given security for the support and proper education of the children whilst minors.

Guardianship of children of deceased husband, on the re-marriage of his widow

IV. Nothing in this Act contained shall be construed to render any widow, who, at the time of the death of any person leaving any property, is a childless widow, capable of inheriting the whole or any share of such property, if, before the passing of that Act, she would have been incapable of inheriting the same by reason of her being a childless Widow.

Nothing in this Act to render any childless widow capable of inheriting

V. Except as in the three preceding Sections is provided, a Widow shall not, by reason of her re-marriage forfeit any property, or any right to which she would otherwise be entitled; and every Widow who has re-married shall have the same rights of inheritance as she would have had, had such marriage been her first marriage.

Saving of rights of widow marrying, except as provided in the three preceeding

VI. Whatever words spoken, ceremonies performed, or engagements made, on the marriage of a Hindoo female who has not been previously married, are sufficient to constitute a valid marriage, shall have the same effect if spoken, performed, or made on the marriage of a Hindoo Widow; and no marriage shall be declared invalid on the ground that such words, ceremonies, or engagements, are inapplicable to the case of a widow.

Whatever ceremonies now constitute a valid marriage shall have the same effect on the marriage of a widow

VII. If the widow re-marrying is a minor whose marriage has not been consummated, she shall not re-marry without the consent of her father, or, if she has no father, of her paternal grandfather, or, if she has no such grandfather, of her mother, or, failing all these, of her elder brother, or, failing also brothers, of her next male relative. All persons knowingly abetting a marriage made

Consent to remarriage of a widow who is a minor.

THE NINETEENTH CENTURY 19

Punishment for abetting marriage made contrary to this Section. contrary to the provisions of this Section shall be liable to imprisonment for any term not exceeding one year, or to fine or to both. And all marriages made contrary to the provisions of this Section may be declared void by a Provise Court of lane. Provided that, in any question regarding the validity of a marriage made contrary to the provisions of this Section, such consent as is aforesaid shall be presumed until the contrary is proved; and that no such marriage shall be declared void after it has been consummated. In the case of a Widow who is of full age, or whose marriage has been consummated, her own consent shall be sufficient consent to constitute her remarriage lawful and valid.

Effect of such marriage.

authority on all matters Hindu; and their authority was being assailed at various points as it was. Then the British supporters of the Bill accepted the orthodox argument that Hinduism forbade widow remarriage, but turned it to Hindu disadvantage. Grant's arguments in support of the Bill, for example, first advanced a biological-determinist reason for permitting widows to remarry: then turned this into a moral reason supported by empirical evidence:

the Hindu practice of Brahmacharya is an attempt to struggle against Nature, and like all other attempts to struggle against Nature, is entirely unsuccessful . . . . In the majority of cases young Hindu widows fall into vice . . . in many cases a licentious and profligate life is entered upon in secret; and in many other cases the wretched widows are impelled to desert their homes and to live a life that brings open disgrace upon their families.

As evidence he quoted two other Englishmen: Ward, who said the ban on widow remarriage forced many women into prostitution; and Major Wilkinson, who claimed he was repeating the opinions of a Brahman he knew in Nagpur, who said that this ban:

inevitably leads to great moral depravity and vice. . . it inevitably causes a frightful amount of infanticides and abortions . . . these widows, inevitably rendered corrupt and vicious themselves by the hard and unnatural laws operating on them cannot be prevented from corrupting and destroying the honour and virtue of all other females with whom they associate.[33]

More than forty petitions against the Bill were submitted by around sixty thousand Hindus of 'the higher class'. The argument that the ban on widow remarriage led to 'depravation' was not referred to by most of these petitions, which set out to prove that it was enjoined by the *shastras*, and any change of the law as it stood would be construed as interference in Hindu custom. One of the petitions pointed out that 'legislative intervention has never yet been able to effect a change in public opinion, while the more such interference is exercised, the more it assumes an objectionable character.'[34] In fact, though the Bill was passed in 1856, very few remarriages resulted from it; social reformers themselves called it a 'dead letter'.

A widow remarriage society did its best to help, maintaining what was practically a Widow Remarriage Bureau. The reformers themselves found practice (as opposed to preaching) difficult. A story was current at the time of a young reformer, who announced to the cheers of his audience, that he would marry a widow, and none other. The Remarriage Bureau fell upon his neck and offered him first choice. Before the marriage actually took place he gave a dinner to his boon companions. 'How many', he asked, 'of you will accept my invitations to dinner after I am married?' Not one was willing. The marriage never took place.[35]

In the 1890s it was reported that in the forty odd years since the Act was passed, there had been five hundred widow remarriages in all. Though social reform organizations had by this time mushroomed all over India, and each one of them was pledged to campaigning for widow remarriages, this was all they had achieved. Moreover, it seems that even these five hundred were remarriages of child-widows or, in the parlance of the day 'virgin widows'. High caste widows who were not virgins did not—and could not—remarry.[36]

Recent research on the functioning of the Act has shown how it often made remarriage more difficult for widows of castes and tribes which had never placed a ban on widow remarriage. Though the Act accorded all Hindu widows the right to remarry, it added a clause classifying the kinds of property the widow had rights to upon remarriage. If her property had come to her from her natal family, or been given to her absolutely, she was entitled to keep it on remarriage. If, on the other hand, it came to her from her husband or his lineal successors it would cease to be hers upon remarriage—unless she was 'expressly permitted' to keep it. That is to say, if she had the right to maintenance, or inheritance, or was willed property, she would forfeit it on remarriage, unless her husband had announced she was free to remarry, or her caste or community rules specified that she could keep her property on remarriage. Both were unlikely eventualities. Lucy Carroll has cited various instances in which this distinction between kinds of property rights for widows was used by relatives to dispossess them, in communities which had by customary law allowed both widow remarriage and the retention of property. Interestingly, one of the examples she gave was of a case brought by members of a tribal family, claiming that on her remarriage one of their widows had forfeited her right to the property she owned. The case was won on a minimal show of evidence that certain Hindu practices had been adopted by some branches of the tribe (the Rajbansis). The Court held this sufficient evidence to bring the entire tribe under the scope of the Act.[37] Thus the Act provided mercenary reasons for non-Hindus to Hinduize their customs; so legislative changes did affect public practice, and thus public opinion, even if not in the way they set out to do.

By the 1860s, several different strands could be distinguished in the social reform movement. An example of this is the wide range of opinion on why women should be educated and what their education should consist of. At one extreme, the Bombay Parsi Framji Bomanji declared 'we want the English language, English manners and English behaviour for our wives and daughters, and until these are supplied, it is but just that the present gulf between the Englishman and the Indian should remain as wide as ever.'[38] Few, however, concurred with this Anglophilia. Though K.C. Sen felt the 'encounter with Christianity' was one of the best moments in Indian history, Bengali literature and Brahmo 'religious instruction' were essential in the curricula of his girls' schools and 'home education' groups.[39] I.C. Vidyasagar gave no religious instruction at all, but had both Sanskrit and Bengali taught in his girls' schools. Sayyid Ahmed Khan, one of the men who started a Muslim social reform movement, and was a loyalist, said that Muslim women should be educated, but at home, and cautioned against the 'Anglicisation' of Muslim girls.[40] At the same time, a new theory for social reform was propounded by Dayanand Saraswati; one which had earlier been outlined by members of the student Society for the Acquisition of General Knowledge, formed in 1838 in Calcutta. Members of the Society, of whom Vidyasagar had been one, said that Hinduism and Islam had both been responsible for the degradation of women in India, and the only way to drag Indian women out of the 'bog of illiteracy and superstition' into which they had fallen was to educate them on secular rationalist lines; yet they also propounded the theory of a golden age in ancient India (Vedic) which had accorded a special place to learned women.[41]

Similar ideas were expressed by members of the Tattavabodhini Sabha, formed by Rabindranath Tagore in 1839. The Sabha was pledged to reform Hinduism, spread knowledge of the *shastras*, especially Vedanta, and propounded a monotheism based on the Upanishads. It was formed in the same year as Alexander Grant's *India and India Missions* was published, which made scathing denunciations of Hindus and Hinduism, saying 'of all the systems of false religion ever fabricated by the perverse ingenuity of fallen man, Hinduism is the most stupendous'. Duff, a propounder of 'aggressive Christianity', signalled the increasing proselytizing drive of Christian missionaries in India, which had aroused alarm not only in the breasts of orthodox Hindus but reformers as well, especially as it was beginning to enjoy a mild success among high-caste students. The 1840s were years of bitter debate between the missionaries on one side and Hindu conservatives and reformers on the other even though the missionaries and reformers agreed that British rule and English education had spread culture and reason among Indians, dispelling 'the darkness of ignorance'. The Tattvabodhini Sabha's defence of Hinduism, in particular, consisted of developing the view of ancient India as 'a great centre of learning and theological study' saying that:

It was a symbol of righteousness and greatness, and among all countrymen the Hindus were given a superior position . . . . Therefore in order to revive our greatness it has become necessary to research the antiquity of India so that it helps and encourages people of the land to respect and love their own country.[42]

Embarking on Indological research, they published their findings on the greatness of Aryan civilization in the *Tattvabodhini Patrika*, and translated various Hindu scriptures from Sanskrit into Bengali.

In this they were not alone. Ram Mohan Roy and Mrityunjaya Vidyalamkara had both privileged the Vedas and Upanishads over other texts; Colebrooke had advanced the theory of an Aryan golden age as early as 1805. As indological research developed in Europe in the nineteenth century, scholars such as Max Muller popularized the golden age theory. Yet in Europe, as in India, these views were to grow in strength in the latter half of the nineteenth century, and to be used in different, often opposed, ways.

Though the Tattvabodhini Sabha's ideas were intellectually influential, they did not attract a particularly wide

Excerpts From Lajpat Rai's
A History of the Arya Samaj

The Relations of the sexes

It must be frankly admitted that when the Arya Samaj came into being the lot of Hindu women was deplorable. In certain respects it was even worse than that of men. A proportion of the men (though comprising only a very small percentage of the population) had received some sort of education, in the schools and colleges opened by the Government, the Christian missionaries and other private agencies, but very little had been done to further the education of Indian women. This system of Government introduced by the British, necessitated the education of Indian men for administrative reasons. Among the agencies that have worked for improvement in this respect, the Arya Samaj occupies a high position in the Punjab and the United Provinces of Agra and Oude. It can be safely said that there has occurred a metamorphosis in the outlook of men towards women.

English education and Western ideas have played an important part in engendering this change, but an equally great, if not even greater, part has been played by an appeal to the ancient Hindu ideals of womanhood and to the teachings of the ancient Hindu religion in the matter of the relations of the sexes. A study of ancient Hindu literature made it abundantly clear that the present unenviable lot of Indian women was due to a deterioration of their old ideal. In Ancient India, both in theory and practice, women were placed on a pedestal in society: equal to that of men, if not higher. As regards education and marriage they held an equal position. The girls were equally entitled to receive education, and no limitations at all were set on their ambition in this direction. Study was equally enjoined for the girls as well as the boys. The only difference was that, in the case of girls, their period of education expired sooner than that of boys. The minimum age of marriage for girls was sixteen, as compared with twenty-five for boys. This was based on Hindu ideas of the physiological differences between the sexes. It is presumed that as regards the choice of a mate, both parties enjoyed equal freedom and equal opportunities. The ideal marriage was monogamic, and one contracted with the mutual consent of the parties. Yet, so many varieties of legal marriage are known to Hindu law as to leave no doubt as to the sensitiveness of the Hindus to the extreme difficulty, and indeed unnaturalness, of attempting to impose a single law upon both sexes. Some forms of marriage suggest that courtship was not altogether unknown in Hindu society, and furthermore, it was not regarded with any grave disapprobation. Though as a rule subject to control by parents, husbands and even sons, Hindu mothers, wives, sisters and daughters occupied a higher position than their counterparts ever had in Christian Europe before the nineteenth century. In the family the position of the mother was higher than that of the father. According to Manu she is entitled to a thousand times greater respect and reverence than the father. She was in supreme control of the house and at the helm of household affairs, including finances.

Hindu law recognizes the rights of the mother, of the widow, of the daughter, and of the sister to possess property in their own right, with exclusive control over it, even when a member of a joint family. A mother has an equal right with the father to the guardianship of her children. On the death of the father her right is absolute. An ideal Hindu wife is never expected to earn her livelihood. She has been exempted from this burden by virtue of the superiority of her mother-function. Male members have been made responsible even for the maintenance, etc. of unmarried girls and widows, though the latter are not debarred from acquiring property by inheritance, by gift, or by their own skill. In no case have males any legal control over the property of females.

The Hindu marriage is a sacrament, and as such, in theory, indissoluble. Says Manu:

"The whole duty, in brief, of husband and wife towards each other is that they cross not and wander not apart from each other in thought, word and deed until death, And the promise is that they who righteously discharge this duty here shall not be parted hereafter, by the death of the body, but shall be together in the worlds beyond also".

Swami Dayanand interprets the ancient Rishis as disapproving of second or third marriages on the death of husbands and wives (Manu is supposed to lay this injuction on widows only). In any case, Dayanand does not lay down any rule for women which he does not apply to men also, and in so doing he is merely following the spirit of the ancient lawgivers. There are certain conditions in which men are permitted to remarry even in the lifetime of the lawful spouse; for example, if she be barren, or addicted to strong drink or guilty of immorality, or even when where is complete incompatibility of temperament. In similar conditions the wife, too, has the option of remarrying in the lifetime of her husband; for example, if he be impotent, or deserts his wife, or falls into dissolute habits, or disappears without trace for a number of years, and so forth.

In special cases, Hindu law sanctions polygamy also, though only under very exceptional circumstances. It follows from what we have stated above that the Arya Samaj is strongly opposed to child marriage. It has conducted a fiery crusade against this unnatural custom, and may be congratulated on its success in rallying public opinion to favour its view. It fixes sixteen as the minimum marriageable age for girls and twenty-five for boys, and it encourages celibacy up to the age of forty-eight.

following. It was left to Dayanand Saraswati and his followers to turn them into fodder for a widespread movement, mainly in north India, and, to some extent, in west India. A peasant from Kathiawar, Saraswati became a *sadhu* and convert to the golden age theory in the course of his wanderings across India. Sent by his guru to spread the message of Vedanta and Arya-dharm, he travelled all over the country, holding public meetings and debates with the pundits, and preaching a doctrine of the egalitarianism and humaneness of Aryan principles: the Vedic *varna* system was based on virtue, not birth; the paths of virtue were open to all in Aryan India, but had been barred in contemporary Hinduism.[43] Saraswati's principles, however, were closer in certain ways to Duff's 'aggressive Christianity' than to the Tattvabodhini Sabha's views: he believed that the preaching of Vedic doctrine must include attacks on the falsity of other religions; in his *Satyarth Prakash*, written in 1875, both Islam and Christianity were subjected to vehement and lengthy criticism. He was, moreover, critical of the Brahmo Samaj for not espousing Arya-dharm sufficiently single mindedly and the founding of the Lahore Arya Samaj in 1877 drew

many Punjabi reformers out of the Brahmo Samaj.[44]

As Uma Chakravarti has pointed out, Saraswati differed from most exponents of the golden age theory in that while they wished to awaken their fellow subjects to pride in their past, he wished to venerate that past in colonial India.[45] It appears that he began to think about the position of women while he was in Calcutta, and that he was especially influenced here by Vidyasagar: despite this, however, he was definite that only widows without children should be allowed to remarry, suggesting that the ancient practice of *niyoga*, or marriage to the dead husband's brother, be revived for this purpose.

According to Saraswati, practices such as polygamy, child-marriage and the seclusion of women did not exist in Aryan India; moreover, men and women had equal rights. In his *Satyarth Prakash* he stressed, as the Tattvabodhini Sabha had done, the parity between learned men and women in Vedic India, saying that: girls were entitled to wear the sacred thread and undergo the initiatory ceremony of *yagnopit*;[46] both girls and boys should start learning Sanskrit, Hindi and foreign languages at the age of five; after the age of eight both sexes should be compulsorily educated, but in separate schools, that true education was part of religion, and *sandhya* and Vedic *yagna* should be performed at the start of every school day. Moreover, both girls and boys should be Brahmacharyas for some years; the minimum age of marriage for girls should be 16, and for boys 25.[47]

In a way, Saraswati shifted the terrain of discussion on women's education: by defining learning as a path to virtue, and virtue as individually acquired. He diverged from the functionalist views of most other advocates for women's education, who argued that women needed education so as to be able to perform their duties as wives and mothers adequately. Saraswati appears not to have made such a connection between education and function, though he too believed that the role of the woman was as mother, laying down a series of guidelines to ensure the birth and post-natal care of her children.

While most advocates for women's education were agreed that it should be functionalist there were certain differences in emphasis when it came to the functions concerned. In perhaps the dominant view the emphasis was on household accomplishments which would benefit both husband and children: The

Herbert Johnson, Mission teachers and scholars at Calcutta, in *Woman in India*

Brahmo schools for girls, for example, especially those run by Keshub Chandra Sen, taught 'cooking, sewing, nursing, and such like . . . (which were) deserving of quite as much encouragement and reward as purely literary proficiency'.[48] A less dominant view at this stage which was later to grow influential, emphasized the role the mother played in forming the child's consciousness, arguing that women should be educated so that they could educate their children. This view was advanced even by so radical a reformer as Jyotiba Phule.

Phule's attitudes towards the reform of women's conditions appear to have been unusual even when compared to those of other reformers of the time. For example, he tried to start a 'home' in which unmarried women and widows could give birth to illegitimate children in secret, promising to then have the children adopted; this was especially radical as the codes repressing women's sexuality were most strongly administered by the upper-castes, so such a home would have been used largely by upper-caste women. Yet his views on women's education were, in certain respects, not very different from those of other reformers. 'Female schools', he observed, 'first of all attracted my notice as, upon mature consideration, they were found to be even more necessary than male ones, the roots of education lying in the proper turn mothers give to the disposition of children between their second and third years.'[49]

The conditions of women's lives, then, needed reform not only because of the hardships women were subjected to, but also for the sakes of their husbands and children. Over the years an increasing emphasis was placed on the latter, so that the rationale advanced for improving women's lives in India was that they were mothers. The importance of this was stressed in the following way: the conditions under which women gave birth to and brought up children were such that the 'Indian race' had 'degenerated', sickly children were born who grew up to be stunted adults; the ignorance and superstitiousness of their mothers led whole generations of Indians to lose the 'entrepreneurial spirit'; this was what had allowed India to be colonized by the British; therefore it was important to the Indian nation that its children be born and brought up in the right conditions.[50]

While in the early nineteenth century women had been the sign of the decline of the community, by the late nineteenth century it was children who reflected the decline of the race. The onus, of course, remained on women, but a spotlight was now turned on children. Philippe Aries has shown how eighteenth century France gave birth to the idea of childhood and adulthood as separate spheres; he describes the way the earlier notion of children as little adults gave way to the notion that children needed protection from the rigours of adult life.[51] By the early nineteenth century this idea had grown enormously: the conditions engendered by

industrialization were so gruelling for childworkers that a host of movements demanding the reform of their working lives arose in Europe.

At the same time, the rapidly growing natural sciences gave rise to new biological theories which drew attention to the development of the human body (including brain), both over the centuries and in an individual's life-span. An adage was coined: 'The child is father of man' (note bias); its formative years were studied; the importance

Herbert Johnson, Three Generations in *Women in India*

of correct nutrition, education and domestic environment were pointed out. While the opposition between theories of genetic determination and theories of environmental influence only really developed in the twentieth century, it was implicit here. Genetics, for example, contributed to the formulation of theories of racial superiority which implied—even asserted—that British rule was ordained by nature (not god-ordained, as in the Crusades or *jiddh*). In other words, the British were genetically fitted to rule; their subjects were biologically inferior races.[52]

No wonder, then, that Indian social reformers turned

Herbert Johnson, Women workers in the Girideh mines, in *Woman in India*

their attention to matters of race and biological definitions of it; nor is it surprising that their efforts were directed towards proving that inferiority was not genetic, but contingent on social practice. Hence the attacks on sati, infant marriage, purdah, and the growth of movements for women's education and widow remarriage. Two campaigns in the 1880s best reflect the development of these ideas in India: the campaign for factory legislation to improve the conditions of industrial labour and the movement against child-marriage.

Though the campaign for factory legislation in India was launched partly by Lancashire mill-owners suffering from Indian competition in the production and sale of cotton textiles, it was supported by both English and Indian philanthropists, who had for some time been agitated by the conditions besetting mill-workers at home and at work. Their attention focussed upon the two groups which had been the most frequent subjects of well-intentioned scrutiny in the period: women and children. High rates of child-mortality were discovered and co-related to gruelling hours of work; at the same time, it was pointed out that women worked such long hours that they were forced to neglect their children.

In 1875, the Government of Bombay set up a Labour Commission to enquire into the need for legislation; though most of the Commissioners saw no need to regulate factory practices, there was sufficient debate in parliament and the press to persuade them otherwise. The first Indian Factories Act was passed in 1881, codifying a distinction between adult and child which had not hitherto been made: a 'child' was defined as 'being any person below 12 years of age', the minimum age for employment of children was fixed at seven years, their hours of work were limited to nine a day, with a one-hour rest interval; and they were granted four days holiday a month. The Act, however, left considerable dissatisfaction at its lacunae: no special regulations for women workers were included, and the protection of children was found insufficient. Agitation for legislation on these aspects was renewed, especially in Bombay, where the Government instituted fresh enquiries into labour conditions. In 1884, the Bombay Factory Commission recommended amendment of the Act, but no action was taken until after the First International Labour Conference of 1890, in Berlin, which recommended the regulation of conditions of work for women and children. The Manchester Chamber of Commerce started to press the Government to apply these recommendations to India; British and Indian factory owners in India opposed them. The Government of India appointed yet another Factory Commission in 1890, and in 1891 the Indian Factories (Amendment) Act was passed. A 'child' was now defined as 'being any person below 14 years of age' and the minimum age of employment of children was raised to nine; their hours of work were correspondingly lowered to seven, but the rest interval was halved. The hours of work for women were limited to eleven a day, with a one-and-a-half hour rest interval—or less for fewer hours of work. Further, the working hours of both women and children had to be between 5 a.m. and 8 p.m., in recognition of children's health requirements and women's domestic and maternal duties.[53]

If the campaign for factory legislation showed first attempts to codify the years of childhood, and regulate working-class family life, the campaign against child marriage showed the increasing obsession of social reformers with the 'debilitation of the race'.

Though in 1860 an Act was passed fixing the age of consent at ten, no campaign as such had been launched until Behram Malabari took up the issue in the late nineteenth century. He canvassed a wide range of Hindu opinion in support of his campaign, though he was not himself a Hindu. Most of the men whose opinion he sought were drawn from professional groups—lawyers, doctors, teachers, public servants. Supporters of the campaign argued, as in the campaign against purdah, that child marriage was responsible for most of the physical and spiritual ills besetting India:

We hold that early marriage weakens the physical strength of a nation; it stunts its full growth and development, it affects the courage and energy of the individuals, and brings forth a race of people weak in strength and wanting in hardihood. (*The Jessore Indian Association*).

With regard to early marriage, I hold it a most pernicious custom which makes the nation very weak. It is necessary that in a country there should be a number of bachelors who would venture upon enterprise, foreign travel, etc. What makes Hindus so feeble is the custom of early marriage. They have hardly any strength either to become soldiers, or to cultivate land, or to go for trade to foreign countries. They are unfit as colonizers. (*G.H. Deshmukh*)

What is good for the individual's health is good for the health of the community, and indirectly beneficial to the State. There is a good deal of sickness and mortality and difficulty in the act of childbirth, due to imperfect consolidation of the bones of the pelvis at the tender age at which women, in consequence of early marriages, give birth to children. The heads of the children of young mothers are also unduly pressed upon and so either the children die prematurely or grow feeble, or both in body and in mind, and turn out helpless idiots. (*Surgeon-Major D.N. Parekh, Chief Physician, Gokuldas Tejpal Hospital, Bombay*).[54]

Malabari himself added a further biological ill of early marriage to the list: quoting from a number of Victorian medics, he adduced evidence to show that early marriage—and, therefore, early proximity between males and females—led girls to menstruate earlier, and this led to early pregnancies and weak children, 'debilitating the race'.[55] Not all social reformers agreed with these views. The British Indian Association, for example, used the same biological terms of argument, but said:

'the Committee deny that it has been proved that early marriage is the sole, the most important cause of the degeneracy of the native race. Climate, food, hereditary predisposition to disease, injudicious selection in marriage, and other causes of arrested growth, are patent factors in the case.'[56]

The Jessore Indian Association, which accepted Malabari's arguments, added that child-marriage should not be discussed solely in terms of its physical effects:

Mr Malabari has considered the institution physically only . . . its moral influence he has not taken into consideration. It is a most powerful check upon our youths against deviating in wantonness and vice . . . . The Hindus are the only *nation* [emphasis mine, to underline that the concept of a Hindu nation already existed] among whom matrimonial scandals, and disgraceful breaches between husbands and wives are rarely heard of.'[57]

Most of the arguments against reform of the age of consent were couched in social and moral terms: they simply ignored the biological arguments of Malabari; if and when they talked of the degeneration of the Indian race, it was in social terms, not physical ones. The nature of the Hindu family was defined as resting on the girl's fusion with her husband and his family; it was only possible for her to look upon them as her own if she grew up with them. Extending this argument, the *Hindoo Patriot* declared: 'Hindoo society is so constituted that early marriage is a necessary institution for the preservation of our social order. Its abolition would destroy the system of joint family and caste'.[58] The debate grew more heated as women entered the fray: women doctors in Calcutta supported the social reform argument for raising the age of consent; and 1,600 'Hindu ladies' sent a petition asking for legislative reform to Queen Victoria in 1890.[59]

Though the campaign against child-marriage was started in Bombay, Poona reformers were less active in support of it, and Poona, in fact, became a major centre of opposition to the campaign. From the 1860s on, opposition to social reform had mounted in Poona; by the 1870s, many prominent social reformers had capitulated to pressure from their caste-brethren. G.H. Deshmukh, who had argued in the 1840s that 'the Brahmins should give up their foolish concepts: they must accept that all men are equal and everybody has a right to acquire knowledge',[60] succumbed to the Chitpavan threat to outcaste him in 1871, and withdrew from campaigns against Brahman social control. M.G. Ranade, an influential Poona reformer, refused to dine intercaste or 'marry a widow' when his first wife died in 1873; bringing home a child bride instead; and, when the Sarvajanik Sabha, a liberal political organization, was formed in 1871, its members decided they would not venture into 'religious' terrain, thus disassociating politics from social reform.[61]

The Bombay social reform movement split into two in the 1870s: in the one, Brahman reformers tended to concentrate on reform within their own community, taking up issues such as widow remarriage; in the other, the non-Brahman movement against the Brahmanic regulation of society developed. In 1873, Phule founded the Satyashodhak Samaj, first in Poona and then in Bombay; among other activities, the organization held widow remarriages and intercaste marriages, using a simplified ceremony, conducted by non-Brahman priests.[62]

The theory of an Aryan golden age began to be increasingly widely accepted in these years; interestingly, two very different versions of it were propounded at the same time, by groups who often opposed each other. The first was largely an expansion of Saraswati's views; but the second was used by opponents of social reform, to evoke a Hindu nationalism which was interconnected with the defence of Brahmanic practices. Aspects of Aryan India which were left implicit by social reformers, were now drawn to the fore. In the one view, Aryan India was an age of learning, and its varna system showed caste mobility; in the other, it was an age of conquest, and its varna system showed racial solidarity between the upper castes. This latter theory drew on some of the ideas developed by Max Muller and other German indologists, which were beginning to attract a wider audience in Europe: that Sanskritic and European languages had similar, 'Indo-European' roots. From this discovery, an 'Aryan theory of race' developed, that the Aryan invaders of India were of Indo-European stock, and thus racially superior to the Dravidians they conquered.[63]

In 1873, most of the Maharashtrian Brahman social reformers joined the newly founded Society for the Vedas and Shastras, which propounded the reformist interpretation of Aryan India described above. When Saraswati came to Bombay Presidency in 1875, his meetings were attended by all the social reformers, from Ranade to Phule. And when Pandita Ramabai founded the Arya Mahila Sabha in Poona, she was helped by many of the Poona social reformers. At the same time, the

Pandita Ramabai, 1858-1922

Pandita Ramabai was born on the 23rd of April in the forest of Gungamal in Western Maharashtra. Her

father, Ananta Shastri, was a learned Brahmin and something of a social reformer. He married a child wife of nine and wished to educate her, which brought the wrath of the Brahman community on his head. As a result, he decided to leave the village and build a home in the forest. His wife, Lakshmibai, hated the loneliness of the forest, but had perforce to accept it. Soon after, Ramabai was born. While she was still a mere child, Ramabai's family started wandering from forest to forest, city to city, village to village. In each inhabited place Ananta Shastri would give lectures on the need for female education. In the 1877 famine both Ananta Shastri and Lakshmibai died. Ramabai and her brother, to whom she was very close, decided to carry on their father's work, and live in the same way as he did. 'Ramabai's fame as a lecturer reaching the ears of the pundits of Calcutta, they desired to hear and see for themselves. She obeyed their summons to appear before them; so astounded and pleased were they by the clearness of her views and her eloquence in presenting them, that they publicly conferred on her the highest title—Saraswati, Goddess of Wisdom.'[1] After the death of her brother Ramabai married a Bengali lawyer, Bipin Behari Medhvi, and they had a daughter whom they named Mano. Bipin was a sudra, so her marriage was inter-caste as well as inter-religious. Husband and wife had planned to start a school for child widows, when Medhvi died in 1882.

After his death, Ramabai moved from Bengal to Poona, where she founded the Arya Mahila Samaj. When in 1882 a commission was appointed by the Government of India to look into Indian education, Ramabai gave evidence before it. She suggested that teachers be trained and women inspectresses of schools be appointed. Further, she said that as in India women's conditions were such that they could only be medically treated by women, Indian women should be admitted to medical colleges. 'Ramabai's

evidence created a great sensation and reached Queen Victoria herself, and bore fruit later in the starting of the women's Medical Movement by Lady Dufferin'.[2] In 1883 Ramabai decided to train as a teacher in England, and join the Episcopalian Church. At their invitation, she went to America in 1886, and it was here that an association was formed to fund her school for child widows. By April 1889 she had started a home-cum-school in Bombay, which she named the Sharada Sadan. This was the first home for widows in Maharashtra—the only other home was in Bengal, started by a Mr Sen. As Ramabai was Christian and the school was funded by missionaries, local citizens viewed it with extreme caution and wariness. Anticipating this, Ramabai had said when opening the school that it 'would not actively preach Christianity or try to make converts.'[3] However, the December 1889 issue of the *Christian Weekly* carried a report that 'at present there are seven young widows in the Sharada Sadan, two of whom have expressed their love for Christianity . . .'

In the revivalist climate of the period this was bound to raise a storm. Public outcry at Ramabai's conversion became so great that Dr Bhandarkar and Justice Ranade, both noted reformers, severed ties with the Sadan. Representations were made to the American supporters of the Sadan, urging them to put pressure on Ramabai to cease from spreading Christianity. Not surprisingly, the Americans refused. Ramabai moved the Sharada Sadan to Poona. As she had been worried about being entirely dependent on American funds, she set up a Trust to collect money for a farm, which would render the Sadan self-supporting. The money, however, had again to be collected in America. By around the turn of the century she had bought land in Khedgaon, and called the farm Mukti Sadan. When they were hit by the 1900 famine, Ramabai and her helpers were able to rescue several hundred women. According to Manmohan Kaur, at the turn of the century these were as many as 1900 people in the Sadan. 'A school was organised . . . . Four hundred children were accommodated in the Kindergarten. A training School for Teachers was also opened and an Industrial School with gardens, fields, oil press, dairy, laundry, ovens, was started. It also taught sewing, weaving, and embroidery.'

1. Pandita Ramabai, *The High Caste Hindu Woman*, 1887, Fleming H. Revell Company, New York. This extract is from the Preface.
2. Manmohan Kaur, op cit., p. 87.
3. Manmohan Kaur, op cit., p. 88.

martial and racist interpretation of Aryan India began to be advanced. V.S. Chiplunkar's 'Nibandhmala' series, published from 1874, was especially influential, invoking bygone Hindu glory, both Brahman and Maratha, and attacking both social reform and individual social reformers. Two incidents in the 1880s brought the revivalists out in full force against campaigns to reform women's conditions: in 1884, one Dadaji Bhikaji filed a suit for the restitution of conjugal rights, because his wife, Rakhmabai, married in childhood and subsequently educated, refused to live with him when she grew up.[64] Though he lost his case in the District Court,[65] he went to the Bombay High Court on appeal. The revivalists mounted a strong campaign against the District Court judgement, saying that 'foreign rulers' had no right to interfere with Hindu customs; and B.G. Tilak wrote that the women's education movement was the route 'for an attack on our ancient religion under the cover of Rakhmabai with the intention of *castrating* (emphasis mine) our eternal religion'.[66] Dadaji Bhikaji won his case on appeal, though the Court made it clear their sympathies were with Rakhmabai. Now the social reformers were up in arms, accusing the Government of 'perpetuating Hindu orthodoxy' and saying the judgement exposed the 'reactionary' nature of the British and their administration of law in India. Rakhmabai herself refused to obey the High Court judgement, was made to pay a substantial fine and excommunicated, went to England and qualified as an M.D., returned to India where she practised medicine, and died at 91.[67]

While debate was raging between reformers and revivalists, Pandita Ramabai converted to Christianity, and began to use the Sharada Sadan, which she had founded in 1889, to convert Hindu women. This was adduced as further support for revivalist claims that reformers were 'anglicisers',[68] and in the ensuing campaign to raise the age of consent, reformers were treated as colonial anti-Hindu propagandists. Though in 1889 Tilak had signed a reformist pledge to educate his daughters, and not have them married until they were 11, by 1891 he led the agitation against the Age of Consent Act, which merely raised the age of consent from 10 to 12.[69]

Among the social reformers, members of the Satyashodhak Samaj were especially active in mobilizing support for the Bill. In Bombay, Lokhande organized a petition in its favour, signed by hundreds of Marathas; the *Din Bandhu* ran a campaign against the shaving of young Brahman widows and exhorted barbers to refuse to perform this act. In response, Bombay barbers resolved at a meeting that they would no longer shave the heads of Brahman widows. Yet reformers were outnumbered by revivalists, whose demonstrations against the Bill swelled to upwards of fifty thousand people.[70]

The period was one of rising fundamentalist, communalist, nationalist and extremist sympathies. British racism in private and public spheres created increasing resentment, and there were protests against preferential treatment to whites in jobs, investment, and under the law; while the sense that Hindu communities were being singled out for attack, which was increasingly articulated as laws concerning women were passed (for most of these were directed at reforming the conditions of Hindu women), was further fuelled by the British introduction of separate electorates for Hindus and Muslims. The demand for a ban on cow-slaughter, raised in the Punjab in the 1870s, was taken up by Hindu groups in various parts of north, east and west India; many U.P. municipalities restricted slaughter-houses and *kabab* shops, to which Islamic fundamentalists reacted by presenting the Bakr-Id sacrifice as an endangered symbol of Muslim identity. Tussles over the issue culminated in riots in 1893, at Azamgarh, Ballia, Saran, Gaya, and Patna. The worst riots were in Bombay city, set off by the issue of whether Hindu processions could play music before mosques. Junagadh and Rangoon were also affected.[71]

Tilak's attack on the social reformers was conjoined with attacks on Christianity and Islam, especially the latter. The Ganpati festivals started by him in 1894 were used to caution Hindus against attending Muharram, saying 'the cow is our mother, do not forget her'; and in the Shivaji Festivals he started from 1896, Shivaji was portrayed as the *go-Brahman-pratipalak* (he who nurtures cows and Brahmans), defender of Hindus against Muslim hordes.[72] In 1895, revivalists led by Tilak succeeded in preventing Ranade's National Social Conference from using the Congress *pandal* (enclosure) for their annual meeting;[73] soon after, they rejected the Maharaja of Kolhapur's claim to Kshatriya status, pushing him into the non-Brahman movement; and created such a climate of intolerance in Poona that in 1908 the reformer D.D. Karve decided to open his widows' home in Higne, outside the city.

In Calcutta, Rabindranath Tagore was one of the liberals who turned to the support of child-marriage, on a nationalist wave to reclaim Hindu tradition. Agitation against the Bill was spearheaded by the newspaper *Bangabasi*, which held huge meetings at the Calcutta Maidan and a puja at Kalighat, at which protest against the 'foreign ruler's' interference with Hindu social customs was mixed with calls for boycott and to organize indigenous enterprises.[74] Revivalism had taken a slightly different form in Bengal, with a greater emphasis on culture than on race, but with an equal anti-'Westernism', together with anti-Muslim feelings.

These ranged from claims of '*shastric* precedents for all the discoveries of Western science', to the search for inspiration in both mythic and real figures, such as Krishna, Chaitanya, and Ramakrishna Paramahansa,[75] a peasant priest who became enormously popular with

The 'marry a widow doctrine'

The tactic of using newspaper advertisements for widow remarriage spread to various parts of India, although, on the whole these were generally placed by men who were looking for widows to marry, not vice-versa. Though most often it was specified that the widow be of the same caste as her prospective husband, sometimes this was not done, perhaps because it was taken for granted, as was the condition that she be a virgin. An anecdote of the south Indian campaign for the 'remarriage of virgin widows', which at first sight may seem frivolous, reveals a mixture of paternalism, Brahmanic Hinduism, and personal courage, which must have been characteristic of several social reformers of the time, even if they were in a minority. By and large, the men who offered to 'marry a widow' tended to specify that these would have to be of the same caste as their prospective husbands, most of whom were high-caste and college-educated. Madras seems to have been no different in this respect, for most of the 'marry a widow' doctrinaires were young college-going Brahmans, some of whom wrote to the *Hindu* advertising their willingness to marry 'Brahman widows'. In 1905, however, when the *Hindu* published a letter from a Brahman called K Subramania Aiyer, saying he wanted a widow to marry, they received a reply from a woman reader who signed herself 'virgin widow' and asked whether 'Mr S A would marry a Sudra widow'. In his reply he said he would, 'as the Shastras provide for the Brahman the privilege of marrying a woman of any of the three lower castes'. Though the implication quite clearly is that it was all right for a Brahman male to marry a woman of any caste as he could only raise her status, while she could not affect his, it is difficult to believe this was the way things were in practice. Other reports show that several South Indian reformers who married widows were ostracized in different ways: many of them found especial difficulty when it came to conducting funeral ceremonies. Surely, then, marriage to a low-caste widow would be treated with even greater severity?

middle class Hindu Calcuttans, especially women, perhaps because he, as he said, 'worshipped all women as representatives of the divine mother'. At the same time, the device of using stories of Hindu resistance to Muslim invasion as a metaphor to stimulate contemporary nationalist sympathy began to be widely used. Tod's depiction of heroic Rajput resistance to Muslim invasion

became so popular that a whole host of plays, novels and songs were written on this theme; and to the glorification of child-marriage was added that of sati. Revivalist literature constructing images of the ideal Hindu woman was often double-edged: if some preferred to dwell on the sweet, flower-like qualities of the child-bride, others approvingly described the great strength of Hindu women when acting as wives or mothers, especially against the Muslims. This was a favourite theme of the literature glorifying the Rajputs, in which the sati was lauded for having preserved the honour of the race, literally and figuratively. B.C. Pal later described the effect Bankimchandra's use of the device, in *Durgesh Nandini* (The Chieftain's Daughter), had on him as a school boy:

The episode of Katlu Khan's assassination in the midst of the revels of his court in celebration of his victory over the Hindu chief of Gar Mandaram left a permanent mark upon my sensibilities. That episode appealed to my boyish imagination as a brilliant example of the courage and cunning of the Hindu woman who had all her life lived in the sacred seclusion of the zenana yet when the occasion called for it, who did not shrink from boldly intriguing for the defeat of the enemies of her clan and country. Bimla, to whose knife Katlu Khan fell, was the widow of the Hindu chief Bir Sinha who had been killed by the Muslim invader. Her assassination of her husband's murderer was justified by her love and loyalty of her dead lord and husband. But behind the personal note there was in this episode the far larger National or Racial issue—the contest for supremacy over the Hindu populations of West Bengal between their own king and the Moslem invader.[76]

It is not surprising, that, paralleling Hindu communalism, there was a rise in Islamic fundamentalism in rural Bengal, where campaigns against syncretic cults began to occur. Hindu-Muslim communalism spread to the industrial suburbs of Calcutta, where many migrant workers from East U.P. and Bihar lived, resulting in riots in 1896–97.[77]

Looking at the example of Maharashtra and Bengal, it could have been argued that the increasingly racist and communalist interpretation of the golden age theory of Aryan India was opposed to most ideas of social reform, especially concerning women. However, developments within the Arya Samaj in Punjab showed that the relationship between communalism and movements for women's rights need not always be one of opposition, for the more moderate College faction of the Arya Samaj was hostile to further education for girls, while the chauvinist Gurukul faction was committed to it. Both, however, emphasized the need for a Hindu consciousness, so that the debate was primarily over what was required of a Hindu girl.

Saraswati's Arya Samaj movement grew rapidly from the 1880s on, moving from a criticism of orthodox Hindu customs to their replacement with 'Aryan' ceremonies. Saraswati's *Sanskar Vidhi* provided a set of ceremonies for Aryas which were now gradually put into practice; beginning with reformed funeral rites, many Aryas moved to using simplified marriage rites. As this immediately made the arrangement of marriages more difficult, the Aryas 'developed a new marriage institution: the newspaper advertisement'. In 1882–83, two tracts were written by leading Arya Samajis, advocating widow remarriage; in the same years Arya journals began carrying accounts of widow remarriages. The Amritsar Arya Samaj was especially active, performing 'widow remarriages' with a great deal of fanfare. Yet the Arya Samaj was able to gain limited acceptance of the remarriage of 'virgin widows' alone, not of those with children.[78] By the mid-1880s, the Arya Samaj grew increasingly active in movements for women's education: an issue which they had earlier shown concern for in a sporadic way. From the late 1880s, various mofussil Arya Samajes began to open girls' schools, largely out of fear that the existing schools were being used for conversion. In 1890, the Jullundhur Samaj opened an Arya Kanya Pathshala; one year later, the school decided to accept widows as well as unmarried girls; and the year after that they announced they would open a Kanya Mahavidyalaya, for higher education. This proposal was supported by the newly- organized Arya Stri Samajes, one of which, in Ludhiana, ran a Female Vedic School and an ashram for widows. Before the Kanya Mahavidyalaya was opened, however, Arya Samajis were divided on the question of higher education for women. Its opponents ranked Lajpat Rai and Lal Chand, both of whom accepted primary education for women but opposed higher education, the former arguing, 'I maintained and do so still, that the spread of education among males has some strong and important inducements to back it, while the education of girls cannot necessarily derive any support from the same motives for education.' Many of the advocates for women's education, too, departed from Saraswati's views, arguing that: 'the character of girls' education should be different from that of boys . . . . The Hindu girl has functions of a very different nature to perform from those of a Hindu boy, and I would not encourage any system which would deprive her of her national traits of character. The education we give our girls should not unsex them.'[79] Though the Kanya Mahavidyalaya was opened, its curriculum was merely an expanded version of the Kanya Pathshala's curriculum, and both were similar to those used by the Brahmo schools. Apart from basic literacy,

arithmetic and some poetry, Arya Samaj religious literature, sewing, embroidery, cooking, 'hygiene', drawing and music were among the subjects taught.[80]

Towards the turn of the century, the Arya Samajis started a *shuddhi* movement, in which purification ceremonies were performed to reclaim Hindu converts; caste barriers were broken by allowing all caste members to wear the sacred thread; and attempts were made to bring outcastes into the fold of caste. Yet there was a certain tension here: outcastes were admitted to the Sanskrit *pathsalas* opened by the Arya Samaj, but could not wear the sacred thread; nor did the Aryas deal satisfactorily with the tricky problem of what Aryan rule over Dravidian subjects consisted of.[81] Even so, the *shuddhi* movement became a means of sanskritization (upward caste mobility), and membership of the Arya Samaj shot up from 40,000 in 1891 to over half a million by 1921.

In the 1890s, the Arya Samaj split, ostensibly over whether meat-eating should be permitted or not, but equally on issues of westernization. The moderate faction were those who supported the Dayanand Anglo-Vedic College, where Western science and Vedic culture were equally taught;[82] the militants were the Gurukul faction, who refused to accept financial support from the government, based education on the principles of brahmacharya, taught only Sanskrit and Hindi, and hired preachers to proselytize for them.[83] Both factions, however, shifted in this period 'from Arya-dharm to Hindu consciousness'. Lekh Ram, one of the founders of the Gurukul faction, conducted a bitter polemic with the Ahmediya Muslims, which resulted in his assassination in 1897; and Lala Lal Chand of the 'moderate' faction attacked the Congress, saying 'the consciousness must arise in the mind of each Hindu that he is a Hindu and not merely an Indian'.[84]

Though social reform campaigns began to develop in South India in the last quarter of the nineteenth century, they remained relatively weak until the turn of the century. In 1871 a widow remarriage association was started in Madras, but was shortlived; it was revived in the 1880s by Dewan Bahadur Raghunath Rao.[85] In 1878, Virasalingam started the Rajahmundri Social Reform Association, which focussed on widow remarriage, and in 1890s K.N. Natarajan started the *Indian Social Reformer*, which became increasingly important in connecting campaigns all over the country. In 1892, the Hindu Social Reform Association was started by young men, calling themselves the 'young Madras party'.[86] Though they were associated with the *Indian Social Reformer*, they formed a radical caucus within it, criticizing older social reformers for the caution and timidity with which they campaigned against polygamy, child marriage, bride price, and the prostitution of temple dancers. At the same time, the Theosophical Society, formed in Adyar in 1882, shifted away from its allegiance to social reform, under the influence of Annie Besant, who, in the early 1890s, attacked social reformers and defended traditional Hinduism.[87]

By the turn of the century, therefore, the search for a Hindu identity had become so important that even the Brahmos were talking of the education of 'Hindu' girls, and not, as they did before, of 'Indian' girls.[88] It is true that while talking of Indian women they were most often referring to Hindu women; in fact, the social reform movement of the nineteenth century has generally been criticized for having taken up issues which largely concerned upper caste Hindu women, such as sati, widow remarriage, child marriage. Yet this criticism ignores the shift that took place within the social reform movement over the course of the nineteenth century: the increasing identification of 'Aryan' with 'Hindu' and the communalization of both; the splitting of movements on lines of caste or ethnicity; and the strange growth of biological-rationalist arguments within 'Hindu social reform'. In the next chapter, we will describe the forms these developments took in the twentieth century.

NOTES

1. This phrase is increasingly used as a better description of the public-private dichotomy in more traditional societies in India. It is also used to historicise the dichotomy as in Kumkum Sangari and Sudesh Vaid (eds), *Recasting Women*, Delhi, Kali for Women, 1989, where a series of articles describe how the world-home dichotomy was affected by the colonial encounter.

2. Richard Tucker, *Ranade and the Roots of Indian Nationalism*, Bombay, Popular Prakashan, 1972, p. 18.

3. Rajat Ray and Sumit Sarkar, 'Ram Mohun Roy and the Break With the Past', in V.C. Joshi (ed.), *Ram Mohun Roy and the Process of Modernization in India*, Delhi, Vikas, 1975.

4. Ashis Nandy, *The Intimate Enemy*, Delhi, Oxford University Press, 1980.

5. Uma Chakravarti, 'Whatever Happened to the Vedic Dasi? Orientalism, Nationalism and a Script for the Past', in Kumkum Sangari and Sudesh Vaid, (eds), *Recasting Women*, op cit, pp. 27–87.

6. Arundhati Mukhopadhay, 'Attitudes Towards Religion and Culture in Nineteenth Century Bengal: the Tattvabodhini Sabha; 183–59', in *Studies in History*, New Series, Vol.3, No.1, pp. 9–28.

7. Ashis Nandy, 'Sati: A Nineteenth Century Tale of Women, Violence and Protest', in *At the Edge of Psychology*, Delhi, Oxford University Press, 1980, p. 21. Henceforth referred to as 'Sati'.

8. Edward Thompson, *Suttee*, London, George Allen and Unwin, 1928, p. 78.

9. Joanna Liddle and Rama Joshi, *Daughters of Independence*, Delhi, Kali for Women, 1986, p.27.

10. Benoy Ghosh, 'The Press in Bengal', in N.K. Sinha (ed.), *History of Bengal, 1757–1905*, Calcutta, 1967, p. 233.

11. Kumkum Sangari and Sudesh Vaid, op cit, 'Introduction', p. 16.

12. Joanna Liddle and Rama Joshi, op cit.

13. Anand Yang, 'The Many faces of Sati in the Early Nineteenth Century', *Manushi*, No 42–43.

14. Ashis Nandy, 'Sati', op cit., p. 7.

15. Ibid, pp. 4–5.

16. J.C. Ghose (ed), *The English Works of Raja Ram Mohun Roy*, Delhi, Cosmo, 1982, Vol. II, p. 363.

17. Ibid.

18. Uma Chakravarti, op cit, pp. 44–46.

19. *West Bengal District Gazetteer*, Hooghly, p. 526.

20. *History of Bengal*, op cit., p. 452.

21. Ibid.

22. The Brahmo Samaj was founded by Ram Mohun Roy in 1828.

23. *History of Bengal*, op cit., p. 452.

24. Sushma Sen, *Memoirs of an Octogenarian*, Calcutta, Elm Press, 1971, pp. 10–30.

25. Usha Chakraborti, *Condition of Bengali Women Around the Second Half of the Nineteenth Century*, Calcutta, 1963, pp. 40–42.

26. Sumanta Banerjee, 'Marginalization of Women's Popular Culture in Nineteenth Century Bengal', in Sangari and Vaid, op cit, pp. 127–79.

27. Gail Omvedt, *Cultural Revolt in a Colonial Society*, Scientific Socialist Education Trust, Bombay, 1976, p. 100.

28. S. Natarajan, *A Century of Social Reform in India*, Asia Publishing House, 1962, p. 53.

29. Cornelia Sorabjee, 'The Position of Hindu Women Fifty Years Ago', in Shyam Kumari Nehru (ed.), *Our Cause*, 1936, p. 5.

30. Gail Omvedt, op cit., p. 107.

31. Ibid, p. 106.

32. Sumanta Banerjee, op. cit, p. 174, f.n. 40.

33. Subal Chandra Mitra, *Isvar Chandra Vidyasagar*, Calcutta, New Bengal Press, 1902, pp. 282–89.

34. Ibid, p. 306.

35. Cornelia Sorabjee, op. cit., pp. 8–9.

36. Mrs. Marcus B. Fuller, *The Wrongs of Indian Womanhood*, Delhi, InterIndia Publications, 1984, pp. 62–69, first published 1900.

37. Lucy Carroll, 'Law, Custom and Statutory Social Reform: The Hindu Widow's Remarriage Act of 1856', *Indian Economic and Social History Review*, Vol. 20, Oct-Dec. 1983, pp. 363–88. Henceforth *IESHR*.

38. C.H. Heimsath, *Indian Nationalism and Hindu Social Reform*, Princeton University Press, 1964, p. 14.

39. Usha Chakraborti, op. cit., p. 42.

40. K.A. Nizami, *Sayyid Ahmed Khan*, Publications Division, Government of India, 1966, p. 12.

41. Gautam Chattopadhyaya (ed.), *Awakening in Bengal*, Calcutta, 1945, pp. 95–97, 277–85.

42. Arundhati Mukhopadhyaya, op cit.

43. Lajpat Rai, *A History of the Arya Samaj*, Delhi, Orient Longman, 1967, p. 45.

44. Kenneth Jones, *Arya Dharma*, Delhi, Manohar, p. 138.

45. Uma Chakravarti, op cit., p. 54.

46. Ganga Prasad Upadhyaya, *Swami Dayanand's Contribution to Hindu Solidarity*, Allahabad, Arya Samaj, 1939, pp. 93–96.

47. D. Vable, *The Arya Samaj*, Delhi, Vikas, 1983, pp. 110–11.

48. Sushma Sen, op. cit., p. 147.

49. Dhananjoy Keer, *Mahatma Jyotirao Phule—Father of Our Social Revolution*, Bombay, Popular Prakashan, 1965, p. 40.

50. See, for example, Dayaram Gidumal (ed.) *The Status of Women in India*, Bombay, 1889.

51. Philippe Aries, *Centuries of Childhood*, New York, Vintage Books, 1972.

52. See, for example, Kenneth Ballhatchet, *Race, Sex and Class Under the Raj*, Delhi, Vikas, 1980.

53. Anna Davin, 'Imperialism and Motherhood', *History Workshop Journal*, n.d. and Rajani Kanta Das, History of Indian Labour Legislation, Calcutta University, 1941, pp. 51–54.

54. Dayaram Gidumal, op. cit., pp. 35, 51 and 55.

55. Ibid, p. 248.

56. Ibid, p. 35.

57. Ibid, p. 36.

58. *History of Bengal*, op. cit., p. 408.

59. Ranade's address to the Fourth Social Conference, Calcutta, 1890, in Y. Chintamani (ed.), *Indian Social Reform*, Pt. II, p. 16.

60. C.H. Heimsath, op. cit., pp. 16–17.

61. Gail Omvedt, op. cit., p. 102.

62. Ibid, p. 107.

63. Joan Leopold, 'The Aryan Theory of Race', *IESHR*, June 1970, pp. 270–97.

64. Gail Omvedt, op. cit., pp. 101–6.

65. Dayaram Gidumal, op. cit., p. 122.

66. Gail Omvedt, op. cit., p. 101.

67. S. Natarajan, op. cit., pp. 85–86.

68. Ibid, pp. 86–87.

69. Ibid, p. 68.

70. Sita Ram Singh, *Nationalism and Social Reform in India: 1885–1920*, Delhi, Ranjit Printers and Publishers, MCMLXVIII, p. 87.

71. Sumit Sarkar, Modern India, (Henceforth MI) Delhi, Macmillan and Co., 1983, p. 80.

72. Ibid, p. 84.

73. Sita Ram Singh, op. cit., p. 88.

74. Sumit Sarkar, MI, pp. 71–72.

75. Ibid, p. 72.

76. B.C. Pal, 'The Freedom Movement in Bengal', *Forward*, No 1138, 26.12.1926, p. 17.

77. Sumit Sarkar, MI, p. 84.

78. Kenneth Jones, op. cit., pp. 99–102.

79. Ibid, p. 106.

80. Ibid, pp. 216–17.

81. Lajpat Rai, op cit., p. 138.

82. Ibid.

83. D. Vable, op. cit., p. 144.

84. Sumit Sarkar, MI, p. 75.

85. S. Natarajan, op. cit., p. 89.

86. Sumit Sarkar, MI, p. 71.

87. Ibid, p. 74.

88. Sushma Sen, op. cit., p. 145.

3. Towards Becoming 'The Mothers of the Nation'

By the late nineteenth century, social reform movements were beginning to show effects: although instances of personal revolt such as Ramabai's were still rare (and perhaps her revolt was made possible by the support her family gave her, as did the missionary community, who paid for her to go abroad), the numbers of women in public spheres had increased considerably. 'Celebrated women novelists' such as Nirupama Devi and Anurupa Devi were being referred to in Bengali literary circles and were members of literary clubs,[1] even though their works were scorned as being 'low', or merely entertaining. Maharashtra's first woman novelist, Kashibai Kanitkar, started writing in the 1890s, and its first woman doctor, Anandibai Joshi, qualified at the same time.[2] Despite these signs of progress the milieu in which such women lived was often a harsh and hostile one: When Kashibai Kanitkar and Anandibai Joshi, who were friends, first ventured out wearing shoes and carrying umbrellas they were stoned in the streets for daring to usurp such symbols of male authority.[3] In 1882, a booklet by Tarabai Shinde, *Stree Purush Tulana*, which was published in Poona aroused heated debate between two members of the Satyashodhak Samaj, Krishnarao Bhalekar and Jyotiba Phule. The booklet, which compared men and women, pointed out that faults commonly ascribed to women, such as superstitiousness, suspicion, treachery and insolence, could be found even more commonly in men. However, though Tarabai Shinde's defense of women was impassioned, she concluded with an exhortation to women, that they should, by the strength of their firm will, remain always well-behaved, pure as fire, and unblemished internally and externally, and shame men into hanging down their heads.[4]

Traditional as these sentiments might seem, the booklet was hostilely greeted even within a reformist organization such as the Satyashodhak Samaj: Krishnarao Bhalekar wrote a blistering attack on it, to which Jyotiba Phule replied equally furiously, accusing Bhalekar of defending a traditional Indian family system which allowed men to enjoy whatever they pleased while women were helplessly tied to their homes. According to Gail Omvedt, to Phule 'the issue was the formation of a new and equalitarian husband-wife relationship; the goal was

the breakdown of the old authority structure within the family.'[5]

Meanwhile, in Punjab and Bengal, both the Arya Samaj and the Brahmo Samaj spawned women preachers, to the consternation of many male reformers. For the Arya Samaj, the accrual of women preachers was an incidental development, consequent on their excessively loose-knit structure, in which many preachers were self appointed. In any case, though women preachers were traditionally accepted in both Bhakti and Tantric movements, they were new to modern reform-based religious organizations such as the Brahmo Samaj and the Arya Samaj. Pandita Ramabai for example, who first gained fame as a preacher in defence of women, was never fully accepted within the reform movement, which was one of the reasons why she converted to Christianity.

One of the women *Upadeshaks* of the Arya Samaj, Mai Bhagwati, spoke before a large public gathering in Haryana; others, apparently, had to speak in private houses. A tongue-in-cheek report of her speech in the *Tribune* implies that its impact on women in Haryana was radical: 'Of late, a correspondent says, it has been difficult to get well-cooked dishes at any house in Haryana, and few people stop at Haryana for fear of indigestion . . . .'[6]

The appointment of women preachers was more controversial in the Brahmo Samaj: In 1881, Manorama Majumdar, educated at home by her Brahmo husband, was appointed *Dharma-pracharika* by the Barisal Brahmo Samaj. Immediately a heated debate arose on whether women should be 'honoured' in this way, which raged for over three years. The matter was eventually settled in her favour at the intervention of an influential Brahmo, Chandicharan Sen.[7] Yet one of the first attempts at public campaigning by women was made under the auspicies of the Brahmo Samaj, in the 1890s. Launching a public campaign against purdah in Calcutta, groups of Brahmo women walked through the city's streets singing, and when crowds collected, addressed them on the evils of purdah.[8]

It was in these years too that women began to get involved in nationalist campaigns and organizations, though they had to overcome a certain degree of resistance from the men surrounding them in order to do so. The report for the 1889 Congress session in Bombay

'Hindoo Ladies' (ca 1900), a photograph showing different forms of attire, reproduced
from *A Second Paradise*, Doubleday, 1985.

Pandita Ramabai with a group of young women from her school.

notes 'that no less than ten lady delegates graced the assembly, one elected by men at a public meeting, the others by various ladies' associations, the Women's Christian Temperance Union, the Bengal Ladies' Association, and the Mahila Arya Samaj.' Among these ten women were Europeans, Christians (presumably native), one Parsi, one orthodox Hindu and three Brahmos. Pandita Ramabai was one of the delegates.[9] In fact, the participation of women in this Congress session appears to have been chiefly Ramabai's doing. Charles Bradlaugh suggested to her, and many others, that women delegates should join the Congress from this time on, so that their concerns would be represented when the Congress constituted independent India's parliament. As Ranade and other leading reformers were opposed to such participation, Pandita Ramabai was the only one who responded to Bradlaugh's suggestion, and it was through her efforts that seven or eight of the women delegates attended the Congress session.[10]

The report did not, however, mention the fact that though the women delegates were allowed to sit on the platforms, they were not allowed to speak or to vote on resolutions.[11] There seems to have been some confusion about exactly when women were allowed to speak at Congress sessions, for one writer says that it was in the 1890 Congress session—at which there were only four women delegates—that one woman was allowed to

speak, or rather, to present a vote of thanks to the President. In her speech, she thanked him for allowing her to speak, saying that this 'raised the status of our Indian women.'[12] Another writer puts the date ten years later, saying 'the first lady speaker of the Congress was Mrs Kadambini Ganguli, who moved the customary vote of thanks to the President of the Sixteenth Congress in 1900 (Calcutta).'[13]

Interestingly, prostitution was one of the first issues concerning women to be referred to by the Congress, and what they had to say about it sheds some light on early nationalist attitudes to the question. At their 1888 session they resolved to co-operate with English 'well wishers' of India in their attempts for 'the total *abrogation* of laws and rules relating to the regulation of prostitution by the State in India' (emphasis mine), and in their 1892 session this resolve was reiterated.[14] In other words, they wanted British laws regulating prostitution in India to be abolished.

First steps to regulate prostitution were taken by the British in India from the turn of the eighteenth century, ostensibly to deal with the venereal diseases which British soldiers were held to have caught from the prostitutes they frequented. In fact, prostitution had rapidly increased in India as the number of British troops stationed across the country increased. A system of *lal bazaars* (red light areas) attached to regimental

"Dancing girl", Jaipur, ca 1885,
reproduced from *A Second Paradise*, Doubleday, 1985.

despair at police harassment;[16] an administrative report for jails in Bengal Presidency said that on an average twelve women were arrested every day for breaches of the Act.[17] Initially protest was concentrated in Britain, where missionaries, non-conformists and Evangelicals campaigned against the Act on the grounds that it virtually legalized prostitution instead of attempting to eradicate it (shades of the sati abolition movement). This argument was taken up in India from the 1870s on, but here it was only one among several arguments against the Act. Another, originally more widely espoused one was that the Act, together with other measures taken by the British, did not distinguish between prostitution and courtesanship, nor between the former and 'kept' women, many of whom occupied places in 'respectable' society. Not only, it was argued, did this give the police scope to harass all classes of women indiscriminately, it also testified to the contempt the British felt for their native subjects, for it reduced courtesans and mistresses to the status of common

"Courtesan of Lucknow", ca 1880,
reproduced from *A Second Paradise*, Doubleday, 1985.

shopping areas developed, and as these markets grew so did attempts to manage them. It was suggested that police checks on prostitution be instituted, that prostitutes be subjected to compulsory medical examination and registration, and that centres for treatment of venereal diseases be established, at which prostitutes could be forcibly detained. Lock hospitals, which originally gained their name from the decision to put lepers and lunatics behind bars, were now established in various cantonment areas for the treatment of venereal diseases, but they had a chequered career. Throughout the century a debate raged over both the ethics and efficacy of thus handling prostitution and venereal diseases: for over a hundred years, therefore, lock hospitals were opened, closed, re-opened and re-closed, largely according to whether their opponents or proponents had greater influence at the time.[15]

Organized opposition to the British regulation of prostitutes really developed after 1864, when the Contagious Diseases Act was passed, making the registration and medical examination of prostitutes compulsory. It was reported that many prostitutes committed suicide in

prostitutes, and thereby reduced the status of the masters of the former to that of the customers of the latter. In effect then, upper-class men felt themselves fallen from patron to client, and felt too that the British had deliberately engendered this fall as a means of rubbing their noses in the dust. Though a nationalist note was sounded here along with one of class, clearly the Congress chose to align with the puritan argument, for its reference was to English 'well wishers'.

First attempts to reform prostitutes were made in Calcutta by Michael Madhusudan Datta, a member of the young Bengali group, who proposed to rehabilitate them by turning them into actresses, and got the Bengal theatre committee to accede to his proposal. This appears to have been the point at which women began to replace men in playing female roles in commercial theatres: several prostitutes turned actresses, and one of them, Binodini, shot into stardom.[18] Datta's move might have been prompted by an *Amrita Bazaar Patrika* report appearing in 1869, which created something of a furore in Bengali reformist circles. According to the report, ninety per cent of Calcutta's prostitutes were widows, of whom a large number came from Kulin Brahman families (Kulin Brahmans practised polygamy).[19] Yet if the report created a furore, the general reaction was to attempt to bury it, rather than act upon it. Though the dangers of widows turning to prostitution had been darkly hinted at in the campaign for the remarriage of widows, Vidyasagar himself disapproved of Datta's proposal, and resigned from the Bengal theatre committee when Datta gained his way. Whether most reformers were made uncomfortable by the thought that many prostitutes came from their own or similar caste and financial communities, or whether they believed that prostitutes should be punished for their choice of a vocation, the fact was that Datta was one of the very rare reformers to attempt positive rehabilitatory action for prostitutes. Most other reformers were more concerned to show their abhorrence for the practice than with what was to happen to prostitutes themselves.

If the Contagious Diseases Act expanded the category of prostitution to cover courtesans, madams and mistresses, the reform movement itself expanded the category even further. Such traditionally accepted expressions of eros as the *nautch*, which was performed at both public and private functions across the country, were now treated as obscene by reformers, and the dancing girls who starred in nautches began to be called prostitutes. Campaigns for a ban on the nautch were first initiated by missionary-dominated organizations, such as the Leagues for Social Purity and Temperance, who petitioned the British government to stop all nautches at public functions sponsored by them.[20] By the end of the century the anti-nautch campaign had become so popular with reformers that in 1897 Ranade declared

that almost all social reform organizations were committed to it, pledging that they would neither allow nautches to be performed at their marriage celebrations, nor attend any functions at which they were performed.[21]

The internalization of Victorian morality grew so deeply that almost any kind of public display of emotion began to be frowned upon, especially if it was physical. Holi celebrations could of course be fairly easily characterized as Bacchanalian or orgiastic, and it is not surprising that at the seventh National Social Conference reformers decided to launch a campaign to 'purify' the Holi festival, so that people would neither drink, nor take drugs, nor dance during it. More revealing of the degree to which reformers were influenced by the nineteenth century British distaste for expressiveness, however, is the veto which they extended even to such traditions as public mourning by women: at the same session of the National Social Conference, a resolution was passed stating that *siapa* (public mourning for a death, by women in Punjab, who beat their breasts and cry aloud), was 'a very objectionable and unreasonable practice, and entailed great misery to the mourners.'[22] All reform organizations were asked by the Conference to campaign against *siapa*.

Predictably, in this context, little support was given by reformers or moderate nationalists to Surendranath Banerjea, himself a nationalist, when he introduced a civil liberties theme into arguments over prostitution. In 1895, there was a government move to expand the scope of the police so that any policeman over the rank of a native constable could arrest a woman for soliciting, without independent evidence. A Bill was tabled to this effect, which Banerjea opposed on the grounds that it threatened individual liberty by giving the police unchecked power. As a result of his opposition the Bill was amended, and police officers were allowed to arrest women for soliciting only if independent complaints were made.[23]

Interestingly, the discrimination which this Bill made between native and British constables does not seem to have been treated as a major symbol of racism. However, other things the British did or said in relation to prostitution aroused considerable resentment. One of the factors prompting the Bill had been the discovery that a number of prostitutes in cities like Calcutta and Bombay were European. The British reaction to this was different from the Bengali reaction to the discovery of Kulin Brahman prostitutes, in being loud where the latter was comparatively muted. A dominant theme in the British discussion of the existence of European prostitutes in India, was how it undermined British 'racial prestige', and blurred the line dividing British rulers from their native subjects. A further irritant was the special treatment they accorded British soldiers, clearing brothels of native men when they were in use by British soldiers, and voicing fears that their men had become the prey of dirty, diseased native women.[24]

Simmering resentment of British soldiers found some outlet in the 1890s, when two incidents became the focus of public outrage: in 1893, a railway gatekeeper named Hampanna was shot by a British soldier for having stopped him from pursuing two women who had come to visit Hampanna. The Government, however, took action against the soldier only after the Hindu Social Reform Association, the missionary-led Social Purity groups, and the *Hindu* took up the issue. Though the evidence given by one of the women was strong, the defence argued that they had encouraged the soldiers to think they were prostitutes (Hampanna, they said, had asked for money and the women had signalled the soldiers), and argued that the soldier had fired in self-defence when Hampanna attacked him with a stick. The judge drew attention to the soldier's youth, and the jury acquitted him.[25]

In 1897, while commenting on the handling of plague operations in Poona, G K Gokhale, a Congressman and social reformer, said in an interview to the *Manchester Guardian* that he had heard that the British soldiers who had been sent in to rescue plague victims 'spat upon idols or broke them. . . and dragged women into the streets for inspection before removal to hospitals. My correspondents. . . reported the violation of two women, one of whom is said to have committed suicide rather than survive her shame.'[26] Gokhale later withdrew the allegation, as his correspondents could not substantiate their reports, but in 1899 another incident aroused indignation—the gang rape of a Burmese woman by British soldiers in Rangoon. In this case, however, the Government, under instructions from Curzon, did take action: the soldiers were dismissed and the regiment received a punishment posting.[27]

By the end of the nineteenth century, therefore, the issues of rape and racism were interlinked. Though this interlinkage was first highlighted by social reformers, it was soon used by nationalists as a weapon against British rule. Cries for the protection of 'our' women from sexual attacks by marauding white soldiers abounded, especially in Bengal. One of the most militantly nationalist women of the period, Sarala Debi Ghosal, who took over the *Bharati* (see below) in 1895, used its pages to harangue young men to engage in 'physical culture', and to start an *antaranga dal* (intimate circle) for self defence and the 'defence of their women from molestation by British soldiers in streets and stations'.[28] The same appeal was made by 'a lady correspondent' in the *Sanjibani*.[29]

Yet if nationalists were beginning to use rape as an example of imperialist barbarism, it was clearly seen as a violation of community—or national—honour, rather than an act of violence against women. Rape, it seems, was a taboo subject, nameable only when committed by outsiders. That this was, at least partly, a deliberate stand taken by nationalists, was shown by their attitude towards the death of Phulmoni Debi, an eleven year old child bride, who died in 1893, when her adult husband raped her. Though the incident caused considerable public outcry, this came mainly from reformist ranks: the nationalists kept mum.

Within the reform movement a certain degree of criticism of earlier methods of campaigning was beginning to take place: Vivekananda, for example, mounted attacks on Bengali social reform for adopting Western values and forms, and being elitist; combining this with paeans to the glory of Aryan India and Hinduism, as well as scathing criticism of latter-day corruption.[30] In 1896 he founded the Ramakrishna Mission in Bengal, which was based on an 'ideal of social service'. The emphasis placed by social reformers on personal practice, as exemplified by the 'marry a widow, be a saviour' dictum of the mid-nineteenth century, now developed into a philosophy of social service instead of legislative campaigns, under the influence of which G K Gokhale founded the Servants of India Society, in 1905.

Similar changes were taking place in the Congress as well, where the moderates were characterized as ponderous and ineffectual by their critics, who included Aurobindo Ghosh, B G Tilak, Rabindranath Tagore, and a host of others. Calls were made for self-reliance and mass mobilization, as well as for 'independent' Indian capitalist development. From the 1870s on, nationalist economic theory had begun to develop an analysis of the birth of British rule as leading to a 'drain of wealth' through creating an artificial export surplus, destroying Indian handicrafts, curbing the development of modern Indian industry, and burdening agriculture with excessive demands for land revenue.[31] This was now translated into two major kinds of campaigns: for the support of indigenous handicrafts, and against malpractices in European and Government-owned enterprises. Rabindranath Tagore's sister, Swarnkumari Debi, who had founded the *Bharati* with him and another brother, was one of the women who acted on calls for *atmasakti* (self-reliance) and swadeshism. In 1886 she started a women's organization called the Sakhi Samiti, which was to train widows to teach, so that they could become self-reliant and aid in the spread of women's education. In the same years, she started to hold annual *mahila silpamelas* (women's craft fairs), at which handicrafts made by Indian women were sold: partly as fundraising for the Sakhi Samiti, and partly to promote indigenous cottage industry as a means of developing both atmasakti and swadeshism.[32] As the nationalist movement grew in strength, annual fairs of this kind began to be held

Swarnakumari Debi, 1856-1932

Swarnakumari Debi was Debendrnath Tagore's fourth daughter, and she married at 13, under the Brahmo marriage rites. She wrote poetry and fiction. Her first novel, *Deep Nirman*, was published when she was 18. In 1877, she joined the board of editors of *Bharati* and became its chief editor in 1884. In all she wrote 25 books in Bengali, including short stories, plays and textbooks. Two of her novels, *Chinnamukul* and *Phuler Mala*, were translated into English, one in 1910 and the other in 1913.[1]

In 1882 she founded the Ladies Theosophical Society, which closed in 1886 for paucity of members. In 1886 she started the Sakhi Samiti, 'so that women of respectable families should have the opportunity of mixing with each other and devoting themselves to the cause of social welfare . . . The first aim of the Samiti is to help the helpless orphans and widows. This will be done in two ways. In those cases where such widows and orphans have no near relations or if these relations have not the means of maintaining them the Sakhi Samiti will take their full responsibility . . . the Samiti . . . will educate them and through them spread women's education. After they have finished their education they will take up the work of zenana education. The Samiti will give them remuneration for their work. In this way two objects will be accomplished. Hindu widows will be able to earn through service to others according to the sanction of Hindu religion an independent living, and a way will be found for the spread of female education.'[2] In order to collect the money to educate women, the Samiti held annual Mahila Silpamelas, at which they exhibited and sold handicrafts made by women to women. Swarnakumari Debi was one of the first two delegates elected from Bengal to represent the state at the 1890 Congress session. In 1927 she was awarded the Jagattarini gold medal by Calcutta University, and in 1929 she became the president of the Bangiya Sahitya Sammelan. She and her daughter Hiranmoyee worked together in the Hiranmoyee Widow's Industrial Home.[3]

1. Lotika Ghose, op cit., p.148
2. Usha Chakraborti, op cit., p. 128
3. Usha Chakraborti, op cit., p. 129

under nationalist auspicies all over the country, and the practice of organizing separate 'women's sections' at these fairs developed. This became an increasingly popular activity for nationalist women.

By the turn of the century, Bengali nationalism had developed in a variety of directions. Influenced by the Italian nationalist movement, Calcutta was, according to B C Pal, 'honeycombed with secret societies'. The Brahmo leader, Sibnath Shastri, was chief of the not so secret societies of the early nineteenth century (the Derozians, for example) who were to 'abjure' idolatry,

caste and child-marriage, in that order of preference.[33]

Despite this indication of loyalty to social reform, revivalism and extremism were now the more dominant themes in Bengali nationalism. It was at this time, in Calcutta, that women began to engage in revivalist and extremist activities, in addition to their earlier involvement in social reform and moderate nationalism. One of the first women to do so, Swarnkumari Debi's daughter Sarala Debi Ghosal, was one of the architects of a militant mother-centred nationalism which was to take to revolutionary terrorism in the twentieth century. By all

Sarala Debi Ghosal (later Chaudharani) 1872–1946

Swarankumari Devi's daughter, Sarala Devi Ghoshal, studied at Bethune school and college and was awarded the Padmabati medal in her B.A. by Calcutta University. She worked as Assistant Superintendent at the Maharani Girls School in Mysore for one year, then came back to Calcutta where she became editor of *Bharati*, a monthly journal, in 1895. Through *Bharati* she organized a physical culture campaign, asking young men to form an *antaranga dal* (intimate circle) for self defence, and for the defence of their women against molestation by British soldiers in streets and stations. She forced her friends and acquaintances to take a pledge on the map of India that they would henceforth be prepared to sacrifice their lives for their country's independence. She tied *rakhis* around their wrists as tokens of their vow.

Sarala Devi was deeply involved in the revivalist movement in Bengal. 'Her declared intention was to remove the historical reproach, perpetuated by Macaulay, that the Bengalis were a race of cowards, and she was avowedly influenced by the success of the Japanese in the war with Russia.'[1] In 1902 she exhorted young men to organize pratpaditya *bratas*, defensive exercises with swords and clubs, as well as wrestling and boxing, and managed to get quite a following. In 1903 she organized *udayaditya bratas* and *birastami bratas*. These latter took the form of a parade of 'physical prowess', on the second day of Durga Puja and were invented by Sarala Devi. In the same year she also opened an academy of martial arts in Calcutta, at which fencing and jiu-jitsu were taught by Murtaza.

In 1904 she celebrated Birastami with a rally at which various competitions took place, a ceremonial vow of the heroes was taken by all champions, and the sword was worshipped as a symbol of ancient heroes. In the same year she 'made Congress history in the session held in Calcutta . . . when she trained a group to sing *Bande Mataram*'.[2] In 1905, the Mymensingh Suhrid Samiti, with which Sarala Devi was closely associated, made the first attempt to 'use the words Bande Mataram as a national call'.[3] Also in 1905 she married and moved to Lahore, where in 1910 she started the Bharat Stree Mahamandal. The chief aim was to be the spread of female education, but as the purdah system and child marriage were the main obstacles to the education of women it was proposed to start organizations in every province whose function it would be to collect money and engage teachers who would be sent to the houses of those who desired to educate their wives and daughters. It was also decided that text books suitable for teaching Indian women should be written or adapted for the purpose, women should try and enrich the vernacular literature, organize selling centres for women's handicrafts and do what they could to afford medical treatment to women.'[4]

1. J.C.Ker, op cit, p.7.
2. M.E.Cousins, op cit, p. 56.
3. Sumit Sarkar, op cit, p. 305.
4. Lotika Ghose, op cit, p. 147.

accounts, Sarla Debi was a rebellious and independent person. While this must have been partly due to her liberal Brahmo background, she had to overcome considerable family opposition when, at the age of twenty-three, she took a job at a girls' school in Mysore. According to Uma Chakravarti, Sarla Debi's own description of why she had fought to take the job was that she 'wanted to flee the cage or prison of home, and establish her right to an independent livelihood like men.'[34] If accurately represented, her words bear an uncanny resemblance to the words used by contemporary feminists to describe the home: 'Caged within the four walls of the home'. (The image of imprisonment has of course been commonly used to describe the human condition: generally, however, men are imprisoned by the world and women by the home).

Sarala Debi's attempt to live and work on her own was brought abruptly and tragically to an end when a young man broke into her room one night,[35] and as a result she gave up her independent life and returned home to help her mother with the Sakhi Samiti and the mahila silpamelas, later taking over the *Bharati*. In 1899 she was one of the nationalists who campaigned vigorously for support to the G.I.P railwaymen's strike;[36] at the same time, stirred by Aurobindo Ghosh's polemic against constitutional paths to independence, she threw herself into mobilizing young Bengali men to revolt against British rule. Clearly, she was a great believer in the agitprop value of rites and symbols: when her calls for an antaranga dal resulted in its formation, she made its members lay their hands on a map of India and pledge that they were ready to sacrifice their lives for the country's independence, tying a *rakhi* around each wrist as a token of the vow.[37] In 1902 she wrote to a cousin saying she intended to move 'from speech to writing and from writing to deeds';[38] in the same year she started a gymnasium in her father's house, at which training in sword and *lathi*-play was given by a 'Professor Murtaza', who also trained various members of Aurobindo's band of revolutionaries. Here she further urged members to leave wrestling and shooting.

With all these activities, Sarala Debi's main thrust was to find ways of actualizing a nationalist warrior-hero, through re-casting local and mythical figures in its image. To this end, she chose a Hindu landlord and parricide, Pratapaditya, whom she elevated to the ranks of warrior heroes, getting members of the antaranga dal to take a vow 'in memory of the Bengali Hindu patriot prince who fought Imperial Muslim power.'[39] In 1903 she added his name to a list of mythic and historical figures, starting a Birastami festival (to commemorate valour) on the second day of Durga Puja, at which a *udayaditya brata* (a vow in memory of bygone heroes) was taken. Sanskrit verses listing these heroes were recited as a kind of litany: The names included Krishna, Rama, Bhishma, Drona, Karna, Arjuna, Bhima, Meghnad, Rana Pratap, Shivaji, Ranjit Singh and Pratapaditya.

The orthodoxy was shocked, and Sarala Debi was criticized in an article in the *Rangalay* of September 1903 for conduct 'unworthy of a Hindu woman.'[40] The *Rangalay* went on to contrast her unfavourably with the wives and mothers of heroes in Sanskrit texts, complaining that the modern Bengali girl could only be satisfied by playing the hero herself.[41]

Though the orthodoxy complained, Sarala Debi's efforts were already both innovative and opportune in a Calcutta swept with admiration for Tod's martial Rajputana, and her Birastami festivals and Pratapaditya *bratas* caught on among groups of young men. In 1904 the Mymensingh Suhrid Samiti started to take the Pratapaditya brata; in the same year, her Birastami festival in Calcutta included the worship of the sword as a symbol of bygone heroes.[42] At the second session of the Mymensingh Suhrid Samiti's Pratapaditya brata, in 1905, Sarala Debi presided, and under her aegis, according to Sumit Sarkar, 'an attempt was made for the first time to use the words *"Bande Mataram"* as a national call'.[43] Bankim Chandra's *Anand Math*, in which the song *Bande Mataram* appeared, was performed as a play at this session: the novel's heroine, Shanti, must have been something of a role-model for Sarala Debi, as must have also been another of his heroines, Debi Chaudharani (in a novel of the same name). Both Shanti and Debi Choudharani were married women who, when required at critical moments to leave their homes, rose unhesitatingly to the occasion and went to war in the interests of a higher good. (Shanti literally donned armour and excelled in the battle to resist Mughal invasion, Debi Chaudharani did not wear armour but carried arms, becoming a bandit queen in order to rejoin her husband). And both women, when the moment of crisis passed, returned to their homes without regret. In other words, when the situation required it, both women sacrificed their 'natural' *dharma* for an ethical way of life, for a masculine warrior ethos, in order to create the conditions for dharma to regain its true nature.[44]

The parallels between this and Sarala Debi's life are irresistible. Not only did her own bid for personal independence grow to be subsumed in a quest for national independence, but, as her activities began to bear fruit, she acceded to family pressure and, at the age of thirty-three, married a widowed Arya Samaji whom her family chose for her, Ram Bhuj Choudhari, then went to live and work in Lahore. After her marriage, she was often referred to as Debi Choudharani. In a way, then, Bankim's reinterpretation of concepts such as dharma allowed women like Sarala Debi to acquire a traditional sanction for their activities. Nor was it only women like Sarala Debi for whom Bengali nationalism created a new space by the turn of the century: it was in nationalist movements to follow that we find women first beginning to be active.

In the same year as Sarala Debi married (1905), Curzon's partition of Bengal provided a focus for the nationalist resentment already aroused by changes in the Calcutta Corporation in 1899, which reduced the number of elected Indian members, and the Universities Act of 1904, which reduced the number of elected Senate members, vested government officials with the final decision on affiliating colleges and recognizing schools, and tried to fix minimum college fees. Though the argument publicly offered for the partition of Bengal was of administrative convenience—that Bengal was too large and Assam would benefit from a maritime outlet for its tea, oil and coal (all European-dominated industries)—intra-government notes on the subject made it clear that 'in this scheme as in the matter of amalgamation of Berar to the Central provinces one of our main objects is to split up and thereby weaken a solid body of opponents to our rule.' At the same time, British propaganda about the advantages for Muslims in a separate province gave credence to nationalist charges that in partitioning Bengal the government was using 'divide and rule tactics', and fostering Hindu-Muslim tensions by dividing the predominantly Muslim-occupied areas from Hindu occupied ones; the decision was, as well, regarded as a high-handed 'national insult'.[45] Though partition was initially received with demonstrations of communal unity, and the nationalists included an extremely dedicated group of Muslim swadeshi agitators, there were a series of riots in East Bengal from mid-1906 through 1907, mostly in Mymensingh district (where Sarala Debi's Pratapaditya bratas had been celebrated from 1904). The targets were landlords and moneylenders, and at many places debt bonds were torn up; but as most of the landlords and moneylenders were Hindus, the effects of the riots were to further intensify communalism in the area. Demands for Hindu self-defence groups began to be made, and the spectre of the British soldier-rapist was now replaced by the spectre of the Muslim rapist of Hindu women, leading to new calls for women to form their own self-defence organizations.[46]

In North India too Hindu-Muslim tensions were exacerbated by increasing competition between educated Hindus and Muslims for Government jobs, the Morley-Minto reform proposals, a Muslim demand for job reservation, and the formation of the Muslim League in Lahore in 1906. A few months after the League was founded, Ram Bhuj Datta and Sarala Debi founded the Lahore Hindu Sahayak Sabha, on the grounds that if Muslims had communal organizations to protect their rights then Hindus should have them too. In the following months, Hindu Sahayak Sabhas were founded in Multan, Jhang, Sialkot, Lyallpur and Gujranwala; at the same time Sarala Debi's Birastami festival began to be celebrated in Lahore. Commenting on this, the *Tribune* said 'we were glad to notice men and women of all classes and persuasions looking at the admirable feats of gymnastics, trials of strength, exhibitions of swordplay, Gatka fights, and other interesting performances . . . and songs exhorted the assembled crowds to sink petty differences and unite in the service of the motherland.'[47]

The 1905–8 Swadeshi movement in Bengal reflects the beginning of women's participation in nationalist activities on a larger scale. From 1904, the moderates in the Congress began a campaign against the plan of partition, consisting mainly of petitions, protests and resolutions; after 1905 these methods dominated the movement against partition for a few months, but their evident weakness led to a dramatic shift in forms of protest after July 1905. A decision to boycott British goods was taken in August, and in October Partition Day was observed by the exchange of *rakhis* to symbolize brotherhood and, in mourning, no hearths were lit.[48] From August onwards, the participation of women was reported: five hundred women watched the laying of the foundation stone of Federation Hall in Calcutta on the 24th; on the same day, Ramendrasundar Trivedi's *Banglalakshmir Brata Katha* (the story of the Bengali women's vow) was read before a women's meeting in his village in Murshidabad district. The *Brata Katha*, intended to translate the swadeshi message for village women, described how the goddess of fortune had been on the point of leaving Bengal once before, because of fratricidal strife between Hindus and Muslims; but Husam Shah and Akbar had made her stay through their tolerant policies. Now she had become restless again as the British were dividing Bengal, separating brother from brother, Hindus in the West from Muslims in the East. But the womenfolk of Bengal could make her stay, through annual *rakhi bandhan* and *arandhan* rites, and above all by taking a vow of abstention from foreign goods. And then Lakshmi would reign forever in the golden fields of Bengal.[49]

It seems also that first steps to woo women were taken in this period. Small though these were, perhaps they were taken because many of the wives, sisters and daughters of nationalists had begun to form support groups for the movement. Middle-class nationalist women contributed jewellery as well as money to swadeshi; there is a report that in some villages women began to put aside handfuls of grain as contribution;[50] and in Barisal, where Aswinikumar Datt had been engaged in 'sustained humanitarian work', many women made over their savings to his Swadesh Bandhab Samiti (this was one of the five principal samitis to be banned in January, 1909. The others were Brati, Dacca Anushilan, Suhrid and Sadhana). In Khulan, women smashed their foreign bangles after a speech given by Kaliprasanna Kabvanisnarod; when B C Pal toured Bengal in 1907, he addressed women's meetings in Habibgunj and Bhola; and when Surendranath Banerjea visited Mymensingh in the same year, he was given a rousing welcome by women.[51] In August 1907, when Bhupendranath Dutta (Vivekananda's brother) was arrested, a Ladies' Meeting was held in his honour, an address of honour was signed by two hundred women and presented to his mother, and contributions were made for his legal expenses.[52] Sister Nivedita, one of Vivekananda's most ardent disciples, stood surety for Bhupendranath. From 1902, after Vivekananda's death, she had grown increasingly close to Aurobindo's group, and was also was reported to have

Sister Nivedita

become a member of his National Revolutionary Council; in 1905, she worked closely with Rabindranath and Hirendranath Datta; and after the 1906 floods and near famine in East Bengal she toured the villages, doing relief work and propagandizing swadeshi, as well as organizing women's meetings at which she asked them to revive *charkha* spinning, among other skills.[53] It seems that there was a move among some zenana bound women to buy and use spinning wheels; and an English critic complained, somewhat improbably:

> the revolt seems to have obtained a firm hold of the Zenana and the Hindu woman behind the purdah often exercises a greater influence upon her husband and her sons than the English woman who moves freely about the world . . . . in Bengal even small boys of so tender an age as to still have the run of the Zenana have, I am told, been taught the whole pattern of sedition and go about from house to house dressed up as little Sanyasis in little yellow robes preaching hatred of the English.[54]

In western India there seems to have been relatively little involvement of women in swadeshism, despite Tilak's popularity; nor do they seem to have been involved in extremist activity. There is just one report of

women's support for the swadeshi movement: on the 6th of October 1905, about 'a hundred and twenty high-caste Brahmin ladies assembled at Natu's temple, Shunwar Peth,' in Poona, for the *halad kunku* ceremony (a Hindu ritual); there was a meeting presided over by Parwati Bapat, essays on the 'Swadeshi Question' were read by Saraswati Bhanu and Miss Bhatkande, and the assembled women resolved that they would not buy glass bangles, 'rock-oil chintz', children's toys, or any other items of European manufacture.[55]

Punjabi nationalists welcomed the Bengali swadeshi movement as one which was taking up Punjab's example, made twenty years ago, when 'a few educated Punjabi gentlemen at Lahore, mostly connected with the Arya Samaj, resolved to eschew cloths and other necessaries of foreign manufacture.[56] Like Tilak's call for boycott of foreign goods in Western India, this had been a protest against the countervailing excise of 1895, but without much success. Punjabi swadeshism from the 1890s consisted largely of founding indigenous capitalist enterprises and educational institutions which were independent of government grants. Their enthusiasm for the Bengal movement did not make much of a change in this activity, though it did receive a fillip. It seems, however, that women now began to join in calls for swadeshism; in Lahore, women organized a Ladies' Section at the Industrial and Agricultural Exhibition of 1909;[57] one Sushila Debi in Sialkot exhorted women to join the movement, organized swadeshi women's meetings and collected funds for 'anarchists' under trial; a woman member of the Hissar Arya Samaj, Purani, toured several districts of the Punjab, exhorting women 'to bring up their sons not with a view to joining government service, but to an independent participation in trade, especially the manufacture and sale of swadeshi'. Moreover, she argued, strict observance of caste restrictions 'prevented women from bringing up their sons, as was done by the women of old, to be warriors and great men.'[58] And in Delhi, a woman called Agyavati was reported to have become an ardent nationalist agitator, and was described by the government, in tones of alarm, as 'a very bold woman'. Agyavati seems to have taken Swarnakumari Debi's ideas one step further: the latter had said that the Sakhi Samiti would train widows to teach, and thereby women's education would spread and widows would become self-reliant. Agyavati started a widow's home (Vidhwa Ashram), at which they were educated to preach nationalist politics; or so the Home Department believed.[59]

Concern for the condition of widows had been renewed towards the end of the nineteenth century. Malabari's campaign had focussed on the problems of widows as well as on child-marriage: the latter became the subject of reformist-revivalist controversy, but the former went unnoticed: perhaps because no moves for

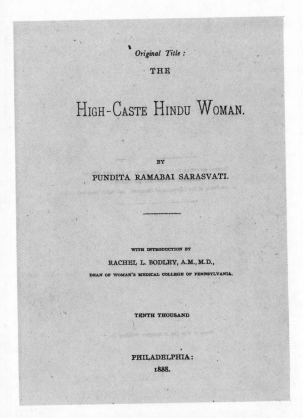

Original Title :

THE

HIGH-CASTE HINDU WOMAN.

BY

PUNDITA RAMABAI SARASVATI.

WITH INTRODUCTION BY
RACHEL L. BODLEY, A.M., M.D.,
DEAN OF WOMAN'S MEDICAL COLLEGE OF PENNSYLVANIA.

TENTH THOUSAND

PHILADELPHIA:
1888.

In Memoriam.

ANANDIBAI JOSHEE, M.D.

DAUGHTER OF GANPATRAO AMRITASWAR
AND
GUNGABAI JOSHEE.

Born in Poona, Bombay Presidency, India, March 31st, 1865. (Child-name, Yamuna Joshee.)

Married Gopalrao Vinayak Joshee, March 31st, 1874. (Wife-name, Anandibai Joshee.)

Sailed from Calcutta, India, for America, April 7th, 1883, being the first high-caste Brahman woman to come to the United States. Landed in New York, June 4th, 1883.

Graduated in medicine, from the Woman's Medical College of Pennsylvania, March 11th, 1886, being the first Hindu woman to receive the Degree of Doctor of Medicine in any country.

Appointed, June 1st, 1886, to the position of Physician-in-Charge of the Female Ward of the Albert Edward Hospital, in the City of Kolhapur, India.

Sailed from New York, to assume her duties in Kolhapur, October 9th, 1886.

Died in Poona, India, February 26th, 1887.

legislation were made. Social reformers had by now come to feel that changes effected by legislation were too slow and too small; they must also have been influenced by new emphasis on service and self-help, as Swarnakumari Debi was. The turn of the century saw a proliferation of widows homes and orphanages, with an emphasis on education, training and employment. Between 1900–3, schemes to train widows as teachers were set up all over the country, including Mysore and Madras.[60] It is not clear whether this shift in aims occurred because reformers were beginning to realize that remarriage was not an option for non-'virgin' widows, or because there was a growing feeling that there should in any case be other options open to widows which would allow them to support themselves. However, whatever the consciousness behind this shift might have been, it did result in the creation of a new category of public activity: social service by widowed women, for themselves and for the country.

This new phase in the campaign for the reform of widows' conditions of existence attracted more and more widows to its fold, and gained new momentum as a result. As with several other social reform campaigns, Poona became a centre for this one as well. Though Pandita Ramabai, herself widowed, had drawn attention to the issue in *The High-Caste Hindu Woman*, published in 1887 and the Sharada Ashram which she started for widows was based on a kind of Tolstoyan concept of the model self-sufficient community, the name most widely associated with the widowhood reform movement of this

time is D D Karve's. Karve it was who was regarded as the parent of the movement to rehabilitate widows in Maharashtra: even roughly contemporary journals espoused this view. A piece in the *Indian Ladies Magazine*, founded in 1907 in Madras, was clearly written under this impression: the writer described how, in 1896 D D Karve had announced in the *Sudharak* (Reformer) that he would donate Rs 1,000 towards the establishment of a widow's home and, even if no-one donated anything, with this money he would be able to at least feed, clothe and educate one widow. Soon after

a letter appeared in the columns of the Sudharak over the signature of 'a widow'. The writer admired the spirit in which Mr Karve had undertaken the cause of her sisters and went on to say: 'If Mr Karve is prepared to upraise one widow, I am sure five-ten humble persons like myself can co-operate and work as cooks, take in washing, clean utensils, grind corn, aye, even beg from door to door, but earn enough to at least support one more of our helpless sisters'. It was a humble appeal—or rather, offer—but it was significant. It pointed to the spirit that was abroad in spite of the ingrained prejudice of centuries. For the time was to come when Mr Karve's remarkable venture had assumed concrete form, when his right hand men, so to speak, were women, widows who had themselves gone through all the iniquitous things that a high caste Hindu widow has to pass through and who

A woodcut of Goddess Kali and a woodcut of a 10-armed Durga from Ashit Paul, ed,
Woodcut Prints of Nineteenth Century Calcutta, Calcutta, Seagull Books, 1983.

were prepared to devote all their lives to the sacred cause which Mr Karve had espoused; to go to the most distant parts of this vast continent to send forth a trumpet appeal on behalf of the helpless widow, to open the eyes of the men of India to all they owed to their women.[61]

Why was no mention of Pandita Ramabai made in this piece, published in a women's journal which was dedicated to women's emancipation? One of the reasons is clearly the increasing marginalization she suffered from the 1890s on, having become a major focus of attack by the revivalists, partly for her radical social reform and partly due to her conversion to Christianity and her post conversion missionary activities. Karve, on the other hand, remained very much a Hindu, though he too had to suffer at revivalist hands. As much a reason for her marginalization, however, was her confident anti-orthodoxy, and independence, truly outrageous in a woman: Meera Kosambi has pointed out how her choice to marry a *sudra* from another region and with a different lan-

guage, when she herself was a Brahman, offended conservative contemporaries, especially Maharashtrian women, 'who projected her as having destroyed her husband and her marriage, and contaminated the rest of society through her unorthodox behaviour.'[62]

In Bengal, meanwhile, goddess-centred nationalist rhetoric gained new ground as nationalism spawned revolutionary terrorism. By 1906 young nationalists began to criticize the notion of *atmasakti*, with its emphasis on gradual, sustained and peaceful work at the local level, and began to call for a struggle to achieve *swaraj* (self-government).[63] In the revolutionary terrorist groups which now started to develop, anti-British feeling was imbued with a Hindu nationalism in which Kali was repeatedly invoked. Kali *pujas* had earlier been put to ideological use in Bengal in the campaign against raising the age of marriage, in 1891. Responding to this, the *Indian Spectator*, a loyalist social reform journal, had crudely quipped when the Bill was passed, 'in the face of Mother Victoria having made up her mind, Mother Kali could do nothing.'[64] Then, however, Kali had been invoked to protect conservative Hindu tradition from Westernized reformers: now she became the liberator of Mother India, and a beacon for her nationalist sons. Sarala Debi, whose links with the Mymensingh Suhrid Samiti had remained strong, began to be lauded for her pujas to Kali as Pratapaditya's tutelary goddess;[65] in Noakhali, a woman named Bhagbati wrote a song saying that thirty-three crores of Indians 'were floating on the bosom of a boundless sea, and weeping day and night', which prayed to Kali to 'save us, we will sacrifice white goats in the Ganges if Bengal prospers.'[66]

Worship of Kali, Durga and Chandi became incumbent for many young nationalists on the grounds that the 'mother' would ease the path to nationalist martyrdom: 'in your right hand shines the sword while the left hand takes away fear; both eyes smile tenderly while the third eye on the forehead glows with fire' (Tagore, speaking of Durga in *Gitabitan*).[67] For many the mother goddess was identified with mother India: 'it is your image we worship in the temples' (Bankim Chandra in *Anand Math*).[68]

In 1907, Kumudini Mitra, the daughter of an illustrious nationalist, started the *Suprabhat*, which reiterated the connection between revolution, mother Kali, and mother India. The journal acquired its name from a poem by Rabindranath Tagore which immortalized death in the cause of liberation; in its second issue, it published a poem called 'The Auspicious Time for Worship', which said that the 'mother's hunger' would only be 'appeased' by blood, heads, workers, warriors, heroes, labour, firm vows and bands of followers.[69] Already in 1906, selected members of the Calcutta Anushilan had made abortive attempts at political assassination; their revolutionary weekly, *Yugantar*, was started some months earlier. Hemchandra Kanungo, a member of this group, went abroad for military and political 'training'. While in Paris, he met the group of Indian revolutionaries of which Madame Cama was a part. Returning in January 1908 to set up a 'combined revolutionary school and bomb factory' in Calcutta, he and other members of the Anushilan were arrested two months later for the Kennedy murders, for which two members of the group, Khudiram Basu and Prafulla Chaki, were responsible. The main target, a racist magistrate named Kingsford, escaped.[70] The May 1908 issue of the *Suprabhat* held laudatory accounts of Prafulla Chaki, who committed suicide soon after his arrest, a photograph of his dead body, and a poem in which both mortal and immortal 'mothers' were united in devotion to nationalist revolutionaries:

The Mother asks - 'Why, oh traveller! have you died an untimely death in this horrible path?' and he answers -
'Where is the pain, oh Mother! Where is the grief?
Daily I play with death; death is no enemy of mine.'

The Mother rejoins,
'Oh child, whose loved one are you?
For your sake I die
The sight of your golden face makes me glad
But why have you become so desperate, and why is there
No fear in your tender heart?'
The dead again replies,
'In this vast world many are the homes that
call me with voices of affection; many are the kind
women who will treat me as mothers.
Death is my bride and my mother!'[71]

Interestingly, Durga and Kali pujas were themselves a relatively modern phenomenon in nineteenth-century Bengal. According to Ashis Nandy, the series of crises faced by Bengal in the mid to late eighteenth century led to a shift in its self-perception as a land of plenty reigned over by a benevolent mother goddess, who represented both fundamental power, or energy, *adyashakti*, and the principle of nature and action, *prakriti*. The Chandi image, a personification of prakriti, bifurcated into, on the one hand, the demon-slaying mother, Durga, and, on the other, the punitive and unpredictable mother, Kali. In the course of the nineteenth century Durga, virtually unknown earlier, became the most popular deity and Durga pujas became the most popular social and religious festivals. Similarly Kali, who was till then the goddess of marginal groups such as dacoits, thieves, thugs and—significantly—prostitutes (themselves symbolic of *vagina dentata*, or devouring sexuality), was forefronted as a goddess. Both rose to dominance primarily in greater Calcutta, where they became the ruling deities of its 'exposed elites and quasi-elites'.[72] In other words, their popularity can be seen as an expression of the crisis in established orders of power and dominance, largely engendered by the British encounter, in which elites sought, and were forced to, redefine themselves. It should perhaps be noted here, that in worshipping Durga and Kali an emphasis was being laid on energy, nature and action: prakriti and the martial aspects of shakti, which can be both protective, as in Durga, and erotically destructive, as in Kali. The question which now arises, therefore, is to what extent can the increasing importance of Kali and Durga be seen as also expressing tensions and shifts in the structure of patriarchy?

Clearly the rising importance of Kali and Durga in an age and place where increasing attention was being focussed on women was not a mere coincidence. At a general level it can be argued that this rise signified the growing dominance of complex images of female power, which represented, in fact, an ambiguous and often polarized vision of femaleness. It is of course fairly common in India to find the image of an uncontrollable and dangerous Shakti (itself female) rising to pre-eminence

Madame Bhikaiji Rustomji Cama, 1861-1936

Bhikaiji Cama (popularly known as Madame Cama) was involved in the revolutionary movement in India, and abroad, with Shyamji Krishna Verma, S.R. Rana, and others. Among other activities she smuggled revolvers concealed in toys (sent as Christmas presents) into India. In 1907 she attended the International Socialist Congress in Stuttgart, where she unfurled the Indian National Flag, and persuaded the Congress to support Indian independence. In 1909, her group started *Bande Mataram*, a monthly organ for Indian Independence, and published it from Geneva. The first issue came out in September 1909. In this issue, an explanation of how to achieve independence was offered; there were three stages which had to be passed through: the first of educating the people; the second of war; and the third of reconstruction: 'These three stages of every national movement must be passed through. History cannot alter its course for India. After Mazzini, Garibaldi; after Garibaldi, Cavour. Even so it must be with us. Virtue and wisdom first, then war; finally independence.'[1] In an editorial comment on a new nationalist journal,

Talwar, which came out from Berlin in 1910, we find some elucidation of the tactics of war favoured by the Bande Mataram group: 'The programme of active resistance with political assassination as a prelude is advocated with splendid earnestness. There is no trace of any inclination towards compromise or hypocrisy in any of its pronouncements. We especially commend to the attention of our readers the admirable article on political assassination in the second number which deserves careful perusal.'[2] From Madame Cama's article in the third issue we see that the 'active resistance' scheduled to follow political assassination consisted of armed revolt: 'I also appeal to your patriotism to make the best of your stay in the West, by taking all kinds of physical training (which is not allowed in our country). Above all learn how to shoot straight because the day is not far when for coming into the inheritance of Swaraj and Swadesh you will be called upon to shoot the English out of the land which we all love so passionately.'[3]

In fact, Madame Cama was a recent convert to armed resistance. In a speech given at India House in 1908, she said, 'Some of you say that as a woman I should object to violence. Well Sirs, I had that feeling at one time. Three years ago it was repugnant to me even to talk of violence. . . But owing to be heartlessness, the hypocrisy, the rascality of liberals, that feeling is gone. Why should we deplore the use of violence when our enemies drive us to it?[4]

The Bande Mataram group was associated with V.D. Savarkar's Abhinava Bharat society which glorified terrorist murders. In July 1909 Madanlal Dhingra, a member of this group, assassinated an Indian Office bureaucrat named Curzon Wylie, and was executed for it. The 1909 issue of *Bande Matram* lauded Dhingra's action both in nationalist and in internationalist terms: 'Dhingra's pistol shot has been heard by the Irish cattler in his forlorn hut, by the Egyptian fellah in the field, by the Zulu labourer in the dark mine . . .'[5]

Madame Cama herself was an internationalist; but she believed that nationalism had to come before internationalism: 'The world is my country, every human being is my relation. But to establish internationalism in the world there must be Nations first.[6] Together with the Bande Mataram group, she felt that nationalist movements all over the world were linked by their anti-imperialism. Her war cry was 'Orient for the Orientals.'

Despite her avowal that Hindus, Muslims and Sikhs should not allow religion to interfere in their brotherhood as countrymen, the 'Indian revolution' to be was defined as a 'Hindi revolution' (she believed that Hindi should be the language of independent India), and revolutionary figures were hailed as re-incarnations of figures in Hindu mythology:

'On the first of July this year, our hero-martyr Madanlal Dhingra attained perfection of character by total renunciation of self . . . in his noble figure, defying death and scorning life, young India saw the incarnation of her highest hopes and her fondest dreams, India waits for the Kalki tenth avatar who should destroy the foreign demon.'[7] In 1913 she herself was described by the Government as 'The recognized leader of the revolutionary movement and was said to be regarded by the people as a re-incarnation of the goddess Kali.'[8]

A Parsi commentator says: 'She was self willed as a child, and as young woman she was hot headed and of independent views.' On 3-8-1885 she married Rustom K.R. Cama, a solicitor and ardent nationalist who was manager of the *Bombay Chronicle* from 1915-18. Her married life was unhappy. He goes on to say that she was good at cricket, and worked as a nurse for some months in 1896.[9]

Madame Cama was only allowed by the British Government to return to India when she was 74 and in failing health. She was admitted to the Parsi General Hospital in Bombay 'where she died lonely and forgotten on 13-08-1936.'[10]

1. J.C. Ker, *Political Trouble in India* 1907-1917, p. 103.
2. J.C. Ker, op cit., p. 103.
3. J.C. Ker, op cit., p. 105.
4. *Proceedings of the Home Department,* July 1913. p. 6.
5. Sumit Sarkar, op cit., p. 145–46.
6. Manhohan Kaur, op cit., p. 112.
7. J.C. ker, op cit., p. 103.
8. *Proceedings of the Home Department,* July 1913, Government of India, p. 6.
9. H.D. Darukhanawala, *Parsi Lustre on Indian soil,* p. 29.
10. H.D. Darukhanawala, op cit., p. 30.

in times of famine, epidemic or other 'natural' disasters. And generally propitiatory offerings to this image are accompanied by retributory or punitive actions against women, who are seen as failing to perform their ritual function of protecting men by manipulating natural events or fate. In other words, the appearance of Shakti in the world in its most threatening form is, and was, regarded as directly related to women's failure, whether deliberate or otherwise, to regulate or channelize their own shakti in the home. Moments of crisis or disorder, therefore, frequently become occasions for the collective punishment of women: bouts of witch-hunting are a prime example. Nandy argues that the rise in the incidence of sati during the first third of the nineteenth century was also an example of this. According to him, as Kali became 'the new symbol of a treacherous cosmic mother', she came to be associated with most of the rituals which both British and Indian reformers cited as instances of Hindu decadence. Nurtured by 'this new psychological environment' the folk theory which grew around sati held it to be a proper form for the punishment or expiation of widows' sins, for they were considered to have caused their husband's deaths by their poor ritual performance as wives.[73]

If this 'epidemic' of sati can, therefore, be seen as a revealing moment of collective hysteria, in which a patriarchal order perceived itself as under threat and reacted violently to reassert itself, by the mid-nineteenth century new attempts were made to contain this threat. It is interesting how crucial the figure of the widow became in this context, almost as if she symbolized the danger which all women might represent potentially. Certainly the view of widows as embodying a volatile and dangerously erotic energy, because unchannelled to their husbands, was often expressed in the campaign for widow remarriage in the eighteen-fifties, and the campaign itself can be seen as attempting to re-channelize this energy by providing the widow with a husband. It is, moreover, significant that in the Act providing for widow remarriage the widow had to lose her rights to her previous husband's property: a measure which both symbolically negated her life before her prior marriage, and rendered her solely dependent on her new husband. In other words, the new agrarian, industrial and social relations engendered by British dominance undermined existing structures of patriarchy, resulting in violent and intensified expressions of patriarchal 'traditions' on the one hand, and, on the other, attempts to reform patriarchy which often amounted to reconstituting it in a Western mould (and, in this process, eroding some of the women's traditional rights).

Despite these elements of the context in which Kali and Durga rose to dominance, or perhaps simultaneously defining and countering it, new spaces for women were also created by the new mother images which were so influential. In many ways the nationalist adoption of these images was crucial in creating these spaces. We have already looked at the kind of sanction Sarala Debi's activities acquired through the nationalist images created by Bankim Chandra. The association of Durga with 'Mother India' and the increasing use of Kali to sanction violence in a struggle for independence from colonial

Annie Besant, 1847–1933

'....the Rights of Man have become an accepted doctrine, but unfortunately, they are only rights of man, in the exclusive sense of the word. They are sexual, and not human rights, and until they become human rights, society will never rest on a sure, just, foundation...to deny these rights (liberty, property, safety and resistance to tyranny) to women is either to deny them to humanity qua humanity or to deny that women form a part of humanity; if women's rights are denied, women's rights have no logical basis, no claim to respect...either all human beings have equal rights, or none have any.

Annie Besant came to India in 1893, by which time she had worked with Charles Bradlaugh on the *National Reformer,* become a critic of British colonialism, and joined the Theosophical Society. In India she lived at Adyar in Madras, which was the headquarters of the Theosophical Society. She supported the Sanatan Dharam movement advocating that Hindu chil-

dren be taught Sanskrit and learn Aryan 'simplicity and spirituality', but despite this revivalist strain she believed in the equal rights of men and women on the equal but complementary basis. Initially she felt that India needed to educate herself before she was capable of self government, but by the outbreak of the First World War she was campaigning for self-government. In 1914 she joined the Congress and in 1916 was one of the founders of the Home Rule League. In June 1917 she was arrested under the Defence of India Act. Her arrest was followed by a series of protest meetings all over the country and abroad. From America President Wilson interceded with the British for her release; in India Subramaniam Aiyar gave up his knighthood. Under pressure, the British announced measures to increase the number of Indians in the administration as a step towards the development of 'self governing institutions' and in September Annie Besant and her two co-internees, Mr Wadia and Mr Arundale, were released.

In the same year Mrs Besant was elected President of the Congress, becoming its first woman president. Under her influence the Congress 'expressed the opinion that the same tests be applied to women as to men in regard to franchise and the eligibility to all elective bodies concerned with local governments and education.' In December 1917, she, along with Margaret Cousins, Sarojini Naidu and eight other Indian women, went to meet Mr Montague to demand votes for Indian women. Her appreciation of the strength of women was remarkably similar to Gandhi's; in her opinion the Home Rule movement was 'rendered tenfold greater by the adhesion to it of large numbers of women who bring to its help the calculating heroism, endurance, and self sacrifice of the feminine nature.' Yet politically she opposed Gandhi, stigmatizing the non-cooperation movement as a programme of revolt 'which must land the country in ruin if successful and almost surely in riot and bloodshed if it fails.' Her opposition made her unpopular, even within the Home Rule League, so that in 1919 she founded the National Home Rule League. In 1924 she led a deputation of home rulers to England to demand Dominion Home Rule for India, and in 1925 she, together with H.S. Gouri, Shivarao, C.P. Ramaswamy Aiyar and others, drafted a Bill on a constitution for self-government which was approved by Gandhi and supported by the Labour Party but never enacted.

rule, moreover, can be read as turning the threat contained in these figures away from the self (of the Hindu male), and directing it instead against the 'other' of the Western colonizer.

To this extent, then, the harnessing of shakti to nationalism was not only a way of making it safer—of containing it—but also a way in which women could find a role for themselves in nationalist struggles. Certainly as the rhetoric of Bengali nationalism grew increasingly mother-centred, more and more women began to get involved in nationalist activities, supporting students rusticated for their participation in the movement against partition, sheltering revolutionaries, and acting as couriers for extremists. Kumudini Mitra herself organized a group of 'educated Brahmin ladies', who liaised between revolutionaries in hiding.[74] Lilabati Mitra, a Brahmo who had helped Vidyasagar in the 1890s to perform widow remarriages under the Special Marriage Act of 1872 (when Vidyasager discovered that the 1856 Widow Remarriage Act facilitated bigamy, as it did not ban polygamy), was one of the women who sheltered students. Her husband, Krishnakumar Bose Mitra, was deported in 1908 for his activities in the swadeshi movement; in protest, she refused to accept a government grant of monthly maintenance. In 1909, she sheltered Aurobindo Ghosh on his release from prison; but after 1911, when her husband was released, she withdrew from nationalist activities and concentrated on spreading Brahmoism.[75] Prabhavati Mirza, one of the most powerful trade-unionists of the 1930s, was influenced as a ten year old girl by her brother's involvement with Aurobindo's group; she fasted, with many others, in protest at Khudiram Bose's hanging, and again when Satyen Bose was hanged. Her comment on the revolutionaries of that period: 'the peculiar thing in Bengal was that mostly the high officials' children became revolutionaries. I don't know why.'[76] The activities of many women in this period show a mixture of orthodox social reform and nationalism, even occasional radicalism: Kamini Roy was active in the Ilbert Bill agitation, organizing girls at the Bethune school to hold meetings and wear badges supporting the Bill, but ceased to be active after she left school; when her husband died in 1909, she joined the Banga Mahila Samiti and worked with them in various social reform projects for women.[77] Aghorekamini Roy, who ran a girl's school and started a social welfare women's organization which later came to be known as the Aghorekamini Nari Samiti, campaigned against the teaplanters' ill-treatment of women workers in Assam, a cause which was first espoused by nationalists in the 1880s, and raised donations for an 'Indian who was falsely implicated in a theft case by the planters', aiding in his release.[78]

Clearly few, if any, of the women who became active in this period remained untouched by proliferating nationalist ideas and campaigns. Interestingly, a number of these women were writers, both reformists and revolutionaries: to refer to only a few, Nagendrakala Mustafi, Mankumari Basu and Kamini Roy published works in Bengali, ranging from poems, novels and plays, to essays on women's education, women's morality and women's duties.[79] In Maharashtra, Pandita Ramabai, Kasibai Kanitkar, Mary Bhore, Godavaribai Samaskar, Parvatibai and Rukminibai were beginning to be known for their writings; Kamala Sathianandan, the editor of the *Indian Ladies' Magazine*, was a novelist.[80] In the north, Rameshwari Nehru founded and edited a journal for women in 1909, *Stree Darpan*; Roop Kumari Nehru brought out a companion journal for girls, called *Kumari Darpan;* of two other journals started for women around the same time, *Grihalakshmi* and *Chand*, one was edited by a woman, and the other had a woman manager.[81] Sarla Debi, Kumudini Mitra and Madame Cama concentrated on exhortatory journalism in the cause of revolution, and all three helped construct the symbol of a Mother India waiting for Mother Kali to liberate her. Madame Cama, a member of the Paris group of revolutionaries comprising Krishnavarma, Har Dayal and S R Rana, was one of the founders and editor of *Bande Mataram*, self-defined as a 'monthly organ of Indian Independence'.[82] Though extremists and revolutionaries had made attempts to use *Bande Mataram*, as a national call from the turn of the century, it was made a major symbol for nationalists by the British ban on this poem of Bankimchandra's in 1909. The *Bande Mataram* was started in reaction to the ban in September 1909; and Madame Cama unfurled a *Bande Mataram* flag at the 1907 Congress of the Socialist International at Stuttgart.[83] While the journal added an internationalist perspective to cries for armed revolt against the British, linking this with anti-imperialist struggles all over the world, and laying down a format for revolution based on the 'three stages' of the Italian nationalist struggle, it used explicitly Hindu symbols, speaking of the 'mighty Hindi Revolution' and saying that 'India waits for the Kalki tenth avatar who should destroy the foreign demon.'[84] (Kalki, a centaur or 'mare goddess' was an incarnation of Vishnu whose purpose on earth was solely destructive. Like Kali she drank the blood of demons.)

A staunch supporter of women's education, Madame Cama's views were that Indian liberation movements would fail without the support of Indian women; and statements to this effect were made by nationalists all over India. Though an essential part of the swadeshi movement was its programmes for 'national education', it was repeatedly criticized for its neglect of 'female and mass education.'[85] The women's education movement was soon given a new fillip by the entry of nationalist women; they, in turn, redefined the rationale for women's education. From its inception, the movement had concentrated on educating women to fulfil their roles as wives and mothers; in 1904, Annie Besant elevated this into a national quest, saying 'the national movement for girl's education must be on national lines; it must accept the general Hindu conceptions of women's place in the national life . . . India needs nobly trained wives and mothers, wise and tender rulers of the household, educated teachers of the young, helpful counsellers of their husbands, skilled nurses of the sick, rather than girl graduates.'[86] By implication, then, Indian women lacked these attributes described above. After 1905, however, this argument was given a new twist: the power and strength of Indian mothers was asserted, rather than their weaknesses; education was a birthright, and those who denied it to their women robbed themselves and the nation, for Indian women were mothers of the nation. Speaking to the Indian Social Conference at Calcutta in 1906, Sarojini Naidu said:

> The word education is the most misunderstood word in any language . . . The instruction being merely the accumulation of knowledge might, indeed, lend itself to conventional definition, but education is an immeasurable, beautiful, indispensable atmosphere in which we live and move and have our being. Does one man dare to deprive another of his birthright to God's pure air which nourishes his body? . . . How then shall a man dare to deprive a human soul of its immemorial inheritance of liberty and life? Your fathers, in depriving your mothers of that immemorial birthright have robbed you, their sons, of your just inheritance. Therefore, I charge you, restore to your women their ancient rights, for, as I have said, it is we, and not you, who are the real nation-builders, and without our active co-operation at all points of progress all your Congresses and Conferences are in vain. Educate your women and the nation will take care of itself, for it is as true today as it was yesterday and will be to the end of human life that the hand that rocks the cradle rules the world.[87]

Education, then, was not only a birthright, it was what sons inherited from their mothers. Henceforth, the place of Indian women in 'national life' was as mothers; this theme was repeated by Madame Cama in 1910, at a meeting of the Egyptian National Congress: 'remember that the hand that rocks the cradle is the hand that moulds the character. That soft hand is the chief factor of national life.'[88] Sarojini Naidu's statements must have been greeted with considerable enthusiasm, for by 1916 she was speaking for all Indian women: 'it is suitable that I who represent the other sex, that is the mothers of the men whom we wish to make men and not emasculated machines, should raise a voice on behalf of the future

mothers of India';[89] in the same year, she asserted that 'women may form a sisterhood more easily because they are bound to every woman in the world by the common divine quality of motherhood.'[90] And Surendranath Banerjea echoed this uncannily when he appealed to all Indians, irrespective of their caste or creed, to 'sink their differences and unite under the banner of [the] religion of motherhood'.[91]

This expanded, semi-mystical vision of motherhood was paralleled by a further growth of the Darwinian 'objective-scientific' views of social reformers described in Chapter I. 'Ancient Indian ideals' had, by the early years of the twentieth century, been appropriated by reformers, revivalists, extremists, nationalists and loyalists alike: each had a different view of Aryan India to offer. Similarly, different kinds of interests in the 'mothers of the nation' were expressed in this period: ranging from the innate biological-spiritual power of motherhood which was assumed by Sarojini Naidu and Surendranath Banerjea, to the biological-rationalist interest of social reformers in the 'healthy development of the race'. The latter was espoused by social reform organizations ranging from the Aryan Brotherhood Conference to the Countess of Dufferin's Fund; the first was a moderate nationalist body, the second a loyalist one. Ranade and N M Joshi were both members of the Aryan Brotherhood Conference; at its first meeting, when discussing reforms in child-marriage, widow-remarriage, etc., one of its members declared:

> Let us no longer live in a fool's paradise in the fond belief that, because we have managed to survive so long as a race under our present social arrangement, we will be able to survive for ever . . . The lessons taught by the lately developed science of animal life are stern, clear, uncompromising. The lesson is (that) this race of animals that could not adapt themselves to changed conditions of existence could not survive long.[92]

The Dufferin Fund was set up to pay for the training of women doctors in India; in 1886, they supported six girls in Madras Medical College, eighteen in Bombay's Grant Medical College, and three in Calcutta Medical College. In 1913, one of its supporters wrote an article in the *Bombay Chronicle* describing the importance of the Fund's work and making it clear that a 'healthy race' was necessary for the creation of the Indian Empire; that women were responsible for the 'production' of a healthy race; and that if boys grew up to be men then girls grew up to be mothers.

> On the woman rests the main responsibility of producing a healthy race. A child who has been subjected to healthy pre-natal influences, both

physical and psychic; a cheerful mother guiding the child's outlook to an optimistic belief in the good and an endeavour to aim at the highest; the growth of such a child into a man, or a mother—all this India knows not. On the contrary, we have women whose period of pregnancy is bound round by traditional maltreatment and ignorance of ordinary laws of hygiene, whose mental outlook is obsessed by the idea of a difficult labour or probable death in childbirth. We have women undergoing the tortures of the rack through ignorant management of child birth . . . . We irrigate, we sanitate; we give free education and encourage industries—all these should be but coping stones to the building of the Indian Empire, the foundations of which should be based on the production of a healthy race.[93]

Women's responsibility for the health of the race was a subject of concern not only for social reformers and philanthropists, but for the Government as well: in 1908, the Indian Factory Commission reiterated the need to restrict women's hours of work, saying 'it will protect to some extent all women operatives who have household duties to perform and will thereby tend to promote the general health of the whole body of workers.'[94]

If the first feelings of concern for the plight of women workers were voiced by Bengali nationalists in the 1880s, by the 1890s this concern had changed in two ways. The campaign of the 1880s was against European malpractice in the Assam tea plantations, and the issues were forced recruitment and harassment; in the 1890s, concern was being voiced for women factory workers per se, irrespective of the race of their employers; the concerned people were loyalists not nationalists; and the issue was women's responsibility for the health of the working class, in particular, for future generations of workers. The long hours of women factory workers were described, and it was pointed out that these were made even longer by their domestic duties; furthermore, factory work adversely affected the performance of domestic work, for the mills gave only two holidays per month, when women could shop for the family's needs.[95] Yet this concern did not result in a significant shortening of women's hours of work, or the provision of more holidays; it focussed instead on improving conditions of child-birth and early care. From the first decade of the twentieth century, 'infant welfare' developed, in which women were active, and which received funding from the government; initially concerned at the high rates of infant mortality, they discovered that these were due 'to causes operating before or during birth', and thus 'antenatal care and supervision of maternity work became part of the infant welfare scheme'.

The role of the working-class mother, thus, was defined as the production of healthy workers. Debates on the nature and importance of motherhood for the motherland, were restricted to defining the roles of middle class women, and whether they were to be mothers of the nation or mothers of the British Indian Empire. These definitions remained paradigmatic in discussions of the nature of womanhood until the 1920s, when the rise of large-scale women's participation in movements effected some changes in consciousness.

NOTES

1. *West Bengal District Gazetteer*, Appendix A, p. 733.
2. Meera Kosambi, 'Women, Emancipation and Equality: Pandita Ramabai's Contribution to Women's Cause', in *Economic and Political Weekly*, vol XXIII, No. 44, Oct 1988, p. WS. 39.
3. Ibid, p. WS. 41.
4. Gail Omvedt, op. cit., p. III.
5. Kenneth Jones, op. cit., p. 108, f.n.
6. Usha Chakraborty, op. cit., p. 119.
7. Ibid.
8. *Source Material for a History of the Freedom Movement in India*: Vo. II, 1885–1920, Bombay, Government Central Press, 1958, p. 95.
9. Meera Kosambi, op. cit., p. WS. 48.
10. Sita Ram Singh, op. cit., p. 206.
11. Ibid.
12. Pattabhi Sitaramayya, *History of the Indian National Congress*, Vol. I, Delhi, S. Chand and Sons, 1969, p. 114.
13. Ibid, p. 51.
14. Kenneth Ballhatchet, op. cit., pp. 12–39.
15. Usha Chakraborty, op. cit., p. 26.
16. Ibid, pp. 28–29.
17. Usha Chakraborty, op. cit., pp. 32–33.
18. Ibid., pp. 17–18
19. Kenneth Ballhatchet, op. cit., pp. 157–58.
20. Sita Ram Singh, op. cit., p. 287.
21. Ibid, pp. 281–82, 286.
22. Kenneth Ballhatchet, op. cit., p. 133.
23. Ibid., pp. 123–43.
24. Ibid, pp. 140–41.
25. Rangaswamy Parthasarthy (ed), *One Hundred years*

of the Hindu, Madras, Kasturi & Sons, p. 112.

26. Kenneth Ballhatchet, op. cit., p. 142.
27. Usha Chakraborty, op. cit., p. 138.
28. Uma Chakravarti, op. cit., p. 62.
29. Sumit Sarkar, MI, p. 86.
30. Usha Chakraborty, op. cit., p. 128.
31. B.C. Pal, op cit, p. 22.
32. Uma Chakravarti, op. cit., p. 62.
33. Ibid.
34. Sumit Sarkar, *The Swadeshi Movement in Bengal, 1903–8*, Delhi, People's Publishing House, p. 192. Henceforth SMB.
35. Usha Chakaraborty, op. cit., p. 138.
36. Sumit Sarkar, SMB, pp. 470–71.
37. Uma Chakravarti, op. cit., pp. 63–64. Sarala Devi elevated this character to the ranks of heroes, because she felt Bengal needed its own equivalents of the Rajputs and Maratha warrior-heroes which were constructed as symbols of nationalism. When her uncle, Rabindranath Tagore, objected that Pratapaditya was a parricide, she retorted that she did not consider him an 'ideal human being', but a brave and manly anti-colonialist.
38. Usha Chakraborty, op. cit., p. 139. See also Uma Chakravarti, op. cit.
39. Sumit Sarkar, SMB, pp. 304–5.
40. Uma Chakravarti, op. cit., p. 65.
41. Usha Chakraborty, op. cit., p. 140.
42. Sumit Sarkar, SMB, p. 305.
43. Robi Chatterjee, 'Anand Math : A Nationalist Text of the Nineteenth Century', unpublished paper presented at the Centre for South Asian Studies, Cambridge, and Nehru Memorial Museum and Library (NMML), Delhi.
44. Sumit Sarkar, MI, pp. 106–9.
45. Sumit Sarkar, SMB, p. 296.
46. Kenneth Jones, op. cit., p. 268.
47. Sumit Sarkar, MI, p. 112.
48. Sumit Sarkar, SMB, pp. 271–72.
49. Manmohan Kaur, *Role of Women in The Freedom Movement, 1857–1947*, Delhi, Sterling Publishers, 1968, p. 97.
50. Sumit Sarkar, SMB, p. 288.
51. Manmohan Kaur, op. cit., p. 97.
52. Ibid, pp. 100–1.
53. Ibid, p. 97, f.n.
54. *Source Material for a History of The Freedom Movement in India*, op. cit., pp. 611–12.
55. Kenneth Jones, op. cit., p. 259.
56. *Indian Ladies Magazine*, Vol. X, No. 6, December 1909.
57. Manmohan Kaur, op. cit., p. 98.
58. Ibid, pp. 98–99.
59. Sita Ram Singh, op. cit., pp. 186–87.
60. *Indian Ladies Magazine*, 'A visit to the Anadha Balikashram', Vol. VIII, 1908–9, p. 8.
61. Meera Kosambi, op. cit., p. WS. 48.
62. Sumit Sarkar, SMB, p. 296.
63. Sita Ram Singh, op. cit., p. 88.
64. Manmohan Kaur, op. cit., p. 103.
65. Ibid., pp. 97–98.
66. Tanika Sarkar, quoting Bankim Chandra and Rabindranath Tagore, op. cit., p. 98.
67. Ibid
68. J.C. Ker, *Political Trouble in India*, 1907–17, Delhi, Manohar Reprints Series, p. 81.
69. Sumit Sarkar, MI, p. 123.
70. J.C. Ker, op. cit. p. 81.
71. Ashis Nandy, op. cit. pp. 8–9.
72. Ibid.
73. Manmohan Kaur, op. cit., p. 97.
74. Usha Chakraborty, op. cit., p. 132.
75. Prabhavati Mirza, 'Interview', NMML Oral History Section, p. 3.
76. Usha Chakraborty, op. cit., p. 133.
77. Ibid., pp. 124–25.
78. All mentioned by Usha Chakraborty, pp. 129–41.
79. Sita Ram Singh, op. cit., p. 169.
80. Vir Bharat Talwar, 'Women's Journals in Hindi, 1910–29', in Sangari & Vaid (eds), *Recasting Women*, op. cit., pp. 206, 210.
81. J.C. Ker, op. cit., p. 102.
82. Sumit Sarkar, SMB, p. 307.
83. J.C. Ker, op. cit., p. 103.
84. Sumit Sarkar, SMB, p. 173.
85. Annie Besant, *Speeches and Writings*, p. 73.
86. Sarojini Naidu, *Speeches and Writings*, Madras, G A Nateson, 1904, pp. 18–20.
87. Manmohan Kaur, op. cit., p. 111.
88. Sarojini Naidu, op. cit., pp. 101–2.
89. Ibid, p. 100.
90. Surendranath Banerjee, *Speeches*, Calcutta, Indian Association, Vol. I, p. 21.
91. Aryan Brotherhood Conference Report, 1912.
92. *Bombay Chronide*, 'Indian Women's Needs: The Dufferin Fund', April 16, 1913.
93. *Report of the Indian Factory Commission, 1908*, Delhi, Government Central Press, 1909, pp. 46–47.
94. Ibid.
95. Bhavani Natarajan, 'Child Welfare', in Shyam Kumari Nehru, op. cit, p. 65.

4. Organization and Struggle

The estrangement of social reform from nationalism, which began towards the end of the nineteenth century, grew greater over the years, expressing itself in the form of a debate familiar to contemporary ears, over the relative importance of social and political issues and their interconnections. Within the debate there were differences in the definitions of social reform and politics. On the one side loyalist social reformers felt that the field of social reform was divided by political allegiances, and politics ought therefore to be eschewed; for the other, reform notwithstanding, many felt that the social and political spheres were distinct but inseparable.

Scattered references imply that the sphere of the social was largely occupied by issues concerning women, unlike the sphere of the political. At the sixth National Social Conference in 1892, Shrimati Hardevi Roshanlal, the editor of *Bharat Bhagini*, insisted that the National Social Conference was a 'more important' organization than the Congress, for it emphasized that:

> The women's cause is man's
> They rise or sink together,
> Dwarfed or god like; bound or free.[1]

According to Sarala Ray, herself a reformer, she and Gokhale often discussed 'social and political improvement and there was always a discussion on which should proceed first. After years of discussion he at last agreed that the two were like the hands and feet of a man—one cannot get on without either.'[2] Not all came to such amiable conclusions. When, in 1895, the revivalists refused to let the National Social Conference use the Congress *pandal* for their meeting, the *Indian Spectator*, a loyalist socialist reform journal, welcomed the split, saying that this would force the Conference to become an independent organization in which all social reformers could come together.[3]

Founded by Ranade, the National Social Conference was itself dominated by moderate nationalists, and its 1895 ouster signalled their defeat at the hands of the extremists. The social versus political debate, clearly, was not merely between social reformers and nationalists, but within nationalism and between two different views of how social change would ensue. Commenting on the different ideologies of Indian moderates and extremists, the *Indian Social Reformer* said in 1906 that 'the Moderate differs from the Extremist in nothing as much as his estimate of the relative influence of social and political institutions on each other. The Bengali held that social democracy came after political democracy. The Reformer held that the verdict of history was that social freedom always preceded political growth.'[4]

Despite these skirmishes, the debate seems to have been both limited and transient as far as women were concerned, though it surfaced again in the late 1920s. We do not find much discussion of the social versus political question in this period in either women's writing or published speeches, nor does it seem to have affected the nature of their activity. As was the case earlier, ideological battles between moderates and extremists did not seem to affect women who became active in any notable way. If, however, the earlier period showed the influence of nationalism on reformist women, from about 1910 on we find that some of the women who were extremist nationalists began to get more actively involved in women's rights issues. In 1913, Kumudini Mitra, a supporter of revolutionary terrorism, was invited to attend the International Women Suffrage Alliance Congress at Budapest, as 'a delegate from India to represent Indian women'. Commenting on this, the *Indian Ladies' Magazine*, a moderate feminist journal, said, 'Miss Mitra has been asked to read in the Congress a paper giving an account of the work that is being done by Indian women. Now is India's salvation at hand!'[5]

The revivalist and extremist, Sarala Debi, had dabbled briefly in social reform, helping in her mother's Sakhi Samiti, but had soon focussed her attention on nationalist activities directed at men. After her marriage, however, she turned some attention both to social reform and women, perhaps unconsciously following the pattern of Bankim's heroines Shanti and Debi Choudharani. In 1910 she formed the Bharat Stri Mahamandal. In 1917, at the same time as a delegation led by Sarojini Naidu waited upon the committee headed by Mr Montague and Lord Chelmsford to demand a series of reforms in the condition of Indian women, Sarala Debi made representations before the committee on behalf of the Bharat Stree Mahamandal. The delegation, organized by an Irish suffragette, M.E.Cousins, who was living in India at the time, comprised fourteen women, and asked that there be better educational facilities for women, improved health and maternity services, and the same franchise rights 'as would be extended to their brothers'.[6] To this Sarala Debi added that in the view of the Mahamandal the Government should set up special educational institutions for widows and enact laws protecting the inheritance rights of Hindu wives and daughters, extend opportunities for women to enter professions, and see that school inspection committees be formed of Indian rather than foreign women. Developing the attack on racism implied here, she added a demand smacking of an inverse racism, that 'The interests of Indian wives be safeguarded by making it criminal and unlawful for a married Indian man to marry an English woman.'[7] Considering that the Gujarati social reformer Dayaram Gidumal had committed bigamy with an Indian woman only a few years earlier, this demand is unpleasantly reminiscent of the double standards adopted by nationalists over the issue of rape in the 1890s. However, it also reflects how deeply painful the British insistence on maintaining a separation between the 'master race' and its subjects was. A less exalted point concerns money: given the way families pooled resources to send their men abroad in order to better their (the men's) and therefore the families' prospects, the loss of so considerable an investment must have generated immense resentment.

The decade 1910–1920 was one in which first attempts at setting up all-India women's organizations were made. The earliest women's organizations were, as we have seen, both urban and sectarian in a non-pejorative sense, for they were Arya Samajist or Brahmo. From the late nineteenth to the early twentieth century they were followed by local or regional women's organizations, such as the Banga Mahila Samaj and the Aghorekamini Nari Samiti in Bengal; the Satara Abalonnati Sabha in Maharashtra, the Mahila Seva Samaj in Bangalore, the Bharat Mahila Parishad in Benares and the Prayas Mahila Samiti in Allahabad. Some of these were practical social reform organizations, others mere discussion platforms for women. The Aghorekamini Nari Samiti, for example, was based on the principle of self-help and trained women to attend the sick and spread education among themselves.[8] The Bharat Mahila Parishad on the other hand, organized discussions on such issues as the codes by which Hindu women should live, and their roles as citizens of modern India. In 1905, the Parishad led a meeting at which twelve women read papers, and their topics included the following: 'The Hindu wife and What She Should Be', 'Female Education', 'The Place of Women in Modern India', 'Matri Puja (mother worship), 'The Responsibilities of Our Sex', '*Grahastha Dharma* and *Pativrata*', 'Brahmacharya and its Advantages', '*Vedokta Sanskar*', 'Relating to Childbirth', 'Advantages of Hawan', 'Injurious Effects of Child-Marriage', and 'The Duty of Indian Women in the Modern Age'.[9]

One of the first attempts at coming together on a larger scale was made in 1908, when there was a 'Mahila Parishad' or Ladies' Congress' at Madras, attended by women from all over South India, at which nineteen papers were presented by women in Tamil, Telugu, Malayalam, Marathi and English.[10] Two years later, Sarala Debi founded the Bharat Stree Mahamandal with the intention of forming an all-India women's organization, with 'the object of bringing together women of all castes and creeds on the basis of their common interest in the moral material progress of women in India.'[11] Whether it was too early for such an attempt to prosper, or whether it was because Sarala Debi did not achieve an all India character, the organization remained largely limited to its three branches in Lahore, Allahabad and Calcutta. Seven years after its formation, in 1917, the Women's Indian Association was founded by Annie Besant, Dorothy Jinarajadasa, Malati Patwardhan, Ammu Swaminathan, Mrs Dadabhoy and Mrs Ambujammal. Perhaps some of the women who organized or attended the 1908 Ladies Congress now joined the Women's Indian Association, for it too was based in Madras, though it had an all-India character. Started at the height of Besant's Home Rule movement, the organization was described as 'the first purely feminist organization to arise in India' by Rajkumari Amrit Kaur in 1932.[12] To M.E. Cousins it represented a new development in women's consciousness, the 'emergence of a consciously fostered unity of Indian womanhood', which began around 1914, when Besant entered Indian politics and delivered a memorable series of lectures entitled 'Wake Up, India.'[13] The lectures combined nationalism, women's issues, and Hindu revivalism in a heady mixture for both men and women. In 1915, Besant announced her intention of starting a Home Rule League, based on the Irish Home Rule movement, and began to canvass support for it.[14] In 1916, some months before she founded the League, Tilak started his own Home Rule League in Maharashtra. At their peak the two organizations commanded a membership of between fifty to sixty thousand people, but their tracts were read by several hundred thousands.[15] When Besant was interned (together with her fellow theosophists, Wadia and Arundale), she became the reigning heroine of the nationalist movement. On her release from internment, she was elected President of the Calcutta Congress session in December, 1917.

In her Presidential address, Besant spoke specifically of the participation of women in the Home Rule agitation, stressing their enthusiasm as activists and assigning them a special role, as women in the movement:

Kamaladevi Chattopadhyaya, 1903–1990

Born in 1903, Kamaladevi Chattopadhyaya was also widowed as a child. Her second marriage was to Harindranath Chattopadhyaya, Sarojini Naidu's brother. Kamaladevi joined the non-cooperation movement in 1921, becoming a member of the Congress. In 1926 she was the first woman to stand for elections in Mangalore (her native state), losing by a narrow margin to a man who had nursed the constituency for years. A very beautiful woman, she aroused fervour in the idealistic and romantic Indian youths who campaigned for her—the extent of their feeling for her can be seen in the name they gave themselves, 'the knights of the blue lotus.' She was one of the founder members of the All India Women's Conference in 1926, and its most active secretary, setting up branches all over India. In 1929 she represented the AIWC at the International Congress of The Women's League for Peace and Freedom in Prague. In 1930 she resigned from the AIWC to become a full-time activist in the Civil Disobedience movement, and was responsible for planning the raid on salt fields in the precincts of Bombay city. '. . . it fell to me to plan it, but unlike Dharasana, where only a small group was entrusted with the task of the raid, here I visualized a mass raid embracing a large part of the city's two million population. I was sure that no force, not even machine guns could stop the raid. On the eve of the raid I was arrested but my parting message to my colleagues and the vast populace was to execute this plan. I was represented by my son of seven who proudly carried the banner and engaged in the drama of his first battle.' At her trial Kamaladevi tried to sell salt in the courtroom and asked the Magistrate to resign his position and join the satyagraha. She was awarded a nine month prison term and a Rs 170 fine. When she was released in 1931 she was put in charge of organizing the women's wing of the Hindustani Seva Dal, an agitational nationalist organization, which was started in 1924. In 1932 Kamaladevi was arrested again, and sentenced to one year's imprisonment. During this period she became a socialist, and in 1934 joined the Congress Socialist Party. She presided over its first all India Conference in Meerut in 1935. During the Quit India movement of 1942 she was arrested and imprisoned in Bangalore.

1. Kamaladevi in Gaig (ed.), op. cit, p. 23
2. Suryanath V. Kamath, op. cit, p. 95

The strength of the Home Rule movement was rendered tenfold greater by the adhesion to it of a large number of women who brought to its help the uncalculating heroism, the endurance, the self-sacrifice, of the feminine nature. Our League's best recruits and recruiters are among the women of India; and the women of Madras boast that they marched in procession when the men were stopped and that their prayers in the temples set the internal captives free. Home Rule has become so intertwined with Religion, by the prayers offered up in the great Southern temples—sacred places of pilgrimage—and spreading from them to village temples, and also by its being preached up and down the country by Sadhus and Sanyasins.[16]

Revivalism was thus, for the first time, explicitly linked with feminine activism by Besant. Like so many nationalists and social reformers who came before and after her, Besant seems to have taken it for granted that the only 'religion' worth talking about was Hinduism: though it was never very clear how she defined Hinduism. Her description of feminine activism was especially interesting, for it dwelt on women's self-sacrificing nature—a theme which was constant from the nine-

Sarojini Naidu 1879–1926

Sarojini Naidu was born in Hyderabad of a Bengali Brahmin family. Her father, Dr Aghorenath Chattopadhyaya was an educationist and a leading scientist. Her mother, though not as well known as the father, was something of a poet and is said to have had a strong influence on Sarojini. After matriculating from Hyderabad, Sarojini went to England, studying at Kings College, London and Girton, Cambridge. However, she fell ill and had to return to India in 1898 in which year she also married. She became a nationalist and supporter of women's rights early, working with the Congress, the Muslim League, and the Indian Social Conference. Among the various campaigns to redress women's lot that she was involved in were campaigns for widow remarriage, women's education and suffrage. In 1914 she volunteered to work with Gandhi. She describes her meeting with him in London in August of that year. Unable to meet

his ship, she went hunting for his lodgings in Kensington in London. When she finally found the place she described the scene thus:

> [she saw] 'an open door framing a living picture of a little man with a shaven head, seated on the floor on a black prison blanket and eating a messy meal of squashed tomatoes and olive oil out of a wooden prison bowl. Around him were ranged some battered tins of parched groundnuts and tasteless biscuits of dried plantain flour. I burst instinctively into happy laughter at this amusing and unexpected vision of a famous leader whose name had already become a household word in our country. He lifted his eyes and laughed back at me saying "Ah, you must be Mrs Naidu! Who else would dare to be so irreverent?"'

That was the beginning of a long and lasting friendship. In 1917 Sarojini Naidu led the delegation to meet Montague for women's suffrage; in 1918 she was instrumental in having a resolution passed supporting women's franchise at the Special Congress session in Bombay; and in 1919, she went to England as a member of the Home Rule League deputation to give evidence before the Joint Parliamentary Committee where she put forward the case for women's suffrage. In 1919 she became a campaigner for women's satyagraha, travelling all over India to propagate the cause. She appealed in particular to women to agitate against the Rowlatt Act. In 1920 Sarojini Naidu was asked at a conference in Geneva why she took to politics. Her answer was: 'I think it is inevitable that one should become interested in politics if one is a true Indian. The importance of Hindu Muslim unity appealed to me. I lived in a Muhammadan city, and you see, I had so many Muhammadan friends.... I have taken part in all their political and educational movements. I have presided over their meetings and spoken at mosques. That is the thing which counts most among men and women, especially men. The first political speech I made was at a meeting of the Muslim League.' In 1920 she joined the non-cooperation movement. In 1921 during the riots in Bombay following the protest against the visit of the Prince of Wales to the city, Sarojini Naidu visited the riot-torn areas to persuade people of the need for Hindu-Muslim unity. Similarly, she went to Moplah during the rebellion to quieten the situation, criticising government action during it. In the 1920s she supported the Akalis, joining their marches to protest the ban against them. In 1924 she went to South Africa, presided at a session of the East African Congress, and criticised the Anti-Historic Bill. In 1925 she was elected President of the Indian National Congress, being the first Indian woman to become so. In 1928 she went to the United States and lectured on Katherine Mayo's *Mother India*, trying to counter the wide impact of that book. Bhabani Bhattacharya, writing about her, remarks: 'On one occasion, speaking at a meeting of the World Aliance of Peace, when the flags of 70 countries bedecked the banquet room she said sharply to the audience; "where is the flag of India?"'

Sarojini Naidu's sense of humour and her fiery oratory were frequently lauded. Along with a love of social reform and politics, she also combined a love of poetry and wrote in English, earning herself the description, the 'nightingale of India.'

teenth century on, though it had, by now, changed in several important ways. If to Ram Mohan Roy it had caused pity, and a desire to spare women at least the horror of forcible sati, to Annie Besant it was a source of strength, both ennobling and sustaining. Sarojini Naidu, too, emphasized the sustenance women could, and would, give to the nationalist movement. In her highly charged prose, speaking, unlike Annie Besant, in the first person, she also addressed the 1917 Calcutta Congress on the subject of women's activism:

I am only a woman, and I should like to say to you all, when your hour strikes, when you need torch bearers in the darkness to lead you, when you need standard bearers to uphold your banner and when you die for want of faith, the womanhood of India will be with you as the holders of your banner, and the sustainers of your strength. And if you die, remember that the spirit of Padmini of Chittoor is enshrined with the manhood of India.[17]

In many ways the Calcutta Congress signalled a new consciousness of and about women. It was, for example, the first time that the role of women in the nationalist movement was emphasized in such a forum and described as being both vital and different from that of men. Yet, at the same time, both Besant and Naidu made it clear that this role was supplementary rather than leading. Perhaps this was a device to render women's activism acceptable, by making it appear unthreatening. Certainly Sarojini Naidu's reference to Padmini of Chittoor was one commonly made by nationalists of the time, who most often referred to her as a 'real' figure. In fact, she appears to have been a mythical rather than historical woman, appearing first in a sixteenth century Sufi poem, where Tod found her. In his *Annals and Antiquities of Rajasthan*, he described her as one of the most brave and beautiful of Rajput satis; during the latter part of the nineteenth and early twentieth centuries she became a symbol of the heroic Hindu woman, especially in Bengal, and was used at least partly to attack the new social reformist or activist woman. To this extent, Naidu's use of the image must have tended to defuse the opposition, whether she intended to do so or not.

At the same time, women were now beginning to create their own real-life and contemporary heroines. If Sarojini Naidu chose a mythical heroine she herself was chosen as a heroine by many. Describing the 1917 Congress, M.E. Cousins said:

I remember vividly being impressed by the three women who occupied the place of power and honour on the platform at that Calcutta Congress—Mrs. Besant in the president's chair, on her right Mrs. Sarojini Devi Naidu, representative of the great Hindu race, on the left Begum Ammam Bibi, mother of the brothers Muhammad and Shaukat Ali, veiled daughter of the strong Muslim people. The three women were deeply significant in the new era in Indian social and political history. Womanhood had come out of its seclusion to share with manhood the struggle for gaining freedom for Bharat Mata—the Motherland.[18]

Kamaladevi Chattopadhyaya, one of the women leaders of the Satyagraha movement of the 1930s, was not only brought up on tales of long-dead Rajasthani heroines, but was also given living examples of heroic women. In an interview with K.P.Rungachary and Hari Dev Sharma, she described how her mother used to talk to her about Pandita Ramabai, the way she had suffered at the hands of many Indians and had turned to Christianity. When Kamaladevi was a little girl, in the 1910s, her mother took her to meet Annie Besant: 'She asked Mrs Besant to bless me so that I also grew up like her, with the same zeal and enthusiasm to bring about changes in our society and position of women. Mrs. Besant, very lovingly, placed her hand on my head and blessed me.'[19] Kamaladevi's mother and maternal grandmother were both educated women; her mother was a nationalist who

Rajkumari Amrit Kaur, Lady Piroj Bai Phiroze
Shah Mehta, Mrs N. Sengupta, all women
activists who were in the forefront of the struggle
for women's rights in the early part of this century.

subscribed to the *Kesari* and *Kal*, and was influenced by Ramakrishna Paramhansa, Rama Tirtha, and Vivekananda. She visited her friends' houses and read to them, while her husband helped widows and destitute women with children.[20]

By the 1920s a second generation of feminists was growing up, several of whom were influenced by their reformer mothers. Sushri Lajjavanti's mother, too, conducted reading circles with women neighbours; it was she who insisted Lajjavanti go to school, just as Kamaladevi's mother had insisted on Kamaladevi's remaining at school though she

Times had indeed changed. Lajjavanti became the Principal of the Arya Kanya Mahavidyala, and in 1919 entered the nationalist movement. Several of the ex-students of the Kanya Mahavidyala were to become nationalist activists (one of them, Parvati Devi, was the first woman to go to jail from Meerut, in the Civil Disobedience movement of the 1920s)[22] though, according to Lajjavanti, the school's objective was to make its students good home-bodies and nation-worshippers: (*grihani va deshbhakth*). Interestingly, Lajjavanti distinguished two kinds of nationalism in the period: *deshbhakti* (for the

Sarojini Naidu on her way to address a public meeting

hated studying. Lajjavanti's mother was a devout Arya Samaji as her father had been; he had wanted to send her to the Kanya Mahavidyala (the Arya Samaj school for girls) but family pressure had prevented her from going, so she was determined her daughter would get the education she lacked. Describing how her great grandfather and her mother had remained silent at her great grandfather's edict, instead of arguing with him and commenting on her mother's silence, she said 'well, in those days girls were just regarded as cows'.[21]

country), and *raj-droh* (against the Empire). Raj-droh was for her associated with Lajpat Rai, Ajit Singh, B.C. Pal and others—of whom, she and other girls at the Mahavidyalaya, had heard only distant murmurs. Devraj, the founder principal of the school, did not mention movements such as the Canal Colonies uprising, nor did he encourage the girls to attend public meetings. Yet they were taught to sing patriotic songs at reform meetings and taught to preach on the need for women's education;[23] while in Calcutta attending one

Nationalist flag-raising demonstrations, place and date unknown

Nationalist demonstrations, place and date unknown

Boycott Day demonstration, Civil Disobedience
Movement, Bombay

such meeting, she and her friends met B.C. Pal in 1913, a year before Gandhi arrived in India.[24] In 1915, he and Kasturba founded the Sabarmati Ashram, and were joined by an increasing number of men and women. The initial agitations he was involved with were local movements in Gujarat: in particular, the Champaran satyagraha of indigo cultivators against planters in 1917, the Kheda satyagraha for non-payment of revenue in 1918, and in the same year, the Ahmedabad mill strike of textile workers against the mill-owners' withdrawal of the 'plague bonus' of 1917. A group of women volunteers worked with Kasturba in the Champaran satyagraha, running schools and ashrams in Bitharwa, Barharwa and Madhuban villages, where they taught women to read, write and spin.[25]

Gandhi was brought into the Ahmedabad mill strike by Anusuya Sarabhai, whose brother, a rich industrialist, owned mills in Ahmedabad. He also donated generously to the Sabarmati Ashram, which Anusuya visited, becoming a Gandhian. On her return from the ashram, she began to work among mill-hands, starting night schools for them.[26] Surprisingly little is generally known about her, considering that she was one of the first women to do such work. All we know is that she remained a Gandhian activist, lived and worked with a fellow Gandhian, Shankerlal Banker, and was a member of the All-India Women's Conference in the 1930s.

The involvement of really large numbers of women in the nationalist movement began sometime after the Rowlatt Act was passed in 1919. Known colloquially as the Seditious Meetings Act, it attempted to extend wartime restrictions on civil rights into peacetime, allowing detention without trial for such 'offences' as the possession of tracts which were officially declared seditious. Gandhi emerged as an all-India leader in the ensuing agitation against the Act. His initial suggestion was that volunteers court arrest by selling prohibited texts in public, but he soon added the plan for an all-India hartal, with the reservation that those who had to work on the day of the hartal (a Sunday) should get leave from their employers to attend it. Coming at the time of a number of post-war economic problems, the hartals were massive, especially in Punjab, and were marked by such an unusual inter-religious solidarity that the government was alarmed. Gandhi was externed from Delhi and Punjab, there were police firings on demonstrations in Delhi, Calcutta and all over Punjab—where, under Lieutenant-General O'Dwyer's administration, repression was particularly brutal. On the 10th of April martial law was imposed on Amritsar, under General Dyer, and three days later his troops fired into a peaceful, unarmed crowd in the walled space of Jallianwala Bagh. Martial law was extended to various parts of the Punjab the next day, including Lahore; Gujranwala and the villages surrounding it were bombed. These events left a stunned and resentful populace. All protests were called off, and the Congress limited itself to asking for an 'impartial' non-official inquiry committee. The December 1919 session of the Congress even passed a resolution thanking Montford for his reforms. Yet the resolutions passed at the session were not representative of the mood of delegates. Delegates came from all over India and according to Lajjavanti, streamed to Jallianwala Bagh, the site of the massacre, 'as if they were on a tirtha yatra' (pilgrimage to a holy spot).[27] Lajjavanti was present as Devraj had sent a group of girls from the Kanya Mahavidyalaya principally to attend the National Social Conference, but also to sing songs at the opening of the Congress session. Several of these songs had been composed by Sarala Devi Choudharani, who was also present.[28] Swami Shraddhanand had set up a fund for the families of those murdered at Jallianwala Bagh, and several women were active in collecting money for the fund. One of the most active was Lado Rani Zutshi, Motilal Nehru's niece-in-law, who set up a stall at the Congress, selling goods made by members of the Kumari Sabha, which she had founded in Lahore and in which her daughters were also active. The Kumari Sabha had, in the same year, rehearsed a play called 'Bharat Mata', based on nationalist themes, which they never performed because Gandhi was arrested on the day they were to open.

According to Lado Rani, the Indians and the English were completely polarized in both Amritsar and Lahore in 1919; the open, and ugly racism of the English was met by intense resentment and a 'we will not put up with it' feeling from the Indians. Tempers ran so high that, more often than not, when members of the two communities met, they quarrelled. Recounting one such encounter with an Englishwoman in a bus, she said she was so furious that when she got off the bus she

Aruna Asaf Ali, 1906

Born into an orthodox Hindu Bengali family, Aruna Asaf Ali (or Aruna Gangulee as she was then) was educated at the Sacred Heart Convent in Lahore and then sent to a Protestant school in Nainital. After graduating she got a job in the Gokhale Memorial School in Calcutta. In Allahabad she met her future husband, M. Asaf Ali, a prominent Congressman, and they were married in the teeth of parental opposition, both on the grounds of religion and of age (She was only 19 and he was 23 years older than she was). Aruna Asaf Ali's first major political involvement was during the Salt Satyagraha, at which time she addressed public meetings, made salt and led processions. She was prosecuted in Delhi 'for being a vagrant having no ostensible means of livelihood',[1] rather than for sedition, and on her refusing to furnish security for good behaviour was sentenced to one year's imprisonment. A few months later, most political prisoners were released on the signing of the Gandhi-Irwin pact, but as she was not a political prisoner she was not released. Her women co-prisoners in Lahore jail refused to leave jail without her, and finally did so only on Gandhi's intercession. Mean-

while, a public agitation for her release was launched, and after some days she was released. In 1932 she was arrested again, and put in the Delhi jail, where she went on hunger strike in protest at the callous treatment of political prisoners. The prisoners' demands were conceded, but Aruna was transferred to Ambala jail, where she was kept in solitary confinement. After her release she dropped out of the national movement for ten years. In 1942 she went to the Bombay Congress session with her husband, and was present at the passing of the Quit India resolution of 8 August. When Congress leaders were arrested the day after this resolution was passed, Aruna presided over the flag-hoisting ceremony at Gowalia Tank Maidan in Bombay, at which the enormous assembly was tear gassed, lathi-charged and fired upon. She became a full-time activist in the Quit India Movement, going underground to evade arrest. Her property was seized by the Government and sold. She became editor of *Inquilab*, the monthly organ of the Congress, along with Ram Manohar Lohia. In its 1944 issue she advised freedom fighters not to 'allow any academic and therefore futile arguments on questions like violence and non-violence to divert your attention from the stern realities of today … I want every student and youth to think and feel as soldiers of the revolution that is to come.'[2] The Government meanwhile announced a Rs. 5000 reward for her capture. She fell ill and hearing of this Gandhi advised her to surrender: 'I have sent you a message that you must not die underground. You are reduced to a skeleton. Do come out and surrender yourself and win the prize offered for your arrest. Reserve the prize money for the Harijan cause.'[3] However, Aruna came overground only when the warrants against her were cancelled on the 26th of January, 1946.

Aruna Asaf Ali came to be known as the Grand Old Lady of the Independence Movement and the Heroine of the 1942 Movement. After she was married, Aruna Asaf Ali also worked in the local women's league, which was affiliated to the All India Women's Conference. In 1954 she helped to establish the National Federation of Indian Women (NFIW), the women's wing of the Communist Party of India. The NFIW was meant to be a radical alternative to existing women's organizations, and one that would reach beyond a mere middle class membership. In 1992 she was awarded the Nehru Award for International understanding.

1. Manmohan Kaur, op. cit., p. 236.
2. Manmohan Kaur, op. cit., p.238.
3. Ibid.

'warned' the Punjabi woman who was getting on at the same time to keep out of the Englishwoman's way. The woman retorted that if 'they' said anything to her, she would throw them out of the window.[29]

The 1920–21 civil disobedience movement which followed seems to mark the time when nationalists began to consciously organize women. Lajjavanti, who met Lajpat Rai in 1920, became a full scale activist in Lahore. She was, by this time, Principal of the Arya Kanya Mahavidyala, and with Lajpat Rai's help, she started classes in *charkha* spinning at the school; becoming, at the same time, a member of the Punjab Provincial Congress Committee. According to her, there were three chief organizers of women in Lahore, all of whom were connected to important men: Purnadevi, Kedarnath Sahgal's daughter; Sita Devi, Chabeeldas' wife; and Parvati Devi, Lajpat Rai's daughter.[30]

Lajjavanti's characterization of most of the women who got involved in the 1920–21 movement in Lahore is interesting: first, most of them were migrants to Lahore, rather than born and bred there; second, most were middle-class rather than rich, though there were a few rich women, like Sarala Devi. Amongst middle-class professionals, she said, the wives of barristers were especially enthusiastic about burning their foreign clothes. The nationalist sympathies of all women 'who were even a little educated' were intense, though there were restrictions on the nature of their participation. Hundreds of women went hawking *khadi* and charkhas from lane to lane in the city; and took out processions to popularize khadi at which they sang songs mocking 'fashion' and collectively burnt their foreign clothes. But they did not go picketing liquor shops, nor did they court arrest.[31] When attempts were made to organize women's demonstrations in violation of the Seditious Meetings Act, only one meeting could be arranged in Haveli Nakain. Yet women came from as far as Jullundar to attend the meeting, and Lajjavanti later discovered that most of the women who had attended the meeting had left word that if even one woman was arrested they would all go to jail, so not to expect them back at any fixed time, or worry if they were late in returning.[32] The local Congress leadership itself, it seems, was divided on whether women should or should not court arrest, for Lajpat Rai did not approve of sending women to jail, and in fact tried to prevent Lajjavanti from violating the Seditious Meetings Act (he stopped his own daughter).[33]

Lado Rani Zutshi, who was also a nationalist activist in Lahore in 1920–21, made no mention of attempts to violate the Seditious Meetings Act, or to court arrest. An anecdote of her daughter's about her mother's work as an organizer during the movement sheds an amusing light on the kind of concern that was felt for 'the ladies' at the time: it seems that the women who went out on demonstrations would often lose their slippers as the pace speeded up, and so Lado Rani would 'depute two or three volunteers with cloth bags' to walk behind the procession and collect all the slippers, taking them back to the District Congress Committee office. When the procession broke up, women marchers would go back to the office, find their slippers and go home.[34]

Interestingly, Lado Rani traced her politicization to Sarojini Naidu's lectures in Lahore, delivered at the time that the Khilafat agitation was growing all over India. Sarojini Naidu was one of the most ardent canvassers for Hindu-Muslim unity in the Congress, and coming at a time when solidarity between the two communities was still fairly strong, she used the occasion of her lectures to get women to make symbolic gestures of solidarity. Clearly these gestures, even when small, had an influence, for some forty years later Lado Rani recounted one such gesture when Sarojini Naidu, at an 'At Home' in her honour, 'joined' the hands of Rani Narendra Nath and Lady Zulfikar Ali.[35]

In both Bombay and Calcutta, women's participation in the 1920–21 movement seems to have been free of the restrictions imposed on them in Punjab. Women picketed liquor shops in Bombay and, on the occasion of a Government auction of liquor licenses, they encircled the Town Hall and prevented the auction taking place. Chief among those in Bombay were Sarojini Naidu, Uma Kundapur, Nanduben Kanuga, Perin Captain (the granddaughter of Dadabhai Naoroji), and Maniben Patel (the daughter of Vallabhbhai Patel). On the 13th of April (the anniversary of the Jallianwala Bagh massacre, now commemorated as Jallianwala Day), women in Bombay founded the Rashtreeya Stree Sabha, an organization devoted solely to nationalist activism. As far as we know, this was the first such women's organization to be founded. Members of the Rashtreeya Stree Sabha engaged in khadi propaganda all over Bombay, including the mill workers' districts, and were involved in organizing a Bombay-wide hartal in boycott of the Prince of Wales' visit to India in November, 1921. Though the Sabha originally concentrated on trying to popularize charkha spinning, they found fairly soon that such efforts would not be successful in Bombay, the home of the Indian textile industry. Some of its members, moreover, were relatives of mill-owners, and this must have further complicated their situation. So they decided that it would be more useful to set up a distribution network for the sale of khadi produced in villages; which they did through organizing khadi exhibitions-cum-sales, and also selling door to door. According to one of their members they sold considerable quantities of khadi in this way, collecting up to Rs 25,000 a year. Furthermore, in an attempt to take up Gandhi's views on the uplift of Harijans the Sabha also started classes for Harijans in Bombay's G ward which they ran from 1921 to 1930.[36] In Calcutta Basanti Devi

Basanti Devi

Durgabai Deshmukh

(Mrs C.R. Das), Urmila Debi and Suniti Debi (who had founded the Nari Karm Mandir, a home for working women), were the most notable women organizers. All three wore khadi and picketed shops selling foreign cloth so energetically that they were arrested for 'obstructing the gentlemen of Calcutta'.[37] Basanti Debi's arrest was described by the *Amrita Bazar Patrika* as having 'had an electric effect on the people. Immediately more than a thousand young men offered themselves for arrest.'[38]

The 1921 Congress session was attended by a hundred and forty-four women delegates; there were a hundred and thirty-one women volunteers and fourteen women on the Subjects Committee.[39] In 1922 Basanti Debi presided over the Bengal Provincial Congress Committee session in Chittagong; and before the 1923 Congress session at Cocanada, a special 'Girl Volunteer Corps' was formed to prepare for it, headed by Durgabai (later Deshmukh).[40] Women were active in the Nagpur Flag Satyagraha of 1923, against a Government order banning the display of the Congress flag in certain parts of the city; and the Borsad satyagraha of 1923–24, against a punitive tax levied on the villagers for payment of the extra police forces drafted to control dacoits. Processions against the Government order in Nagpur were led by a woman, Bhaktiben Desai.[41]

Lajjavanti has described the intensity of nationalist-feminist feelings amongst women in the 1920–21 movement, saying that while it did not show the kind of mass women's activism that the 1930s movement did, the fervour and anticipation with which women joined the movement was greater in the 1920s.[42] That there was a sense of great achievement by women, of new spaces opening up for them, is shown in the 'Dance of Liberation' written by the Tamil nationalist poet, Subramanya Bharati, sometime in the 1920s:

> *Dance! Rejoice!*
> *Those who said*
> *it is evil for women to touch books*
> *are dead,*
> *the lunatics who said*
> *they would lock women in their houses*
> *cannot show their faces now.*
> *They showed us our place in the home*
> *as if we were bullocks, bred*
> *and beaten to dumb labour.*
> *We have ended that*
> *Sing and dance!*

Vir Bharat Talwar and Indrani Chatterjee have described how a discourse of equality began to develop in the late 1910s and 1920s, amongst women who had been active in nationalist or women's rights campaigns. Not only did they link women's rights with nationalism, they used nationalist arguments to defend demands for women's rights to equality with men. Urmila Debi, one of the militants of the 1921–22 movement, declared that swaraj meant self rule and *swadhinata* the 'strength and power to fulfill ourselves', while Amiya Debi said 'swadhinata cannot be *given*, it has to be taken by force . . . the responsibility for this swadhinata cannot be with well-wishing men—if it does, then adhinata alone will be strengthened.' A series of questions were put to male nationalists who either opposed women's rights or counselled caution in the matter of fighting for them: those who said women would be given their rights in due course were reminded of their own arguments that rights had to be fought for; those who advised a gradual method of gaining these rights were reminded that the Congress moderates had been criticized precisely for advocating this, and so on. Moreover, some women now began to express the view that women, in order to be free, had to engage in a struggle with men. And the demand for equality between the sexes was itself based on the principle of sameness rather than complementarity.[43]

Thus, by the 1920s, two quite different rationales for women's rights were being expressed: the one that women's rights should be recognized because of women's socially useful role as mothers; the other that women, having the same needs, desires and capacities as men, were entitled to the same rights. The former held that the biological difference between men and women affected the sexes qualitatively; the latter that biological differences did not determine the 'nature' of each sex.

Meanwhile, Indian women abroad were also beginning to engage in nationalist activities. Prabhavati (later Mirza), who had supported the 1905 Bengal revolutionaries, worked with a group called 'Freedom for India and Ireland' in the United States; while Renuka Ray, Sarala Ray's grand-daughter, worked with the League Against British Imperialism in England. Prabhavati moved to Germany to do her doctorate in 1923, where she met M.N. Roy, Virendranath Chattopadhyaya and other Indian revolutionaries and communists. She returned to Calcutta in 1926, stopping en route at Benares in order to meet communist and revolutionary groups there. Through them she got in touch with the Workers and Peasants' Party, formed in Benares by Muzaffar Ahmed, Nazrul Islam and Hemantakumar Sarkar, and began to work with them. Together, they decided to start organizing the scavengers in Calcutta, and began to haunt the teashops 'day and night', hoping to strike up acquaintance with scavengers. The scavengers, at first, laughed at them, asking teasingly if they were lovelorn to be sitting in tea-shops the whole time. Later, though, when

there was a scavengers' strike, the group put forward certain demands for the strikers. The strike, however, fizzled out. Some time after, Prabhavati was arrested and jailed during another strike which was successful, partly because it was in the summer.[44] In the years to follow, she became one of the most important trade-unionists in Calcutta, representing jute and textile workers as well as scavengers, and establishing an empire on both sides of the Ganges. The workers called her Mataji, and it appears that she was something of a matriarch, for she had a gang of *dadas* (goons) posted at various strategic points of 'her' territory, who would report to her if any strangers happened to encroach.[45] In 1928 she was involved in organizing the Calcutta scavengers' strike, in which women played a leading—and radical—role. Tanika Sarkar has described how women scavengers threw excreta at policemen, characterizing this as a 'symbolic demonstration of how their very degradation, related to impure caste and lowly tasks, might be turned into a weapon of strength.'[46]

The 1920s also saw a shift in consciousness of and about working class women. Where formerly attempts to work amongst them were rare and strictly reformist, now reformist activities were expanded in both scope and scale: while within workers' movements women began to be seen as a special category with distinct rights and a distinct role. As before, the emphasis was on their roles as wives and mothers, but there were by now certain changes in the way this role was defined.

The 'health and sanitation' stream of voluntary work expanded as women's organizations grew all over the country, at the same time as the Government too took an increasing interest in the conditions of the Indian working class. When, in the mid-1920s, the loyalist National Council of Women in India was set up, with Lady Willingdon and Lady Stephens as its patronesses, a major part of its energies were devoted to maternal and child welfare. Its Patna branch alone founded two maternal and child welfare clinics, one named after Lady Willingdon and one after Lady Stephens. At both free milk and medicines were distributed, 'maternity benefits were provided for the mothers', and classes were held for them 'to learn how to bathe, clean, feed and treat the children'.[47]

Nationalists too, for the first time, began to show an interest in health and sanitation—as the concern of women—but this concern was defined as a kind of national service by the women, not merely for them. When, for example, C.R. Das died, leaving his money 'to the nation', Gandhi, Surendranath Banerjee, Lord Sinha and other trustees decided that the house and money would be used for maternal and child welfare in Bengal. The house was converted into a hospital and a nurses' training institute was attached, with the idea that nurses trained there would set up in Calcutta and different parts of the province. Unlike the National Council of Women, however, the Chittaranjan Seva Sadan offered neither free milk nor 'maternity benefits': it held out, instead, an ideal of social service, in which the recipients of the Trust's service would in turn become donors of service:

> It will not ordinarily be the object of this Institution to afford training to women who are anxious to make a living out of it, but the Institute will welcome women who are prepared to take instruction for the sake of utilising such knowledge in their homes and imparting it to others so that they may get an opportunity of taking their legitimate share in the building and upliftment of the nation.[48]

In a way, this ideal of social service done by one's self for those who are one's self drew from the tradition of the widowhood reform movement: Karve's home, for example, was run and supported by widows who had themselves trained at the home; it had, moreover, been founded with the idea that those who trained there would go on to impart their knowledge to sisters in misfortune. But it was through Gandhi that this idea of self-help became truly popular, and the Gandhian feminism which developed in the 1920s became majority feminism in the 1930s.

Interestingly, conscious attempts to expand the scope of nationalist activity so that poor women were included in the 'task of nation-building' were based on the image of women as nurturers rather than wage-earners. None of the nationalist women of the time seems to have made mainstream attempts to organize women workers; even their few attempts at 'employment generation' for women, made along swadeshi lines, seem to have assumed that women's wage-work was subsidiary activity to supplement the male wage rather than to earn a living wage. The Rashtreeya Stree Sabha, for example, started classes for poor women in Bombay, at which they were taught to embroider khadi; these embroideries were hawked by Rashtreeya Stree Sabha members along with other khadi goods, as part of their programme to popularize swadeshi. Most of the women embroiderers earned between Rs 5 to Rs 15 a month from this work, but the meagreness of this wage does not seem to have caused the members of the Sabha any concern. Similarly, the Patna branch of the Aghorekamini Nari Samiti founded an Industrial School for Women in the 1920s, at which they were taught handicrafts; the objects produced were sold at annual exhibition-cum-sales, called 'Ananda Bazaars'. Proceeds of the sale, however, were not divided by the producers, but given to charity.[49]

In South India, women seem to have been more active at this time in social reform campaigns than in nationalist ones. M.E. Cousins was now working for the Women's Indian Association, whose branches held regular meetings at which such subjects as domestic economy and human physiology were discussed, 'and some religious books were read and explained'.[50] Though they canvassed support for Dr Gour's Civil Marriage Bill in 1921, their energies seem to have been concentrated on expanding the organization, for branches were set up in such distant places as Jaffna and Rangoon, and by 1926 they had sixty five branches, with three thousand members.[51] They seem also to have taken up the ideas of the co-operative movement in the early 1920s, for their Salem branch opened a women's co-operative bank, which met once a month and had thirty members (only five or six, however, attended regularly, the 'others transact[ed] business by proxy').[52]

Yet the Women's Indian Association was the first women's organization to take up women workers' demands, and the group of moderate nationalists that they were associated with were the first to raise the issue of maternity leave and benefits for women workers. In fact, the demand for maternity leave was first put forward in the 1921 Jamshedpur strike, but came to nothing. It was again mentioned in the All India Trade Union Congress charter in the year that the organization was founded. Gandhi interestingly, never joined the AITUC, though Annie Besant, Wadia, N.M. Joshi and a whole host of moderate nationalists, social reformers and workers' representatives did. In 1924 the Bombay social reformer S.K. Bole, moved a resolution in the Legislative Council urging the Government of India to enact laws for the granting of maternity leave and benefits to women workers; in 1926 the Government of India requested provincial governments to collect information on this question; in 1928, R.S. Asavle introduced a Private Member's Bill for Maternity Benefit in Bombay, with ardent support from N.M. Joshi; in 1929, the Bombay Maternity Benefit Act was passed. The Government of India had decided to leave the question of maternity benefits to be sorted out by provincial governments; so the Bombay Act was followed by similar legislation in the Central Provinces in 1930, in Ajmer-Merwar in 1933, in Madras in 1935, in Delhi in 1936, in Bengal in 1937, and in the United Provinces in 1938.

Sometime in the early 1920s members of the Women's Indian Association in Madras got involved in developing a kind of association of women workers: 'on account of the difficulties women had in one of largest mills employing female labourers. When a woman had worked for six months and she was in a delicate state she was dismissed with no compensation whatsoever, and that was the time she needed extra money'.[53] It seems, moreover, that in order to be re-employed by the mill after pregnancy, women had to pay bribes of between Rs 3 to Rs 10. According to Dorothy Jinarajadasa, women had come together because they were beginning to see that

The All India Women's Conference

In late 1925, or early 1926, Margaret Cousins, the founder-Secretary of the Women's India Association, and editor of *Stri-Dharma*, wrote a letter which was sent to several women's organizations and many individuals, in which she asked women to come from all over the country to discuss women's education: 'There is undoubtedly a need for women to express their considered views clearly on the subject of present-day education for boys and girls in India, and specially for girls. If these opinions are formulated in a memorandum women will be doing a service to the future and be helping those who are at present in charge of the educational destinies of young India.'

She then suggested what she considered to be the most practicable way of 'collecting the assistance of women to this end', and asked women to cooperate in bringing the project to success, and also asked that they write and give their opinion as well as extending their active support. Her suggestion was:

'As problems connected with girls' education are different in different provinces and localities, it is thought necessary that there should be a women's conference on educational reforms in each province and in clearly defined districts which will facilitate local solutions and will also give views which would be all-India as well. From each of these, conference representatives should be elected who will attend an All-Indian Conference which may take place in Poona at the end of December next or at the end of January. The conference of representatives consisting of forty or more women will have the duty of synthesizing from the proceedings of the preliminary constituent conference an authoritative and representative memorandum by women on educational reform which will be published widely and sent to all the Indian educational authorities.'[1]

The first conference at Poona was a spectacular success, with 2000 people attending; it was held at the Fergusson College Hall in Poona University—on the opening day the top gallery was filled with male students, the lower gallery with women students and the main hall with delegates from all over India. Among the recommendations were: that primary education should include handwork, manual training and domestic science which would later be followed by vocational training, and that the dignity of labour be emphasized; that college courses should include social service, journalism, politics as practical sciences, and women's colleges should become centres of active corporate life. One of the delegates

commented: 'One felt awakening spring, a promise in the air. The discussion sessions on the following days gave achievements in formulation of the memorandum, and the opening sessions fused the women, young and old, into a spiritual sisterhood....'

In the memorandum the following points were stressed: (a) that the child's talents should be developed in the service of humanity; (b) that secondary schools should also have courses in domestic science, journalism, social science and architecture; (d) that women students should be given scholarships to encourage them to study law, medicine, social science and architecture. Lotika Ghose adds 'the only resolution of a general social nature was the support of Rai Sahib Harbilas Sarda's Bill for the restraint of early marriage.'[2] At their second conference there was wide and extensive debate on whether the Conference should remain a single issue organization, or should widen its scope, the latter view eventually winning majority support with the decision to campaign for the Sarda Bill. At the third conference in Patna this decision was ratified and a separate committee was appointed for the purpose of dealing with all issues concerning women other than education. At the fourth conference the campaign for reforming women's inheritance laws was discussed, and subsequently meetings were held all over the country to lobby for legislative change in inheritance rights. At the fourth conference they decided to observe March 1 as Women's Day, celebrating it in Lahore in 1931.[3] In the fourth, fifth and sixth conferences women's conditions of labour and the Maternity Benefit Act were discussed, further safeguards to the Sarda Act passed in Baroda explored. The debate on reform versus political involvement, started in the second conference, continued; where earlier members had decided that the conference would not engage in any political activity, this ban was now lifted. The conference had drawn up a memorandum on women's franchise, jointly with the Women's Indian Association and the National Council of Women in India. It was decided that this memorandum would be placed before the Franchise Committee, explicitly and continuously refusing that votes for women be subject to the communal award. In 1928 the Conference started collecting funds to open the Lady Irwin College of Domestic Science in Delhi opening it in November 1932; in 1933–34, three women representing the All-India Women's Conference, the Indian Women's Association and the National Council of Women were invited to London to give evidence before the joint parliamentary committee on women's franchise. In the next three years, the Conference campaigned for the setting up of a commission to look into the legal disabilities of Indian women, which would recommend reforms from a modern point of view; brought out a report on the conditions of women mine workers, concluding that women should be legally prevented from doing underground work; and presented a memorandum on women's political, social and educational status in India to the League of Nations and the Government of India. In 1938, the Conference started publishing a bulletin in English with the Hindi title *Roshni* (light). During the Bengal Famine of 1943 the All India Women's Conference did relief work in Calcutta and its districts. A 'Save the Children Fund' which received major funding from abroad was also started, under Vijay Lakshmi Pandit's presidency.

By this stage many of the earlier and more radical members of the Conference had become full time nationalist agitators, resigning from the Conference for this purpose. The organization itself settled into a solid reformist patten, representing the more conservative currents in the nationalist movement. At the same time women were pouring into the nationalist movement and joining the Congress in large numbers.

Today the AIWC continues to exist, with its headquarters in a huge building in Delhi, but has little connection with latter day feminist movements.

1. Lotika Ghose, op. cit., pp. 158–59.
2. Lotika Ghose, op. cit., p. 160.
3. R.K. Sharma, *Nationalism, Social Reform and Indian Women*, Janaki Prakashan, Patna, 1981. p. 118.

'through co-operation they could improve their position'.[54]

By the late 1920s the presence of women in workers' movements was noticeable; not only were there several prominent women trade-unionists, but women workers began to be consciously organized and a special role began to be given to them in the workers' movement. Bombay was in some ways the centre of this development, with Maniben Kare emerging as a socialist leader of railway workers, and Ushabai Dange and Parvati Bhore as communist leaders of textile workers. In the 1928–29 Bombay textile strike women were placed at the head of demonstrations in the belief that the police would not lathi-charge them; and were used to picket the mills to prevent strike-breakers from entering. It seems they stood at mill gates with brooms in their hands, and when moral suasion failed to win over errant workers, they were not above using their brooms to belabour them.[55] As in the Calcutta strike of the same period, women seemed more aware of the tactical uses of humiliation as a weapon—possibly because it was an ancient ar.d common experience for their sex. The awareness that different classes of women had different conditions and needs also began to influence the women's movement, albeit in a limited way. When, in 1926, the All India Women's Conference for Educational Reform was formed, its charter uneasily juxtaposed the statement that they wanted an education which would fit Indian women to best perform their roles in the home, with a demand for vocational training for poor women.[56] The nature of arguments on education amongst the middle-class women who constituted the AIWC is shown by the following exasperated comment by one of the organizers of the first conference in Poona:

I find it almost impossible to make them think of education nationally, that is, of the education of the princess down to that of the sweeper's daughter, including, on the way, that of the most numerous class of all, the daughters of eighty per cent of the population, the raiyats and agriculturists generally. Both consciously and unconsciously they think only of the professional classes to which they belong.

One young lady yesterday wanted the sons of the agriculturists all to take the Matric: 'otherwise they could not be considered educated' . . . (yet) these eighty per cent (of agriculturists and raiyats) constitute the foundation on which the upper classes rest. . . India is on the brink of a French Revolution unless the senseless worship of Matriculation not only ceases for the boys but is cut out at once for the girls.[57]

At their 1930 conference in Gwalior, the AIWC held a special session on 'labour questions': and at their 1931 conference in Lahore they passed a string of 'Resolutions on Labour', saying that all factories employing considerable numbers of women should provide a woman doctor for ante and post-natal care, a creche and nursery school, and a maternity home. Moreover, a central maternity benefit act should be passed by the Government of India, and in every industrial area there should be at least one woman factory inspector; local authorities should provide playgrounds and ensure better housing for workers; there should be part-time education for half-timers and a Government scheme for adult education. They also asked for an enquiry into the conditions of women mine workers, following a memo-

A BILL TO
Restrain the solemnisation of child marriages

WHEREAS it is expedient to restrain the solemnisation of child marriages; It is hereby enacted as follows:-

1. (1) This Act may be called the Child Marriage Restraint Act, 1928.

Short title, extent and commencement. (2) It extends to the whole of British India, including British Baluchistan and the Santhal Parganas.

(3) It shall come into force on the Ist day of April, 1930.

2. In this Act, unless there is anything *Definitions.* repugnant in the subject or context,—

(a) "child" means a person who, if a male, is under eighteen years of age, and if a female, is under fourteen years of age;

(b) "child marriage" means a marriage to which either of the contracting parties is a child;

(c) "contracting party" to a marriage means either of the parties whose marriage is thereby solemnised; and

(d) "minor" means a person of either sex who is under eighteen years of age.

3. Whoever, being a male above eighteen years of age and *Punishment for male adult above twenty-one years of age marrying a child.* below twenty one, contracts a child marriage shall be punishable with fine which may extend to one thousand rupees.

4. Whoever, being a male above twenty-one years of age, *Punishment for solemnising a child marriage.* contracts a child marriage shall be punishable with simple imprisonment which may extend to one thousand rupees, or with both.

5. Whoever performs, conducts or directs any child marriage shall be punishable with simple *Punishment for parent or guardian concerned in a child marriage.* imprisonment which may extend to one month, or with fine which may extend to one thousand rupees, or with both, unless he proves that he had reason to believe that the marriage was not a child marriage.

6. (1) Where a minor contracts a child marriage, any person having charge of the minor, whether as parent or guardian or in any other capacity, lawful or unlawful, who does any act to promote the marriage or permits it to be solemnised, or negligently fails to prevent it from being solemnised, shall be punishable with simple imprisonment which may extend to one month, or with fine which may extend to one thousand rupees, or with both:

Provided that no woman shall be punishable with imprisonment.

(2) For the purposes of this section, it shall be presumed, unless and until the contrary is proved, that, where a minor has contracted a child marriage, the person having charge of such minor has negligently failed to prevent the marriage from being solemnised.

7. Notwithstanding anything contained *Imprisonment not to be awarded for offences under section 3.* in section 25 of the General Clauses Act, 1897, or section 64 of the Indian Penal Code, a Court sentencing an offender under section 3 shall not be competent to direct that, in default of payment of the fine imposed, he shall undergo any term of imprisonment.

8. Notwithstanding anything contained *Jurisdiction under this Act.* in section 190 of the Code of Criminal Procedure, 1898, no Court other than that of a Presidency Magistrate or a District Magistrate shall take cognizance of, or try, any offence under this Act.

9. No Court shall take *Mode of taking cognizance of offences.* cognizance of any offence under this Act save upon complaint made within one year of the solemnisation of the marriage in respect of which the offence is alleged to have been committed.

10. The Court taking cognizance of an offence under this Act shall, unless it *Preliminary inquiries into offences under this Act.* dismisses the complaint under section 203 of the Code of Criminal Procedure, 1898, either itself make an inquiry under section 202 of that Code, or direct a Magistrate of the first class subordinate to it to make such inquiry.

11. (1) At any time after examining the complainant and before issuing process for compelling the attendance of the *Power to take security* accused, the Court *from complainant.* shall, except for reasons to be recorded in writing, require the complainant to execute a bond, with or without sureties, for a sum not exceeding one hundred rupees, as security for the payment of any compensation which the complainant may be directed to pay under section 250 of the Code of Criminal Procedure, 1898; and if such security is not furnished within such reasonable time as the Court may fix, the complaint shall be dismissed.

(2) A bond taken under this section shall be deemed to be a bond taken under the Code of Criminal Procedure, 1898, and Chapter XLII of that Code shall apply accordingly.

This Bill was passed at a meeting of the Legislative Assembly on the 23rd day of September, 1929.

V.J. Patel,
President, Legislative Assembly.
The 25th September, 1929.

STATEMENT OF OBJECTS AND REASONS.
The object of the Bill is twofold. The main object, by declaring invalid the marriages of girls below 12 years of age, is to put a stop to such girls becoming widows. The second object, by laying down the minimum marriageable ages of boys and girls, is to prevent, so far as may be, their physical and moral deterioration by removing a principal obstacle to their physical and mental development.

2. According to the Census Report of 1921 A.D., there were in that year 612 Hindu widows who were less than one year old, 2,024 who were under 5 years, 97,857 who were under 10 years, and 332,024 who were under 15 years of age. The deplorable feature of the situation, however, is that the majority of these child widows are prevented by Hindu custom and usage from remarrying. Such a lamentable state of affairs exists

in no country, civilised or uncivilised, in the world. And it is high time that the law came to the assistance of these helpless victims of social customs, which whatever their origin or justification in old days, are admittedly out of date and are the source of untold misery and harm at the present time.

3. According to the Brahmanas, the most ancient and the most authoritative book containing the laws of the Hindus, the minimum marriageable age of a man is 24 and a woman 16. And if the welfare of the girl were the only consideration in fixing the age, the law should fix 16 as the minimum age for the valid marriage of a girl. But amongst the Hindus, there are people who hold the belief that a girl should not remain unmarried after she attains puberty.

And as in this country, some girls attain puberty at an age as early as 12, the Bill fixes 12 as the minimum age for the valid marriage of a Hindu girl.

4. In order, however, to make the Bill accessible to most conservative Hindu opinion, provision is made in the Bill that for conscientious reasons, the marriage of a Hindu girl would be permissible even when she is 11 years old. No Hindu Sastra enjoins marriage of a girl before she attains puberty, and the time has arrived and public opinion sufficiently developed, when the first step towards the accomplishment of the social reform so necessary for the removal of a great injustice to its helpless victims and so essential to the vital interests of a large part of humanity, should be taken, by enacting a law declaring inva-

lid the marriages of girls below 11 years of age.

5. With regard to boys, the Sastras do not enjoin marriage at a particular age. Thoughtful public opinion amongst the Hindus would fix 18 as the minimum marriageable age for a boy. But as some classes of the Hindus would regard such legislation as too drastic, the Bill takes the line of least resistance by providing 15 years as the age below which the marriage of a Hindu boy shall be invalid. Even in England, where child marriages are unknown and early marriages are exceptions, it has been found necessary to fix the ages below which boys and girls may not marry.

M. HARBILAS SARDA.

randum submitted to the Bombay Conference on Labour, called by the National Council of Women in India. The memorandum, sent by a visitor to the Asansol mines, said that though attempts were being made to give women lighter work overground, neither the men nor the women wanted the sexes to be separated in this way, for when underground, they engaged in 'immoral' acts. The Memoramdum ended with the pious statement that 'the place for women is in the home in this day of building New India.'[58]

Interestingly, the increase of interest in women workers came at a time when large numbers of them were being retrenched from textiles and mines, the two major industries employing women. It has been shown that as industrialization proceeded and labour markets were established, a reserve army of labour power began to be made. These were accompanied by what Marx called a 'gospel of abstention', in which women's role in engendering habits of thrift, sobriety and loyalty among present and future generations of workers was stressed. Studies were conducted showing that women's wage work separated them from the home, leading to neglect of themselves, their husbands and children, resulting in a poorer quality of wage work and generations of reckless and undependable workers. The bourgeois ideology of motherhood was now expanded to include working class women. Perhaps it was because of this that no real attempts were made to canvass against women's retrenchment from industrial employment: instead, attempts were made to carve out the space of 'women's work' which, for both middle class and poor women, centred on her biologically defined qualities of mother-

hood. Women's skills, it seems, were seen as 'nurturing' ones, such as nursing, cooking, cleaning, teaching; or those which followed from their traditional household duties, such as food processing and handicrafts. Even when not so narrowly confined, there was an assumed boundary curtailing women's work; the AIWC, for example, collected money for scholarships for women studying law, medicine, architecture and the social sciences, but not for physics or chemistry. Coming at a time when the burgeoning nationalist movement began to publicly espouse women's causes, and women's own public presence had forced a certain measure of acceptance of this presence, the AIWC expanded rapidly, growing to be the one organization representing the women's movement of the 1930s and 40s. While it had initially been founded as a single issue organization, within a year or two it had expanded its purview to a host of issues concerning women, though not without considerable debate. Several issues were brought up and conflated, but basically the argument was about tactics, with one side arguing that it would be better to stick with 'safe' objects, such as the need for women's education, than alienate large sections of women by taking up contentious issues; and the other side urging the need to take up all women's issues. Underlying the debate was the question of whether to campaign for Harbilas Sarda's Bill against child-marriage, which attempted to raise the age of marriage for girls from 10 to 12 years. A formal statement of support for the Bill had already been made by the Conference, with the caveat that Hari Singh Gour's Bill of 1924, which attempted to raise the age of girls at marriage from 10 to 14 years, was preferable. Sarda's watered down Bill, however, aroused a storm of protest from both Hindus and Muslims of all classes all over the country, whose demonstrations often swelled to over fifty thousand. Opposition to the Bill again stated (as in the 1890s) that the Government had no right to 'interfere' in what was the purview of religion, but this time the question was not so much a matter of foreign interference as one of defining the boundaries between civil and religious laws, and of asserting that no state could codify the latter without the sanction of religious leaders. It was, therefore, in the context of a new wave of religious fundamentalism that the AIWC debate took place. The question of whether to campaign for the Bill or not, however, became secondary in the ensuing debate, which focussed more on the method the AIWC should employ in order to work effectively among Indian women, with one side arguing that the AIWC would isolate itself if it threw itself into the agitation over the Sarada Bill, and the other arguing not only that it was vital to agitate for the Bill, but that the scope of the Conference be widened to include 'all questions affecting the welfare of women'.

Interestingly, in the debate which followed this proposal (which was made by Kamaladevi Chattopadhyaya and supported by Rameshwari Nehru and Maya Das), the old argument about the social versus the political surfaced again, but with a new twist. Arguing against the widening of the AIWC, Sarala Devi Choudharani and Lakshmi Kutty of Bengal said that the social would lead to the political, while the novelist Anurupa Devi said, 'members carrying the banner of education will have easy access to every home. But if you associate politics or social reform all our members will be viewed by suspicious eyes.'[59]

The old argument, thus, of social reform versus political reform, had now given way to the idea, that far from being opposed, the two were inextricably linked, for the one led to the other. Although neither Sarala Devi, nor Lakshmi Kutty or Anurupa Devi defined their stand, it was possible that for them the old ideal of social service rather than reform now replaced the earlier opposition between the 'social' and the 'political'. Eventually, a kind of compromise was arrived at, with the Conference accepting the need to get involved in all issues concerning women and expanding its name to the All India Women's Conference for Educational and Social Reform, but refusing to get involved in political issues and placing a ban on the involvement of its members in political movements. Within another two or three years, this ban too was lifted; for, by then, thousands of women all over the country had been swept into the civil disobedience and non-cooperation movements of the 1930s.

NOTES

1. Sita Ram Singh, op. cit., p. 93. Smt Roshanlal was quoting Tennyson.
2. Sarala Ray, 'Notes on Gokhale', Sarala Ray Papers, NMML, New Delhi.
3. Sita Ram Singh, op. cit., p. 88.
4. Ibid, p. 94.
5. *Indian Ladies' Magazine*, 'News & Notes', Vol. XII, April 1913, No. 10, p. 223.
6. M.E. Cousins, *Indian Womanhood Today*, Kitabistan, 1947, p. 29.
7. Sita Ram Singh, op. cit., pp. 206–7.
8. Usha Chakraborty, op. cit., p. 125.
9. Vir Bharat Talwar, op. cit., p. 206.
10. Sita Ram Singh, op. cit., pp. 197–88.
11. Ibid, pp. 190–91.
12. Manmohan Kaur, op. cit., p. 106.
13. Rajkumari Amrit Kaur, *Challenge to Women*.
14. M.E. Cousins, op. cit., p. 24.
15. Sumit Sarkar, MI, p. 151.
16. Ibid.
17. Pattabhi Sitaramayya, op. cit., p. 131.
18. Sarojini Naidu, op. cit., p. 246.
19. M.E. Cousins, op. cit., p. 58.
20. Kamaladevi Chattopadhyaya, 'Interview', NMML Oral History Section, p. 6.
21. Ibid, pp. 1–2.
22. Sushri Lajjavanti, 'Interview', NMML Oral History Section, p. 3.
23. Ibid, pp. 12–15.
24. Ibid, p. 20.
25. Sita Ram Singh, op. cit., p. 330.
26. Pattabhi Sitaramayya, op. cit., p. 142.
27. Lajjavanti, 'Interview', p. 32.
28. Ibid, p. 31.
29. Lado Rani Zutshi, 'Interview', NMML Oral History Section, p. 4.
30. Lajjavanti, 'Interview', p. 45.
31. Ibid, pp. 46–47.
32. Ibid., p.52.
33. Ibid., p.61.
34. Manmohini Sahgal, 'Interview', NMML Oral History Section, p. 54.

35. Lado Rani Zutshi, 'Interview', p. 3.
36. Information on Rashtreeya Stree Sabha given to me by Kamaladevi Chattopadhyaya, November, 1977.
37. R.K. Sharma, *Nationalism, Social Reform, & Indian Woman*, Delhi, p. 61.
38. Ibid, p. 97, f.n.
39. Ibid, p. 60.
40. Durgabai Deshmukh, 'Interview', NMML Oral History Section, p. 2.
41. R.K. Sharma, op. cit., p. 63.
42. Lajjavanti, 'Interview', p. 61.
43. Vir Bharat Talvar in Sangari and Vaid, (eds), op. cit.
44. Indrani Chatterjee, 'The Bengali Bhadramahila— 1930–34', unpublished M.Phil thesis, JNU 1986, pp. 91–94.
45. Prahhavati Mirza, 'Interview', NMML Oral History Section, pp. 5–10.
46. Ibid, pp. 13–14.
47. Tanika Sarkar, 'Politics and Women in Bengal: the Conditions and Meaning of Participation', *IESHR*, Vol. XXI, No. 1, Jan-March, 1984, p. 92.
48. Sushma Sen, op. cit., pp. 312–13.
49. *Forward*, Special Number on Deshbandhu C.R. Das, July 1927, p. 55.
50. Sushma Sen, op. cit., p. 313.
51. Paper Relating to the Salem Branch of the Women's Indian Association, 1918–30, Muthulakshmy Reddy Papers, NMML, file No 3, p. 5.
52. Muthulakshmy Reddy Papers, NMML, file No 5, p. 7.
53. Muthulakshmy Reddy Papers, NMML, file No.5, p. 15.
54. Lecture by Dorothy Jinarajadasa to the National Council of Unions, Rangoon, press clipping September 11, 1926, Muthulakshmy Reddy Papers, NMML, file No. 5, p. 5.
55. Ibid.
56. AIWC Papers for 1927–28, NMML, Microfilm Section.
57. Letter from Mrs Huidekopar to M.E. Cousins, AIWC Papers for 1930–31, NMML, Microfilm Section.
58. AIWC Papers for 1930–31, NMML, Microfilm Section.
59. Sushma Sen, op. cit., p. 328.

5. Constructing the Image of a Woman Activist

Constitutional reforms again became a rallying cry for nationalists in 1927, when the Government sent an all white enquiry commission to look into the reforms promised by the Montague Chelmsford Committee. A boycott of the Simon Commission was organized all over India, which was supported by all the major political groups in the country. An All-Parties' Conference was held in the same year, in which the first really serious attempt to draw up a constitution for India was made. Known as the Nehru Report (because it was drafted by a group headed by Motilal Nehru), it was finalized at the All-Parties' Conference in 1928: though it did not demand total independence, asking for Dominion status instead, it raised the demand for adult suffrage for both men and women. In 1929, Lord Irwin, the Viceroy of India, declared that Dominion status would 'naturally' result from constitutional reforms, and promised a Round Table Conference after the Simon Report was published; the Congress accepted this offer on condition that details of the conference be worked out beforehand, an amnesty declared, and Congress given majority representation at the conference. Irwin refused to consider these conditions and the talks broke down. In the December 1929 Lahore Congress the demand for *purna swaraj* (total independence) was finally adopted and suggestions for a renewal of civil disobedience were made, though the planning of an action programme was left to the All India Congress Committee, under Gandhi, to do later. In January 1930 Gandhi issued an eleven point ultimatum to Lord Irwin, combining general and specific demands: total prohibition, the release of political prisoners, cuts in army expenses and civil service salaries, changes in the Arms Act, reform of the C.I.D., lowering of the rupee-sterling rate, textile protection, reservation of coastal shipping for Indians, a fifty per cent reduction in land revenue, and abolition of both the salt tax and the government salt monopoly. Roughly a month later Gandhi announced that he would launch a salt satyagraha by marching from Sabarmati to Dandi (a Gujarati coastal village), and illegally manufacturing salt there. On the eve of the march he declared that country-wide illegal salt manufacturing would begin after he had broken the law at Dandi, accompanied by the boycott of foreign cloth and liquor; moreover 'everyone

(would have) a free hand', provided they were non-violent, truthful, and obeyed their local leaders.

The Dandi march began on the 12th of March and ended on the 6th of April. All along the route, as Gandhi and other satyagrahis passed through their villages, local officials began to resign; and midway through the march *patidars* 'in Borsad taluka' solicited and won Gandhi's permission for an immediate cessation of revenue payment.[1] No woman had been included by Gandhi in his chosen seventy-one marchers and this aroused considerable resentment among nationalist women. Kurshed Naoroji, Dadabhai's granddaughter, wrote angrily to Gandhi that his edict was unfair, while Margaret Cousins protested the decision in *Stri Dharma*.[2] Gandhi remained firm however, offering in exculpation the plea that he had allocated a 'greater role to women than the mere breaking of salt laws'.[3] According to Kamaladevi Chattopadhyaya, Gandhi's decision to exclude women applied only to the march; it was the Congress Committee rather than Gandhi, that decided to exclude women from the salt satyagraha. As its organizers, she said, refused to accept women's demands that they be 'allowed' to participate, she went to meet Gandhi on the Dandi march and asked him to make a special appeal to women to join the movement. Gandhi apparently laughed and said that they would do so anyway, but on Kamaladevi's insistence he wrote a brief appeal. This she took to the Congress Committee and upon reading it they withdrew their veto.[4]

On the last day of the salt march, Sarojini Naidu joined it at Dandi, and was the first woman to be arrested in the salt satyagraha. On the day the march ended, groups of volunteers from all over the country broke the salt laws, picketed the legislatures, and began the boycott of liquor and foreign cloth. Having withdrawn their veto, the Congress Committee chose women to lead satyagrahas all over the country. Cells were formed to organize the satyagrahas, and their leaders were named 'dictators', probably under the influence of the Stalinist and fascist ideas of the period. Sarojini Naidu, Lado Rani Zutshi, Kamala Nehru, Hansa Mehta, Avantikabai Gokhale, Satyavati, Parvatibai, Rukmini Lakshmipaty, Perin and Goshiben Captain, Lilavati Munshi, Durgabai Deshmukh and Kamaladevi Chattopadyaya, were all among

Banglan peasants preparing to participate in the
5 August Satyagraha, 1930.

Tribal women manufacturing salt,
Ghansoli, Maharashtra.

Koli girls manufacturing salt, Ghansoli, Maharashtra.

Manufacturing salt at Madras beach.

Returning from the sea with salt pots,
Vile Parle, Bombay.

Kamala Nehru, Swarup Rani Nehru and other women
manufacturing salt, Allahabad, Uttar Pradesh

Salt manufacturing, place and date unknown.

THE ILLUSTRATED LONDON NEWS

302

AUG. 16, 1930

THE ENGLAND OF 1893–1910 AND 1930:
A STUDY IN CONTRASTS.

By SIGNOR GUGLIELMO FERRERO,

the distinguished Italian Philosophical Historian ; Author of "The Greatness and Decline of Rome," "Ruins of the Ancient Civilisations," etc.

We continue here our monthly series of articles by Signor Ferrero, dealing with world politics as that famous modern historian sees them and interprets them. The views set forth in the series are personal and not necessarily editorial.

PEOPLE are fond of saying that the modern world is in a state of perpetual revolution. Although civilisation was static in old days it is now dynamic. In that incessant transformation of everything, we see the decisive superiority of our epoch over those which have preceded it, and the supreme standard by which we can judge the merits of modern peoples. Is there not perhaps a little illusion in that flattering opinion, which we have formed of ourselves and of our transformation? Do we not sometimes mistake what is really only the acceleration of the previous movement for a change of direction? That acceleration is real, for a century past each generation has lived more hurriedly. But the tendencies and aims—what the English call the "drift"—of our civilisation change perhaps less than a superficial examination would have us believe.

There are, however, exceptions; countries in which the direction changes in the midst of the accelerated pace. It appeared to me that England was one of those countries. I spent nearly a year there, in the days of my youth, in 1893–1894, during the last period of the Victorian era. Up to 1910 I frequently returned there on short visits. After 1910 my visits were suspended for twenty years. But what a contrast I found to my recollections of 1910, and especially to those of 1894, when I once more crossed the Channel in the spring of this year! In 1893 Great Britain was still, for a Continental European, a lost island in an immense lonely ocean, lying at an incalculable distance from all inhabited countries. I shall never forget the impression of isolation in which I lived in London during my first stay there. I felt much closer to continental Europe in the United States in 1893 than in London in 1893. And on that lonely island, work, riches, political liberty, were wrapped in a strong religious spirit, as if it were sunk in a rather sad austerity, but which afforded a stranger a wonderful spectacle of rigid hierarchism which was at the same time original and solid.

The England which I found again in 1930 seemed to me much gayer, more supple, living, profane and continental. The religiosity of the Victorian era seems, to a great extent, to have evaporated. Social rank is no longer so sharply divided; everywhere one finds traces of the dumb but continuous working of a process of levelling and fusion. A breath of gaiety, a ray of elegance and grace, a new spirit of liberty and equality have given greater suppleness and softened, at least in external life, that *je ne sais quoi* of rigidity and almost sombreness, which thirty years ago struck a Frenchman or Italian so forcibly. Europe is no longer an incalculable distance away, as in 1893. One need only walk in the old parts of the City or in those parts which are being rebuilt: everywhere one sees on one side the American influence and on the other the Continental, French or German. Sometimes I felt as if England were held as in a vice between the two continents. The triumph of the Feminist movement, which in 1893 had hardly begun, and the appearance of all those elegant and often pretty young women who now mingle in every department of life, have contributed much to that transformation. Those English people to whom I communicated these ideas and who, on account of their age, were in a position

to give an opinion from their recollections, agreed with me, only remarking that the change was more accentuated in London than in the rest of England. That is natural. The great capitals are like a kind of megaphone of contemporary life: they enlarge the tendencies of the epoch by exaggerating them. If in London one sees a vivacity, a gaiety, a liberty of modes and manners greater than there was thirty years ago, it is because all England is more or less transformed in the same way. Is the "Merry England" of old days, which Protestantism and industrialism seemed to have extinguished for ever, about to reappear?

I do not know. What struck me most during my last visit to England was a curious contradiction of the outside and the inside. That outward gaiety and vivacity seemed to cover to-day preoccupations and anxieties which did

not exist in 1893. Under the slightly melancholy rigidity of the end of the Victorian epoch lay hidden a tranquillity, security and confidence in the future which was simple and robust, which struck and rather irritated the young traveller who had come from the anxious Continent. It would be vain to seek for the signs of an analogous state of mind to-day. One cannot help perceiving this if one talks with people belonging to all sorts of different classes and professions, if one reads for a few weeks the newspapers of different political parties, and follows the debates in Parliament, and the incidents of political life.

The reasons for these preoccupations are numerous. The one which is immediately obvious to the eyes of an observant stranger is the economic crisis, with its multitudinous manifestations; from the crushing weight of taxes, to the question of unemployment. It is a long while since England went through such difficult times. The weight of taxation is so heavy that the newspapers end by openly deploring that England did not follow the example of France, Italy and Belgium, and reduce by at least one half the legal value of the pound sterling. Even those industries by which England made her fortune, coal, cotton, wool and iron, are at grips with the gravest difficulties. But the most agonising problem of all is that of unemployment. It was thought at first that it was due to one of those recurring crises of production to which the industrial world is everywhere subject. Consequently, confidence was felt in the *vis medicatrix naturæ*, and it was hoped that the crisis would gradually decide itself. People are now beginning to see that the cause is more deeply seated, and that it is part of a universal perturbation of the ancient economic balance, under which and thanks to which England had so marvellously prospered up to 1914. Add to all this the anxieties about India, Egypt and China,

the continued uncertainty of the European situation, and the Naval policy of the United States. . . . This is enough to trouble the sleep of the Nation, whose power and riches are charged with such great responsibilities. But if these preoccupations are visibly manifest, if they are easy for an earnest observer to note, it seems to me that they are multiplied by a deeper, hidden anxiety, the cause of which it is more difficult to ascertain, but whose action is perhaps more intense.

Great Britain up to 1914 had been governed by the superior classes. When universal suffrage was extended the Conservative and Liberal parties tried, by different methods, to capture the sympathies and votes of the masses; but both of them drew their support from the superior classes—their doctrines, programmes, animating passions, directing officials—and from financial means. Outside these two parties no third party existed which could be compared to the numerous parties by which the middle classes and the popular classes are represented on the Continent as independent political forces. The Labour Party in 1914 was still very small, and had only a modest political influence. Organised as trade unions, the working classes defended their professional interests, and did not draw back from long and desperate struggles with the forces of Capital. But in politics they followed the superior classes, voting like the middle classes, sometimes for the Conservatives and sometimes for the Liberals.

In fact, up till 1914 Great Britain was the one of the European States which politically could count more on the docility of the people and the lower middle class. It was this that excited the admiration and envy of the rest of Europe. But that privilege had not fallen from the skies upon the big island enveloped in fog. In the second half of the 19th century the people and the lower middle class had greatly benefited by the growing prosperity. All the Governments, Conservative and Liberal alike, had taken much trouble to improve their material and moral condition. They had given them education and increasingly perfect forms of help, political liberty, and numerous facilities for raising themselves on the social ladder. The rich classes had taxed themselves considerably in order to help the masses. Up to 1914 there was no great country in Europe where the masses paid fewer taxes than in England. And there was no conscription. It was the British State and not the people who made war; the repercussion of war upon the masses was limited to a light imposition of taxes. As the people were not forced to go out and fight, wars might break out, but the majority of the British people lived under a régime of perpetual peace.

That happy past is now only a memory. The world war introduced conscription into the country. Millions of Britons had to go and fight in Europe, in Asia and Africa, like the French, Germans and Italians, as a duty and not by their own free choice. An enormous shock overthrew the depths of society, traditions, ideas and inclinations. And so the same rupture has come about in England during the last ten years, as it did long ago on the Continent; the middle and popular classes have detached themselves from the superior classes and are trying to conquer political autonomy by organising and attaching themselves to new parties. Small and without influence as it was in 1914, the Labour Party has since twice governed the Empire. Why? What does this somewhat brusque interruption of the game of see-saw between the Conservatives and Liberals, which they had carried on for so long, signify? The impressions which I gathered

(Continued on page 312.)

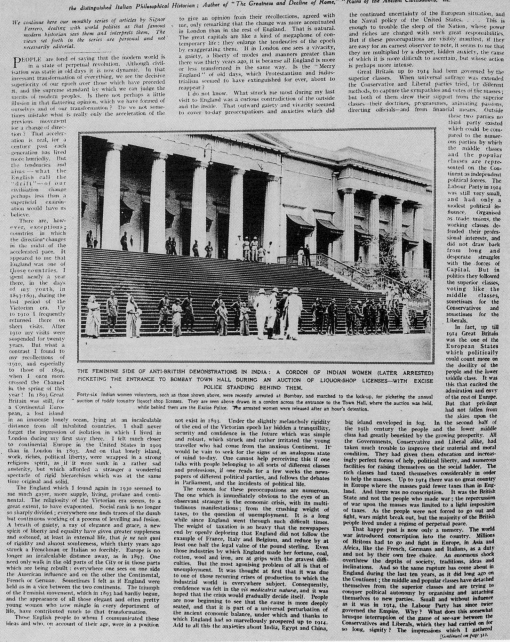

THE FEMININE SIDE OF ANTI-BRITISH DEMONSTRATIONS IN INDIA : A CORDON OF INDIAN WOMEN (LATER ARRESTED) PICKETING THE ENTRANCE TO BOMBAY TOWN HALL DURING AN AUCTION OF LIQUOR-SHOP LICENSES—WITH EXCISE POLICE STANDING BEHIND THEM.

Forty-six Indian women volunteers, such as those shown above, were recently arrested at Bombay, and marched to the lock-up, for picketing the annual auction of toddy (country liquor) shop licenses. They are seen above drawn in a cordon across the entrance to the Town Hall, where the auction was held, while behind them are the Excise Police. The arrested women were released after an hour's detention.

Picketers at the Town Hall in Bombay, demonstrating against liquor licenses.
From *The Illustrated London News*, August 1930

A hundred women broke forest law
(August 1930) and cut sandalwood trees
in Sirsi, North Kanara.

Satyagrahis defying British soldiers
at the liquor licence auction outside the
Town Hall in Bombay.

the women chosen to act as dictators; as the leaders were being constantly arrested, the life of a dictator was fairly short.

Thousands of women joined in the salt satyagraha, manufacturing and selling salt all over the country; in fact, this agitation marked a new level of participation by women in the nationalist movement, and is generally remembered as the first time that the 'masses of Indian women' got involved in the struggle for independence. The impact this had on many nationalist women is shown by the highly charged prose with which Kamaladevi described the first day of the salt satyagraha; reminiscent in tone of Annie Besant, Sarojini Naidu and Margaret Cousins, she again stressed that Indian women were simple and valiant:

Even though only a few women were chosen officially to take part in the salt satyagraha with which the Indian revolution opened on the morning of

April 6, 1930, by sunset of that first day it had turned into a mass movement and swept the country.

On that memorable day thousands of women strode down to the sea like proud warriors. But instead of weapons, they bore pitchers of clay, brass and copper; and, instead of uniforms, the simple cotton saris of village India.

'. . . Women young and old, rich and poor, came tumbling out in their hundreds and thousands, shaking off the traditional shackles that had held them so long.

Valiantly they went forwards without a trace of fear or embarrassment. They stood at street corners with little packets of salt, crying out: 'we have broken the Salt Law and we are free! Who will buy the salt of freedom?' Their cries never went unheeded. Every passer-by stopped, slipped a coin into their hands and held out proudly a tiny pinch of salt.[5]

A confrontation with the police and the army.

Picketing women being arrested by British Officers.

Prabhat Pheri, Sangamner, Gujarat.

The image that Kamaladevi chose to glorify was, however, different from those chosen by Annie Besant, Sarojini Naidu, or Margaret Cousins: Besant glorified the self-sacrificing Hindu woman; Naidu the self-sacrificing Indian mother; and Cousins the proud representatives of 'the great Hindu race' and 'the strong Muslim people'. Kamaladevi, on the other hand, here glorified the self-sacrificing peasant woman. Congress activity amongst the peasantry had always been vastly greater than amongst the working class; as more and more women turned nationalist, their attention too turned naturally towards peasant women: especially as Gandhi, in the late 1920s, began to lecture them on the need to 'descend from their western heights and come down to India's plains', adding that 'these questions of the liberation of women, liberation of India, removal of untouchability, amelioration of the economic condition of the masses, and the like, resolve themselves by penetration into the villages, and reconstruction, or rather reformation, of village life'.[6]

As the movement snowballed, the Government's alarm grew. When in May they arrested Gandhi, it only had the effect of intensifying the movement. There was a wave of resignations of Indians who held government posts: Muthulakshmy Reddy and Hansa Mehta were among those who resigned. The Congress Working Committee sanctioned non-payment of revenue, no *chaukidari* tax, and the violation of forest laws; and organized a massive salt raid in Dharasana in mid-May. Led by Sarojini Naidu, the raiders were met by such police ferocity that most observers were stunned. Several of the male satyagrahis, according to an American reporter, were beaten to a 'bloody pulp'. In an account of the first day of the Dharasana raid, Kamaladevi Chattopadhyaya said that the salt pans had been fenced off with barbed wire and the satyagrahis were cut off from the mainland by the police, so they sat down on the sand and stayed there the rest of the day. Though it was at the height of

summer, the police not only refused to allow them water to drink, but actually 'drove water carts through the thirsty crowd'.[7] At the end of the day the satyagrahis were arrested, but at dawn a new group took their place. Dharasana became a symbol of the struggle for independence of the country.

The British suddenly found themselves facing a situation of mass civil unrest amounting, in certain areas, to war. In rural Gujarat there were massive and successful non-revenue campaigns and resignations of village officials; in Maharashtra, Karnataka and the Central Provinces there were forest satyagrahas and camps were set up to train satyagrahis; and in Bihar and Bengal a no-*chaukidari* tax campaign took place. The picketing of liquor shops and excise license auctions spread across cities, small towns and villages; the boycott of foreign cloth was especially successful in Bombay, Amritsar, Delhi and Calcutta, with merchants taking collective pledges not to sell foreign cloth.[8]

Separate women's organizations to mobilize and co-ordinate women's participation in these activities were now set up; the Desh Sevika Sangh, the Nari Satyagraha Samiti, the Mahila Rashtriya Sangh, the Ladies' Picketing Board, the Stri Swarajya Sangh and the Swayam Sevika Sangh.[9] Most of these bodies not only mobilized and organized women's processions, pickets, and *prabhat pheris* (literally, greeting the dawn, here a symbol of the dawn of independence, generally ending with hoisting the Congress flag), they also trained women in charkha spinning, hawked khadi and engaged in publicity and propaganda. The Ladies' Picketing Board, for example, which was formed in Bengal, roughly one year after the order, in 1931, had the following objectives: to struggle against the use of foreign goods; to popularize home industries and help develop cottage industries, especially of spinning and weaving khadi; to arrange processions and meetings demonstrating the greatness of liberty and equality of nations; to preach to the people

Volunteers presenting themselves to Nehru.

the need for the removal of untouchability; to enlist as many people as possible as members of the Congress; and to work in accordance with the direction of the Indian National Congress and in affiliation with the Bengal Provincial Congress Committee. To facilitate organization, the Board was divided into five sections; the Boycott and Picketing Section; the Swadeshi Prachar Section; the Prabhat Pheri section, the Constructive Workers' Section, and a General Section.[10] Several women mill-workers were active in the Bombay Desh Sevika Sangh, which was banned in 1931; the others were banned a year later.

In the countryside the government reacted to the no revenue and no tax movements by confiscating household goods, implements and even land, which they later auctioned. In the boycott of these auctions which was organized, women were especially active, persuading so many not to attend that only a few loyalists and government servants bid for the goods, which had therefore to be sold cheaply. Those who bought the goods soon came to regret it, for women satyagrahis, often with babies in their arms, would camp outside their houses until the goods were returned to their rightful owners. Sometimes women satyagrahis even occupied the houses of the buyers, going on stay-in hunger strikes there; the more persistent buyers would throw mud at the hunger-strikers, insult them, and even occasionally hire thugs to beat them up. Sometimes women sat on satyagraha outside a house for upto a month before the goods were returned, but generally their quarry were shamed into returning the goods after a day or two of satyagraha.[11]

The tactic of non-violent protest used at Dharasana now became a standard one, as did the government's response of lathi-charges and mass arrests. It was at this time that nationalist women encountered police repression for the first time. The special role sought for them in the 1920s had been partly predicated on the assumption that women would be protected from physical violence by their sex—and so, to a large extent, they were—but in the 1930s this assumption no longer held good. In April 1930 the police lathicharged a procession led by Jawaharlal Nehru's mother, Swaroop Rani Nehru, at which she was hit on the head and fell unconscious. In Delhi, a women's procession was lathicharged, and ten women were injured. In Borsad, a procession of fifteen hundred women was lathicharged, and the woman leading the procession was injured, but 'with blood stained sari she proceeded on again until disabled by further beating. At Viramgaon, two hundred women took water to the railway station to quench the thirst of volunteers, a simple act of human kindness. The police set upon them and beat them mercilessly.'[12] In July 1930, a procession led by Hansa Mehta in Bombay, to commemorate Tilak's anniversary, was lathicharged and

one hundred women were arrested, including Kamala Nehru, Amrit Kaur, Maniben Patel and Hansa Mehta.[13] In Madras, the police experimented with methods other than the lathicharge: 'one of the methods adopted by the police against women picketers was to train a water hose on them . . . The Hindu reported that on January 25, 1932, two women volunteers who were subjected to this treatment fell down unconscious and the police prevented anyone rushing to their help'. This was, however, given up when the Madras Corporation protested against it.[14] And, in a police firing in October 1930, on satyagrahis breaking forest laws in Madhya Pradesh, two women, both Gond tribals, were shot dead.[15]

Incidents of this sort not only deeply shocked public opinion, they also provided a fillip to the nationalist movement. The press were full of reports of police brutality on Indian women under the British; social reform and nationalist journals alike decried the police; Congress bulletins ran special articles on the maltreatment of women volunteers; and the AIWC prepared a special report on this for the 1931 session at Lahore.

The number of women arrested mounted rapidly: four hundred women, who were picketing election booths in Bombay, as part of the election boycott in 1930, were arrested; their picketing had been so successful that the elections had to be postponed till the next day.[16] Stiff sentences were imposed on women who were arrested: Indumati Goenka, for example, was given nine months' imprisonment for hawking khadi door to door, and Jayalakshi Keshavarao was given seven months' for violating prohibitory orders in Hospet.[17]

When, in response to large scale prohibitory orders, the Congress had issued calls to court arrest, the rush to obey came from women in both urban and rural areas: in 1932–33, Girijabai, Manorama Naik and Ambabai Pai from Udipi picketed foreign cloth shops, and courted arrest; Ambabai Kilpadi, a sixty-five year old woman from Bantval, and Kamalabai Talchekar, an eighteen year old girl, were among the dozen women who courted arrest in South Kanara. From the Maralingannavar family in Gokok taluka three women courted arrest in 1932. In Coorg, Dalyatanda Mudamma and Pandyanda Seethamma courted arrest. Savitriamma Hosamani and three other women courted arrest at Haveri and were jailed for six months' each. Gangubai Ambli of Bijapur courted arrest and was sentenced to nineteenth months' imprisonment. It was reported that between 1930–31 twenty thousand women satyagrahis were arrested and sentenced to imprisonment.[18]

The experience of being jailed was, if anything, conducive to an intensification of earlier views and feelings. Margaret Cousins referred to the political discussion groups which were formed in her jail; Durgabai Deshmukh talked of how she learnt charkha spinning there; and both Manmohini Sahgal and Margaret Cousins described the feelings of solidarity there were among women satyagrahis of different class, linguistic and caste backgrounds.[19] This solidarity was not always extended to non-political women prisoners: Kamaladevi Chattopadhyaya described how in 1932 she and the Captain sisters were together in Arthur Road jail, where, as it was next to the red light area, a number of prostitutes were also jailed. As the jail was overcrowded by an influx of political prisoners, they were kept with the non-political women prisoners: 'the political prisoners objected to being kept with the ordinary prisoners . . . particularly the prostitutes, on *health* grounds, so we carried out some protests'.[20] Feminist women were anxious to make it clear that they had no moral aversion to prostitutes, though they might deplore prostitution itself: Margaret Cousins recounted how warmly a group of *devdasis* were welcomed by the women satyagrahis that she was in jail with.

The involvement of women in nationalist-feminist activities was beginning to arouse a certain degree of hostility from some husbands. Kamaladevi Chattopadhyaya described how a session of the AIWC in Mysore in the 1930s sparked trouble for her with Sir Mirza Ismail. She was close to his wife, who was 'very active in the women's movement', and was a frequent visitor at the Ismail's house. Yet it was only after the AIWC session that he 'somehow began to take note, and he saw that it was creating not only political trouble but also social trouble by bringing in this question of women's freedom movement'. According to Kamaladevi, Sir Mirza Ismail was alarmed to find that his wife was 'now showing a degree of independence, thinking on her own', and, blaming Kamaladevi for this, he banned all visits from her.[21]

Though Manmohini Sahgal found that most of the husbands of the women who were jailed with her were very proud of their wives, she recounted the following story about a woman who was in jail with her mother:

Her husband was a clerk in a shop. When he heard that his wife was in prison, he sent word through somebody that she need not return home. So the poor lady was much worried, and she used to weep. My mother was an acknowledged leader of the women in prison, whether they were in A, B, or C class. When she heard of it, she sent for some Congress leaders, and sent them to this lady's husband, with a message saying, 'she has done such a fine job, which you should be proud of, and it was of no use sending such a foolish message'. He replied, 'I am very proud of her, but she did not go with my permission. She should have taken my permission first, and I would certainly have permitted her. She went while I was at office, and that is why I am not taking her back'. Then of course everybody said, 'you must not behave so

foolishly'. Thereafter he started coming to jail to visit her.[22]

For most of the women who were active in 1930s, nationalism had a beneficial influence on feminism, drawing it out of its upperclass enclave. Kamaladevi, for example, talked of how the first presidents of the AIWC were Maharanis, but in the 1930s members of AIWC decided that such presidents were mere 'figureheads', and as the AIWC was to be an organization of activists, it needed an activist president. Sarojini Naidu was then elected, in 1931.[23]

Nationalism was also beginning to create major rifts between feminists. When the first Round Table Conference took place, from November 1930 to January 1931, the Congress boycotted it, as it only allowed discussion of a possible dyarchy, giving limited political and administrative control to Indians. Among the small number of Indians who attended the Conference (most of whom were liberals), were Begum Shah Nawaz and Kamala Subbaroyan, both of whom belonged to the pro-reservation lobby for women's franchise, on the grounds that women would reach parity with men only through initial reservation. Nationalist women opposed this argument, and the Rashtriya Stree Sabha and Desh Sevika Sangh both held demonstrations against the participation of Begum Shah Nawaz and Kamala Subbaroyan in the Conference.[24] But a few weeks later, nationalist women changed their tune, when Gandhi signed a pact with the Viceroy, Lord Irwin, in February 1931, only days after he had criticized the agreements reached in the first Round Table Conference. The most likely explanation of Gandhi's volte-face seems to be the pressure Indian capitalists put on him to make an 'honourable' settlement with the British, who had recently placated Indian mill-owners by imposing a five per cent surcharge on cotton piecegood imports. The Gandhi-Irwin Pact achieved little beyond the release of Congress civil disobedience prisoners: Lajjavanti later described her shock at his refusal to make any effort to secure a pardon for Bhagat Singh, the communist who was hanged for his activities in Punjab.[25]

Both Begum Shah Nawaz and Sarojini Naidu attended the Second Round Table Conference. Nationalist-feminists now dominated the scene, presenting a memorandum to the Conference which rejected all suggestions of concessions to women, whether of reservation, nomination or co-option, and declaring that, 'to seek any form of preferential treatment would be to violate the integrity of the universal decision of Indian women for absolute equality of political status'.[26]

It is generally acknowledged that the main influence on this increasing participation of women in the struggle for independence was Gandhi's. He had, by this time, become a legendary figure, even in areas which he had never visited, and rumours of his imminent arrival as liberator caused outbreaks in many areas. The kinds of sentiments he aroused can be seen in the following anecdote of Margaret Cousins:

A white haired grandma, a sturdy and literate peasant woman, and her middle-aged daughter, unexpectedly arrived amongst our political group in prison one day. Their story was that they used to hear from their menfolk of the Swaraj movement and how Gandhiji was also in prison. They said to one another: "if he is in jail then let's go there too!" They waited till their menfolk had gone to the fields next day, then went off to their nearest temple to worship god, walked seven miles to the nearest town and there picketed a foreign cloth shop till they were arrested. They were contented only when they were behind prison bars.[27]

Gandhi's attention was first drawn to the potential militancy of women in South Africa, where he found that his political ideas were espoused by large numbers of women, who joined the agitations led by him, went to prison, served sentences of rigorous imprisonment without complaint, and brought out the miners in a protest strike. According to Gandhi, there were two major influences on the development of his concept of satyagraha: his wife, Kasturba, and black women in South Africa. The former was a 'woman always of very strong will, which in our early days I used to mistake for obstinacy. But that strong will enabled her quite unwittingly to become my teacher in the art and practice of non-cooperation. The practice began with my own family. When I introduced it in 1906 in the political field it came to be known by the more comprehensive and specially coined name of satyagraha'.[28] Interestingly, but not surprisingly, Gandhi did not see his own refusal to be or do as Kasturba would have liked him to in the same light.

The participation of women in the South African satyagraha agitation, said Gandhi, showed him the extraordinary capacity women had for self-sacrifice and suffering. In the years to come he was to elaborate this into a theory of women's nature as essentially self-sacrificing and thus ideally suited to non-violent war, based on moral principles:

I have suggested in these columns that woman is the incarnation of ahimsa. Ahimsa means infinite love, which again means infinite capacity for suffering. Who but woman, the mother of man, shows this capacity in the largest measure? She shows it as she carries the infant and feeds it during nine months and derives joy in the suffering involved . . . Let her transfer that love to the whole of humanity, let her forget that she ever was or can

be the object of man's lust. And she will occupy her proud position by the side of man as his mother, maker and silent leader. It is given her to teach the art of peace to the warring world thirsting for that nectar. She can become the leader in satyagraha which does not require the learning that books give but does require the stout heart that comes from suffering and faith.[29]

In emphasizing the self-sacrificing nature of Indian women Gandhi was not being original, for the same had been done by the reformers and revivalists. He did, however, transform attitudes towards it. While reformers saw self-sacrifice for women as ritually enforced and deplorable, and revivalists said that sacrifices enjoined by rituals conferred glory upon Hindu women, Gandhi detached it from Hindu ritual and defined it as a special quality of Indian womanhood, based on the woman's existence as mother. For Gandhi, the experience of pregnancy and motherhood especially qualified women to spread the message of peace and non-violence. If they could endure labour pains, they could endure anything.

According to Gandhi, the biological differences between men and women not only determined masculinity and femininity, they meant that each had a different role to play. The roles were complementary and each was equally important. The man's role was as breadwinner, the woman's as housewife and mother. Here too Gandhi transformed earlier terms of debate on the nature and role of motherhood. The revivalists and extremists had used the images of the mother as victim (mother India, ravaged and depleted by rampaging foreign hordes), and the mother as warrior-protector (mother Kali); reformists and nationalist feminists had used the image of the mother as nurturer, socializer and supporter of men; Gandhi created the image of the mother as repository of spiritual and moral values, as a preceptor for men. Earlier arguments for changing the condition of women had tended to imply that Indian women were backward, ignorant and generally unsatisfactory. Gandhi, on the other hand, not only emphasized the virtues of Indian women as they were but said that they were worth learning from for there were certain things that only they could do. It is noteworthy that Gandhi said this not only about Indian women in relation to men, but also to Western women, telling American women, for example, that they had a lot to learn from the pure, noble and non-violent Indian women. Notably, in the search for a national identity to oppose British colonialism, Gandhi turned political method into a means of expressing Indianness, particularly for women (satyagraha, for example).

In a perceptive article on Gandhi, Madhu Kishwar has described how Gandhi found 'for women a new dignity in public life, a new confidence, a new self-view', concluding that 'from passive objects women became active subjects or agents of reform'.[30] Yet it must be acknowledged that Gandhi's views were expressed at a time when women had already begun to find these attributes for themselves, not only in public professional life, as doctors, teachers, social workers, etc., but also in public political life, in nationalist and reformist campaigns, as well as in worker and peasant agitations. While not wishing to undervalue the importance of Gandhi's role in the women's movement, his most important contributions were to legitimize and expand women's public activities in certain ways, extending the latter so that it cut across class and cultural barriers. At the same time, his definition of women's nature and role was deeply rooted in Hindu patriarchy, and his inclinations were often to limit the women's movement rather than push it forward. Though he spoke of how struck he was by the qualities displayed by women in the South African satyagrahas, it took many years of pressure from nationalist women before he was to appeal to women to join in public campaigning. In the early years, he consigned the 'special role' of women to the home: if, on the one hand, he turned the private area of the family into an arena for women's public action, through emphasizing the importance of the family as a site for social change, he also, on the other hand, made it clear that further expansion of their role into the field of public action was wrong. Thus, for example, he stated that the role of women in the swadeshi movement was a home-based one, to use the *charkha* and see that she and her family wore khadi: 'the swadeshi vow cannot be fully kept if women do not help. Man alone will be able to do nothing in this matter. They have no control over the children, to dress them is the mother's duty, and, therefore, it is necessary that women should be fired with the spirit of swadeshi'.[31]

By the late 1920s Gandhi had changed his tune to calls for women to come out of their homes and join in the civil disobedience movement, but he sought to restrict their participation to mass picketing of drink and drug shops, as to him this was an issue ideally suited to women, not only because they suffered from their husbands' patronage of such shops, but also because the issue was one of purity and morality in personal life; salt, however, was an issue symbolizing the economic hardship Indians suffered under British rule: as such, it was an issue relating to public life, and not therefore suitable for women to take up. If some nationalist women protested against this dichotomy, others welcomed the calls for women's pickets: to Hansa Mehta, the shift from asking women to support swadeshi in the home to asking them to picket in the streets represented a move towards purna swaraj.[32] Actually, the idea of using all-women pickets first appeared in the workers' movement, when, in the 1928–29 general strike in the Bombay cotton

textile mills, communist trade unionists decided to post all-women pickets at mill-gates in order to prevent blacklegs from entering. It was found that very few men were able to resist women's taunts, especially as these were most often directed at their lack of manliness; at the same time, the police were reluctant to manhandle women. This initial reluctance was very soon overcome, as we have seen.

By the 1930s, Gandhi's attitude had changed considerably. He was willing in 1930 to accede to Kamaladevi's request that he appeal to women to join in the salt satyagraha; by the mid-thirties he was lauding the part that women had played in the civil disobedience movement: 'the women in India tore down the purdah and came forward to work for the nation. They saw that the country demanded something more than their looking after their homes . . . .'[33] He had found that women adhered more closely to his creed of non-violent war, for it 'calls into play suffering to the largest extent, and who can suffer more purely and nobly than woman?'[34] This emphasis on the need for, and virtue of, suffering was central to Gandhi's thought: his ideal activist was the 'voluntary widow', who was a 'gift to humanity', for she had 'learnt to find happiness in suffering'. *She* was a true sati; not the woman who burnt herself on the pyre:

> A sati has been described by our ancients, and the description holds good today, as one who, ever fixed in her love and devotion to her husband, signalizes herself by her selfless service during her husband's lifetime as well as after, and remains absolutely chaste in thought, word and deed . . . . She would prove her satihood not by mounting the funeral pyre at her husband's death, but she would prove it with every breath that she draws from the moment that she plighted her troth to him at the saptapadi ceremony, by her renunciation, sacrifice, self-negation and dedication to the service of her husband, his family, and the country . . . and by completely identifying herself with her husband (she would) learn to identify herself with the whole world.[35]

No woman who was not 'chaste in thought, word and deed' was to be allowed into *into his movement*. When in 1925, the Bengal Congress Committee organized some women prostitutes under its banner, Gandhi was almost hysterical with rage. The women had been asked to do such Gandhian 'humanitarian' work as helping the poor, nursing, promoting khadi spinning and weaving, etc.; all this was, however, dust and ashes to Gandhi, for the women had not given up their wage-earning work of prostitution itself. The idea of their engaging in 'humanitarian work' before they reformed themselves and 'lived like Sanyasins' was described as 'obscene' by

Rani Gudiallo

In the North Cachar hills of Nagaland, a woman named Gudiallo became famous for her part in

the civil disobedience movement. Affectionately titled 'Rani' Gudiallo, she had first got involved in the struggle for independence when she was thirteen, joining her cousin, Jadonang, who had started mobilizing villagers into satyagraha campaigns in Manipur District in 1925. In 1931, the British arrested Jadonang, summarily tried and sentenced him, and hanged him. Gudiallo now took over the reins of the movement, shifting its base from Manipur district to the North Cachar hills, inhabited by the Zeliagong tribe. Between 1931–32 she led a no-tax campaign there: when the British imposed collective fines on the villages which were active in the campaign, and seized both unlicensed and licensed guns, the campaign developed further into refusing to pay compulsory porterage levies, or work as forced labour. The British tried various methods of catching Gudiallo, ranging from a fake proposal of marriage to stationing troops in all the Zeliagong districts. Gudiallo and her gang retreated into the jungles bordering the river Barak, where they were hunted unsuccessfully by the British for many months before she was arrested and jailed.[1]

As happened in most of the tribal agitations in the civil disobedience movement, they could not be restricted to the lines laid down by Congress leaders, and were often not, therefore, given their place in the nationalist hall of fame. Gudiallo, for example, has been more often acclaimed by communist historians than by nationalists or Gandhians.

1. Vimla Farooqi and Renu Chakravarty, 'Communism and Women', *Communism Today*, November 5, Delhi, New Age Press, pp. 33–34.

Gandhi, who said these women were worse than an 'association of known thieves', for they stole 'the virtue of society'. Only through reforming themselves, taking to the charkha and khadi, and welcoming suffering and self-denial, could they be accepted.[36]

Suffering and self-denial meant, above all, the ability to control—and eventually transcend—all desire for another person: those who joined the Sabarmati ashram were doused with buckets of cold water morning and evening to dampen their passions; married people were expected to live unmarried *brahmacharya* (sexless) lives and the unmarried were neither to marry nor fall in love. Sucheta Kripalani remembered, some forty years later, how she went to the Wardha ashram and met Gandhi's disciple Vinobha Bhave: 'When I was taken to him, he

was fasting. He had undertaken the fast to expiate for the sin of two young people living in the ashram complex, who had fallen in love with each other! These two were going about the ashram with small, hurt faces. The whole thing appeared to me rather uncalled for.'[37] Her own marriage to J.B.Kripalani was opposed by Gandhi, who told her that if she married J.B., she would be breaking Gandhi's 'right arm': 'I asked him why he didn't think that, instead of one national worker, he would gain two. But he just brushed aside the idea and said, "I have seen many cases, they just get embroiled in the family and household".' Not only was Gandhi unhappy and restless until he had persuaded her to agree to neither marry J.B. Kripalani, nor meet him, nor write to him, 'the next day he come out with something more outrageous. He said, "if you remain unhappy it will oppress Kripalani; so you must marry someone else."'[38] She refused to do this, and in 1936 she and Kripalani got married, without Gandhi's permission. Later they were forgiven, took the *brahmacharya* vow, and worked with Gandhi. Gandhi himself constantly tested his *brahmacharya* principles, going so far as to sleep in the nude with this neice in order to show that he could resist women's sexual potency.[39] What his niece must have suffered was not described by Gandhi; he did not enquire into it.

The Gandhians were not the only ones to fear women's sexuality. So deep was the fear that male activists would turn away from the struggle if they got involved with women, that in the revolutionary terrorist movement of the twenties and thirties, 'it was an iron rule for the revolutionaries that they should stay away from women'.[40] In a book on Bhagat Singh, Manmathnath Gupta recounted the following incident while discussing the part played by women in the communist movement in Punjab:

One of the interesting episodes of the revolutionary movement was that Yashpal was found to be more intimate with Prakashwati (not yet married) than the rules of the revolutionary party would allow. Chandrashekhar Azad, the Supremo, sentenced Yashpal to death for this breach of rules and Virbhadra Tiwari was entrusted with the work of carrying out the sentence. But Tiwari informed Yashpal, who took to his heels.[41]

Gupta adds, writing in 1977, that though it was a good thing that Yashpal escaped 'because Hindi literature would have lost a giant', Azad 'acted according to the best traditions of the revolutionary movement, with firmness and malice towards none'.[42] He says nothing at all about Prakashwati. Interestingly, it was the men who were in need of protection; the women were dangerous, even if unwittingly so, for their very being constituted a sexual threat. Gandhi clearly felt that Kripalani would only be safe if Sucheta transferred her affections, and became an object of desire for someone else; he implied at the same time that she was incapable of transcending desire herself. Similarly, Azad chose to punish Yashpal but no mention was made of Prakashwati, almost as if she, being a woman, could not help herself.

Yet this definition was limited only to those women who got involved with male activists of their own choice. Women who were prepared to dedicate themselves to the cause alone were being admitted into both nationalist and revolutionary folds. Within the latter, a new kind of women's participation was developing: where earlier women had been restricted to tasks of shelter and propaganda, now they were turning to direct action and

becoming members of the core, rather than remaining at the periphery. In the 1920s many of the revolutionary terrorists had joined the Congress, but by the thirties a dissatisfaction with this kind of work was being felt, and in Bengal there was a move towards direct armed action. The centre of these activities was Chittagong, where a band of revolutionaries had formed; on the 18th of April they set out to capture the police and Auxiliary Force armouries, destroy the Telegraph Office and Telephone Exchange, and perform exemplary assassinations of Europeans by bombing their club. The group was successful in raiding the police armoury and destroying the telephone board at the exchange, but fled after setting fire to the Auxiliary Force armoury, upon the arrival of the police. Many of them were subsequently tracked down and shot; others went into hiding.[43]

As news of the Chittagong Armoury raids travelled through the province, more and more people were moved to enthusiasm. 'Recruits poured into the various groups in a steady stream, and the romantic appeal of the raid attracted into the fold of the terrorist party women and young girls who from this time onwards are found assisting the terrorists as housekeepers, messengers, custodians of arms and sometimes as comrades'.[44] Following the police shootings of so many of their members, the revolutionaries decided that the Commissioner of Police would be killed, and two of their members, Dinesh Majumdar and Anuja Sen, were instructed to bomb his car on August 25. Majumdar's bomb succeeded in bringing the car to a halt, but Anuja's exploded as she threw it, and she died on the spot. In the same month, another woman was one of the three revolutionaries arrested at a place called Sarishbari, 'with explosive materials which they were taking from Calcutta to Mymensingh'.[45]

In October 1931, the government passed an Act banning the publication of matter inciting or encouraging people to violence, and promulgated an ordinance which conferred special powers on the police to arrest or detain people on suspicion of terrorist activities; the schedule of offences was also widened, so that people giving shelter to revolutionaries would be liable to punishment. In November, the district of Chittagong was declared to be under a state of Emergency, and the police and military were given special powers to round up 'terrorists and absconders', while the District Magistrate was empowered to commandeer property, limit access to certain places, regulate traffic and transport, and impose collective fines on recalcitrant inhabitants 'to render the operations effective'.[46] This method had been used in curbing the incidence of sati, and had been found to be extremely effective.

Terrorist activities, however, continued, and increasing numbers of girls joined revolutionary groups, or engaged in direct action on their own. In December

Preetilata Wadedar

I got to know her when both of us were very young. We went to school together—she was only a class ahead of me . . . when we got to the senior classes, both of us joined the Girl Guides. We used to tell each other that it was our duty to learn all the methods of the 'other side'. It would be useful to us for building up our own strength. We wanted to get the pledge 'To be loyal to God and the King Emperor' changed into 'To be loyal to God and Country!'

Preeti used to tell us that in her family they had the true Indian way of life. They all used swadeshi goods. I used to feel rather small—because our family was rather loyalist in trend then—right from the use of foreign cloth downwards.

But we had no clear idea in our school days about our future. Sometimes we used to dream of becoming great scientists. Then the Rani of Jhansi fired our imagination with her example. Sometimes we used to think of ourselves as fearless revolutionaries . . .

Both Kalpana and Preeti joined nationalist groups at college and learnt how to wield lathis and swords. Kalpana went to Calcutta University and Preeti to Dacca.

In our vacations we two and two other girls got in touch with Chittagong revolutionaries. Preeti didn't trust the others too much—although they were her friends at school. She used to say 'I'm afraid they'll desert—they are soft'. She hated the slightest touch of cowardice.

A tiny incident—not big in itself—brings out Preeti's extremely gentle character. During the Puja holidays in 1930 she had asked me to go to their place for a feast. We were discussing whether either of us could slaughter a goat for mutton. I said, 'of course I can! There's nothing much in it.' Preeti said, 'there's nothing frightening in it, of course, but I won't be able to slaughter a poor, innoffensive creature in cold blood.' Somebody asked at once, 'What do you want for to fight for? Reply, 'when I am ready to give my own life for the country's freedom I won't hestitate a bit in taking somebody's life too if necessary. But I shall not be able to kill a poor harmless creature just like that.' Within two years she proved by her death that she believed in what she said then.

Preetilata was the only child of her parents, and their joy, later their martyrdom. She was always their pride.[1]

1. Kalpana Dutta, *Chittagong Armoury Raiders—Reminiscences*, People's Publishing House, Delhi, 1945, pp. 51–6

1931, two girls, Shanti Ghosh and Suniti Chaudhary shot the district magistrate of Tipper, Mr Stevens, who was one of the magistrates who had taken advantage of the government promulgations to harass women. According to Ela Sen:

In the hilltracts no Bengali girl of good family was free from the attention of magistrates, who ex-

ploited their position of authority. Therefore two young girls sought to end the degradation by making an example of a certain magistrate. To them it appeared that brutality must be paid back in its own coin, and boldly they walked up to him in his office and shot him dead. They knew they would be immediately arrested but preserved a calm and courageous attitude then, as later when under

Gandhi addressing women.

trial. Their courage did not desert them even when they were transported for life. The whole world was shocked by this 'revolting' incident, by what was called the 'shameless' conduct of these girls, but none knew what was behind. Even when a member said of another at the Assembly: 'Let him go and ask the brave girls of Bengal why they have committed these deeds', it was slurred over and no proper investigations were made.[47]

Shanti Ghosh and Suniti Chaudhary were sentenced to transportation for life; they had acted on their own, as did Bina Das, who attempted to shoot the Governor of Bengal, Sir Stanley Jackson in February 1922. Bina Das was a member of a women students' society, the Chhatri Sangh, of which her sister, Kalyani, was secretary. Members of the Sangh were taught *lathi-khela* by Dinesh Majumdar, the revolutionary terrorist, and formed a kind of support-cum-recruiting group for revolutionary activities. Kamala Dasgupta, who was a member of the Sangh, joined the Yugantar Party in 1929, and was told by its leader, Rasik Lal Das, that she would have to move to a hostel, as it wasn't possible to live at home and do revolutionary work. The hostel which she moved into was run by Bina and Kalyani Das' mother: it was a centre of women's revolutionary activity, for both Kamala Dasgupta and its previous student manageress, Suhasini Devi, had used it for that purpose. Kamala kept bombs in the store room, and Suhasini went off to 'shelter' terrorists in hiding after the Chittagong Armoury raid.[48]

Bina Das confided her intention of shooting the Governor to Kamala Dasgupta, asking her to find her a revolver. As she was a member of a different revolutionary group from Kamala's the latter suggested she ask her own 'party seniors', but Bina explained that her own group had disintegrated, some were under arrest and others in hiding, so she had decided to go ahead on her own, especially as this meant that no one else would have to take responsibility for her action. According to Kamala she argued with Bina, warning her of the darkest possible consequences of such an action, testing her to see if she would go through with her plan, and when Bina remained firm, she decided to help her. So Kamala Dasgupta collected money from the girls, and she and a male comrade bought the gun. He taught Bina Das how to use the gun. When the attempt failed and Bina Das was arrested and questioned, she did not give the others away. She was sentenced to nine years' rigorous imprisonment.[49]

Kamala Dasgupta was herself arrested some days later, and was jailed for six years on March 1st 1932, the same day that the Chittagong Armoury raiders were sentenced. Seven months later, in September, another young woman, Preetilata Wadedar, led a raid on the Pahartali Club, which Europeans frequented; the raiders threw a bomb into the main hall of the club, one person was shot and four were wounded. Most of the raiders escaped, but Preetilata Wadedar was found dead outside, 'clothed in male attire'. She had taken cyanide rather than be arrested. 'A statement was recovered from her person, stating that the raid was an act of war. On the same day four types of pamphlets had been distributed exhorting teachers, students and the public to join in a campaign against British rulers and Europeans'.[50]

Ironically, both Preetilata Wadedar and Kamala Dasgupta had been inspired by Bankimchandra and Saratchandra in their adolescence; reading their novels, both resolved that they too would give their lives for the country. Tanika Sarkar has shown how, as young women grew to be involved in revolutionary terrorist activities in Bengal, there was a growing opposition not only to women's activism, but also to any form of activity outside

Jhanda Vadan (flag hoisting) at a youth conference in Mangalore

the home for them. In *Char Adhyaya* Tagore's revolutionary heroine came at the end of the novel to realize that she was 'mistaken' in engaging in political activities, a confession which was welcomed by the hero: 'At last I see the real girl . . . you reign at the heart of home with a fan in your hand and preside over the serving of milk, rice and fish. When you appear with wild hair and angry eyes on the area where politics has the whip hand, you are not your normal self, but are unbalanced, unnatural'.[51] The words used were clearly intended to summon the image of a demonic, sexually abandoned woman (wild hair, angry eyes, unbalanced, unnatural), reminiscent of Kali, symbolizing the ravenous sexuality of women and counterposing this to the subdued domesticated sexuality which sublimated itself by nurturing the male. At the same time, Saratchandra too ridiculed both the political woman and 'the educated, Westernised, emancipated woman who seeks a role outside the home'.[52]

The Westernized woman was becoming the focus of opprobrium from nationalists all over the country. Sarojini Naidu and Begum Shah Nawaz both declared that the Indian women's movement was not a 'feminist' one like the Western movement;[53] V.Ramakrishna Rao displayed an unequivocal distaste for 'the sheer, grasping suffragette', bemoaning the loss of Sita and Savitri;[54] and Cornelia Sorabjee linked the newfound assertiveness of many Indian women with the 'Western Influence':

The Pioneers of 1885 were impelled to service by their hearts: they talked little of 'women's rights': they were stirred to the core by women's needs. Feeling filtered through the heart. In 1935 feeling would seem to filter through the mind. Service is inspired and directed to a great extent by Politics . . . . Women's Rights have become a slogan— rights visualized out of focus because of the belief

Nehru being welcomed by women
Congress workers

Vijayalakshmi Pandit hoisting the national flag at the Mahila Vidyalaya Girls College in Lucknow.

that Western methods were to be clearly imitated, and that the final achievement of English Feminists was to be our starting point. This get-rich-quick procedure has been applied to the social evils which are still with us.[55]

Debates on the question of collaborating with English feminists had begun in the AIWC in the late twenties. When Eleanor Rathbone, who was president of the National Union of Societies for Equal Citizenship (which represented the moderates amongst the suffragettes) wrote to the AIWC suggesting that the two organizations work together on a handbook on the evils of child marriage, in 1927, Kamaladevi Chattopadhyaya opposed her proposal, saying 'we must realize the entire consequences of a responsible body like the AIWC taking such a step as co-operating with an organization outside India'.[56] Rathbone had been influenced into taking up the cause by Katherine Mayo's *Mother India*, a book which had aroused considerable nationalist rage by its scathing comments on Hindu 'barbarism'.

If Mayo's book was one of the reasons why Indian nationalist feminists distanced themselves from Western feminists, the unthinking arrogance of many well-intentioned Western feminists was another. Barbara Ramusack has described how Dhanvanthi Rama Rao, a moderate feminist herself, attended a conference of British feminists interested in social reform in India, organized by Rathbone: 'Rama Rao had once sought the assistance of the wives of British officials in India, but now she was angered by Rathbone's stress on the responsibility of British women for the extermination of social evils in Indian society'. Angered as much by the discovery that most of the speakers were English women who had never been to India, Dhanvanthi Rama Rao told the Conference that Indian women were already working against 'social evils' all over the country, adding 'we are

Durga Bhabi,
a contemporary of
Bhagat Singh
who helped him to
escape from Lahore.

Bina Das
who tried to shoot
the Governor of Bengal,
Stanley Jackson.

Matangini Hazra, a Gandhian leader who was killed by police bullets
during the Quit India Movement, when she was 72 years old.

Shanti Ghosh
and
Suniti Chaudhary,
who were
sentenced to
life imprisonment
for their
'terrorist'
activities.

Accounts of Preetilata Wadedar's 'terrorist' actions

On the 6th February, 1932, 'While his Excellency the Governor of Bengal Sir Stanley Jackson was addressing the convocation of Calcutta University, a girl graduate, Bina Das, originally of Chittagong, rose from her seat, walked up the aisle and when a short distance from His Excellency, took a pistol from her robes and fired three times. Luckily the shots went wide, and, before she could take another deliberate aim, she was overpowered by Sir Hasan Suhrawardy, the Vice Chancellor, although she managed to discharge two more bullets which passed harmlessly over the heads of the assembly ... Bina Das was sentenced to 9 years rigorous imprisonment.' On the 1st of March, 1932, 12 of the accused in the Chittagong armoury raids were convicted of conspiracy to murder, two on lesser charges, and 16 acquitted. Terrorists activities continued. 'On the 13th June, 1932, when Captain Cameron was leading a search party at Dhalghat, shots were exchanged and he was killed as were the terrorists Nirmal Sen and Apurba Sen. Suraj Sen and Pritilata Wadedar, another girl who was in league with the gang, escaped.'[1]

This is Ewart's account. Here is Kalpana Dutta's: 'In May 1932 Preeti had gone to see Masterda in a village in Dhalghat. At dusk a police force led by captain Cameron surrounded the house. Cameron opened fire with machine guns. Our side also fired back with revolvers. Preeti had never been in action before. But within a few minutes she had sized up the situation and began firing herself. Cameron was shot and Nirmalda was fatally wounded. Cameron's force was confused for a while. The order came 'Escape'! The same Preeti who had been in the thick of the shooting suddenly became soft and could not tear herself away from a wounded comrade ...

Preeti got away from the Cameron shooting incident. Her clothes were found in the house. But the police did not suspect her, although she came back home. They could not dream of this quiet girl being mixed up with the revolutionaries.

Mastarda sent word that she had to be kept safe in the town ... she went underground. On the 5th of July the D.I.B. Inspector went to arrest her and found she had disappeared. He came to our house to tighten the grip on me, and said 'she's such a quiet girl, speaks so well, I could not imagine she had so much in her. She's outwitted us all night.'[2]

On the 24th of September 1932, Preeti later led a raid on the Pahartali Club 'where bombs were thrown into the main hall and shots were fired from guns and revolvers during a whist drive, at which some 40 Europeans were present. One lady was killed and four were wounded, but further causalities were certainly avoided by someone's presence of mind in turning out the lights. In the confusion the raiders escaped but Preetilata Wadedar, clothed in male attire, was found dead outside. She took cyanide rather than be arrested. A statement was recovered from her person, stating that the raid was an act of war. On the same day four types of pamphlets had been distributed exhorting teachers, students and the public to join in a campaign against British rulers and Europeans.'[3]

This is what Kalpana Dutta said about Preeti's death: 'Eight boys made the attack under Preeti's leadership. All the boys went back unhurt—but Preeti never came back. She took potassium cyanide and collapsed, dead, about 10 yards from the club house. A splinter wound on her breast had soaked her shirt in blood. Plenty of men had mounted the gallows, had been killed in action in the struggle of the terrorist revolutionaries. But Preeti was the first woman known to have been in action and to have died in action ...

From Preeti's actions, people were convinced for the first time that Indian women can do what our men have done. They can give their lives for their country as easily as men can. Whatever criticism there may be of the methods of the terrorists, all Chittagong remembers Preeti as their brave daughter. They say with deep reverence: 'she did not give herself for the police ..'[4]

1. J.M. Ewart, Director, Intelligence Bureau, Home Department, Government of India, compiler, *Terrorism in India*, 1917–36, Government Central Press, 1973, P.31.
2. Kalpana Dutta, *Chittagong Armoury Raiders: Reminiscences* People's Publishing House, 1945, pp. 54–55.
3. Ewart, op.cit., pp. 33–34.
4. Kalpana Dutta, op.cit., pp. 51–52.

sure we could be more successful than any outsiders, especially those ignorant of the cultural patterns of our society.[57]

Despite the prevalence of these views, they were not shared by all feminists or social reformers. In the 1930s Rathbone again proposed collaboration to the AIWC, offering to share the costs of employing a full time worker to set up a single issue organization, campaigning against child-marriage. The then president of the AIWC, Rajkumari Amrit Kaur, turned down this offer,

Extracts from Bina Bhowmick's statement made after shooting at Bengal's ex-Governor, Sir Stanley Jackson, on Convocation Day, Calcutta University Hall, 6th February, 1932.

I confess I shot the Governor on the last Convocation Day at the Senate House. I hold myself entirely responsible for it. My object was to die, and if to die, to die nobly fighting against this despotic system of Government, which has kept my country in perpetual subjection to its infinite shame and endless suffering—and fighting in a way which cannot but tell . . .

I have been thinking—is life worth living in an India, so subject to wrong and continually groaning under the tyranny of a foreign Government or is it not better to make one supreme protest by offering one's life away? Would not the immolation of a daughter of India and a son of England awaken India to the sin of its acquiescence to its continued state of subjugation and England to the iniquities of its proceedings? This was the question which kept thundering at the gates of my brain like the incessant hammer blow that could neither be stilled nor muffled ...

The series of ordinances savouring of martial law, to my mind showed nothing but a spirit of vindictiveness and were only measures to crush down all aspirations for freedom. The outrages perpetrated in the name of the Government at Midnapore, Hijli and Chittagong (my own District), the refusal to publish the official enquiry reports, were things I could never drive away from my mind. The outrages on Amba Desai of Contai and Niharabala of Chittagong literally upset my whole being. I used to help the wife of a detenu in her studies, as a work of love. Every day I saw with my own eyes the sufferings of the poor girl who was leading the life of widowhood in the lifetime of her husband, the almost demented mother, and the father every day sinking into the grave, without their having the faintest notion of the nature of the supposed guilt of their son. I attended the Court during the trial of my own sister, Kalyani. Her punishment was to serve a term of rigorous imprisonment for attending a meeting which could not be held, and

for being a member of an unlawful society (which she was not), without any evidence thereof except a leaflet which was published and circulated without her knoledge—[it] was to my mind grossly unjust . . .

I can assure all, that I have no grudge against any person or thing on earth; I have no sort of personal feeling against Sir Stanley Jackson, the man, and Lady Jackson, the woman. But the Governor of Bengal represents a system of repression which has kept enslaved three hundred millions of my countrymen and countrywomen.

Accounts of some of the activities of women in the Chittagong Armoury Raids

In January, 1933, the trial of Ambika Chakravarty and two other raiders began, ending on 1st February, 1933, with the conviction of Ambika Chakravarty, who was sentenced to death, although the High Court commuted this sentence to transportation for life by the tribunal. On the 16th of the same month, a military party surrounded a house at Gariala and, after an exchange of shots, Suraj Sen and Brojendra Sen were arrested while trying to break through a cordon. The former was in possession of a revolver stolen in the Armoury raid. Kalpana Dutta and others escaped. Tarakeshwar Destidar now became the new president of the Chittagong branch, and active preparations were made to rescue Suraj Sen. On the 20th of March, 1933, Sailesh Roy, who was arrested near the jail when talking to a warder, was found to be in possession of suspicious slips of paper which led to the recovery of a revolver and bombs from a granary, and on the 18th of May 1833, a party of military surrounded the group's headquarters at Gahira. After an exchange of shots, Tarakeshwar Dastidar, Kalpana Dutta and others were arrested. Three stolen revolvers were recovered and later a tin box containing explosives and materials for bomb making were found. A third case was instituted which resulted in the conviction of Suraj Sen and Tarakeshwar Destidar to death, while Kalpana Dutta was transported for life.[1]

1. Ewart, op.cit., pp. 33–34.

but not before a debate had taken place within the AIWC executive, with some members arguing that if nationalists could ask for foreign aid to rehabilitate the victims of an earthquake in Bihar, then why could not they accept Rathbone's offer?[58]

That the debate was an important one can be seen by Muthulakshmy Reddy's reference to it in her speech at the eighth annual AIWC session, held in Calcutta on

RamMohun Roy's centenary:

The AIWC itself is an inter-communal and international assembly of women bound together by common ties of service to our sex and to our country. The women's movement from its very beginning has been international in its scope and even this very organization has been brought into

existence by the joint consultation and co-operation of our sisters both of the east and west.

. . . It is true that nationalism should precede
internationalism and for us to participate in international assemblies and gatherings we should be a
nation . . . . So far as this conference is concerned,
there is no doubt that women, Hindus, Muslims,
Christians and Parsees, etc., think only in terms of
our sex and country, and not of our creeds and
communities. We hope that our men also, ere
long, would realise the strength, the glory and the
honour of belonging to a nation and not to communities.[59]

The issue of communalism was taken up by the AIWC
in the thirties: in 1932 both their district branches and
their annual conference organized protests against the
reservation of separate seats for women in the legislatures on a communal basis; the Bombay branch reported
at the annual conference that their members had been
involved in riot-relief work, and the Andhra Pradesh
branch reported that they had called on 'managers of
schools to see that prayer conducted in schools is made
agreeable to people of all religious beliefs without being
denominational, and that the prayer is worded in the
vernacular only'.[60] In 1932–33, they held 'echo-meet-
ings' all over the country to mourn the death of Sir Ali
Imam. At the same time, they raised the demand for a
uniform civil code, which would apply to all 'citizens',
irrespective of communal, religious or regional differences (including caste).[61] Their work, however, remained largely limited at this stage to calls for
Hindu-Muslim unity, and the general notion that a
solution to communal warfare could be found in the
construction of a national identity. That most nationalist
constructions of identity had been based on communal
distinctions was not, however, recognized.

By the 1940s communal tension was being manifested
within the AIWC. According to Kamaladevi Chattopadhyaya, as relations between the Congress and the Muslim
League became increasingly hostile, Muslim women in
the AIWC drew away from the others. From 1941 'for the
first time we noticed that they felt they were a separate
group, and had to sort of stand together'.[62] This 'we' and
'they' had been present right from the start of national-
ist-feminism: Sarojini Naidu had joined the hands of a
Muslim and a Hindu woman as symbolic of Hindu-Muslim unity; both Margaret Cousins and Muthulakshmy
Reddy spoke of individual women as 'representatives' of
their respective communities, though Cousins used the
adjective 'proud', and Reddy 'enlightened'. By 1944 the
AIWC had split, and most Muslim women left. After the
partition of India, they formed the Pakistan Women's
Conference.

From the late thirties onwards communists entered

the feminist field. The Communist Party of India was
founded in Tashkent in 1920 by M.N.Roy, Abani Muckerjee, Muhammad Shafiq and others, but its real foundation was in 1925, at the Indian Communist
Conference in Kanpur. Communist women like Ushabai
Dange started organizing women workers in the Bombay
textile industry from the early thirties, largely because it
was considered easier for a woman to 'organize women',
but it was only many years later that concerted efforts
were made to organize women independently, and this
was in many ways a sequel to the increasing involvement
of women in the struggle for independence. The first
joint involvement of communist and nationalist women
was in the campaigns for the release of political prisoners which were launched all over the country in the
1930s. In 1939 women political activists came together
to form the Congress Mahila Sangh: in Bengal its constituents were from the AIWC, the radical Stree Sangha
group, Yugantar, and the communist underground.
They decided to bring out a magazine called *Mandira*,
and to organize street corner meetings demanding the
release of political prisoners. A separate 'mothers of
political prisoners' group was also formed. Women students had by now become so active in the struggle for
independence that the All India Students' Federation
set up a separate Girl Students' Committee, which participated in the first women students' conference at
Lucknow in 1940.[63]

Though the Communist Party was now accepting
women activists within its fold, it still was not easy. Sushila
Chain, who worked on the Kisan front of the Communist
Party in Punjab described the problems she had in
becoming an activist.

. . . Chain Singh Chain, the secretary of the polit-
buro . . . lectured me for two hours on how difficult it was for a woman to face the political
hardships involved in the life of a revolutionary . . .

I . . . asked him whether the communist party
made any distinction between men and women,
and whether they did not allot political work to
women . . . He was put in a quandary and consulted the other political leaders . . .

They decided to send me to the home of one
comrade, Mohabhat Singh, who was then in jail.
They hoped that the women of his family might be
able to persuade me to abandon my plans . . .
Then I received a letter from the party, telling me
that I was not yet an adult since an unmarried girl
became an adult only at the age of 21. . . They
advised me to get married, because if I got married
I would be considered independent.[64]

Meanwhile, the breakdown of most negotiations between the Congress and the British in the 1930s had

created considerable bitterness amongst nationalists, which was further fuelled by British practice in India when the Second World War began. The Congress had repeatedly condemned fascist aggression, showing solidarity both with Spain and China, and in 1939 they proposed full support to the British on their entry into the war provided they agreed to the post-war creation of a constituent assembly to decide a political structure for free India and the immediate formation of a representative government at the centre. Both proposals were rejected by the Viceroy, Linlithgow, and some years later by Winston Churchill. Following their defeat in South Asia, Europeans in Malaya, Singapore and Burma 'commandeered all forms of transport in their ignominious flight and left the Indian immigrants there to make their way by trekking in atrocious conditions through forests and mountains'.[65] Allied troops stationed in India behaved as all soldiers appear to do, with a casual brutality towards their hosts. There were innumerable cases of molestation and rape, against which the Congress repeatedly protested, but with little action by the government. Prices shot up and there were food shortages, especially in rice (where Burmese imports had stopped) and salt. It was in this context that, on the 8th August 1942, the Bombay session of the All-India Congress Committee passed the famous 'Quit India' resolution, calling for a mass non-violent struggle, but adding that if Congress leaders were arrested 'every Indian who desires freedom and strives for it must be his own guide . . . .'[66]

When, on the 9th of August 1942, Congress leaders were arrested, a 'country-wide wave of mass fury' began, initially in the cities, but spreading to the countryside. In Bombay, Calcutta, Delhi and Patna there were strikes, and clashes with the police and army; in Ahmedabad the textile strike lasted for three and a half months. Communist opposition to the Quit India movement, following Hitler's invasion of Russia in 1942, played some part in stilling working class involvement in the movement, but a major part was played by the government's swift, and brutal, repression. Sumit Sarkar describes how in Tamluk, where an underground 'national government' of Congress functioned, the Congress listed 14 cases of police rape, in one of which 46 women were raped in one village on January 9, 1943.[67]

Though thousands of women all over the country were involved in the Quit India movement, going underground, helping form parallel governments, leading 'illegal' activities in the course of which several women were killed, feelings ran especially high in Bengal. The discovery that the British, fearing their inability to defend Bengal and Assam in the face of a Japanese invasion, were prepared to withdraw to the Chhota Nagpur plateau defence line, outraged Assamese and Bengalis. Black marketeering and food-profiteering led to the

Bengal famine of 1943. The large-scale mobilization of women for self-defence now began.

In Barisal women's self-defence committees were set up, to equip women to face Japanese bombs and British and American molesters. Here they were taught first how to wield a lathi. In Sherpur, in Mymensingh district, several *baithaks* (closed door meetings) were held, in which the role of women in the war against fascism was discussed. In Patna, women organized *prabhat pheris* and poster exhibitions. In Hooghly, Bally, Chinsurah and Maheshtala, all in 24 Parghanas district, women's self-defence committees were organized. In Calcutta several women's meetings were held, at which it was decided to form an organizing committee to co-ordinate the self-defence committees. This organization became the Mahila Atmaraksha Samiti (The women's self defence committee), and Ela Reid was appointed its first organizing secretary. According to Renu Chakravarthy:

> There were three main planks of the women's movement in this period. First, defence of the country; second, release of the leaders and the formation of a national government; and third, defence of the people from starvation and death. With the war came the question of survival for our people. On the other hand, the frightening scarcity of food was engulfing the whole of Bengal. The national leaders were in prison. Their release and Hindu-Muslim unity for maintaining communal harmony took on great urgency. In trying to tackle these three main tasks, a big mass women's movement came to be born.[68]

It seems as if the Mahila Atmaraksha Samiti was formed as a kind of separate, communist dominated women's organization. Not only were most communist women in Bengal now working full time in MARS, there seems to have been some sort of competition between the Congress Mahila Sangh and MARS. When in May 1943 the Surma Valley and Shillong women's self-defence conference was held in Sylhet, it was organized jointly by the AIWC, CMS and MARS, but the CMS 'dictator', Suprava Putakayestha, expressed fears that communist separatism was being practised, and a minor fracas ensued. Yet the struggle for independence had now grown so intense that the MARS could not keep out of nationalist activity, and in the same year was heavily involved in the 'release Gandhi' campaign of 1943.[69] At the same time, MARS had established such a solid base in Bengal that Congress women could not keep communist women out of nationalist campaigns.

By the 1940s there was a sense of seeing independence on the horizon, and the women's movement was absorbed into the struggle for independence in such a way that the issue of women's emancipation was felt to have been resolved. With independence the inequalities between men and women would be righted, and all would be well with India. The nationalist feminist woman activist was seen both as a symbol and a bulwark of women's emancipation: the fact that the image of a woman activist which had been constructed in this period itself limited and restricted women was not questioned. Though activist women did not themselves dwell on this, clearly nationalists, revolutionary terrorists and communists saw a certain threat in women's activism, for each, in their different ways, tried to restrict it. Their chief desire seems to have been to somehow divest women of the sexuality associated with them: either through total de-sexualization, as preached by Gandhi, or through domestication and subjugation, as for example, in the communists' preference for women activists who were married to male activists.

Feminists themselves seemed to have held conflicting views on the subject: if some asserted that men and women were complementary, others asserted that they were the same. The tension between notions of complementarity and notions of equality was, however, only to be articulated by the second wave of feminism in India, in the 1970s.

NOTES

1. Sumit Sarkar, MI, p. 286.
2. Ibid.
3. Madhu Kishwar, 'Gandhi on Women', cyclostyled paper circulated as *Readings in the Women's Movement–1*, by Bombay feminists, p. 12.
4. Kamaladevi Chattopadhyaya, 'Interview', op. cit., pp. 72–73.
5. Ibid.
6. Madhu Kishwar, op. cit., p. 8.
7. Kamaladevi Chattopadhyaya, in Baig, op. cit., pp. 20–21.
8. Sumit Sarkar, op. cit., p. 293.
9. R.K. Sharma, op. cit., p. 76.
10. Manmohan Kaur, op.cit., p. 183.
11. Ibid.
12. R.K. Sharma, op. cit., p. 67.
13. Pattabhi Sitaramayya, op. cit., p. 413.
14. *100 Years of the Hindu*, op. cit., p. 413.
15. R.K. Sharma, op. cit., p. 75.
16. Ibid.
17. Usha Bala, *Indian Women Freedom Fighters.*
18. Ibid.
19. Margaret Cousins, op. cit., p. 5; Durgabai Deshmukh, 'Interview', p. 7; Manmohini Sahgal, 'Interview', pp. 30–37.
20. Kamaladevi Chattopadhyaya, 'Interview', pp. 84–85.
21. Ibid p. 169.
22. Manmohini Sahgal, 'Interview', pp. 37–38.
23. Kamaladevi Chattopadhyaya, 'Interview', p. 48.
24. Gail Pearson, 'Reserved Seats—women and the vote in Bombay', *IESHR*, vol. XX, No 1 pp. 53–54.
25. Lajjavanti, 'Interview', pp. 62–63.
26. Gail Pearson, op. cit., p. 55.
27. Margaret Cousins, op. cit., p. 65.
28. *100 years of the Hindu*, op. cit., p. 596.
29. M.K. Gandhi, *Women and Social Injustice*, Ahmedabad, Navjivan Publising House, 1954, pp. 26–27.
30. Madhu Kishwar, op. cit., p.9.
31. Ibid, p. 11.
32. Ibid, p. 13.
33. M.K. Gandhi, op. cit., pp. 18–19.
34. Ibid.
35. Ibid., pp..119–20.
36. Madhu Kishwar, op. cit., p. 7.
37. Sucheta Kripalani, *Sucheta—An Unfinished Autobiography*, Ahmedabad, Navjivan Publishing House, 1978, p. 20.
38. Ibid pp. 21–22.
39. M.K. Gandhi, *My Experiments with Truth*, Ahmedabad, Navjivan Publishing House.
40. Kalpana Dutt, *Chittagong Armoury Raiders–Reminiscences*, Delhi, People's Publishing House, 1945, p. 16.
41. Manamathnath Gupta, *Bhagat Singh and His Times*, Delhi, Lipi Prakashan, 1977, pp. 122–23.
42. Ibid.
43. J.M. Ewart, op. cit., pp. 27–31.
44. Sumit Sarkar, MI, p. 252.
45. Kamala Dasgupta, 'Interview' NMML Oral History Section, p. 10.
46. Ibid, p. 46.
47. Ela Sen, *Testament of India.*
48. Kamala Dasgupta, 'Interview', pp. 8–9.
49. Ibid pp. 15–20.
50. J.M. Ewart, op. cit., pp. 33–34.
51. Tanika Sarkar, op. cit., p. 99.
52. Ibid.
53. Gail Pearson, op. cit., p. 48.
54. V. Ramakrishna Rao, *Altar Stairs*, Madras, 1936, p. 386.

55. Cornelia Sorabjee in Shyam Kumari Nehru, op. cit., pp. 20–21.
56. Barbara N Ramusack, 'Women's Organisations and Social Change' in Naomi Black and Anne Baker Cohrell (eds.), *Women and World Change*, London, Sage Publications, 1981, pp. 205–6.
57. Ibid. pp. 206–7.
58. Ibid. pp. 210–11.
59. Muthulakshmy Reddy Papers, 'Speeches and Writings', NMML, Vol II, p. 593.
60. AIWC papers for 1932–33, NMML, microfilm section.
61. Ibid.
62. Kamaladevi Chattopadhyaya, 'Interview' pp. 45–46.
63. Renu Chakraborthy, *Communisim and the Indian Women's Movement, 1940–50*, Delhi, People's Publishing House, 1980, pp. 8–16.
64. Sushila Chain, Interviewed by Mridula Muckherjee, *Manushi*.
65. Sumit Sarkar, MI, pp. 391–92.
66. Ibid, p. 388.
67. Ibid p. 396.
68. Renu Chakraborthy, op. cit. pp. 20–23.
69. Ibid, pp. 24–25.

6. The Contemporary Feminist Movement

Bidi workers from Nipani, Maharashtra

After Independence the Congress made certain attempts to ratify their promises to women, declaring the equality of men and women in the Constitution, and setting up various administrative bodies for the creation of opportunities for women. Yet these attempts were at best partial, and to many the years after Independence seemed the site of a severe setback for feminists. The Hindu Code Bill was heavily opposed by a number of influential Congressmen, including the then President of India, Rajendra Prasad, and had eventually to be treated in a piecemeal fashion, with some sections of it being passed as separate Acts only many years later, in the mid-fifties. Demands for a reformed, uniform and all-encompassing codification of Hindu personal laws had been first raised by feminists in the thirties, and a committee was appointed to look into the matter, under the chairmanship of B.N. Rau, which submitted a draft code in 1944. No further action was taken until after Independence, when another committee was appointed under the chairmanship of B.R. Ambedkar, the then Law Minister. The Bill produced by this committee raised the age of consent and marriage, gave women the rights to divorce, maintenance and inheritance, and treated dowry as *stridhan*. Though the feminists and social reformers welcomed the Bill, and the majority of Congressmen supported it, the opposition of men such as Rajendra Prasad and Sardar Patel was enough to pressurize Nehru into stalling the Bill until 1955–56, when sections of it were passed as four different Acts: The Hindu Marriage Act, the Hindu Succession Act, the Hindu Minority and Guardianship Act, and the Hindu Adoption and Maintenance Act. Ambedkar resigned in protest and there was an outcry from some feminists, but the Government took no further action on the question of a uniform Hindu code, the outcry receded, and the matter was dropped.[1]

In post-Independence India, feminists were more fragmented than ever before, for they no longer saw a common enemy. Political divisions became more important than they had been earlier, especially since feminists had neither openly sought nor identified the enemy in gender terms, due partly to the exigencies of colonialism, and partly to the complexities of a culture in which gender relations were not as clearly distinguished as in the West. Many pre-Independence feminists were now members of the Congress government; more than any other political bloc, the Congress stood for an improvement in women's condition, and if disillusionment was setting in, it was doing so gradually. In the fifties and sixties, therefore, there was a lull in feminist campaigning, and the movement which started in the seventies and eighties was a very different one, growing out of a number of radical movements of the time.

The immediate aftermath of Partition and Independence saw a steadily increasing sense of betrayal on the part of workers and peasants, communists and socialists. The delays of the Congress in the fulfilment of its promises of speedy and effective land redistribution infused the Kisan Sabhas with a new spirit of opposition at a time when the impact of the Chinese revolution was being felt by Indian communists, and there were sharecroppers' rallies, strikes and demonstrations, led by the Kisan Sabhas, criticizing Government measures as insufficient and demanding land reform. Most of these agitations were suppressed by the Government through the arrest of peasant leaders, but this was not possible in the case of one of the earliest and most militant sharecroppers' movements, the 1948–50 Telangana movement in Andhra Pradesh. Under the leadership of Maoist-influenced members of the CPI (Communist Party of India), some two thousand five hundred villages in Telangana district were 'liberated', sharecroppers' debts were cancelled, rent payments were suspended and land redistributed. In September 1948, Indian troops took over the state, arresting peasant leaders, and firing upon demonstrators. The CPI was outlawed, and the movement forced underground, where it took to guerilla tactics.

Though thousands of women had been active in the strikes and rallies, and the leaders of the Telangana movement were unusual for their time in the attention they paid to such 'women's problems' as wife-beating, making it known that they would chastise offenders, the attitude towards women remained one of benevolent paternalism, and when the movement went underground women were not allowed to join the guerillas but were expected to perform the ancillary tasks of providing shelter, acting as messengers, etc. The exceptional women who did manage to push themselves into the guerilla movement later confessed how lonely they had felt, for while they were treated as having shed their womanliness they were never accepted as being on par with the men.[2]

Meanwhile, struggles within the CPI led to a shift in policy, with emphasis being placed on working class agitation rather than peasant insurrection, and in 1951 the CPI decided to cut their losses and called off the Telangana movement, leaving Andhra communists feeling betrayed.

In the wake of the Telangana movement, Vinobha Bhave, a nationalist leader influenced by Gandhian ideals of *sarvodaya* (self-help), started a movement to persuade landlords to donate land for redistribution to the landless. Known as *bhoodan* (the gift of land), the movement did not take off in any big way in Andhra Pradesh, but it had some success in Bihar. When Bhave went to Bihar in 1955, Jai Prakash Narayan, a Gandhian-socialist leader from the time of the Quit India movement, joined the bhoodan movement, vowing to give his life to spreading the message of bhoodan and sarvodaya. In Bihar the movement collected considerable amounts

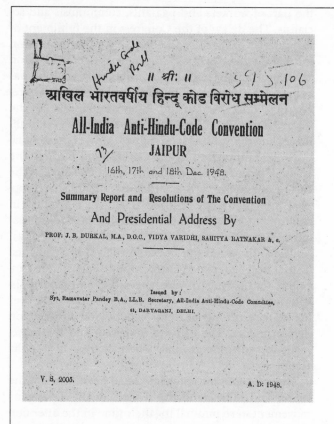

RESOLUTIONS

Passed at the All-India Anti-Hindu-Code Convention held at Jaipur on the 16th, 17th & 18th December 1948

1. Resolved that this All-India Anti-Hindu-Code Convention held at Jaipur enters its emphatic protest against the Hindu Code Bill for the following among other reasons and requests that it should be dropped:

(a) That it cuts at the root of the Vedic and Shastric origin of the Hindu Law and will seriously and inevitably undermine the foundations of the Hindu religion, Hindu culture and Hindu Social structure.

(b) That the Bill introduces sweeping, fundamental and revolutionary changes in the Hindu Law against the solid opposition of almost the whole Hindu Society.

(c) That the provisions relating to marriage, divorce, inheritance etc. are opposed to salutary and long established conceptions of Hindu Law.

(d) That the introduction of women's share in the inheritance will lead to fractionization, and the disruption of the Hindu family system which has throughout the ages acted as a cooperative institution for the preservation of family ties, family property and family stability amongst the Hindus.

(e) That this is a major bill, highly controversial and of far reaching effect on the Hindu Society and should not be passed without full consideration by the vast body of Hindus who will be profoundly affected by it.

(f) That the present Constituent Assembly was elected only for a specific object, namely to frame a constitution for India and it may at the most consider and pass Legislation of a routine or urgent and non-controversial nature.

(g) That the present Assembly, not being elected by adult franchise and for other constitutional reasons, should not pass a legislation of such serious magnitude and character as pointed out by the President of the Indian National Congress and President of the Constituent Assembly.

(h) That the Bill should be withdrawn for the time and provisions of the same be put before the electorate at the next election and it can, if at all, be taken up for consideration thereafter if sanctioned by the electorate.

II. The Convention hereby declares its considered view that:

(a) If in spite of the protest of the entire Hindu Community, the sponsors of this Bill persist in pushing the Code Bill through the Legislature, the members of the Assembly are requested in a body as well as individually to oppose the same.

(b) If the members of the Legislature are unable to oppose the Bill, the electorate may be given a chance in the election to express their views.

(c) The President of the Constituent Assembly has already pointed out that the bill has not been circulated by the Assembly for public opinion. Even evidence was not taken from the residents of the States as the Hindu Code was not then to apply to the States. Now if it will be applicable to the whole of India including the States, the Public Opinion is to be invited from the States and India and evidence is also to be sought in the States.

(d) The bill contemplates a flagrant and downright interference with Hindu religion in violation of the fundamental principles of a salutary constitution.

III. This Convention recommends to the Constituent Assembly that there should be perfect and inviolable guarantees in the new constitution for religious and cultural protection and the legislature should not interfere in personal law.

IV. That a chain of meetings should be held throughout the country to oppose the Hindu Code Bill and arrangements should be made to send telegrams and letters and signatures should be obtained against the Bill. All the resolutions etc. should be communicated to the Government.

V. Certain films are being exhibited in the country touching the social and religious matters which wound the feelings of the Hindus; so, this convention requests the Government to ban such films.

Daryaganj
Delhi

RAMAVATAR PANDEY
Secretary
All-India Anti-Hindu-Code Committee.

of land, but some were uncultivable, some were snatched back by landlords after they had been made cultivable, and some were lands over whose ownership legal battles were being waged at the time that they were given.

In the northern hill areas of Uttarakhand too, the sarvodaya movement gained a fillip through Bhave, under whose instructions attempts were made to organize people against the degradation of forests and the increasing consumption of alcohol. The Gandhi ashrams which had been started in this region after Independence, by Mira behen and Sarala behen, were the loci for these attempts, which resulted in a women's anti-alcohol agitation in the early sixties. Led by Sunderlal Bahuguna, who also used the Gandhian method of fasting in protest against alcoholism, the movements focussed on action against the manufacturers and sellers of alcohol, and were successful in creating widespread disapproval of alcohol consumption and sale, but could not banish either alcohol or alcoholism from the area.[3]

On the left, simmering resentment at the official communist line came to a boil in the sixties. The Sino-Soviet split, followed by the 1962 war between India and China, polarized communists, and in 1964 the CPI split and a new party, the Communist Party of India-Marxist (CPI-M), was formed which was at the time regarded as a pro-China faction. In 1967 both parties contested the elections and the communists was fairly evenly distributed between them, as were Assembly seats. Subsequently, communist-dominated coalition governments were formed in West Bengal and Kerala which were viewed suspiciously by radicals in the CPI-M, who felt that the times called for revolutionary uprisings, especially in the countryside. Soon after the elections, an agricultural tenants' movement began in Naxalbari village, in Bihar, where landlords' holdings were forcibly occupied. Under the communist organized *kisan samitis* (peasant organizations), the movement spread rapidly to other areas of Bihar and Bengal. Radio Peking hailed Naxalbari as a 'liberated zone', the Indian Government reacted with alarm, and the communists in the coalition were faced with the problem of how to contain the situation. In disgust with the official party stand of containment, many members and supporters of the CPI-M left, joining radical student uprisings, workers' agitations, and, most of all, peasant agitations. New sharecroppers' movements started in many areas: in Bihar the veteran CPI-M organizer, A.K. Roy, led a movement to liberate zones in Dhanbad district and set up communes; in Andhra Pradesh a second wave of the Telangana movement started, in which women were very active; and in Kerala Maoists attempted to establish a 'Red army base' in Malabar. While these groups were different, they were clubbed together by the state and media as 'Naxalites', and held to espouse a terrorist ideology, for from 1966–67 a tendency had developed within the Indian Maoist movement which preached an 'annihilation line', holding that exemplary assassinations of individual landlords and capitalists would engender a revolutionary uprising.

In 1969–70 Maoists came together to form the Communist Party of India-Marxist-Leninist (CPI-ML). State repression of Maoist movements began one year later, culminating in particularly brutal repression in 1972, when annihilationists and non-annihilationists, peasant insurgents, militant students, and others were indiscriminately murdered by the police and army. The myth of the 'armed encounter' was born: a tale of shootouts between 'Naxalites' and the police, which provided suitable cover for all sorts of repressive activities.

From the early seventies onwards, the movement broke into increasingly small fragments, many of which began to question their earlier analysis of the processes of revolution. This led to bitter intrafeuds and to the development of a host of new ideas and movements on the radical left, which paid attention to issues which had hitherto been neglected such as culture, gender, caste or tribe. Corresponding to these developments on the radical left, within the socialist movement too, new ideas and movements developed, albeit on a smaller scale, on the nature of the State and revolution, environment, trade-unionism and gender. Among these various new ideas and movements, the most interesting ones for feminists were the Shahada and anti-price rise agitations in Maharashtra, and SEWA and Nav Nirman in Gujarat.

Shahada, which acquired its name from the area in

Being trained as guerillas, Telangana, 1946–52

which it occurred, in Dhulia district in Maharashtra, was a tribal Bhil landless labourers' movement against the extortionate practices of local landlords, most of whom were non-tribals and treated the tribals as sub-human. First attempts at ameliorating this condition were made by a local *bhajan* singer called Ambarsingh, who started an Adivasi Seva Mandal in 1977, on hearing of the rape of two Bhil women by a local landlord; in the same year some sarvodaya workers learnt of an incident in which rich farmers had fired on Bhil workers in Shahada, and went down to investigate. They met Ambarsingh, and with him formed the Grain Swarajya Samiti (district organization for self-governance); soon after, they were joined by members of the far left from Pune and Bombay. According to Maria Mies, this move represented an indirect criticism of the Naxalites' 'annihilation line', in particular, their assumption that mass uprisings could occur spontaneously: 'one of the main points of criticism against the Naxalites was their neglect of mass mobilization. In Shahada, therefore, the "mass line" was the guiding principle of action.'[4]

In 1972 the Shramik Sangathana was formed in Shahada, and the 1972–73 drought and consequent famine led to the rapid growth of the movement, which had then taken up struggles against land alienation through occupying and cultivating fallow lands (many of which had been reserved by Government as 'forest lands'). Through gheraos and satyagraha, the Shramik Sangathana managed to get more famine relief work from the Government for Shahada than any other area in Maharashtra received.

Among the labourers who were active in the movement, women apparently played the most militant role. They led the demonstrations, invented and shouted militant slogans, sang revolutionary songs and mobilized the masses. They went from hut to hut to agitate the men and persuade them of the necessity to join the Shramik Sangathana. In the negotiations with the landlords they proved to be 'more adamant than the men'.[5]

Within two years, therefore, a movement involving thousands of women had grown out of activities which shifted fairly rapidly from indigenous social reform to sarvodaya to the far left. As women's militancy developed in the movement, gender-based issues began to be raised by them, following a pattern we have seen earlier and will see again and again: where a community expresses consciousness of its own oppression as a community through a protest movement in which women are acknowledged to be active; at a certain stage women apply this consciousness to questions of their oppression as a sex. Interestingly, women in the Shahada movement raised the same question as some women in the pre-Independence communist movement had done: the problem of wife-beating.

According to Mira Savara and Sujata Ghotoskar, the raising of this issue led to the development of a women's anti-alcohol agitation, with groups of Bhil women going to liquor dens and breaking all the liquor pots, for many men got drunk and beat their wives. Beginning in late 1972, the anti-alcohol agitation continued into 1973, growing in strength so that women from one village would go to others to break liquor pots. In March, the Shramik Sangathana organized a women's *shibir* (camp), at which 'women from Karamkheda village described how their husbands drank and beat them up and they asked the women at the camp to help them eradicate liquor from their village'.[6]

There and then, it seems, the women got up and marched to the village, and on the way they were joined by more and more women from villages along the route. On first entering Karamkheda, they went and broke all the pots in the liquor den, then went and gheraoed the police inspector and asked him why the liquor dens were not closed down. Further, Mira Savara and Sujata

Women's battalion, Telangana, 1941–52

'Give us water, not alcohol' Junagadh, Himachal Pradesh

Ghotoskar described how, in a village named Moad, 'women moved around in bands to break liquor pots and terrorize the ruffians of the village'.[7]

In the following months, it seems that some sort of organized network of women within and between villages had formed, and if any woman reported that her husband had beaten her, the others would get together and beat him in public, and force him to apologise to his wife in front of everyone. The Shahada movement, thus, moved from protesting against alcohol vending and consumption to attacks on wife-beaters; from an indirect protest against violence in the family to a fairly direct one, making a public issue out of what is generally regarded as a private problem. In fact, the spheres of public and private were not as sharply demarcated in tribal communities as in mainstream ones, for the property form was not as prevalent in the former. Hence there was not the same herding of women behind a 'protective barrier, nor the same elevation of the passive, nurturing, qualities of 'motherhood', nor the same insistence that a woman's sexuality be shaped by patriarchal norms and fears. These spaces may have made it easier for the women in Shahada to challenge some of the aspects of the patriarchy they did suffer from.

A comparison of the Shahada anti-alcohol agitation with the one in Uttarakhand several years earlier is interesting, for the difference in both methods and attitudes towards alcohol was quite pronounced. Though both concentrated on protesting against the vendors rather than consumers of alcohol, the Uttarakhand agitation relied largely on shaming the vendor and arousing his better feelings, through non-violent satyagraha while the Shahada agitation seems to have relied primarily on material punishment, breaking liquor pots, chastizing errant husbands, and so on. Again, the Uttarakhand agitation seems to have seen alcohol as the chief evil, whereas in Shahada they moved from protests against alcohol sale and consumption to direct attacks on wife-beaters. Moreover, the remarks of a woman activist in the movement, quoted by Mira Savara and Sujata Ghotoskar, imply that there was some recognition that wife-beating was not caused solely by drunkenness: 'our opposition was not to alcohol as such but to the beating of wives which was the inevitable result of liquor drinking'.[8]

Anti-patriarchal sentiments, it seems, were expressed in the Shahada movement, but remained dormant in Uttarakhand, probably due to a combination of factors;

the difference in time between the two movements; the difference in social structure and attitudes towards women, the one being a traditional caste society and the other tribal; and of course, the ideological difference between the activists in the respective movements.

Meanwhile, in Gujarat, what was probably the first attempt at a women's trade union was made in Ahmedabad, by Gandhian socialists attached to the Textile Labour Association (TLA), originally founded by Gandhi. Formed in 1972 at the initiative of Ela Bhatt, who worked in the women's wing of the TLA, the Self-Employed Women's Association (SEWA) was an organization of women who worked in different trades in the informal sector, but shared a common experience of extremely low earnings, very poor working conditions (most of them either worked at home on the putting out system, or in streets as vendors or hawkers), harassment from those in authority (the contractor for home workers and the police for vendors), and lack of recognition of their work as socially useful labour. The aims of SEWA were to improve these conditions of work through training, technical aids and collective bargaining, as well as to 'introduce the members to the values of honesty, dignity and simplicity of lifegoals reflecting the Gandhian ideals to which TLA and SEWA leaders subscribe'.[9] In keeping with their Gandhian views, SEWA preferred the term 'association' to 'union' though it is possible that the acronym's oral similarity to *seva*, the devoted care of other people, played a part in this choice as well. In any case, SEWA had a difficult time getting registered as a trade union, for under the Indian Trade Unions Act official recognition is granted only to unions of workers in a particular factory or under a particular employer, and SEWA fulfilled neither condition. Supported by the TLA, SEWA argued that a trade union need not conform to these regulations but could be based on the 'development' of its worker members, defining development as the 'freedom from exploitation, assurance of regular work, and access to opportunities for advancement'. Eventually, they won their way and were registered.[10]

Interestingly, some sections of the feminist movement which arose in the late seventies, did not claim SEWA as a precursor, criticizing it instead for its reformism.

Anti price-rise demonstration, Gujarat, 1973

Anti price-rise demonstration, Bihar

SEWA itself maintained a distance from the feminists, perhaps because it felt they were 'westernized', or too radical. Shahada, on the other hand, was definitely claimed by the feminists, partly because of its direct attack on male violence and partly because it spawned many of the feminists of the late seventies. In a rather different way, the feminists of the seventies also noted the anti-price rise agitation in Bombay and the Nav Nirman movement in Gujarat as precursors, but more because they had involved thousands of women in activism than for the nature of this activism.

The conditions of drought and famine which had affected Shahada, among other areas in Maharashtra, also led to a rise in prices which affected urban areas. In 1973, Mrinal Gore of the Socialist Party and Ahilya Ranganekar of the CPI-M, together with many others, formed the United Women's Anti Price Rise Front, 'to mobilize women of the city against inflation just as women . . . of the rural poor had been mobilized in the famine agitations'.[11]

The movement grew rapidly, becoming a mass women's movement for consumer protection, demanding that both prices and distribution of essential commodities be fixed by the Government. So many housewives were involved in the movement that a new form of protest was invented, with housebound women expressing their support for women demonstrating

against price rises and hoarding by beating *thalis* (metal plates) with *lathas* (rolling pins). The demonstrations themselves were huge, with around ten to twenty thousand women going to gherao M.P.s and industrialists and offer them bangles as a token of their (the industrialists') emasculation or to raid warehouses where goods were being hoarded.

Soon after, the movement spread to Gujarat, becoming known as the Nav Nirman movement of 1974. Nav Nirman was originally a students' movement against soaring prices, corruption and black-marketeering, which became a massive middle-class movement joined by thousands of women. In its course the movement shifted from protesting on these issues to an all out criticism of the Indian State, which they saw as venal and undemocratic. Their methods of protest ranged from mass hunger strikes to mock courts passing judgement on corrupt state officials and politicians, mock funerals celebrating the death of those condemned by their courts, and *prabhat pheris* to greet the dawn of a new era. Women also 'rang the death knell of the Legislative Assembly with rolling pins and *thalis.*' It took the police some three months to crush the Nav Nirman movement, in 1974, and between ninety to a hundred people were killed.[12]

Nav Nirman activists were influenced by Jai Prakash Narayan's concept of 'total revolution', fighting to reform as well as to limit State power, arguing that the *rajniti* (State rule of law) had become corrupt and decayed, and the time for *lokniti* (people's rule of law)

Rolling pins and empty tins of ghee (clarified butter), symbols of the anti price-rise agitation

had come. Central to their definition of lokniti were opposition to the caste system and religious ritual, and an emphasis on changing personal and familial relationships as well as political or economic ones. The major focus of the Nav Nirman movement however was on corruption of the rajniti, and the formation of 'people's courts' to pass 'people's verdicts' on the rajniti was seen as a step towards the building of a lokniti. The movement did not, therefore appear to stress the importance of changing caste, religious, personal or familial relationships.

Thus, whether the anti-price rise and Nav Nirman movements can be called anti-patriarchal or not is an open question. Neither of them seems to have asked, for example, why an increase in domestic expenditure should be the concern primarily of women rather than men, and to this extent they seem to have accepted that the family was women's sphere. Nor do they seem to have challenged women's role as consumers rather than producers, or to have asked why the family should be tended as a unit of consumption rather than production. Moreover, their use of a gender defined sign of contempt, offering bangles to men to signify their womanly unworthiness for public office, would seem to reinforce rather than challenge patriarchal stereotypes. Yet women's collective public action is generally regarded as posing an implicit threat to patriarchy, and both the anti-price rise and Nav Nirman movements involved thousands of women in public action. Perhaps both movements allowed anti-patriarchal ideas to germinate indirectly for several of their activities emerged as feminist activities in the late seventies.

In the same year as the Nav Nirman movement developed and was crushed, the first women's group of the contemporary feminist movement was formed in Hyderabad, the Progressive Organisation of Women (POW). Comprising women from the Maoist movement, the group was another exemplar of the process of rethinking within the movement after its savage repression. As in the Shahada movement, Maoist women were beginning to stress the existence of gender oppression, and to organize women against it; but while in the former the question came up through a single issue, the latter (POW) attempted holistic analysis through its Manifesto, which gave an indication of the feminism to come. We have argued in the introduction that an idea of equality based on sameness underlies many of the feminist movements of the nineteen-seventies, distinguishing them from anti-patriarchal women's movements. The POW made the connection between feminism and this idea of equality explicit in their manifesto:

the concept of the Indian woman as an equal partner of man and as an active participant in all walks of life has never been so clearly shattered as

today. We have, on the one hand, our Constitution mouthing pious platitudes about the equality of women, and a few women scattered here and there as leaders, and on the other hand, the terrible conditions of the majority of Indian women . . . . Feudal culture preaches to women seclusion at home and restriction from active participation in public life. Increasingly, penetrating foreign culture, on the other hand, has reduced women to nothing more than decorative sex objects. Obscenity in art and literature are rampant. Aggressive male supremacy has led to the sickening practice of eve-teasing and one step further, rape. Some of us are not allowed to work for our own living, while others who work on a par with men are not treated on the basis of equal pay for equal work. The position of the housewife is no better. Confined to her home, working from morning to night in back-breaking chores, she has neither independence nor dignity.[13]

The two primary structures of women's oppression were thus, according to the POW, the sexual division of labour, and the culture which rationalized it. The former was the base of women's oppression, rendering them economically dependent on men, and the latter was the superstructure, providing justificatory theories which argued that the biological differences between

Anti-alcohol agitation, Himachal

men and women were such that women were naturally inferior. Both were modified by the epochs in which they existed, and both stood revealed in moments of contradiction: between feudalism and 'increasingly penetrating foreign culture', for example. The implication here was that such a contradiction, through revealing the truth, created conditions for a women's liberation movement, though this was not actually stated in the Manifesto, which moved instead into an outline of how women's oppression could be brought to an end. This was, firstly, through attacks on the 'base of economic dependence and private work at home', and secondly, through spreading an 'ideology of equality', which could be found in socialism: 'Women should be encouraged to participate in all walks of life and their potentialities in all spheres should be developed. Socialism, being the ideology of the oppressed class, will also create the necessary and genuine climate for the equality of women'.[14]

1975 saw the sudden development of a whole spate of feminist activities in Maharashtra. This has been seen by some feminists as being partly due to the U.N's declaration of 1975 as International Women's Year, and perhaps the declaration did provide a kind of focus for activities centering on women. But it seems likely that these activities would have taken place even without the declaration, for an interest in women's problems had started developing in Maharashtra from the early seventies, as we have seen through the Shahada and anti-price rise agitations. Influenced by the POW, Maoist women in Pune formed the Purogami Stree Sangathana (progressive women's organization), and Maoist women in Bombay formed the Stree Mukti Sangathana (women's liberation organization). March 8, International Women's Day, was celebrated for the first time in India by a number of both party-based and autonomous organizations in Maharashtra; and the Lal Nishan Party brought out a special issue of their party paper. In August, the Marathi socialist magazine *Sadhana* brought out a special women's number; in September, dalits and socialists organized a conference of *devadasis* (literally, servants of the gods; used to mean women who have been 'given' to the temple); in October, a number of organizations which had developed out of the Maoist movement, such as the Lal Nishan Party, the Shramik Sangathana and Magowa, organized a 'United Women's Liberation Struggle' conference in Pune. It was attended by women from all over Maharashtra, some of whom were CPI-M, others in the Socialist and Republican parties.[15]

Especially interesting was the connection which was now being made between the anti-caste dalit movement and feminism. *Janwedana* (distress of the people), a dalit Marathi newspaper, brought out a special women's number, entitled 'In the Third World Women Hold Up Half the Sky', a statement borrowed from the Chinese to make clear their difference from first world feminism; and some months later an intriguing new group was formed by women from the *dalit* (the word chosen by the anti-caste untouchable movement in post-independence India to describe themselves) movement, calling itself the Mahila Samta Sainik Dal (League of Women Soldiers for Equality). The name itself, which stressed equality and conjured up images of a women's crusade, was faintly reminiscent of the Black movement in the United States of America, and in fact the Dal's Manifesto claimed Angela Davis as a sister. Though the Manifesto stressed the sexual oppression of women as did the POW, its analysis of women's oppression was radically different from the POW's. The Dal saw religion as a major agent in the oppression of women as well as dalits, and the caste system as the source of inequality in India:

People are labelled by their caste and crippled and enslaved. Therefore, until the caste system is torn up from the roots, the caste ideology which discriminates among people will not die. Complete equality will not be established. This is our firm opinion. The caste system has been constructed by a handful of selfish people for their own interest. We have become soldiers to destroy it.

It is the custom here to nourish this slavery under the name of religion. It is this religion which has enslaved women. The . . . holy books, which made women and shudras inferior and deprived us of education, knowledge and independence, are selfish. All these books were written by men and have enslaved women.[16]

Further, the Manifesto drew parallels between caste oppression and women's oppression, seeing in the latter a caste division between men and women, in which notions of purity and impurity were used to repress women:

The idea of *pativrata* (devotion to the husband) is based on the purity of a single organ . . . the idea of family purity is decided not on the basis of the purity of a special organ of men but only on the basis of the purity of a special organ of women and so she is locked up inside the house. The male caste has done a gross injustice to women by this mistrust. It is our firm opinion that men have kept women deprived of freedom and apart from knowledge and have made them slaves only for sexual pleasure.[17]

Both the POW and MSSD Manifestoes stressed the sexual oppression of women in a way that earlier social reform or feminist groups had not done, except in relation to certain categories of women: prostitutes and temple dancers, for example, in whose cases the question of sexual oppression could hardly be avoided. The emphasis laid by POW and MSSD, on the other hand, was on the sexual oppression of all women; and is an emphasis which quite clearly distinguishes the contemporary feminist movement from those that preceded

Poster, Maharashtra

it—even though it was, and is, differently viewed by different groups within the contemporary movement. The POW, for example, felt that all forms of male domination were based on women's economic dependence on men; whereas the MSSD felt that men's base desire for 'sexual pleasure' had led them to 'enslave' women. Underlying these two different statements was an age-old argument within the socialist-feminist movement all over the world: whether the biological difference between men and women was the root of women's oppression or not. The POW took the view that 'the sex stereotype was not due to basic biological differences but due to the thousands of years in which the division of labour has prevailed, and men and women were conditioned to the ideology of male supremacy'; while the MSSD asserted that women's oppression was predicated on their reproductive capacities: 'it is not necessary to treat women as inferior because they have accepted the responsibility of bearing children'.

The declaration of the Emergency in 1975 led to a break in the development of the fledgeling women's movement, for many political organizations were driven underground, thousands of activists were arrested and many who remained at liberty focussed their energies on civil rights groups. The lifting of the Emergency in 1977, and the formation of the Janata Government in 1978,

led to a renewal of some of the movements of the early to mid-seventies and women's groups were formed all over the country, but mainly in the major cities.

The distinguishing features of the new women's groups were that they declared themselves to be 'feminist', despite the fact that most of their members were drawn from the left, which saw feminism as bourgeois and divisive; that they insisted on being 'autonomous', though most of their members were affiliated to other political groups, generally of the far left; and that they rapidly built networks amongst each other, ideological differences notwithstanding. All three were, however, defined—and, in certain ways, limited—by the background and evolution of the groups.

The first year or two in the life of these groups was spent mainly in attempts at self-definition. Most of their members were drawn from the far left and belonged to the urban educated middle-class, and these two factors influenced the feminist movement of the late seventies and early eighties in fairly complex ways. On the one hand, there was considerable debate on the class basis of women's oppression, the road to women's liberation, and the role feminists themselves could play in this; on the other, the awareness of their basically middle-class background led many feminists to feel that their own needs were minor and different compared to the needs of the vast majority of women in India, who belonged to the working/labouring/toiling classes. Consequently, the feminism culled from their own experiences could never be 'true' or even 'real'. In effect, this meant a kind of objectification of both working-class and middle-class women, for the self-awareness which generally facilitates intimacy was invalidated. Emotional needs or desires were thus relegated to the personal or individual sphere, and the sort of public-private dichotomy which feminists

Poster, Maharashtra

'We will only rest after having broken this prison' Women's Liberation Group poster for
International Women's Day, Bombay, 1982

Poster made by the National Coordinating Committee, Kerala, for the Fourth
National Conference on Women's Movements, Calicut December, 1990

A joint demonstration of different groups, Delhi

opposed in their campaigns against rape or violence in the family, appeared in a different form within their own groups.

Within a few years a third view was offered on this argument, saying that while the root of women's oppression lay in the biological differences between men and women, it was only as the mode of production and reproduction changed historically that these biological differences became important enough to subjugate women:

> One of the first dualisms in human history was the sexual division of labour, which evolved due to women's reproduction ability. The large periods for which women were engaged in childbearing and childcare—and therefore less mobile—led to the growth of units of domestication (the nest, the hut, the house and family), and as societies grew first agricultural, then mercantile and industrial, to the privatisation of women's work, centering it around the duties of maternity, childcare, etc . . . The appropriation of control over women's bodies has been one of the most significant forms of our oppression under capitalism. Where pre-capitalist societies also felt the need to regulate their popu-

Young women forced into prostitution recovered from a house in Uttar Pradesh, 1976

lation, capitalism has found that the need for regulating the labour force and for maintaining a balance between production and consumption, requires a more systematic control over women's reproductive capacities. These needs become fundamental ones to ensure the smooth functioning of the capitalist economy, which is threatened as much by overemployment as by underemployment on a large scale.[18]

Though the Marxist affiliations of most of the feminists led to a kind of broad agreement that a materialist framework was necessary for the analysis of women's oppression, there were fairly wide differences over what this meant, and debates arose over such questions as whether certain forms of women's oppression—the connection between male or familial honour and the control of women, for example—were 'remnants of feudalism' or present in an altered form under capitalism; whether the family should be seen as a homogenous structure of oppression for women, or differentiated according to class: that is, whether the working-class family should be seen as quite different from the middle-class family, as the former provided a kind of supportive nucleus against the alienation engendered by the capitalist mode of production, while the latter was completely oppressive, existing primarily as a means of consolidating and preserving private property. Underlying these debates was an argument over how far, and in which ways, commonality of women's experience could be sought, and whether at all it could cut across class, and to a lesser extent caste or community, boundaries.

Theatre groups demonstrate in Delhi

Posters by Ahmedabad Women's Action Group, Gujarat

It was only in the debate on what the role of feminist groups was, however, that this argument came to a head.

Historically, the experience of the Maoist insurgency of the late sixties, and its repression and disintegration in the early seventies, had led many to believe that a revolutionary transformation of society could only come into being if different oppressed groups, such as tribals, subordinate castes and women, were organized and represented separately, and then coalesced to fight their common enemies. The question before the women's groups in the late seventies was, therefore, of how women could be organized and represented. Interestingly, the feminists did not take it for granted that they would be proper organizers and representatives of women: on the contrary, there was a general agreement that this was not the task of feminist groups, though the conclusion was reached in a variety of ways. For some, feminist groups could not organize and represent women because they were primarily urban and middle-class and therefore could not become working-class or peasant women's organizations; others believed that while autonomy was necessary for the development of socialist-feminist theory, it would be detrimental in mass organizations or movements, and thus women should not be separately organized. The task of feminist groups, therefore, was to raise feminist issues in mass organizations (such as trade unions, kisan samitis, etc.) which would then undertake to organize and represent women as well as men. Yet others propounded a spontanist argument, that once a socialist-feminist movement began, it would naturally spread and grow in multiple ways, and throw up its own organizations and representatives, and thus it was not necessary for the feminist groups to debate whether or not they should organize and represent women.

The three arguments were neither as abstract nor as crude as they sound: by and large, those advocating the former two had been, or were, active in radical and far left organizations, and felt that they contained space for the raising of feminist demands; while those espousing the latter had not been, or were not then, involved in such organizations, and felt that negotiating within them would yield small gains compared to those won by an independent women's movement, which through its very existence would force political organizations to take note of it.

As the majority of the new feminist groups comprised women from diverse sections of the far left, few of them were ideologically homogenous, and this was a source of distress to many, partly because it meant that no uniform perspective on women's oppression and liberation was offered, and partly because differences in political faiths led to constant argument and disagreement within and between groups, resulting in the formation of ideological blocs which caused majority-minority problems. The sectarianism of the far left, which was part of the heritage feminists brought with them, further exacerbated these problems, leading to a suspicion of individual feminists' motives, and a defensive fear of being overwhelmed by opportunism both within and outside the feminist movement. This was to cause really severe problems in a few years' time, when the movement had grown considerably larger, but in the late seventies feminists were dominated by fear that to recognize sectarianism within their ranks would allow anti-feminists to declare that they knew that women were incapable of working together. The recognition of sectarianism was therefore suppressed, and most often treated as a 'personal problem' between individuals rather than as a conflict of ideas and attitudes.

Poster by Ahmedabad Women's Action Group,
Gujarat, date not known

The lack of ideological homogeneity which was a
source of distress to so many was also a source of comfort
to some, who saw in it examples of the potential plural-
ism of feminism and its ability to provide grounds for
women with different ideas to work together, despite the
sectarianism which existed within the movement. At one
level this was true, for a majority of feminists rejected the
policy of achieving homogeneity through expelling dis-
sidents: for example, in Delhi in a feminist group, Stri
Sangharsh, formed in 1979, there was a majority-minority divide which became so acute that some members of
the majority wished to expel the minority, and were
opposed by others, who felt that feminism could not
resort to such methods as expulsion in order to resolve
a crisis. The anti-expulsionists won, but the crisis
remained unresolved, and though the minority was tol-
erated, only occasional feeble and individual efforts
were made to have a dialogue. Many groups opted for
autonomy, which was defined as consisting of separate,
women-only groups, without any party-political affiliation or conventional organizational structure, for these
were hierarchical, created self-interest and competitive-
ness, were fairly loose, without formal structures or
funds and reproduced the division. The only party-based

women's organization to be formed in the late seventies,
was in fact, the Mahila Dakshata Samiti (MDS), which
was founded in 1977 by socialist women in the coalition
Janata Party.

While there was, therefore, some sort of feminist
critique of party politics, the terms of criticism varied
widely: some were critical of the existing practice of
political parties but believed that reform was possible
and could fulfil feminist aims; others were critical of
traditional and entrenched political parties, but believed that genuinely representative political parties
could be created; and yet others argued that political
parties were so structured that they would never fulfil
feminist, or indeed socialist, aims. While these three
arguments can be characterized as belonging to the
liberal-reformist, left, and libertarian schools, there was
also a regional variation in the terms of argument. In
Delhi, which as the capital views party-political sectarianism, opportunism and factionalism on such a scale and
frequency as to be blasé about it, it was more or less taken
for granted that feminism and party-affiliation were
mutually opposed. Neither Samta nor Stri Sangharsh,
the two major feminist groups of the late seventies in
Delhi, had any members who were party-affiliated; both
developed out of university-based feminist discussion
groups, in Delhi University and Jawaharlal Nehru University, and while some of their members had been active
in student politics, none of them had joined any party.
In fact, Stri Sangharsh decided it would not extend a
welcome to party-affiliated women, in the unlikely event
that any such should wish to join the group.

The first feminist groups in Bombay, on the other
hand, were neither university-based not composed
mainly of students. Most of their members came from
the far left, from civil liberties' organizations, revolutionary groups, independent trade unions, etc., and had
some experience of organizing, campaigning and negotiating, both as members of political groups or organizations, and in joint party and non-party fronts. While
critical of the orthodox parties of the left as well as of the
right, they were able to work in joint left and socialist
fronts, and several of them were affiliated to small parties
on the radical left.

That this difference between the Delhi and Bombay
groups was an important one became clear at the first
national conference of socialist-feminists in India,
organized by women in Bombay in 1978 and attended
by women from all sections of the left, and even some
Gandhians. The contingent from Delhi was the largest
one from outside Bombay, and the conference was
dominated by the Delhi and Bombay groups. The Delhi
feminists, among whom the first rifts were beginning to
appear, had for some months previously been meeting
to plan a feminist magazine, and one session of the
conference was devoted to discussing their proposal. In

the course of the discussion it appeared that most of the participants felt that a distinction had to be made between activists and the general body of women, and thus two kinds of publications were needed: a magazine for 'consciousness-raising', and a bulletin for activists, which would provide a forum for them to come together, report on their activities, and discuss strategies for a movement. As the Delhi feminists had proposed the former, they would bring it out, but the latter was the responsibility of the Bombay group, as they were the ones who had considerable activist experience. That this experience had been garnered on the left and far left, during a period of repression and disarray for both, was not seen as being of particular consequence, even though the feminist groups had grown out of these fragments and represented to some extent a reaction against certain of their practices.

Furthermore, a double distinction was made, not only between activists and the general run of feminists, but between consciousness-raising and theory generation. A three-tiered heirarchy now developed, consisting of theory generators (usually the most articulate), activists (consciousness-raisers), and the subjects of their attention.

Meanwhile, the influence of feminist ideas was beginning to grow. Though the feminist campaigns in the late seventies and early eighties were dominated by the new city-based groups, similar developments of feminist consciousness had also taken place in certain rural movements. The Telangana movement in Andhra Pradesh was again renewed after the Emergency was lifted, and the area was declared a 'disturbed zone' by the Government. In Karimnagar district, where women had been especially active in the landless labourers' movement from the sixties on, the new wave of agitation began with a campaign against the kidnapping of a woman called Devamma, and the murder of her husband, by a local landlord. The Stree Shakti Sanghatana, formed in the late seventies in Hyderabad, by women from the erstwhile POW, described how this agitation led to the development of women's organizations in the area:

> The villagers, mostly women, caught the landlord, surrounded him, mounted him on a donkey and led him around the village, abused and humiliated. The police intervened and Lalita (the local CPI-ML activist) was arrested. In the neighbouring villages, solidarity protest marches were held, an increasing number of women were being politicised and the Ryotu Coolie Sangam (agricultural workers' organization) was forced to recognise the need for separate or autonomous women's organisations, and by 1979 the first Mahila Sangam was formed in Kodurupaka with about one hundred and fifty members.[19]

According to the Stree Shakti Sanghatana, the demand for independent women's organizations came from the 'women themselves', who raised the issues of wife-beating and landlord rape through the Mahila Sanghams. Describing the development of the Mahila Sanghams in a paper read at the 1980 socialist-feminist conference in Bombay, organized by the Forum Against Rape, the Stree Shakti Sanghatana concluded:

> We have seen how women's organizations affiliated to political parties (even in socialist countries) have become mere appendages of those parties. In post-revolutionary periods, women's movements have been relegated to the background. It is important that women's organizations guard against such a danger, but without isolating themselves from the masses, and from other revolutionary movements.[20]

University students' demonstration against sexual harassment, Delhi, 1982

Forum against the Oppression of Women, Bombay

Interestingly, one of the central issues of debate during the 1980 conference was on the role of feminist groups and the relationship they should have to party and mass based organizations. Allied with this was the issue of how a women's movement would and should develop. Basically, the debate was within the Marxist tradition, representing perhaps different streams of it. Excerpts from two of the papers presented around the debate follow, which show the kinds of premises which were dominant in the movement at the time:

I believe that socialist-feminist groups should work on the following principles:

They should *not* try to 'organize women', they should not aim at being 'organizing centres' or a nucleus of a developing women's movement; they should not try to become themselves mass organizations of women. A natural tendency for women in such organizations is to say: 'We must organize women, we must build up our mass base among working class women', etc. I believe this is a mistake. It is true that we should go among toiling women—the question is how. It is true that a working class-based, rural poor-based movement must be built—but who will build it and how will it be built?

These are different issues. As organizations, middle class socialist-feminist organizations cannot and *should not* try to be organizing centres for such work. Many of their members, as individuals, may be doing part time or full time work in slums, etc., but this work will be guided by/directed by the political group responsible for work in that area (or the political group to which they are committed) and cannot be done under the *authority* of a middle class women's organization, however progressive or revolutionary its ideology may be. Instead, such organizations should be political *organizations* of a particular type, organizations of activists and not mass organizations.

Their goal should be to help build up a women's liberation movement linked to the revolutionary struggles of the toiling masses—but their role in that process should be to present *before the masses* a political line of women's liberation, i.e., a line which links women's liberation to the fight for revolution, and to spread this as much as possible among the masses of working women and men, rural women and middle classes and party and union activists.[21] (Gail Omvedt)

****

The question may arise, why form an autonomous organization, why not function in political trade unions? It may be answered that it is a historical fact that trade unions do not give credence to women's questions, that they are dominated by men, that the tendency to bureaucracy is greater.

This is valid, but it is also true that it is only within such groups (women's groups) that the contradictions and tensions faced by women can be fathomed. For example, hostels, women's unions, even bhajan mandals can become centres of struggle, the starting point of an acquisition of an identity.

Because of the capacity of the constraints of the social structure our immediate task is to develop intellectuals from all sections of the oppressed classes. By the term 'intellectual' one does not mean intellectual in the traditional sense but those who are able to reveal and articulate the tensions in society. It is only when the specific alienating nature of our society, which is bogged down by colonialism, imperialism, Hinduism, is understood that a perspective can emerge.[22] (Manju Upadhyaya)

At around the same time, in the Bodhgaya district of Bihar, feminist issues were raised by women in the J.P.-influenced Chhatra Yuva Sangharsh Vahini, which was involved in an agricultural labourers' struggle against the temple priests who owned most of the land in the area. According to the pamphlet brought out by the Vahini in 1980, titled *Aurat* (woman), J.P.'s concept of total revolution, propagated in 1974, was based on three theses: firstly, that individuals will change only if society changes; secondly, that society will change only if individuals change; and thirdly, that relationships between men and men, men and women, and women and women, will have to change. Further, all relations between human beings were based on *dharma* (religion), *nasla* (race), *rang* (colour), and *linga* (gender). Despite this, it was only in 1979 that questions of male dominance were raised, resulting in the Vahini's organizing a women's shibir in Bodhgaya, at which a demand was made for women, as well as men, to have land registered in their own names.

The Vahini was different from other organizations in that it did not set up separate women's organizations, though there was a sort of uncodified women's wing, with women activists organizing women, and so on. According to one of its activists, Chetna, though the Vahini 'had an understanding of women's problems . . . it is not easy to be accepted as a woman with her own independent thinking . . . People usually think I must be under the influence of some man or other'. Conversely, their understanding of women's problems could in turn create problems for the women in the Vahini: for example, while the institution of marriage was criticized for the way it oppressed women, many of its male critics felt that if women 'were really liberated they should not object to being physically approached by boys'.[23] In other words, some of their male comrades used ideological pressure to try and make the women sleep with them. As Chetna hastened to add, this was not a problem specific to the Vahini, but was faced by women from all sections of the left—though few of them would say so publicly.

For most feminists, including Chetna, the chief problem in this context was the way in which men used ideology as a tool to further their own ends. While this was indeed a problem and probably still is, this view glossed over other questions concerning sexuality, for it looked upon women as objects of sexual desire rather than subjects of it. In so doing, it implied that women either did not have such desires or that they were not problematic, even in relation to the institution of marriage. Underlying this were further questions on the relation between activism and self-fulfilment for example, was it permissible for activists to display sexual desire or should they suppress it?

The image of the activist as one who had transcended all considerations of self had long been part of the political culture of India, though it was translated differently by Gandhians, socialists, communists and Maoists. Given that most feminists belonged to one or other of these political traditions, it is not surprising that they felt an urge to conform to the image, though it conflicted with the feminist view that ideals of feminine purity and selflessness were a part of the structure, of women's oppression. In a way, the conflict was resolved by pushing it into abeyance, through focussing on forms of violence against women, rather than the less obvious ways in which they were oppressed. In this context, it is not simply coincidence that the two campaigns which, in effect, 'launched' the contemporary feminist movement, were the campaigns against dowry-deaths and rape, both of which focussed on especially brutal forms of violence against women. Detailed descriptions of the two campaigns, and their significance for feminists, follow.

NOTES

1. Indu Prakash Singh, 'Dialectics of Law and the Status of Indian Women', unpublished Ph.D. thesis, Centre for the Study of Social Systems. J.N.U., Delhi 1985, pp. 97–107.
2. Stree Shakti Sanghatana, *We were making history ... Life stories of women in the Telangana People's struggle*, Delhi, Kali for Women, 1987.
3. J. Bandopadhyay and V. Shiva, 'Chipko', in *Seminar*, Feb. 1987, p. 35.
4. Maria Mies 'The Shahada Movement: A Peasant Movement in Maharashtra, its Development and its Perspective' in *Journal of Peasant Studies*, Vol. 3, No. 4, July 1976, p. 480.
5. Ibid, p. 478.
6. Mira Savara and Sujata Ghotoskar, '*An Assertion of Womanpower*' in Madhu Kishwar and Ruth Vanita (eds), *In Search of Answers: Indian Women's Voices* from *Manushi*, London, Zed Books, 1984, p. 135.
7. Ibid, p. 145.
8. Ibid, p. 144.
9. Devaki Jain, 'The Self Employed Women's Association, Ahmedabad', in *How*, Vol. 3, No. 2, Feb. 1980, p. 14.
10. Ibid.
11. Gail Omvedt, 'Women and Rural Revolt in India', cyclostyled paper, later published in *Journal of Peasant Studies*, p. 22.
12. Vibhuti Patel, *Reaching for Half the Sky*, Antar

Rashtriya Prakashan Bawda, 1985, pp. 8–10.
13. Gail Omvedt, *We Will Smash This Prison*, London, Zed Press, 1980, Appendix II.
14. Ibid.
15. Collected from Gail Omvedt, op. cit., *Manushi, Baija, Feminist Network*.
16. Gail Omvedt, op. cit., p. 174.
17. Ibid, pp. 174–5.
18. For an elucidation of these views see two papers presented at the National Conference on a Perspective for a Women's Liberation Movement in India, Bombay, November 1980: Gail Omvedt, 'Social-Feminist Organisation and the Women's Movement', and Sujata Ghotoskar and Vibhuti Patel, 'Social-feminism and the Trade Union Movement'.
19. Stree Shakti Sanghatana, 'The War Against Rape', in Miranda Davies, ed., *Third World, Second Sex*, London, Zed Books, 1984, pp. 199–200.
20. Ibid. p. 201.
21. Chhatra Yuva Sangharsh Vahini, *Aurat*, Chotanagpur Yuva Chetna Prakashan, Giridih, 1980, pp. 1–2.
22. Manimala, 'Zameen Kenkar? Jote Onkar', in *In Search of Answers* op. cit., p. 150.
23. Madhu Kishwar, 'She Works for Change—an Interview with Chetna, a Sangharsh Vahini activist', *Manushi*, No. 27, March-April 1985, p. 12.

7. The Campaign Against Dowry

Aftermath of a dowry demonstration, Delhi, 1983

I have been working for 10 months on children's classes, adult literacy programmes and health camps, in addition to taking up local issues, in Chembur slums in Bombay.

In the course of working in the slum Pancha Seela Nagar, we were introduced to Malarkodi, a young woman who lived in the slum and was a potential leader among the women.

Some time ago, Malarkodi had run off to Madras with a former boyfriend. Her husband went and brought her back, promising to behave well. But

after that he continued to remind her of her elopement. He used to drink and beat her up. All the neighbours knew this since it was an everyday routine. But this Sunday the routine took a fatal turn. She died.

When I asked some of the men why they had not intervened, their reply was that it was a 'family quarrel.' A step ahead was the reply: 'She was killed by her husband. So why should we interfere?'

I found that almost all men, whatever their class,

job or status, thought in the same manner. When we went to the police inspector of Tilak Nagar to demand Malarkodi's body, he said: 'Why are you taking up this issue? She was an immoral woman. Otherwise, no sane husband would do this.'... Later, when I was narrating the incident to somebody who studies in my class, they too offered the same consolation: 'Oh, it was her husband who killed her. Then what can you do about it?'[1]

This kind of 'family quarrel' is common to all classes, religions, and communities, all over India. Indeed, the term dowry has become a euphemism for wife-battering, a practice so familiar that such violence has become a key issue in practically all movements in which women have been active.

Thus communists and left parties have been embarrassed into admitting it exists even among their members (see Renu Chakravarty). It became a central issue of the Shahada movement, and of feminist movements all over the country. And yet, until recently, violence within the family remained hidden and even now, women hesitate to speak of it for a variety of reasons.

The first time he said I'll beat you, I thought he was joking. No one had said these words to me all my life. When he beat me the first time, with his hands, I was shocked. The second time—with a wooden hanger, I said: 'No this can't be true. It cannot happen to ME!' The third time it was the belt, the buckle hurt the nose, and the bridge broke. I was numb not so much with the pain, but despair. No one had warned me marriage included this. He said: 'You are a sick curse, you are an idiot. You are good for nothing. I could have got a better girl and a lot of dowry too.'

I pointed out: 'It was you who approached my mother. You were most keen. You told my mother you didn't want dowry.'

I got beaten.

He said: 'I will never pay for your expenses... Your clothes... your medicines...'

Then he said: 'You think too much of yourself.'

I said: 'But so do you.'

He said: 'You grew up the easy way. I am a self made man.'

A couple of times, after fierce fights, and a lot of

Anti-dowry demonstration, Delhi, 1980

battering I left the house and took shelter with a relative. But each time, the faces of my children would haunt me, and I would return the next day or the day after. Sometimes I left with the children, but how long can one stay with a relative with three small children? So I returned. If any relative tried to intervene, he would break off relations with them. With the result that the number of friends who dropped in became less. I was afraid of making new friends (what will they think when they find out my husband beats me?) So I started living in isolation, a social outcaste with a stigma attached to my name.[2]

Although there are countless incidents of such violence, it is seldom that we see women giving up their oppressive situations and moving out. Partly this is because, in many families (particularly middle class) a woman's life is defined only in the context of a man's. The following statement provides an example: 'I was twelve or thirteen when I was married... don't remember exactly when. He beat me from the very beginning. He used to drink, come home, and beat me. He used to burn me too—and kick me mercilessly. I suffered very badly... He beat me up brutally, it's true; but at least he was there.'[3]

Over the years, feminists have heard these saddest of words used time and again and have grown to understand their full significance; indeed, it is only by coming across this again and again that women have grown to recognize their own helplessness in view of the daunting situation they face in this country. It is impossible to live in India without being aware of the gruelling hardship people have to face to survive, the paucity of food and clothing, or education that are part of everyday life. The situation is made more difficult because of the years of conditioning which do not allow a woman to see her husband as anything other than a god. Thus, women will protect men even at the cost of their own lives. The incredible mental cruelty that some families inflict upon their daughters-in-law is tragically revealed in a series of letters published in *Manushi*, written by a young girl who killed herself two months after she was married. The following extract is from her farewell letter to her husband:

My Raja (Lord)

I am going away. Forgive me...
Ever since I came to your house your family has had difficulties. My coming into your house was not auspicious for you. So I am going away. I will make every effort to see that I do not survive, because if I do, not only will my life be ruined, but so will yours. Do not take me to hospital...

I am taking your child along with me in my womb. Forgive me for this too. You had a desire to marry again. Do marry again. You can either burn the clothes I brought in my dowry, or return them to my parents. The clothes which were given to me by your family can be ironed and kept for the new bride...

When the new bride comes, try and listen to what she says, and do not quarrel with her. Even if her relatives do not pay much attention to you, you should try to stay happy. You should ignore these things. Otherwise, her life will be ruined. And if she talks to you privately about anything, never tell anyone else in the house what she says...

Only yours

Tato[4]

Tato committed suicide because her husband and his family tortured her for having brought so little with her by way of goods; mocking her and her family for the quality of food at the wedding and presents to the bridegroom's family. We do not know whether her ex-husband took a formal dowry when he remarried, which he did a few months after her suicide, but there is no doubt that in contemporary India families who might not formally ask for or even take dowry, make known their expectation that the bride's family will help maintain a standard of life which the bridegroom's family find mandatory.

The first protests against dowry in the contemporary feminist movement were made by the Progressive Organization of Women in Hyderabad in 1975. Though some of their demonstrations numbered as many as 2000 people, the protests did not grow into a full fledged campaign.

After a lull of around two years, a new movement against dowry started in Delhi. This time it was against violence inflicted upon women for dowries: especially against murder and abetment to suicide. Though there have since been protests against dowry harassment and murder in several parts of India (Punjab, Maharashtra, Karnataka, Gujarat, Madhya Pradesh, Bengal), the emphasis on action has been infrequent. Only in Delhi has there been a sustained agitation against dowry and dowry-related crimes. Among the reasons for this is that Delhi seems to have the highest number of murders of women for dowry. In 1979 a Delhi-based feminist group, Stri Sangharsh, made the following analysis of dowry:

As Engels pointed out in his classic work, property relations within the family were mediated through the development of private property, and ques-

Anti-dowry demonstration, Delhi, 1980

tions of inheritance became paramount. Engels used this to differentiate between middle-class and working-class families, saying that as working-class families did not own private property, inheritance was not important and thus the material basis for women's oppression did not exist in working-class families. In doing this he not only wrongly identified women's oppression by missing the sexual division of labour, the need for reproductive control, the patriarchy, and the existence of female labour power as property under capitalism, but also conflated the question of private property with that of inheritance. While the question of inheritance remains an insight into women's oppression, it is not the sole relationship of private property to this oppression. The example of dowry in India is a clear one of relationship with private property in which this becomes a bridegroom price and is added to the immediate, consumable family capital, used either to further business ventures, to educate younger sons, to buy a promotion, or to furnish a daughter's dowry. In many cases it does

not remain within the immediate family, but becomes someone else's private property.[5]

Further, they suggested that in the present situation the bridegroom husband became a conduit for the transfer of liquid capital, noting that in this case the sale of the bridegroom did not confer right of ownership on the buyer; on the contrary, the transaction was closer to the payment of blood money. In an exhibition on dowry murder they showed that such murders were committed by middle class entrepreneurial families, who killed so that their sons could remarry and amass more wealth.

Though the Mahila Dakshata Samiti was the first women's organization in Delhi's contemporary feminist movement to take up the issue of dowry and dowry harassment, it was Stri Sangharsh whose campaign made dowry murder a household term. The Mahila Dakshata Samiti had organized a demonstration in Delhi and also published a booklet on the issue. On June 1, 1979 Stri Sangharsh organized a demonstration against the death of Tarvinder Kaur, a young woman who lived in Delhi,

A member of the audience telling
her story, Delhi, 1980

Parents of dowry victims join women's organizations in demonstrating
against the increasing numbers of dowry deaths in the capital, 1981.

saying that her death was murder and that she was killed because her parents could not fulfil the ever-increasing demands of her in-laws. Impetus for this demonstration came, in fact, from the Indraprastha College Women's Committee, formed in 1978, who told Stri Sangharsh of the murder and suggested that they demonstrate. The Indraprastha College Committee, and the Progressive Students' Organisation all marched under the Stri Sangharsh banner, adding both numbers and militancy. The demonstration was widely reported by the national press and in the next few weeks there was a spate of demonstrations against dowry deaths, one of the biggest ones being organised by the Nari Raksha Samiti, on June 12, through the alleys of old Delhi. Each one hit the headlines.

Until this time women's deaths-by-fire had been put down as suicide, and even these suicides were rarely seen as being due to dowry-harassment. No-one (including the police) had ever bothered to investigate them, or even categorize them. And mostly they had been passed off as 'private' affairs which took place within the family and which were no concern of the state. Within weeks, however, feminists reversed the indifference of decades,

linking death-by-fire with dowry harassment, showing that many official 'suicides' were in fact murders. In some cases, victims of dowry murder had often lived long enough to indict their husbands and in-laws of murder (in their dying declarations), but the obligatory police follow-up had been so delayed and so cursory as to yield little or no evidence; such cases were then written off as suicide and the whole matter forgotten.

However, when feminists raised their voices against this situation, insisting that dying declarations be treated as evidence, that police procedures be tightened up, and these murderers be confronted by society, some people did listen, and some joined in the protests as well. The first Stri Sangharsh demonstration had trebled by the time it reached Tarvinder Kaur's in-law's house: not only did neighbours join in with their children, but so did sweepers, domestic workers, and passers by.

On the 30th of June residents of Malviya Nagar demonstrated against the murder of Kanchan Chopra, another young woman, the previous night. Kanchan had visited her parents on the 29th morning and had said then that she was afraid because her in-laws were demanding more dowry and threatening to kill her if it was not forthcoming. Her brother went that afternoon to the Malviya Nagar Police Station to lodge a complaint against her in-laws for dowry harassment, but the police refused' to intervene in what they said was a 'family quarrel', and did not register the complaint. That night she died. And the next day the residents of Malviya Nagar, along with Kanchan's distraught family, surrounded the police station, demanding that they file a charge of murder against her in-laws. When reports of this incident appeared, feminists were encouraged to find that people had been disturbed enough by this issue to take action. This lent momentum to the campaign and very soon after, another group, the Nari Raksha Samiti, demonstrated outside the house of a young man called Narang, whose family had stepped up their demands for dowry on the eve of his marriage to Premlata. Two days before the scheduled wedding, Premlata's family broke off her engagement because of increased dowry demands. They contacted the Nari Raksha Samiti and asked them to stage a demonstration outside the Narang's house, as public denunciation.[6] This too was remarkable, for normally the scandal accruing from such publicity adheres longer to the girl than to the man, whose sins are in any case blamed on his family, and soon

forgotten. That Premlata and her family were willing to brave this publicity in order to humiliate the Narangs for their avarice roused admiration among women's groups.

After some months of campaigning however, several groups began to feel the need for a more direct method of communication with people when raising the issue of dowry. Discussions on this gave rise to the idea of having a street play and some months later Stri Sangharsh gave the first performance of its street play, *Om Swaha,* an attack on dowry and dowry murder, based on the lives of two women.

The play proved enormously popular and soon people from all over began to ask the group to visit their locality and perform the play there. For many middle class women who were in the play, this was a first attempt at activist work.

One year after the agitation began, governments started to legislate against dowry murders. In fact in 1978 Charan Singh, then prime minister, had said that measures to stop the 'maltreatment of women for dowry' would be introduced in the next parliamentary session. He made this assurance to a delegation of the Mahila Dakshata Samiti. The Samiti also met the Inspector

Protesting the commercialization of marriage, Delhi, 1980

Taking a break during the Dahej Virodhi Chetna
Manch demonstration, Delhi, 1982

for the anti-dowry cells to begin functioning, and at
present they deal mainly with complaints of dowry de-
mand/harassment and not with dowry murders. In practice the anti-dowry cells more often perform the
function of marriage counselling bureaus. Given the way
most women are treated in India when they lack the
'protection of a man' (be they single, divorced, deserted,
or widowed), it is hardly surprising that so many women
choose to suffer at the hands of their families rather than
of all society. The Mahila Dakshata Samiti, for example,
found that the first question confronting them when
they spoke to women who were being harassed for more
dowry was: if we encourage her to leave her family, where
will she live? For if she were to return to her parents'
house she would 'endanger' the chance of her (inevitable) younger sister's suitable marriage (presumably because other eligible boys' parents would then fear that
the girl's would not fulfil their dowry demands) and no
landlord willingly rents to a single woman, for fear of her
being a prostitute—or thought to be one so, as most
cases of dowry harassment seemed to occur in joint
households, the Mahila Dakshata Samiti and other
women's organizations found themselves suggesting
that the 'young couple' move out and live by themselves.

Many feminists have chafed at having thus to aid in
the nuclearisation of the family instead of filing complaints of assault against the people who burned brides
for dowry, but they have had few alternatives. Ironically
enough, it is easier to prove dowry assault than dowry
murder for in death-by-fire there is almost always no
evidence to show that it is murder and not suicide or
accident. 'Her sari pallav caught fire,' 'there was a stove
accident in—' The two main kinds of evidence in such
cases are a) dying declarations made by the victims when
they survive long enough to be rushed to hospital; b)
circumstantial evidence: letters, neighbours' testimo-
nies and so on. Dying declarations have frequently been
completely ignored by the police, as in the Tarvinder

General of Police (Delhi), who agreed to set up a standing committee consisting of the Superintendent of Police and a Deputy Superintendent, who would deal with
cases of dowry harassment. However it took many years

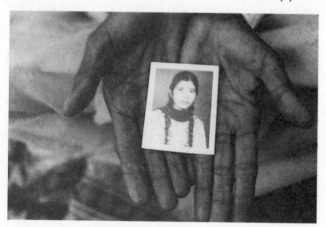

A mother shows a picture of her dead
daughter, date not known

'Burned her', slogan painted on wall of alleged
dowry murderer's house, date not known

Another scene from 'Om Swaha'

Kaur case, where she declared her mother-in-law and sister-in-law had together set fire to her but the police dismissed this declaration and registered a case of suicide. When the police have registered a case of murder against sundry in-laws and husbands on the grounds of a dying declaration, the case has most often been dismissed for insufficient evidence. That the victim's testimony cannot be regarded as sufficient evidence to convict the accused of murder is only fair; what is shocking is that in most cases dying declarations are not treated as sufficient reason for a thorough investigation by the police. The most frequently cited reason for this cavalier attitude of the police is that they were bribed by the murderers to delay investigation or else to ignore evidence. In most cases the victim's parents would arrive too late to offer counter-bribes for the scene for suicide/accident would have already been set. But one is also constrained to ask: would the police recognize evidence when they saw it, in cases of death-by-fire? How many methods of collecting circumstantial evidence do they use? What practice do the police have in building detailed circumstantial cases against dowry murderers—

and what resources do they have to do so? Why haven't they got more investigators, more doctors, more machinery, to build up an adequate case? Why haven't they asked for them?

Members of the police force also seem to believe that this is a matter that is outside their purview. The policemen escorting a demonstration against a dowry-murder asked: 'What is this demonstration about?' When told it was to demand police action against a man thought to have murdered his wife for dowry, one policeman said that had he been in our place he would have burnt the accused's shop and his house. He recounted a similar murder in his locality where the community had burnt down the suspected murderer's house. Feminists have been variously advised by policemen and politicians to use 'social pressure' against dowry murderers rather than to take recourse in the law. They have, however, done both. Anti-dowry demonstrations have always been outside the homes or workplaces of dowry-demanders or accused dowry murderers as well as at police stations; the names of both the victims and the accused have always appeared in slogans; neighbourhood groups have been formed to boycott dowry harassers; accused husbands of dowry victims have had their faces blackened (this has happened only once or twice); public meetings have been arranged at which people have pledged neither to give nor to take dowry, and so on. In June 1982 two things happened which showed new developments in the movement against dowry murders: first, on the 3rd of June, the residents of a South Delhi locality got together to protest against the death-by-fire of Bharati Narula, who lived with her in-laws in the same area. Under the auspices of the local Welfare Association, Karmika (a feminist group based in Gulmohar Park), and the Women's Club, volunteers went from house to house mobilizing for a public meeting on June 8th, at which it was decided to a) ostracise Bharati Narula's husband and in-laws; b) send a memorandum to the Prime Minister demanding action in the case; c) provide a list of people willing to help in cases of dowry harassment or murder; d) to have sundry meetings in June in Gulmohar Park to publicise the anti-dowry movement by performing plays and inviting lawyers and policemen to discuss the problem.

Under this kind of pressure the Narulas were arrested and charged with murder, but were released on bail in October. Subsequently, the chief witness against them withdrew her statement.[7]

Though the residents of other areas had some years earlier expressed their disapproval of dowry murder in a more vehement fashion by demonstrating against it, the decision to ostracise this family showed a determination to express disapproval in a more personal and more sustained way. The idea of a list of people to contact in need and to have meetings about dowry problems showed an inclination for self-education and self-help which had so far been absent in local areas.

Secondly, on the 11th of June women teachers of S.P. Muckerjee College (for women) in Delhi demonstrated against the death-by-fire of one of their colleagues, Shakuntala Arora, on June 5. Shakuntala killed herself because her husband beat her up regularly for not supplementing her dowry sufficiently. The teachers demonstrated outside police commissioner Bajarang Lal's office, demanding that a case of abetment to suicide be registered against Shakuntala's husband, Subhash Arora, a teacher in Hansraj College. Though Bajarang Lal promised swift action, no investigation was conducted into Shakuntala's death. In mid-July the District commissioner of Police, West Delhi, met the teachers of Muckerjee College and told them no case could be registered against Subhash Arora unless he had been seen handing Shakuntala a tin of kerosene and a matchbox. So on July 17 the teachers decided to 'join hands to seek social boycott of Mr Subhash Arora and to curb the vice of dowry before it assumes uncontrollable proportions.' Their first step was to demonstrate outside his house in Multan Nagar. They were joined by many residents of Multan Nagar, several of whom had seen Arora beating his wife. After this, on July 24, they went to Hansraj College to ask teachers there to press for an investigation of the case, and suggested that a joint action committee be formed of Hansraj College teachers. But Hansraj College teachers were reluctant to take any action, and eventually nothing happened.[8]

Thus a protest began in the victim's workplace and moved to the neighbourhood she lived in. This may not have been the first workplace protest at the wrongs done to a woman/colleague domestically (that is, in the private family sphere), but it was sufficiently unusual to show another new direction in the movement against dowry deaths. Moreover, like the Gulmohar Park agitation, it showed more sustained effort: attempts to extend the protest, both into the area where she lived and into her husband's workplace. Finally, it was also interesting as a protest against abetment to suicide, not murder. As this incident shows, the evidence required to prove abetment is virtually impossible to collect. This is why feminists demanded that proof that a woman killed herself because of dowry harassment should be considered adequate evidence for a charge of abetment. Naturally this proof would consist of neighbours' and

Mother of a dowry victim calling for police action, Delhi, date not known

'Om Swaha', Delhi 1980

visitors' statments as well as those of the victim herself (letters,etc.).

The law has been a considerable disappointment to feminists. The single judgment which caused women to rejoice was soon reversed, and when they expressed disapprobation at this decision, contempt of court was slapped upon them. Early in November 1983, Justice R.N. Aggarwal of the Delhi High Court reversed the judgement of S.M. Aggarwal in the Session Court, on the death of Sudha Goel. Justice S.M. Aggarwal had found those accused guilty of murder, but Justice R.N. Aggarwal let them off because he said the evidence was inadequate. Women's organizations protested against the acquittal on November 7th, in the High Court compound. A contempt of court petition was filed against three of these organizations, the Janwadi Mahila Samiti, Karmika, and the Mahila Dakshata Samiti, although a larger number had been involved. When asked why only three had been indicted, the petitioners said it was because they only recognized those three, which seems unlikely since the National Federation of Indian Women is an old established and fairly well known organization, and Saheli had been in the news recently. Justices Sachar and Sen, who heard the petition, seemed sympathetic to the women, for they acquitted Brinda Karath and Subhadra Butalia of the Janwadi Samiti and Karmika respectively. Suman Krishan Kant of the Mahila Dakshata Samiti was held guilty because her defence made various personal digs at the judges.[9]

However legal attitudes to dowry deaths have been changing since then. In December 1983 the Criminal Law (second amendment) Act was passed. It introduced section 498-A to the Indian Penal Code. Under this, cruelty to a wife was made a cognisable, non-bailable offence, punishable by upto three years' imprisonment and a fine. Cruelty was redefined to include mental as well as physical harassment. Secondly, Section 113-A of the Evidence Act was amended so that the court could draw an inference of abetment to suicide. Technically this is called shifting the burden of proof, and thus it lessens the burden upon the complainant. Both these changes in the law relating to suicide were exactly what feminists wanted. Finally, the Act amended Section 174 of the Criminal Procedure Code, making a post mortem examination compulsory on the body of a woman who died within seven years of marriage. Since most dowry deaths occur in the early years of marriage, this too was a welcome amendment. In fact in November 1980, the

'Om Swaha', Delhi, 1980

central government had ordered compulsory investigation and post-mortem in cases of married women dying under unnatural circumstances during the first five years of marriage. And in September 1980 the Haryana Government had ordered the police to register unnatural deaths of married women under Section 302 of the Indian Penal Code, that is, as murder. Cases of suspected abetment to suicide (however indirect) were to be registered under Section 306 of the Indian Penal Code (forced to commit suicide).

In 1985, the Supreme Court reversed the High Court acquittal of the accused in the Sudha Goel case, sentencing her mother-in-law and husband to life-imprisonment, and letting her brother-in-law off for lack of evidence. And in the Hardeep Kaur (Hardeep was a friend of Tarvinder Kaur's who was killed soon after Tarvinder was) case, her mother-in-law was judged guilty by the High Court. In Rajasthan a two judge bench sentenced the two convicted of dowry murder to hanging, again as an 'exemplary punishment'. The sentence, however, is likely to be reversed. Finally, in a case of dowry harassment in Delhi, the magistrate refused bail to the accused, directing the woman to collect those items she brought as dowry.

What is fascinating about the movement against dowry and dowry violence is how it has woven together several different kinds of attitudes towards women in India: from feminist to anti-patriarchal to anti-capitalist to utopian patriarchalism. The latter is held largely by men who feel it is their duty as good patriarchs to protect and care for their wives; it is not strong in the women's movement against dowry and dowry-deaths. Many women active in this movement relate the incidence of dowry murder or suicide to the way capitalism is developing in India, as described by the Stri Sangharsh analysis quoted earlier. On the other hand, most of them see this as an anti-patriarchal issue rather than a feminist one: while protests are mounted against the subordination of young women—and sometimes young men—few would stress the contractual nature of marriage itself or publicly say that they themselves dislike marriage for this reason. This is due more to the kind of gap feminists feel between their aspirations and most women's experience in India; a gap which is also reflected in the difference between the language they use and the language used by politicians, social reformers, etc. In the next section, which is a chronology of the rape agitation, we see this difference most clearly.

NOTES

1. Alfie, in *In Search of Answers*, op. cit., pp. 215–16.
2. Flavia, *My Story... Our Story, of Re-building Broken Lives,* Women's Centre, Bombay, November 84, pp. 11, 12, 18.
3. Rohini, Sujata S.V. and Neelam C, *My Life is one Long Struggle*, Pratishabd, Madras, p. 72. The speaker is the widow of a railway worker.
4. *In Search of Answers,* op cit., 'Letters Written at Death's Door', pp 204–5. It is interesting that of the eleven pieces in the section of the book entitled 'Family Violence,' six are on dowry torture and murder.
5. Stree Sangharsh, 'Draft Manifesto.'
6. Subhadra Butalia, 'The agitation against dowry', in *How*, March 83, Delhi.
7. Deepthi, 'Women Lecturers Mobilise Against Dowry Deaths' *Times of India.*
8. *In Search of Answers*, op. cit. P. 213
9. Information from Subhadra Butalia.

8. The Agitation Against Rape

**A state-wise break-up of rape cases
reported from 1986 to 1988, according to the Home Ministry**

STATES/UNION TERRITORIES	RAPE 1986	1987	1988	MOLESTATION 1986	1987	1988
Andhra Pradesh	301	335	455	989	853	1,168
Arunachal Pradesh	9	11	16	6	9	12
Assam	354	379	278	139	101	81
Bihar	563	580	623	411	244	182
Goa	–	12	20	–	10	9
Gujarat	144	159	130	637	663	600
Harayana	144	14	90	265	41	153
Himachal Pradesh	52	34	45	117	122	134
Jammu & Kashmir	187	171	211	899	850	956
Karnataka	137	164	184	557	807	843
Kerala	133	188	197	494	488	594
Madhya Pradesh	1,526	1,695	NA	4,698	4,871	NA
Maharashtra	800	781	830	2,724	2,417	2,646
Manipur	10	9	9	27	21	24
Meghalaya	19	19	10	10	10	18
Mizoram	46	62	56	29	NA	30
Nagaland	8	11	9	Nil	Nil	Nil
Orissa	164	184	180	583	524	554
Punjab	49	47	49	37	37	21
Rajasthan	598	604	578	939	964	1,072
Sikkim	5	8	6	6	12	14
Tamil Nadu	231	231	252	750	726	669
Tripura	38	43	43	26	26	123
Uttar Pradesh	1,192	1,291	1,437	1,591	1,795	1,948
West Bengal	503	491	529	304	346	276
Andaman & Nicobar Islands	2	6	4	22	23	20
Chandigarh	4	4	4	1	5	8
Dadra & Nagar Haveli	Nil	2	3	5	4	6
Delhi	89	103	111	112	95	121
Goa, Daman & Diu	8	NA	3	8	NA	Nil
Lakshadweep	Nil	Nil	Nil	Nil	Nil	Nil
Pondicherry	5	7	5	7	7	7
Total	7,317	7,645	6,367	16,393	16,060	12,289

- Figures are based on monthly crime statistics and are to be treated as provisonal.
- NA stands for Not Available.
- Figures of Harayana for 1987 are upto February, 1987 only.
- Separate figures for eve-teasing are not available. Cases of eve-teasing are included in the cases of molestation in Bihar.
- Figures of molestation and eve-teasing are excluding the months from April 1987 to June 1987 in Bihar.

Source: Bureau of Police Research Delhi. Taken from *The Illustrated Weekly of India*, Bombay, 1990.

Rape is one of the most common and frequent of crimes against women in India, as can be seen by the enormous number of forms in which it is committed, and, indeed, in which it is classified. There is, for example, the category of 'landlord rape', exercising the *droit du seigneur* (right by rule of the lord) to rape 'his' women wage slaves, or the wives of his male wage slaves. There is the category of 'rape by those in authority', comprising the exercise of power within the workplace to rape women employees or juniors. There is the category of 'caste rape', in which caste hierarchy is exercised to rape lower-caste or outcaste women (such as 'tribals'). Similarly, there are also the categories of class rape, police rape, and army rape. There are also forms of rape which are yet to be fully recognized within our law, such as marital rape, rape within the family, rape of minors, rape of prostitutes, etc.

Rape is also one of the most under-reported of crimes in India. According to figures provided by the Bureau of Police Research and Development (New Delhi), in 1972 there were 2,562 cases of rape reported from all over India; in 1975 there were 3,283, and in 1978, 3,899. By the late 1980s, these figures had more than doubled, to 7,317 in 1986, and 7,645 in 1987 (see box). Many feminists feel that this stupendous rise in numbers does not actually reflect the rate of increase in rape per se, but reveals that social attitudes towards rape are changing, so that more women now have the courage to report it.[1]

The issue of rape has been one that most contemporary feminist movements internationally have focussed on, firstly because sexual assault is one of the ugliest and most brutal expressions of masculine violence towards women, secondly because rape and the historical 'discourse' around it reveal a great deal about the social relations of reproduction, and thirdly because of what it shows about the way in which the woman's body is seen as representing the community. In India, it is the latter reason which has been most dominant in the taking up of campaigns against rape. In pre-Independence India, as we have seen, the nationalist-feminist movement raised the issue largely to point to 'excesses' committed by the British state as foreigner-colonizer. In post-Independence India, the left and far left raised the issue both to point to 'excesses' committed by the Indian state, and by the 'ruling class'. The two major categories of rape which were singled out were those of police rape (here defined as including the army and security forces), and the *droit du seigneur*. Theoretically, this was because both could be treated holistically as part and parcel of the exploitation of the 'weaker sections of society', and thus consciousness of women's oppression could be created amongst the men, and a consciousness of class oppression could be stimulated amongst women. In practice, however, the focus on such issues often worked in a different way, as the agitation against rape has shown.

In effect, this agitation began largely with campaigns against police rape. Broadly, there are two kinds of police rape in this country: one, incidents of mass rape which are acts against a community or class which is engaged in a struggle with those who hold power over it, the other, the rape of individual women, who generally belong to relatively powerless or marginal groups and communities. This latter is not so much an act of reprisal against a community as an exercise of the rights which are seen as automatically accruing to the police, that is, it is a kind of *droit du seigneur*, in which the police are themselves *seigneurs*.

The scale and frequency of police rape are quite startling in India: police records themselves show that the number of rapes by 'government servants' in rural and tribal areas exceeds one a day.[2] This figure vastly understates the actual number of such rapes, for it does not cover incidents of mass rape by the police, and even in the case of individual or gang rape it cannot cover unreported incidents, of which there are likely to be at least as many as reported incidents.

When the new feminist groups were formed in the late seventies, they were already familiar with the categories of police and landlord rape, for both, especially the former, had been protested against by the Maoist movement. Moreover, the issue of police rape achieved new significance in 1978, just as feminist groups were in the process of formation, through an incident in Hyderabad, where a woman called Rameeza Bee was raped by several policemen, and her rickshaw-puller husband murdered because he protested at his wife's gang rape. Following this rape and murder, twenty-two thousand Hyderabadis went to the police station, laid the rickshaw puller's dead body in the station verandah, set up road blocks, cut the telephone wires, stoned the building and set fire to some bicycles in the compound. Two platoons of armed police were called in to quell the crowd's fury. Politicians entered the fray and the Chief Minister was *gheraoed* the next day by members of the opposition. In the course of the gherao the police fired on the crowd, further exacerbating the situation. The next day a Hyderabad *bandh* (closure of all services) was called to protest the firing, curfew was declared in sixteen areas, and nine people were killed and eighty injured by police firing in Hyderabad and Secunderabad. The agitation continued even when the Army was called in, and could only be repressed after President's rule was declared, and a commission of enquiry into the rape of Rameeza Bee and the murder of her husband was appointed.[3]

To many feminists the Hyderabad agitation was a sign of great hope, showing that police rape could become a 'mass issue', though it was not quite clear on which terms, for newspaper reports gave the impression that while the agitation was sparked off by an incident of rape and murder, this was sidelined as the agitation grew.

When, despite the report of the commission of enquiry which established the policemen's guilt, they were acquitted by the Session Court, the only people to protest were feminist groups: the Stri Shakti Sanghathana in Hyderabad, Vimochana and the Women Lawyer's Association in Bangalore, demonstrated against the judgment and went on appeal against it to the High Court and then the Supreme Court. The case is still pending.

Given the far left affiliations of most of the feminist groups of the late seventies, it is not surprising that police rape was one of the first issues to be taken up by them. Not only could they synthesize class and gender perspectives through it, it was somehow a 'safe' issue.

In 1979 there were women's demonstrations against incidents of police and landlord/employer rape in Sangamner, Patiala and Malur village and Karnataka, while in Guwahati there were huge rallies protesting the rape of women by the army in Kamrup. As part of the Jharkhand movement, a move to campaign against mass rape was started in the Santhal Parganas, and the Delhi feminist group, Stri Sangarsh, was asked to do a report on

Street play on domestic violence, Delhi 1987

incidents which had occurred there in mid-1979 (see appendix). Campaigns against these incidents, however, remained isolated from each other until 1980, when an open letter by four senior lawyers against a judgement in a case of police rape in Maharashtra sparked off a campaign by feminist groups. Known as the Mathura rape case, the incident had occurred several years earlier, when a seventeen or eighteen year old girl, Mathura, was taken by local policemen to the police station and raped there.

Under pressure from her family and the villagers, a case was registered against the policemen, who were acquitted at the Sessions Court, convicted on appeal at the High Court, and later acquitted by the Supreme Court. The defence argument for the policemen was that Mathura had a boyfriend and was thus a loose woman who could not by definition, be raped. The open

letter was in protest at the Supreme Court's acceptance of this argument.

Coming upon this letter in February, 1980, the Bombay feminist group, Forum Against Rape (which now calls itself the Forum Against Oppression of Women—FAOW), decided to campaign for the reopening of the case, and wrote to feminist groups all over the country to propose that demonstrations be held on International Women's Day

Demonstration outside Police Headquarters demanding arrest of police official Azad Singh Bhardwaj, for alleged involvement in incidents of rape and abduction, Delhi, 1982

(March 8), to demand a retrial. In effect, this was the first time that feminist groups came together across the country to co-ordinate a campaign. While preparations were under way for the March 8 demonstrations feminist groups tried to meet Mathura to find out what her own views on the matter were. Two women from the Bombay FAR then went to meet her and found that though she did not object to the campaign, she was not particularly hopeful of it either. Though this was a relief, many were shamed by the realization that they had gone so far into a campaign without even wondering what one of its main subjects felt. This raised the question of representation in a different—and for many, more painful—way: who were we to protest until we had met the woman who was raped and found out whether she wanted a protest or not? Supposing the protest brought upon her, again, the stigma of being a 'dishonoured' woman?

When this question arose it led to another: supposing Mathura had been reluctant to have the issue raised again, would feminists have called off the campaign, even if it had not already been under way, as it was? (For in several cities there was a build up to the demonstrations, generally consisting of a week-long series of activities, exhibitions, plays, street corner meetings, area mobilization, etc.) Opinion was sharply divided on this question: many felt that the decisions of the courts were matters of public significance and could not simply be ignored because of the wishes of the victim which had to be respected, even if she was wrong, and even if the failure to protest against legal decisions in her case meant that such decisions would be perpetuated.

It was with a sigh of relief, therefore, that feminist groups shelved the issue and returned to their campaign. Groups in seven cities had responded to the FAR letter and on March 8 there were women's demonstrations in Bombay, Delhi, Nagpur, Pune, Ahmedabad, Bangalore and Hyderabad, demanding a retrial of the Mathura case, the implementation of relevant sections of the Indian Penal Code (IPC), and changes in the law against rape. In both Bombay and Delhi joint action committees of feminist groups and socialist and communist party fronts, mainly student, were formed to coordinate the campaign. Thus the campaign against rape marked a new stage in the development of feminism in India; the networks which had begun to form in 1978 were now being consolidated and expanded, and used to co-ordinate action; at the same time, through joint action, feminism began to be drawn into mainstream political activism.

Coordinated action, however, was not to last long. There were several reasons for its breakdown between the cities. First of all, the pressures of developing a campaign with limited resources were such that attempting to maintain co-ordination between far-flung areas, given the ever-present difficulties of efficient or speedy communication, was impossible. Some degree of contact was maintained, through the exchange of pamphlets, posters etc., as well as the occasional visit. Co-ordination, however, was not really possible to any significant extent.

Within cities too, joint action was not easily maintained. Given the differences in attitude and analysis of women's oppression, as well as general ideological

'From the darkness of the womb to the silence of the grave,' a poster made by
Stri Sangharsh for International Women's Day, Delhi 1982

differences on such questions as the importance of organizational identity, it was inevitable that joint action could only be maintained at a formal level, with groups and organizations also being left to act independently. But the 1980 campaign was the first attempt at joint action within the contemporary feminist movement, and this kind of more liberal position could not be adopted then. I can still remember how annoyed many of us in Delhi felt when, on March 17, the NFIW, which was a member of the Joint Action Committee Against Rape and Sexual Harassment in Delhi, held a *dharna* (sit-down protest) outside the Supreme Court to demand a review of the Mathura case, without even informing the Joint Action Committee of their plan. At the same time, the AIWC, the Bombay FAR, and the NFIW all separately filed petitions in the Supreme Court asking for a review, and a few days later, on March 21, the Maharashtra Government followed suit.

Meanwhile, protests against incidents of police rape began to be reported from all over the country: only some of which were organized by feminists. In April, women students in Patna protested against the rape of a rickshaw puller's wife, Bachiya; and in the same month but on the other side of the country, in Vijayanagar, in Rajasthan, villagers surrounded the police station and stoned it, following the 'molestation' of a widow by the Station House Officer. The police retaliated by lathicharging the irate villagers, and the situation was 'brought under control' after senior police officials rushed down to the village and announced that the SHO (Station House Officer) had been suspended pending an inquiry. In May angry mobs attacked the Bankura police station and set fire to some houses and shops in protest against the 'molestation' of a girl: the mob was teargassed, sixteen were arrested and indefinite curfew declared. And in June, the subdivisional magistrate of Dhunda town, in Uttarkashi, was gheraoed after he attempted to rape a twenty year old woman in the district

Demonstration against
violence against women, Patna 1988

hospital. The gherao was only lifted when the commissioner of Garhwal ordered the transfer of the SDM (Sub-Divisional Magistrate), Kulbe.[4]

It seems unlikely that these protests were stimulated by the feminist campaign against police rape, for, in contrast to the campaign against dowry-deaths, they did not arise in the cities in which the feminists were active. What did happen, however, was that the protests got more news coverage than they would otherwise have done, for the feminist campaign had been received with considerable enthusiasm by the press, and as a result the problem of police rape was acknowledged in a new way. The kind of press coverage that was now given to incidents of police rape and protests against them, created the impression that the issue was one which aroused anger all over the country, and was therefore of political significance. From now on the national political parties entered the fray.

When in June policemen arrested a woman called Maya Tyagi in Baghpat (Haryana), stripped her naked, raped her and paraded her through the streets, the incident aroused such furore from women's organisations and political parties that the Union Home Minister, Zail Singh, went down there with ten women MPs, and ordered a judicial inquiry into the incident. While they were in Baghpat, the Lok Dal staged a 'noisy demonstration' against the incident. Referring to it on the same day, Khan Abdul Ghaffar Khan, the 'Frontier Gandhi', said that only 'capital punishment would act as a deterrent' to crimes against women. Roughly a week later, the Lok Sabha debated the 'large-scale increase in the incidents of rape and atrocities against women', with several MPs, and others using the issue to demand the resignation of the Home Minister and suggesting that the death penalty be introduced. Perhaps the only sensible suggestion to be made came from Jagjivan Ram, who said that the law against rape should be changed so that the onus of proof would be on the accused and not on the woman, as the current regulation was borrowed from British jurisprudence and 'did not suit the prevailing situation in the country.'

The day after the debate a scheduled CPI meeting in Baghpat, to protest against the incident, was banned, but when, a few days later, nine hundred Lok Dal volunteers assembled in Baghpat to court arrest they found, to their chagrin, that prohibitory orders had been lifted. The next day thirty organizations, mainly party-based, including the All India Congress Committee, sat in a dharna to protest the Baghpat rape. The dharna was attended by women from Baghpat, Baraut, Chaprauli, and surrounding areas, including some from Maya Tyagi's village. After the dharna there was a rally, and then they marched to the Prime Minister's house, where twenty-three were arrested for violating prohibitory orders.[5]

Street play, Section 304, (on rape) being enacted by Stri Sangharsh members, Delhi, 1981

Around the same time another incident of rape in Haryana was made prominent by a local protest: five thousand residents of Dahwali demonstrated against the rape and alleged murder of Shiela Devi, the wife of an orderly serving the District Magistrate, who was raped by a police constable in the police station. Twenty-two were injured when the police opened fire upon the demonstrators. This time the Haryana Government responded fairly promptly, transferring the Dabwali police force to the police lines in Sirsa, ordering a judicial inquiry into the firing, and registering cases against the constable for rape, the Dabwali police force for attempted murder, and against the demonstrators for alleged unlawful assembly, illegal confinement, illegal use of firearms and attempted murder. Furious at the incidents in Dabwali, Sirsa town went on a one-day *hartal* (strike), all the shops were closed, and when the Chief Minister Bhajan Lal, went through Sirsa on his way to Dabwali his car was stoned. There were again noisy scenes in the Lok Sabha, with Congress members trying to shout the opposition down when they raised the issue, and the opposition members shouting each other down while trying to prove their rage over Dabwali. The Bharatiya Janata Party (BJP), which had earlier demanded the resignation of the Home Minister, now demanded the resignation of the Haryana Government for failing to protect the 'lives, property and honour' of the residents of Dabwali. And their Delhi unit launched a one week campaign against the 'increasing number of dacoities, robberies, and attacks on women in the city.'[6]

A final touch was added by the comic politician Raj Narain, who resigned from leadership of the Janata (S) on the grounds that he was going to launch a 'struggle to protect the dignity and honour of women' by going on an indefinite fast from the 3rd of August, unless the Government took appropriate action in Haryana. On the morning of the 3rd a letter from the Prime Minister to Raj Narain appeared in the press, in which she rebuked him for taking 'political advantage of incidents of the type of which had happened in Baghpat'. Undeterred, Raj Narain embarked on his fast after a *havan* (fire ritual) was performed, as well as a medical examination. At a little over five foot in height, his weight was then 82.5 kg: after one day of fasting he lost four kilogrammes![7]

Thus, within a couple of months, the campaign, against police rape had not only been joined by the centre-right national parties, but taken over by them; and the feminist discussion of rape as an expression of class and gender-based power was shouldered aside by the patriarchal view of rape as a violation of honour, accompanied by demands for the 'protection' of women. Working with the entrenched and hierarchical organizations of the orthodox left and finding their own voices increasingly drowned by the cacophony of competing centre and right parties, feminists discovered the ironic process whereby an agitation gained numerical strength by being joined by political blocs, but at the same time found itself constrained morally, and strategically—by them.

over, it added the categories of mass and gang rape to that of individual rape. The Bill further laid down that for cases of custodial rape there was to be a mandatory punishment of ten years imprisonment, trials would be *in camera*, and the onus of proof would be shifted onto the accused.

The Bill thus codified distinctions between different categories of rape in a fairly radical way, though it refused to include familial rape in custodial rape. If anything, it leaned the other way, for it reiterated a

An activist from Sabla Sangh, Delhi, explains an anti-violence poster, 1982

Soon after Raj Narain's hunger strike, the government introduced a Bill to amend the existing law on rape. The Bill had been on the anvil for several months before this, as the government had accepted the feminists' demand for a change in the anti-rape law. The Law Commission had been instructed to draw up a Bill, which they took several months to do, but when it was finally produced, the Bill was based largely on the suggestions that feminist groups had made to the Commission. Because the campaign had focussed on police rape, the major clauses of the Bill were devoted to defining the category of custodial rape, and treating it as a more heinous crime than other forms of rape. The category itself was now fairly widely defined, as consisting of state functionaries, employers, immediate superiors: more-

distinction made in pre-Independence India, between the age of consent for married and unmarried girls, saying that for the former intercourse below the age of sixteen would be regarded as statutory rape, while for the latter the age limit would be fifteen years.

Interestingly, none of these distinctions was challenged in the controversy following the Bill, though feminists did protest, in a rather half-hearted way, against the distinction between married and unmarried girls. To a slightly greater extent there was also controversy over the clause saying that trials would be *in camera*, with civil libertarians, the far left, and some feminists, arguing that this would make any public monitoring of rape trials impossible, and was therefore dangerous; while those who were for *in camera* trials argued that this

A discussion on violence against women on March 8, 1981 near Delhi

would at least protect the women from the harassment and humiliation which was contingent on the trials being open.

The clause over which controversy raged, however, was the Burden of Proof clause, which said that if the woman could prove intercourse with the accused, at the time and place she alleged, and if it had been forced upon her, then the accused would be presumed guilty until he could prove himself otherwise. Immediately there arose the cry that this violated the legal principle that a man was innocent until proved guilty, and the papers were full of articles vehemently protesting the clause, some of which exclaimed that this paved the way for every revengeful woman to frame innocent men.

A similar controversy over the clause arose amongst feminists as well, though in a somewhat different way. The 1980 socialist-feminist conference in Bombay, a few months after the Bill had been produced, set aside a special session for discussion of the Bill and recommendations on it, at which debate centered mainly on this clause. Various groups, including the Lawyers' Collective and Stri Sangarsh, had proposed that the scope of the Burden of Proof clause be extended to cover all cases of rape, not custodial rape alone, as the kind of evidence required by the courts, under the existing law, made convictions virtually impossible, for in most cases rape was considered proven only when physical signs of forcible entry were found on the woman's body. Members of the Stri Shakti Sanghathana, as well as others, argued against this that if the clause were to be extended it would provide opportunity for the state to embroil male activists in false cases of rape, to which some people responded that the state had sufficient powers to frame activists under any laws, if it so wished.

The debate grew increasingly charged, with one side accusing the other of being anti-feminist and belittling the horrors of rape and its aftermath (social disgrace, humiliation in the courts, penury), and the other side accusing the former of being bourgeois idealists, unconcerned with the larger political issues and realities on the ground. After some four or five hours of the debate, a vote was taken, and those who were against the extension of the clause won with a thumping majority. Yet the debate had taken such a hold of the participants at the conference that they voted to re-open it immediately after the vote, for another couple of hours, and then take another vote. When the second vote was taken the anti-extensionists won again, but this time by a very narrow margin, and even after the second vote many wished to re-open the debate, having changed their minds yet again. Time, however, would not permit a reopening.

Interestingly, all the Delhi feminists voted for expansion of the clause, even though there were tremendous rifts between several of the Delhi groups, and they were thus not voting as a bloc. Having been one of the Delhi feminists, I can remember feeling at the time that there was some consolation in this fact, albeit small, for the voting showed that there was a basic consensus in Delhi on what constituted feminism. No other region showed a similar consensus on the question, for different groups from the same region voted differently; and, in fact, many did not vote as groups or organizations at all, for their members were left to make individual decisions. The Bombay Forum Against Rape was one such group: some of its members voted one way, others another, and many abstained.

Soon after the Bill was introduced in parliament, it was referred to a Select Committee of both houses of Parliament which then spent the next couple of years travelling around the country, 'collecting evidence' on various clauses. Eventually, a truncated version of the Bill was passed in 1983, which included the 'Burden of Proof' clause in cases of custodial rape, but left out many others recommended by both the Law Commission and women's groups (see Appendix). The joint action campaign had already begun to fizzle out by the time of the conference, and thus no attempts were made to speed up the passing of the Bill.

In a way, the government had taken the wind out of feminist sails by responding to their demands so promptly. But this was, at most, only one of the reasons why the campaign faded so rapidly. The highly publicized nature of the campaign, the rapidity with which it became a mainstream political issue, even the fact that it began with joint action rather than growing into it—all contributed to the downfall of the feminists. Moreover, the nature of the issue, the kind of social sanction accorded to rape, together with the problem of acquiring medical evidence to prove it in a country where only the big cities are technically equipped to provide such evidence, constituted formidable obstacles. Finally, those very aspects which had led feminists to take up the issue of custodial rape also made it most difficult for their campaign to sustain itself, for they were in no position to struggle successfully against those in power. In a recent incident of mass rape in Bihar, the doctor who examined the women victims said that some of them did appear to have been raped, but there was no way of medically proving who the culprits were. The

Women activists get together to appeal for humanity and solidarity, Delhi 1983

DESCRIPTIONS OF DIFFERENT INCIDENTS OF RAPE FROM THE NATIONAL MEETING ON RAPE, BOMBAY 1990

Case 1: Rural Women's Labour Movement (Tamil Nadu)

A construction worker is forcibly taken into a room and raped. She brought her rape to the notice of the Rural Women's Liberation Movement (RWLM) who took the case before the village panchayat. ("Our strategy is never to go to the police.") The woman asked for, and obtained, compensation in the form of a share of the rapist's property. Asked if she would like him to marry her, she refused.

Generally, however, in the experience of RWLM, the rapist is made to marry his victim, after they have the woman's consent: if she is willing, the group arranges the marriage. Sometimes, she may even be the rapist's second wife. Women feel they cannot live with dignity after a rape; no-one will agree to marry them, they are like social outcastes—and so are open to such marriages. The question arose about how a woman can agree to marrying her rapist. The women replied: She has been made socially unfit, she cannot live in the same village, "so he better marry her and take away some of her shame. We make him sign an undertaking that he will not abuse or mistreat her." In many instances women would otherwise see suicide as the only way out for them. "Even in Tamil films, so deep is the hold of the concept of 'honour' that, at the end of the film, the rapist marries the woman—these are the messages."

Case 2: Elphinstone College Rape, Bombay

At a *dandia raas* programme organised by the College, a student was raped by six fellow students. The girl's father swiftly removed her from college and denied she had been raped—said it was just "misbehaviour". Other students took up the case, protested vociferously and boycotted the exams. It was picked up by the press and given wide coverage. The gang-leader was expelled from college (although he still visits the place) as were three others, but they got admission elsewhere. Women's groups wanted very much to take up the case, but the girl's family ensured that she was silenced and not traceable.

campaign of 1980 had so far receded that one of the points made during it, that semen analysis could be used as a method of identifying the rapist, had been completely forgotten. And Maya Tyagi's rapists were only convicted by the sessions court in early 1988, almost eight years after agitating organizations had made her a household name; moreover as only the first stage of the legal process has now been completed, there is no knowing whether or not the convictions will stand.

Further, the recent Supreme Court judgement in another case of custodial rape (known commonly as the Suman Rani case) has shown precisely how clauses in the law which are intended to ensure fairness allow scope for interpretations which the main thrust of that particular law is intended to disallow. The Rape Law Amendment which the 1980 agitation had fought for included a clause saying that the mandatory ten year sentence prescribed in cases of custodial rape, could be reduced by the bench if the latter found 'adequate and special reasons' for doing so. What these could be is anyone's guess. The law, however, illustrates this point by giving an example of a rape case in which the rapist and the victim may, subsequent to the rape, develop relations with each other and perhaps wish to marry. In such a case, the court may, if it sees fit, reduce the punishment of the rapist in order to give the relationship a chance.

However, the use to which the Supreme Court put this clause militates against the entire reasoning which led to the passing of the Bill in the first place. According to Justice Pandian's bench, the sentence against Prem Chand and Kushi Ram, Suman Rani's rapists, was reduced because of the 'conduct' of the victim; when asked to define 'conduct' the judge held that because the victim had let five days pass before she reported the case, and filed an FIR (first information report), she had conducted herself badly and therefore the rapists' punishment could be reduced by half. Apart from the fact that the victim could not file the FIR because she was put on a bus to her home village and it took five days to get back to file one in the relevant police station, what outraged feminists was that while the entire earlier agitation had taken as its main thrust the argument that neither the character nor conduct of the victim should be taken into account in cases of rape, because they had no relevance at all to the matter of assault, this was completely forgotten here. Further, it was pointed out that such a use of character or conduct was made only on the assumption that if a woman had 'illicit' sexual or even social relationships then any man was free to forcibly violate her; in other words, the assumption was that no woman is free to choose her lovers, and if she does so then it is permissible to punish her as violently as you choose.

This was a staggering setback for the feminist movement, which in 1980 had appeared to have gained—at least partially—its point that character and conduct should be deemed irrelevant. Feminists reacted with a storm of protest, held several meetings and a dharna and burnt an effigy of 'the law' in front of the Supreme Court. The National Front Government responded promptly with the promise of yet another amendment on rape, this time concerning the rules of evidence, but the key question, of implementation and interpretation of the law, still remains open. In a way, every case that has come up has made it a more crucial issue, and made us more aware of the great need for attempting to place our views within public consciousness.

Summing up, then, it would be unfair to say that there were no gains made by the 1980 campaign. First of all, it was the first attempt at formal joint action, and set a pattern for many subsequent campaigns, developing a 'left and democratic' pro-feminist lobby. Secondly, it dragged rape out of the closet, so that people became aware of the nature and extent of its occurrence in India. Thirdly, it added the category of 'custodial rape' to the already existing categories, getting it legally recognized as special and distinct. In a way, the recent Suman Rani case has not only focussed attention again on many of the issues raised in the course of the 1980 agitation, it has also led to a renewed debate on the nature and problem of rape. Significantly, one of the major questions being discussed today is not only the whole issue of freedom of choice concerning husbands or lovers, but also of the definition of rape itself. The issue of freedom of choice has come up in the course of investigations of particular custodial rapes: in Delhi, for example, the People's Union of Democratic Rights has discovered that several of the cases were ones in which the victims had run away from home with the men they loved but whose marriages were not permitted by their families; that they had newly arrived in the city; and that the police, having stopped them, had used their 'runaway' status as a reason to separate them from their men, and rape them.[8] This is an interesting new dimension to freedom of choice: earlier arguments on this issue had tended to dwell more on prostitutes as an example.

On the definition of rape, the most interesting questions which are now being raised are directed towards challenging the limited genito-centric definition of it. On the one hand, if 'penetration' of the woman's vagina is forcibly effected by the man's using a stick, bottle, etc., rather than his phallus, then this does not fall under 'rape', but under 'molestation', for which the punishment is lighter. Molestation, in fact is much more common, according to police reports (see box). On the

---

Case 3: Kashtakari Sanghatana activist's rape by CPM cadre members, Dahanu (Maharashtra)

The issue of rape by party workers was highlighted in the case of an activist of the Kashtakari Sanghatana being raped by CPM workers, and the party taking no action at all against them. Although the issue was raised repeatedly by women and men activists from a range of groups, to date the question has not been resolved satisfactorily. The CPM in Dahanu has denied responsibility, women's and other groups have held morchas and issued a fact-finding report, but there has been no impact on either the CPM or the legal machinery.

Some of the broader questions that arose from a discussion of these and other cases were:

— Should one take recourse to the law or not?
— How should women's groups respond when conflicting demands are made on them?
— In cases of marital, familial, minor rape what should our response be?
— How does one deal with mass-gang-political-communal rape?
— How do we work with the law, as is?
— What alternative strategies have proved more effective than legal remedies?
— If the woman doesn't want to file a case, how should women's groups proceed?
— How effective have our forms of protest been?
— Have we made any headway in providing counselling, crisis centres, support, to rape victims?

---

other hand, if the male, for example, forces his phallus into the woman's mouth, then this is not regarded as 'penetration', and therefore again would be defined as molestation. Yet both are extremely violent acts. The new issue therefore is: in distinguishing between categories of sexual crime, surely the principle must be that of violence, and not of which organs are involved.

At the present moment, these issues are subjects of discussion, rather than action. Whether, how, and in which ways feminists shall seek to modify them, or what kind of form subsequent agitation on the rape will take is an open question.

NOTES

1. See Flavia Agnes, interviewed by Radha Rajyadh-yaksha, 'Rape' *Illustrated Weekly of India*, Jan 28–Feb 3, 1990.

2. Figures of reported rapes in India, year by year, are provided by the Bureau of Police Research and Development in Delhi. Evidence for the statement made here is in their report for 1983.

3. Account compiled from reports in the *Times of India, Statesman, Indian Express,* and *Patriot,* April 2–12, 1978.

4. See newspaper reports of April 4–5 for reports of the Patna and Vijayanagar demonstrations; May 2 for Bankura, and June 30 for Garhwal: all in 1980.

5. See newspaper reports of July 2, 6, 11–12, 18–19, 1980.

6. See newspaper reports of July 17–21, 1980

7. Raj Narain's decision reported on July 29, Indira Gandhi's letter on August 4, and his loss of weight on August 5, 1980.

8. People's Union for Democratic Rights, *Custodial Rape,* Delhi March 1990.

APPENDIX: A
MASS RAPE IN SANTHAL PARGANAS

Police repression against a tribal movement to reclaim land
A study by Stri Sangharsh

The story we are about to tell is not a new one. All of us live in fear of rape. In cities and in villages girls are told not to go out after dark, never to go into deserted areas, always to be under the protection of men. Many of us are not raped because we have bartered our freedom for protection. Must we always live in cages? For tribal women these cages are being specially built by men of 'our' civilization—both Hindus and Muslims. For most non-tribals in the area, tribals are sub-human creatures, whose land is to be usurped, whose possessions are to be looted, who can with impunity be laughed at and pushed aside. As for tribal women, they are prostituted, raped, beaten and discarded: objectified in every way. These conditions govern their lives not only in Bihar, but also in other parts of our country: truckloads of them are sent regularly to Punjab, Delhi and Tripura, to work as domestics or construction labourers and are kept there as concubines and slaves; many have not been paid by their contractors for years.

A racket of this nature has been recently discovered by the Tripura Government and the enslaved tribals were sent home. This is the first sign of official cognizance that has been shown—Bihar itself will probably be one of the last to follow. None of the officials we met showed any sympathy for the tribals, many of them actually denying incidents of rape, beating and molestation. Our police have already achieved a certain notoriety as outlawing the law in acts of illegal detention and rape, but the volume and frequency of their atrocities in tribal areas would probably achieve a place in the Guinness Book of Records. The excuse for these atrocities is the land problem.

Traditionally all the land in the Santhal Parganas has belonged to Santhals and Sauri Paharias, but the 'dikus' (non-tribal outsiders, who are moneylenders and landlords) who come in over the borders from Bihar, Bengal and Orissa, have been steadily alienating tribal land over a hundred year period. Under the British, sporadic attempts were made to resist the entry of dikus and protect the land. As early as 1872, they passed a regulation forbidding any non-tribal from owning land in the Santhal Parganas. This regulation was later passed as an Act and stands as one today. It has never been properly implemented. This is largely due to the working of law itself both under the British and under the Indian Government. For the implementation of the Act, the Santhals need land ownership papers which they can show when Government settlements are made. But the Santhals don't understand the importance of such papers. They have never had papers, and their laws are unwritten codes administered by the panchayat. The only people who could make use of such laws were—and are—the dikus, who know where to get papers and when to present them. Thus most of the land is controlled by upper caste Hindus and a few Muslims, who have forged papers in false names.

Tribal Movement to Reclaim Land

Because they have no papers to prove their ownership, the Santhals have had to resort to methods like forcible harvesting in order to reclaim their land. This movement started only in late 1977, when the Jharkhand Mukti Morcha (a tribal party) took up a radical land programme in the Santhal Parganas. Under their direction, the Santhals forcibly harvested land which should legally be their own. Each attempt to reclaim their land, is followed by a large scale reprisal in which the police plunder, burn and rape. They destroy every little bit of property belonging to the men—and for them women come under the heading of property.

'Law and Order': A Bitter Echo in Santhal Parganas

It is not an accident that CRP men conduct these reprisals in numbers which are never less than a hundred. What justification does the State offer for keeping so many CRP men in each sub-division? None other than that hoary old claim 'the needs of law and order'. The phrase has a bitter sound in the Santhal Parganas: it is under this phrase that protracted police atrocities devastate the countryside, destroying the last vestiges of any citizen's birthright: the freedom to live unmolested, protected by the law and the State.

As one of the traditional means of repression, rape appears to be of the same order, just another spice in the titillating broth of atrocity. But in fact it is qualitatively different from plunder, arson and assault: where the latter three are directed against an entire community, rape is directed against one sex only and at first sight it becomes difficult to understand why it is so widely practised when women have not been directly responsible for sparking off the incident.

One explanation lies in the ideology treasured by all patriarchal societies: the women are raped to humiliate the community and this is an act against the men, through the women: they are the means of revenge, having traditionally been seen as belonging to the men, like their fields, their houses, etc. Women are also objects with a difference: things which can be dishonoured by rape for no fault of theirs and this brings dishonour to the men, their families and the community.

This is the ideology behind the widespread use of rape by dominant communities to suppress the weak. However, in the Santhal Parganas, there are also distinct sexual and cultural norms. In Santhal society, rape has never been common and women have not been kept in fear by the threat of rape. Pre-marital sex is the norm among tribal Santhal women who go about freely, sell food and wood in the markets, work in the fields, marry as they wish and get divorces easily. At the same time, relationships with dikus are taboo, and reactions to such relationships are violent within the community.

For non-tribals, the conflict between this taboo and the open sexuality of tribal women is an explosive one. The freedom of tribal women is a threat to diku morality—be it Hindu, Muslim or Christian. Unlike diku women, Santhali women are not ashamed of being women nor afraid of their sexuality. The dikus hate this freedom and say that they are 'loose women'. They rape Santhal women to force them into fear, shame and subjugation. They rape to show their hatred and contempt for tribal society.

Defenceless in their mud walls, Santhal women are the natural victims of the hob-nailed arrogance of the dikus. From village to village, they say the same thing: '*be-izzati kiya . . .zabbardasti kiya . . .*'

Beldiha is a village in Godda sub-division of the Santhal Parganas. It has about 300 inhabitants, all of whom are Santhals. Except for one—the local mahajan—a Rajput ironically named Bhagwan Singh, who lives in the basti. It was over a few bighas of land, occupied and cultivated by him, that the dispute began. One day, in late November, the Santhals harvested this land:

> We harvested the land sometime towards the end of November, but the CRP men came only at the end of December. We did not know they were coming. I was at home grinding spices when I heard a noise outside my door, as if someone was calling the cows. . . I went out to see and the CRP men grabbed me and pushed me outside. They drove my mother-in-law out and threw my baby on the floor. Four men raped

> me and two kept watch at the door. They beat me again and again . . . . They took all the grain and cows . . .

The CRP men came to Beldiha at 4 p.m. They left at 8-9 p.m. There were about 150 of them. They drove the men out of the village, arresting 19, before they started on their five hour voyage of plunder, arson and rape, going from house to house, in groups of five to six, beating the women and children, raping the younger women. One old woman was so badly beaten that today she lies all day and all night on her khat, shivering and moaning. We went to see her—one year and three months after the events—and she cringed away from us: 'I haven't done anything . . . don't touch me, please don't beat me . . .'

Another woman, Sona Soren, had just delivered. Five CRP men shoved their arms up her vagina and then raped her. She died 20 days later, on the 10th of January.

Phulki Membrun was savagely beaten and raped. She was in a state of mental shock afterwards and suffered from constant headaches. She died one year later, in January 1980.

The old Mahajan who called in the police, still lives in the basti. There is not one villager there who doesn't hate him—not one whom he hasn't harmed. Yet he continues to live, survey his fields, drive to the market in his horse and cart—untouched by the community he has devastated.

Pakadiya, 17 March, 1979

Three months after Beldiha, in the same Godda sub-division, a similar pattern was repeated. The horror of what happened on 17, 18 and 19 March, 1979, drives home the nature and extent of police brutality and their complicity with the mahajans of the Santhal Parganas.

The initial act concerns two villages in Godda sub-division: Saraikita and Pakadiya. But the reprisal that followed swept seven more villages into the net of police terror: Kerwar, Bakhadda, Phulwadiya Gangarampur, Digghi, Bishaha and Rajaon.

The incident that sparked off this particularly gruesome episode in Santhal history was a land dispute between the Santhal landowners and the sharecroppers. The showdown was over 1.5 bighas of land which belonged to the Santhals, was claimed by the Brahmins, and was cultivated by Harijans. The land itself was in Saraikita, bordering Pakadiya.

On 16 March, at about 7 a.m., all three groups

turned up for the harvesting: the Santhals with the Harijans, and the Brahmins with a police escort of one havaldar and five cops. It is worth noting that the police had come without a warrant, in fact without official orders, as the SDO (Sub-Divisional Officer) was absent from Godda. Even so, they fired upon the Santhals when they began to cut the crop. An 11 year-old child looked up in wonder at the whizzing bullets and saw two of his fingers fly off. After one man had been killed and several wounded the Santhals fled, and re-assembled two miles away.

Basti set Ablaze

By the evening all Pakadiya was ablaze. To vent their fury against the Harijans for having sided with the Santhals, the Brahmins allegedly set fire to the Harijan basti, and then set fire to their own homes, claiming that the Santhals had done it with flaming arrows. The Santhals deny this, and are supported by the Harijans. Santhal arrows have a range of only 150 yards and all the men were at a distance of two miles from the basti.

Thus began the familiar pattern of police reprisal, an operation which stretched over three days.

In the early hours of the 17th, CRP trucks began to rumble towards Pakadiya. By 9 a.m. a massive police force has assembled there. Though all the Santhals had gone into hiding in the fields and hills, the Harijans were still there. They were savagely beaten, the little property which they had salvaged from the fire was looted, and the charred floors of their huts were defecated on. Empty Santhal huts were given the same treatment.

In search of the Santhals, the CRP and the Brahmins set out on an extensive combing operation. Over the next two days they fanned out towards the adjoining villages, destroying everything they could lay their hands on, regardless of the innocence of the villagers.

Kerwar

The CRP men came first to Kerwar. One of the leaders of the tribal movement lives in this village. Most of the villagers had run away, but a few women remained behind. They were raped.

A group of five women was caught while running towards Bakhadda. 'We heard that the CRP was coming so we ran . . .But they caught up with us—eight of them surrounded us. They were laughing. They beat us with their lathis. Two men held me down, and two

raped me. They did it with all of us. Then they took our jewellery. We went away and hid in the hills for three days. There was no food and no water . . . '

Bakhadda

'They snatched my baby from my arms and threw him on the ground . . he was only six days old. They asked me to show them my vagina and threatened to shove their lathis up me if I didn't.' The CRP came from Kerwar to Bakhadda at noon, there were around 150 of them. They surrounded the village. In a pitiful hope that numbers would protect them the women had gathered under the peepal tree. The CRP men swaggered up to them, saying, 'Is this a dharamshala?'

Item by item, their jewellery was stripped off them. Their houses were broken into, their vessels stolen and their grain stores plundered. What the CRP did not want to steal they smashed. Almost all the women were raped—sometimes by two, sometimes by three and a few by five men.

Only two women remained at home. They too were beaten and raped. 'I was suckling my child when the CRP men burst in. They grabbed me, saying, "So you have come back after looting Saraikita?" I told them, "How could I have gone to Saraikita with a baby at my breast?! But they didn't listen, they kept beating me, telling me to 'confess.!"

In the melee created by the CRP men, her young daughter disappeared. For eight days Marangmai wandered the neighbouring hills and fields dementedly searching for her daughter.

'We never found her—not even her body . . .'

APPENDIX: B
THE BAGHPAT RAPE CASE

The Baghpat incident has triggered off the strange phenomenon of politicians of various hues falling over themselves to protect the honour of women. Parliament echoes with their strident calls to flog, stone and hang rapists. The same Charan Singh under whose administration circulars were issued banning women IAS officers from serving in his state, is today beating his chest about atrocities against women. The Janata Party which hushed up incidents of mass rape in the Santhal Parganas today condemns the 'humiliation' of women. Raj Narain has been heard saying that a 'wave of rapes' has swept the country since Mrs Gandhi came to power, and is demanding her resignation.

Has he forgotten Narianpura? And Basti?

For the Congress-I of course all this talk about rape has blown the issue out of proportion—their history does not record Telangana, Bailadilla, the 1974 railway strike rapes . . . the Goonda incident . . .

Rape is not only a Matter of Honour

The vocabulary of Indian politicians has always been limited. From the BJP to the Congress-I, key terms in their sound and fury are 'honour and humiliation'. They say the 'dishonouring of women' is the 'dishonour of our country'—they say the 'honour of our women is the honour of our country'. Yet it is in this country that women are forced into prostitution, sold as slave labour, killed for dowry and raped by their husbands, brothers-in-law and fathers-in-law. Recently a man committed suicide because his wife had been raped. Two months ago a woman killed herself instead of telling her husband she had been raped. Families have thrown out their sisters, daughters, and daughters-in-law for having been raped. How can your honour be taken away when you yourself have committed no crime? It is in this country that the State itself allows mass rape by its Police, CRPF, and BSF. If these are honourable actions, then we spit on honour.

For us rape is an act of hatred and contempt—it is a denial of ourselves as women, as human beings—it is the ultimate assertion of male power.

Rape is not a Law and Order Problem

The Opposition says that the law and order situation has worsened under the Congress-I. The Congress-I says 'mischievous elements' are using rape to 'demoralise the police'. Both agree that it is a party political problem. Both simply imply that they can solve the problem of police rape.

Yet for women in Bailadilla and the Santhal Parganas, for Rameeza Bee, Mathura and Maya Tyagi it is not a question of who is in power—Congress-I or Janata. For them the sight of a policeman implies fear, intimidation and sexual violence. The authority that a man acquires when he puts on a police/CRPF/BSF uniform and picks up his lathi/gun itself allows him to beat, to torture and to rape. It is an authority given by the State, and in most cases torture, arson and rape are the weapons of his authority. It is the defender of law and order who commits rape; in working class houses and peasant villages, law and order means police atrocities.

For decades our history has endlessly repeated this truth—we cannot fight it by pretending, as the politicians do, that this is false. If today we allow them to turn our truth into their lie we will have lost what few gains we fought for on March 8.

9. The Nineteen Eighties

Chhatra Yuva Sangarsh Vahini, Rajasthan to Delhi march against increasing
violence against women, Gurgaon, Uttar Pradesh, 1980

The experience of the campaigns against rape and dowry deaths led many feminists to question their methods and tactics on a wider scale than before. The discovery that there was no connection at all between the enactment of new laws and their implementation had left many feeling rather bitterly that the Government had, with the greatest of ease, sidetracked their demands, and this gave rise to further questions about the efficacy of basing campaigns around demands for changes in the law. On the one hand, this strengthened decisions to take up individual cases and follow them through the intricacies of the courts, no matter how long it took; on the other, feminists began to move away from their earlier methods of agitation, such as public campaigns, demonstrations, street theatre, etc., feeling that these had limited meaning unless they were accompanied by attempts to develop their own structures to aid and support individual women. In the early eighties, women's centres were formed in several cities, which provided a mixture of legal aid, health care and counselling; one or two of them also tried to provide employment, but as they lacked sufficient resources to sustain their schemes, these foundered.

Though women's centres to provide aid, counselling,

Women educationists demanding their rights,
date and place not known

health care and employment had existed from the early twentieth century on, these new centres were different in several important ways. First of all, most of the earlier centres had concentrated on one or two issues, whereas the new ones attempted to provide help on a whole range of issues which they saw as interlinked. Secondly, the earlier centres had a social-welfare ideology, while these were explicitly feminist: for example, while earlier centres which provided health care had concentrated on maternity and child welfare alone, the new centres looked at women's health in a more holistic way, providing not only information on all gynaecological problems but also looking at the socially structured ways in which women treated their own bodies. Thirdly, while the earlier centres tended to approach women's problems in an already defined, blanket way, the new centres had a more flexible, individualist approach; for example, those of the former which provided counselling for marital difficulties based this on the belief that reconciliation was the most desirable thing in all cases, whereas

What do we want? 'Justice'. Demonstration
against the alleged murder of Jaswanti,
for dowry, Delhi, date not known

the latter discussed the problems with the men and women concerned before advising either reconciliation or divorce.

Finally, the new centres represented an effort to put feminist concepts of sisterhood into practice, as well as to redefine these concepts through basing them on traditionally accepted structures of friendship among women. In both Delhi and Kanpur, for example, the names of the centres symbolized moves to locate notions of sisterhood in a specifically Indian context. Both chose to focus on—and thereby re-interpret—the traditional concept of a girlfriend; in Delhi, the name chosen was Saheli, and in Kanpur, Sakhi Kendra.

Saheli, with its association of playfulness, was deliberately chosen by the Delhi feminists who set up the centre, to signify that they were not only concerned with

Nari Mukti Sangharsh Sammelan (women's liberation
conference) rally, Patna, 1988

women in distress, but also with sharing moments of play and pleasure. The idea underlying this was to give an equal weight to the positive aspects of women's lives in India, particularly their forms of celebration and creativity. This led Saheli to host a workshop for feminists from all over India, in 1983, at which there were sessions on song, dance, drama and painting. For most of the feminists who attended the workshop this emphasis on exploring their own, often traditionally defined, creativity was a liberating one, and from now on solidarity and intimacy were increasingly, and more joyously, expressed through non-verbal forms, especially music and dance, than through words. Discussions, conversations, written statements, and so on, now grew to represent 'politics' in a public context; dancing and singing, on the other hand, were both means and signs of immediate, personal, culturally rooted and collective warmth.

This had both its good and bad sides. The good sides, which are perhaps more obvious, were that dance and song, and to a more limited extent painting, allowed a short-cut to communication, which cut across class barriers and, in fact, reversed the normal pecking order, for often it was upper-class women who were learning forms of singing and dancing from working-class or peasant women. At the same time, it instilled a sense of confidence among the verbally less articulate women, who found that what they had to contribute to feminism was special, and valued. Moreover, the emphasis on traditionally defined forms of women's expression, which accorded a formal recognition to folk cultures, gave Indian feminists a sense of regional, ethnic and national identity. Simultaneously, through familiarizing them with different cultural forms in India, it allowed them to experiment with these forms in a feminist context.

Thus a whole new set of personal relationships developed in the feminist movement, of friendships which cut across class and cultural barriers, even though, to some extent, these friendships remained unequal, for the middle-class women acted more out of a sense of duty and the poor women out of a sense of gratitude. Even so, this signified the growth of a new sense of individuality within the movement, qualifying stereotypes of the battered wife, the rape or dowry victim, the woman worker, the student, housewife or professional woman.

The bad sides of this separation between verbal and non-verbal communication were more complex: the relegation of the verbal to the public-political sphere re-inforced the dichotomy between the political and the personal, so that neither informed the other, and thus ideas of personal ethics and behaviour could not be lifted into political life, nor vice versa. The fact that it was not felt to be necessary to articulate the lessons learnt from non-verbal communication meant, similarly, that the sphere of the verbal was so severely restricted that the development of feminist ideas was stunted and their impact on political life was minimized: so that, more often than not, feminist politics had little to sustain itself on. This, in turn, meant that feminists tended to fall back on orthodox political ideas and methods in a detrimental fashion. In the women's centres, for example, attempts at legal aid and health care became attempts to put individual women in touch with lawyers and doctors who were already over-burdened and who had often not been able to develop feminist legal or medical views or practices. Not only did the 'do it yourself' ideas never gain any ground, eventually attitudes towards women in distress degenerated into seeing them as so many 'cases' to be dealt with.

The attempt to re-appropriate traditionally accepted women's spaces grew in the eighties, through attempts to re-interpret myths, epics and folktales: to critique mainstream religious and cultural texts or practices and search for alternative texts or practices; and to discover historical or particular methods of women's resistance in India. To some extent an interest in tradition had been present in the Indian feminist movement from its inception: the street plays *Om Swaha* (against dowry deaths, first put together in Delhi in 1979, and performed all over the city and in several parts of northern India), and *Mulgi Zali Ho* ('A girl is born', put together in Bombay in 1979–80, and performed all over Maharashtra), had both used traditional songs and dances; while the exhibitions mounted by feminists had similarly used traditional images. At this stage, however, the main effort was to detail traditional forms of women's subordination in India, from birth to puberty, marriage, maternity, work, old age and death; as well as to search for traditional comments on women's suffering, placing both in an orthodox socialist-feminist framework. As against this, in the eighties the emphasis changed to looking for traditional sources of women's strength, rather than suffering. For some this consisted of identifying images of women warriors, to be used as a battle cry for the latter-day women, within which an attempt was made to appropriate and recast Kali, the all-powerful ravening mother goddess, in a feminist mould. Interestingly, the best known image in this context, by the dancer and artist Chandralekha, was of a Kali from whom all traces of manic bloodlust had been removed, though she continued to wield weapons of destruction, chosen by Chandralekha to represent the different religious communities of India. Thus the feminist reinterpretation of Kali negated the view of her as symbolizing a devouring female sexuality, and turned her, in fact, into an a-sexual and aseptic figure. Though the image came in for considerable criticism from the feminist left, this took the form of rejecting the idea of using the image of Kali at all, because she was seen as revealing male attitudes towards women (seeing them as essentially threatening).

Intriguingly, when Indira Gandhi was assassinated in 1984, the Congress(I) picked up the idea of depicting her as a mother goddess, and huge hoardings went up all over the country, proclaiming that she was the mother of the nation, murdered by her ungrateful children, and showing her with blood dripping from her hand. And her burial ground was named Shakti Sthal. Thus she was, after her death, turned into a female symbol of considerably greater power than Chandralekha's Kali.

If the interest in traditionalism led some to create images for feminists, others were more interested in defining the ways in which ordinary, or unexceptional, women used the spaces that were traditionally accorded them to negotiate with their husbands, families, communities and so on. Special attention was now paid, for example, to the way in which women simulated possession by the *devi* (goddess), particularly at times of pregnancy, in order to wrest concessions from their

husbands or families which would not otherwise have been given. Though this tactic was more commonly espoused by pregnant women to get special food during their pregnancy, accounts now began to circulate of women who had simulated possession in order to reform alcoholic husbands, or get money for household expenses, and this began to be recommended as a means of gaining some degree of power. The search for traditional women's tactics developed within the feminist movement in concurrence with attempts to celebrate courage and gaiety, inventiveness or strength in Indian women. The *shibir* or camp was, in areas like Tilonia in Rajasthan, transformed into the *mela* or festival, and to

discussions of rape, wife-beating or unequal wages were added, on the one hand, sessions of singing, dancing and making merry; and on the other, of examining traditional female devices as potentially feminist tactics.

The search for historical examples of women's resistance led feminists to scrutinize the distant and immediate past, to look at the role women played in general movements for social transformation, and to reclaim some of the movements predating contemporary feminism. Two movements were of especial interest in this context: the landless labourers' movement in Telangana, and the forest protection movement in the north-Indian hill areas of Garhwal, and to a

Above and below: a series of posters produced by the Ahmedabad Women's Action Group (AWAG) on the theme of violence against women

limited extent Kumaon, popularly known as the Chipko movement.

The Mahila Sanghams which had begun to be formed in Telangana in the late seventies had proliferated by the eighties, and within them there was a fusion of far left and reformist views, for on the one hand they participated in struggles against landlords and the State, and on the other, formed co-operative societies through which they got certain benefits from the State. At the same time, the Stree Shakti Sanghatana, a Hyderabad based group, developed an understanding of the specificity of women's experience in the Telangana movement, and embarked on an oral history of them; while in Bombay a similar attempt was made at an oral history

of women textile workers by Rohini Banaji and Sujata Ghotoskar, who had been involved in setting up the Trade Union Research Group, and Neelam Chaturvedi, who had been involved in setting up the Sakhi Kendra in Kanpur. Though the two histories were different, the former being more comprehensive than the latter, both were part of the new consciousness which was developing in the feminist movement, of the ways in which they had tended to objectify women, especially as peasants and workers.

Though the Chipko movement had begun in the mid-seventies, and was carried forward largely by women, these was little or no discussion of it as a women's movement at the time. In the early eighties,

Above and below: different posters on varying themes produced by women's groups in different parts of the country

however, feminists began to celebrate it as a mass women's movement, and theories of women's special relation to their environment began to be advanced. Leading women activists of the movement were interviewed, and articles about women in Chipko abounded. In consequence a new awareness of women's role and problems developed within the movement, and the hitherto defunct Mahila Mandals (Government sponsored village and district level women's organizations) were revitalized, while in the neighbouring Kumaon region, where Chipko had not been especially strong, a women's anti-alcohol agitation began, following the pattern of Shahada, where too the development of a 'women's consciousness' had led to an anti-alcohol movement.

By the early eighties feminism had branched into a series of activities, from the production of literature and audio-visual material to slum-improvement work, employment-generation schemes, health education, and trade unions. Barriers against feminism were increasingly eroded within the political sphere, and, though 'feminism' still remained largely a term of abuse, the need to take up women's issues gained far greater recognition than before. New attempts to organize women workers' unions were made in the south, where the first attempts to unionize women workers had been made in the early twentieth century, under the aegis of the moderate trade union headed by Annie Besant. Interestingly, these attempts focussed largely on the unorganized sector, as Sewa had done; unlike Sewa, however, they grew out of campaigns for an improvement in the conditions of living rather than in the conditions of work. In Bihar, the far left trade union leader, A.K. Roy, attempted to organize a campaign against the retrenchment of women mine-workers, which had been a consequence of Government moves to modernize the mining industry; a similar attempt was

An activist explains one of the visuals at an exhibition on women in Delhi, 1980.
This exhibition accompanied the demonstration on violence against women

made by feminists in Bombay, to organize women textile workers against their retrenchment. Both attempts failed, partly because women workers were not as confident of their right to work as male workers were, and partly because the threat of joblessness caused by the decline in these two industries led workers to feel that they had to unite around the minimum demand of one wage per family, even if that was a male wage. Though feminists argued against the patriarchalism implicit in such a demand, asking why then could not demands be raised for a female family wage, their pleas went unheeded, for they were seen as idealistic rather than pragmatic.

Attempts to unionize women within the skilled working class were also made in Bombay, especially in the free trade zone, but these were largely unsuccessful, partly because women had short working lives in such industries as micro-chip production, and partly because trade-unionism was yet to develop there.

As a result of these experiences, feminists began to conclude that poor women were more militant when it came to issues concerning their conditions of living as *families* than around issues concerning either work, or the specific problems they faced as women. The Chhattisgarh Mine Workers Shramik Sangh was noted as an example of how successfully women were unionized when equal attention was paid, by the union, to creating better housing, schools for children, and health care for the family. And, in the early eighties, a public statement of the involvement of workers' families in their working lives was made for the first time, when the wives of textile workers in Bombay organized support demonstrations for the general strike of 1981–82. At the same time, feminists also noted that once women had got involved in general movements for social transformation, they began to raise problems concerning them as women within the family. This, as we have seen, was a pattern in most movements from the early twentieth century on, but recognition of the pattern has largely been voiced only by the contemporary feminist movement.

City bred and based feminists were now gaining enough confidence to move into unfamiliar areas and co-ordinate activities with other groups. This process was most noticeable in Maharashtra, where women's organizations from all over the state were able to form joint action platforms with socialists and the left, resulting in the constitution of local and district level joint action fronts in 1983, under the umbrella name Nari Sangharsh Manch. Vibhuti Patel has pointed out that even when their party executives issued directives for separate party building work, local activists worked together with others on women's issues: she situates this in the long tradition of independent social reform and left wing activity in Maharashtra.

The situation was more complex in areas which had

Women workers at a union demonstration, Arwal, Bihar, 1987

Women's wing of the Chhatisgarh Mines Mazdoor
Sangh, flag rally celebrating foundation day of union,
Chhatisgarh, Madhya Pradesh, June 1982

When Neelam continued to raise these issues, together
with questioning the hierarchical structure of most
working-class organizations, and actually discussed them
in public at the Bombay Feminist conference in 1980,
the party ordered her either to apologize or declare she
had nothing to do with CITU or the Kamgar Mahila
Samiti. She chose the latter course.

For Kiran Shaheen the problem arose at a more
painful personal level. Her boyfriend was a member of
the CPI and she was attracted by the feminist ideas of
women in the JP (Jai Prakash Narain) influenced CYSV
(Chhatra Yuva Sangharsh Vahini), whom she met at
college. In fact, the tradition of sectarianism between
communists and JP-influenced organizations was an old
one, for the Bhave and JP led Bhoodan movement had
arisen at a time when extremely militant communist-led
movements were being brutally crushed and disintegrat-
ing, in the late forties, and neither Bhave nor JP had
expressed support or sympathy for the communists.
Similarly the CYSV movement too had started around
the time of the repression and fragmentation of the
Naxalite movement, leaving many feeling that these
were deliberate attempts to move into communist spaces
on an anti-communist platform. The success of the JP
influenced CYSV movement was an especial threat to the
CPI, for whom Bihar had provided some of the strongest
bases since the forties, but which was currently in the
doldrums. The CPI had elaborated a critique of the
movement, and Kiran felt, after meeting many of the
women activists of the CYSV that:

Though the leadership may be reactionary the movement couldn't be called that. When I said this to my
boyfriend he started shouting at me and telling me
to keep away from the girls and personally attacking
the girls, which upset me a lot. At first I had felt what
he said was right because he was logical and I didn't
have any logical alternative. But when he couldn't
answer my questions logically I began to wonder how
I could be dependent on him emotionally and intellectually; this dependence was becoming empty.
When I began to assert myself he got domineering,
and started to make my decisions for me. Yet I
couldn't assert my anger at this because my own
family life had been so empty, and I couldn't just
break off. But because of this a kind of resentment
started building up in me.

In 1978 Kiran started the first women's printing press
in Bihar, from which she and Madhu Singh published a
feminist monthly paper in Hindi; years later, she joined
the CYSV women's section. It must be said that the
women's section was not particularly anti-communist,
though their feminism was in advance of orthodox
communist attitudes towards women.

either had no such tradition of activity, or in which
feminist ideas were only just developing for the first
time. In Kanpur, for example, where workers from different parties had come together in an agitation against
police firings on textile workers who were protesting the
closure of the Swadeshi Polytext factory in 1977, the
daughter of a leading activist, Neelam Chaturvedi, grew
interested in feminism through meeting some Bombay
feminists who were active in organizing support for the
Swadeshi agitation in 1978. Gradually she started working with working class women in Kanpur, and got involved informally with the CPI-M trade union, CITU.
When she discussed the possibility of starting a local
women's wing of the union, the CPI-M leaders were most
encouraging, and Vimal Ranadive herself came to discuss issues with Neelam, though at the same time she
also warned her that the struggle for women's liberation
had to be fought in gradual stages, and such issues as
rape were divisive because they were 'family problems'.

Bombay textile workers strike, 1981–82

Being arrested at a demonstration for
the textile workers

By this stage the feminist movement had undergone a process of spread and fragmentation, which took a variety of forms, from the development of profession and issue-based groups to the development of distinct and organizational identities. The first professions to feel the influence of feminism were journalism, academics and medicine. Soon after the feminist movement began, most of the major English language dailies had deputed one or more women journalists to write exclusively on feminist issues, and a network of women journalists evolved, which in Bombay was formalized into a women journalists' group in the mid-eighties, with the purpose of lobbying for better reporting on 'women's issues', such as dowry, or rape, or sati; rather than for a change in what constitutes mainstream journalism, that is to say, the reporting of 'events'. A change here would entail in feminist terms, not only the analysis of the structure of the event, but of its subjectivity; the ideas, emotions and relations engaged in it, for example.

Many of the women involved in founding the first contemporary feminist groups were themselves academics who chose to study different aspects of women's lives with the idea that this would be useful to the development of the feminist movement. 'Women's studies', however, really took off in the eighties, initially under the aegis of independent research institutes such as the Centre for Women's Development Studies (CWDS) in Delhi; though an attempt to fund research at the University level was made by the SNDT Women's University in Bombay, which set up a Women's Research Unit. Together with the CWDS, in the mid-eighties they began to jointly host annual national women's studies conferences. An interest in women's studies grew so rapidly that today the University Grants Commission, a Central

Wives of textile workers demonstrate
solidarity with the strike

Prostitutes meet to discuss forming a union,
Maharashtra, Circa 1982

Domestic workers in Pune went on strike to demand better working conditions, 1982

government body, is planning to set up women's studies courses at the college level. As, however, women's studies proliferated, it became a separate sphere, and the initial, rather utopian-vision of it as aiding in the generation of feminist theory to inform feminist practice, was relegated to the background. Thus a somewhat paradoxical situation arose, in which much knowledge was produced which had great significance for feminist activity, but which remained, by and large, disconnected from the activity itself. Today, women's studies has become a sort of activity in itself, though there are a few feminist groups, such as Stree Shakti Sanghatana, which attempt to synthesise feminist research, theory and practice, within an activist perspective.

While the influence of feminism in medicine has been less effective than in journalism or academics, the connection between theory and activity has been closer here than in the other two. On the one hand, feminists have been unable to actually change medical practice; their campaigns against the dumping of drugs, such as Net-en and Depo Provera in 'developing' countries like India, by multinationals, have failed, as have their campaigns against the misuse of new diagnostic techniques such as amniocentesis. On the other hand, radical medical organizations, such as the Voluntary Health Association of India, or the Medico Friends' Circle, have worked closely with women's organizations in these campaigns, and together they have generated both analysis and campaigning tactics around the issue of women's health. Thus, for example, through the campaigns against Net-en and Depo-Provera (which began in the mid-eighties), feminists developed an understanding of some of the international processes of capital accumulation, and of the way in which many developing countries permitted certain 'imperialist' practices to continue, such as the creation of markets in their countries for products which no longer had a market in their countries of origin. At the same time, through their connection with radical

medical organizations, feminists were able to generate much more detailed information on issues of health (such as the effects of Net-en and Depo-Provera, and the alternatives to them), than on most other issues. Similarly, because of this connection, a wider range of tactics could be tried than in other campaigns. For example, in the campaign against the widespread use of pregnancy-inducing drugs for pregnancy-testing, feminists were able to argue their case before the drug-controller in 1986–87, and to force him to arrange a series of hearings about these drugs all over the country; they were also able to produce lists of doctors and medical centres which prescribed these drugs without warning their patients of the side-effects, among which was an effect on the development of the foetus, so that the risk of producing spastic or retarded children was much greater once the drug had been taken. Finally they were also able to show that medical evidence given by doctors in favour of the drugs was not impartial, for the Delhi Science Forum discovered that the doctors who gave this evidence attended the hearings in cars provided by the pharmaceutical companies which produced the drugs.

Thus, by the mid-eighties, feminism had not only spread into a variety of different areas and developed profession and issue based groups, within it three major streams of feminist though had developed, which can be generally characterized as being liberal, leftist and radical feminist. The liberal stream concentrated primarily on demanding reforms in those aspects of the polity which specifically affected women; the leftists situated the oppression of women within a holistic analysis of the general structures of oppression and called for a coming together of specific movements for social change in order to effect the revolutionary transformation of society; and the radical feminists concentrated on defining the development of femininity and masculinity in society as fundamental polarities, and experimented with reclaiming traditional sources of women's strength, creativity, etc.

Textile workers welcoming released comrades, Rajnandgaon, Madhya Pradesh, November, 1984

A woman activist of the Mazdoor Kisan (farm workers) union in Arwal, Bihar, 1980

Baiyeja Marathi feminist magazine for working class women, one of the earliest feminist magazines in India

In practice, however, there was often a considerable degree of overlap between these three streams, and, if looked at another way, it could be argued that different permutations and combinations of all three could be found both among feminists and within the movement. In their demands of the state, for example, most feminist campaigns could be characterized as belonging to the liberal stream; while attempts to link up with anti-caste, working class and landless labourers' movements were made by women from all three streams, as were attempts to re-interpret and reclaim traditional spaces.

The process of political clarification and differentiation which took place within the feminist movement as it grew was, thus, a fairly complex one. From its inception the contemporary Indian feminist movement had been self-consciously non-cohesive, and the existence of different steams of feminist thought had always been emphasised. At the same time, a certain commonality of women's experience had been stressed, as a point at which political differences could be transcended and joint action could be undertaken, however limited it might be. The problems of group formation, splits and reformation, which are common enough in all democratic movements for social change where there is a conflict between individual and collective being, had been dismissed largely as 'personal problems', though within groups there was often considerable discussion of the political implications of these problems. By the mid-eighties, however, there was a much greater awareness of these problems as problems, and it was felt that they could not be subsumed in the way they had earlier been.

Sadly, this public recognition of the importance of personal and collective relationships within feminism was arrived at only through a process of splits, schisms and feuds, leaving huge residues of pain and bitterness. This meant that the problems were either approached at such a level of abstraction that they had little effect on the groups or individuals concerned, or, when more directly confronted, they were expressed through accusations—which led the groups or individuals into adopting defensive postures, so that the problems were reinforced rather than resolved.

A feeling now grew that the quest for unity was not only futile but also counter-productive, for it allowed all sorts of evils to be glossed over: especially the way in which the movement was used to further either individual or organizational ambitions. This affected the movement in various ways, for it paved the way for an open display of sectarianism. First moves towards this were made largely by the party-political women's organizations, who took to print in order to express their differences from each other. While the left concentrated on

**Text of a leaflet published by Vimochana,
a women's group in Bangalore, for the 1989 elections**

TO ALL WOMEN VOTERS

Vimochana is not a political party. Why then do we reach out to you at the time of general elections? In 1979 when we first intervened in the political process, we did so to raise women's issues and put them on the political agenda. We had asked you then to vote for candidates who would recognize and talk about violence against women—dowry, rape, sexual harassment, exploitation in the media, shelter, fuel, water . . . questions on which politicans were totally silent.

We have come some way since then. Women's issues have become more 'visible'. We are now an essential part of political rhetoric—no speech or manifesto is complete without a formula to draw women into the political and national mainstream. Why then do we need to reach out to you once again?

Perhaps because we all know that in an age of false promises and hollow utopias, this rhetoric too hides the everyday reality of a majority of the women in India. We write to you this time to ask you to expose the hypocrisy behind political promises. All parties speak glibly about giving full representation of women in politics–some have gone so far as to promise 30% reservation in these elections. How many parties have fulfilled this promise? In fact this year the number of women candidates has drastically decreased.

We ask you expose this hypocrisy because we all know that most of our 'representatives' rarely practice at home what they preach on the streets—they cleverly separate private ethics from public morality. Today wife beaters and rapists can talk of equality of women; mafia dons can talk of justice; fundamentalists can preach secularism. . . . As women and 50% of the electorate we have to exercise our vote to transform this degenerate political culture. Let us all take a strong stand against 'leaders' like:

- Z.R. Ansari, the Union Minister of State for forestation, who despite being directly implicated in an attempt to rape charge by Mukti Datta, a woman activist working in Himachal Pradesh, has been given a Lok Sabha ticket.
- Kalvi, a Janata Dal leader from Rajasthan who openly came out in support of the murder of Roop Kanwar, a young widow burnt alive on her husband's pyre in 1988.
- The 19 CPI (M) activists arrested in connection with the gang rape of a young woman activist of Kashtakari Sanghatana, an organisation working with the tribals in Dahanu District, Maharashtra.
- Suraj Singh Deo, Bihar's mafia king, who is the trusted lieutenant of Chandrashekar, senior leader of the Janata Dal.
- H.K.L. Bhagat, who has been directly named by a number of the post-Indira Gandhi murder riot victims in Delhi in 1984 as the man behind the mass killings of Sikhs and yet continues to be a Union Minister and a senior Congress (I) leader.
- R.L. Jalappa, a Janata Dal candidate from Doddaballapur, who has been implicated in the murder of a lawyer.
- Dr. Venkatesh, a former Janata Party M.P., at present contesting on a Congress (I) ticket from Bethamangala to the Karnataka Assembly, who has not only deserted his wife and child without paying any maintenance despite a court order, but also has a criminal case of assault on his wife pending against him.

This list is endless. . . .

The irony is that none of the political parties involved i.e., the CPI (M), Janata , or the Congress (I) have thought it fit to initiate any enquiry against these individuals who have all been implicated in serious crimes. The greater irony is that some of these are not even seen as crimes—deserting a wife is seen as a 'personal' domestic issue. Society too sanctions such acts with its silence and cynicism about the 'criminalisation of politics'.

— Boycott these candidates in your constituency who get up on a public platform and speak of equality for women while denigerating and violating them in their personal lives.
— Support those candidates who you are assured will respond positively to issues of violence against women.
— Support those candidates who genuinely ateempt into put to practice what they speak, both in their public and in their private lives.

It is a small step but the first one.
Let us vote with our conscience and bring conscience back to politics.

VIMOCHANA
Forum for Women's Rights
P.O. Box 4605

November 1989

Dalit women's organization demonstration,
Delhi, date not known

'Find a people's solution to the Punjab
problem' Delhi, date not known

Forum against Rape demonstration demanding
re-opening of the Mathura rape case,
March 1980, Bombay

Activists of Pennuramai Iyakkam, Madurai, 1989,
at a demonstration

attacking autonomous feminist groups through their papers, pamphlets and other publications, the socialists concentrated on attacking the left, ostensibly for dividing the feminist movement, but actually because they were engaged in a struggle with the left over representation as the 'leaders' of the women's movement. More subtle and more scrupulous than they, autonomous feminist groups did not attack other women's organizations in public, but most of them began to devote considerable energy to establishing separate identities from each other, and now specific organizations were held to represent different strands of feminist practice, rather than ideology, as had earlier been the case.

Unfortunately, the logic of this development was such that organizational needs began to be privileged over the needs of the movement, and the identity of an organization was judged as much in terms of its clout as its ideas. Cynicism and bureaucratism both entered the movement, for it began to be assumed that self-interest was the order of the day, and the only difference was between those who operated on individual self-interest and those who were concerned with organizational self-interest. An

ugly divide now developed within the feminist movement, with one side feeling that the emphasis on organizational identity reflected a growth of Stalinism posing as collectivity, and the other side feeling that individualism was merely a mask for egotism. This was further compounded by a problem which is common to many developing countries, of aid for 'developmental activities' being poured into social movements, creating competition, schisms and bitterness.

The bureaucratism which generally complements the development of organizational identities was seen at its worst in joint action fora, where struggles over analyses, demands and strategies were relinquished on the assumption that the 'others' were closed to all argument, and thus attempting to discuss anything would be a waste of time; yet there were redoubled struggles over the division of spoils, such as the allotment of areas of campaigning, time and space for speeches, which banners were to be carried, and in what order organizations would march. Even worse, a kind of division of labour now developed in these fora, so that areas of interest were distributed between organizations without any attempt to achieve, or even discuss, commonality of interests.

Shahjehan Begum 'Apa' with photograph of her daughter, allegedly murdered for dowry

Satyarani Chhada at a demonstration protesting the alleged dowry-murder of her daughter, Kanchan, Delhi 1982

As a result of this, autonomous feminist groups lost much of the space which they had earlier occupied on the premise that they were different from party-political women's organizations. Moreover, their shift away from agitational activities in the early eighties not only left an empty space for party-political women's organizations to move into, but also led to a significant loss of presence through the media.

Meanwhile, women's issues had become so widely recognized that the centre and right parties also formed women's fronts, and special attention began to be paid to women in most general movements of the eighties, though this was more noticeable in peasant movements than in workers' ones. In Maharashtra, a peasant movement led by an independent, Sharad Joshi, found an especially strong base amongst women, which was further expanded by his working with locally based feminists such as Gail Omvedt and Chetna. As a result, such 'women's issues' as wife-beating and sharing control over the household income began to be raised within the movement; while women activists began to be given more place within the hierarchy of leadership. Today, they plan to field women candidates in the forthcoming local elections. In Bihar, moves started to be made by various Marxist-Leninist fragments to come together in the early eighties, resulting in the formation of the Indian Peoples Front (IPF) in 1984, which rapidly grew to lead the strongest peasant movement in the state in the eighties. Again, special attention was paid to organizing women; about fifty thousand women took part in their campaigns, and links were forged with the autonomous feminist groups, resulting in the IPF's getting involved in jointly organizing (with several other women's groups) the national-level feminist conference in Patna in April 1988.

At the same time the extreme right began to organize their own bases amongst women: in 1982 the Maharashtra-based Hindu chauvinist Shiv Sena formed a women's wing whose primary activity was anti-Muslim propaganda. Interestingly, they focussed on arguments which had been advanced over a hundred years ago and which have had an enduring success in India; that the Muslim rate of reproduction was so prolific that in a year their population would be larger than that of Hindus. The year, of course, never comes.

An even more interesting—and worrying—development took place in Delhi, Rajasthan and parts of Bengal, where under the aegis of the Marwari-funded Rani Sati Organization, feminist discourse was used to propagate a cult of widow immolation from 1982–83. Women's demonstrations were organized in various parts of the country to demand women's 'right' to commit sati: in Delhi, the organization, which already ran a couple of sati-temples in the city, was granted land to build another temple by the municipality, and it was only after a furore ensued, initiated by the feminists and supported by the then Prime Minister, Indira Gandhi, that this grant was withdrawn.

Simultaneously, counter-movements against feminist (or women's rights) ideas began to be initiated by sections of traditionalist society, which took the more normal course of using an anti-feminist discourse based on demands for religious or cultural autonomy. The rise of these counter-movements was partly related to the spread of feminism and the influence it was beginning to have on women's attitudes, especially within the family. The kind of individual support work that women's centres did, for example, involved them with people's lives in a way that was more intimate, and therefore more threatening, than their earlier agitations. Unsurprisingly, this provoked a considerable degree of both public and private hostility, and feminists began to face attacks from irate families, in person and through police and courts.

However, where earlier such attacks would have led to a wave of sympathy for the feminists, from the mid-eighties on they were accompanied by a public, and increasingly sophisticated, critique of feminism. Interestingly, the arguments against the feminists were remarkably similar to those advanced against social reformers in the nineteenth century: that they were westernized, upper-class and urban, and therefore ignorant of, and unsympathetic to, traditional 'Indian' society. It was further argued, both then and now, that the reformers of feminists could not claim to represent any large category of society, and therefore their demands should be ignored by the state. Unlike the nineteenth century, however, when anti-feminists had not organized their own representative fora, in the nineteen-eighties almost every political tendency had its own women's organization, and claimed to represent the desires of 'Indian women'.

What this meant, in effect, was that the category 'Indian women' itself was broken down into several constituents, of which the most important became communal identity: that is to say, while the feminists had attempted to distinguish between women on lines of caste and class, and later region and culture, counter-movements against feminism now imposed communal distinctions instead, so that Indian women were distinguished from each other as being Muslim, Christian, Hindu, and so on. Not only were attempts to better the conditions of women of any one community treated as attempts to impose alien norms and interfere with communal autonomy, communal offensives were now launched against laws which had existed over a century, under the somewhat arbitrary banner of 'religion in danger'. From the days of the British, secularism had been interpreted in India as the State's recognition and codification of different religion-based laws, but these had not, by and large, been used to take away rights conferred under civil law. This, however, happened in the mid-eighties, when under pressure from Muslim religious leaders, the government passed a law which deprived divorced—and destitute—Muslim women of the right to maintenance by their husbands. How this came about, and what the reactions of the feminists were, will be described in the next section.

NOTES

1. Stri Shakti Sangathana, 'We were Making History ...' op.cit; Rohini P.R., Sujata S.V., and Neelam C., 'My Life is One Long Struggle' op.cit.
2. A classic example is Vandana Shiva, Staying Alive; Women, Ecology and Survival in India, Delhi, 1988, Kali for Women.
3. Neelam Chaturvedi, interview, December 10, 1987.
4. Kiran Shaheen, interview, March 5, 1986.

10. Personal Law and Communal Identities

Hyderabad during the riots, date not known

Not surprisingly, both the pre and post-Independence feminist movements have seen the family and home as the single most important structure ordering women's lives. In the late seventies feminists had focussed on the dowry form as an expression of the subordination of women within the family, and had seen dowry-murder as one of the most brutal manifestations of violence against women. By the early eighties, attempts to analyse the relationship of women to and within the family had led to examining the codification of women's rights in marriage, divorce, property, maintenance, etc., as in India most family law is differentiated on the basis of religion, as well as community. This entailed investigation into different 'personal' laws. (By a curious feat of meaning, the term 'personal' when conjoined with law means the different family laws of different religious communities).

The issue of personal law became especially controversial for feminists in 1985, with what is now referred to as 'The Shah Bano case'. On the 23rd of April, a five member Constitution Bench of the Supreme Court led by Chief Justice Chandrachud, ruled that a 75-year old woman, Shah Bano, was entitled to maintenance by her husband under Section 125 of the Criminal Procedure Code. Shah Bano's husband, Mohammad Ahmed Khan, an advocate, had divorced her after roughly a half-century of marriage. Ten years earlier, under pressure from her husband, Shah Bano and her children had moved out of the main house, into a sort of annexe. For two years her husband gave her Rs 200 per month, and then abruptly stopped. In 1978 she filed an application in the Indore Magistrate's Court, under Section 125 of the Criminal Procedure Code (Cr. P.C.), asking that her husband be ordered to pay her maintenance. Intended to prevent vagrancy due to destitution, this section entitles destitute, deserted, or divorced women to support from their husbands, provided they (the husbands) are not destitute themselves. Destitution thus defines the provisions in this section. The maximum amount allowed by it as 'maintenance' was Rs 500 a month, certainly not adequate for both shelter and subsistence. Shah Bano asked for the maximum, on the grounds that she was old and could not work to support herself. In other words, under section 125 she had to show that she was destitute in order to claim support from her husband.

While Shah Bano's application was still pending, her husband decided to divorce her, using the triple *talaq*, which the Koran names the most lowly form of divorce.[1] At the same time, he deposited Rs 3000 in court, claiming that he was returning the *mehr* agreed upon at the

time of their marriage. According to Shah Bano, however, the *mehr*, a sum meant to be given to the bride as 'a mark of respect', was 3000 silver coins. Meanwhile, the magistrate ruled that Shah Bano *was* entitled to maintenance under section 125, but fixed the amount at a ludicrous Rs 25 per month. She went on appeal to the Madhya Pradesh High Court, which raised the amount to Rs 179.20. Now Mohammad Ahmed Khan went on appeal to the Supreme Court arguing that the High Court judgement exceeded its jurisdiction and violated Muslim personal law as stated by the *Shariat*. In effect, several statements made up this contention: first, that as a Muslim he was bound primarily by Islamic law; second, that as maintenance from a husband related to the laws of marriage and divorce, which in his case fell under Muslim personal law, Shah Bano's application should be judged by this law and no other; and third, that if marriage, divorce and maintenance regulations fell under personal law, then criminal law should not enter the picture at all. In support of these arguments, he produced written statements acquired from the Muslim Personal Law Board, which said that under the *Shariat* the husband was not obliged to pay maintenance for more than three months after the divorce (the *iddat*

National Federation of Indian Women solidarity demonstration with Pakistan feminists, around 1986

A poster made by Saheli, a women's group
showing how religions can be used to entrap
and exploit women, Delhi 1985

period): with this, and with giving his ex-wife her *mehr*,
his duties towards her ended. Moreover, said the Board,
the *Shariat* did not deal with the question of how the
woman was to support herself after the *iddat*, and therefore the question was outside the purview of the court.

By the time the case was before the Supreme Court,
therefore, the distinction between maintenance on destitution (section 125), and maintenance on divorce
(which falls under personal law), was largely blurred. By
virtue of this the distinction between criminal and civil
law was also blurred: at the same time, criminal law was
banished from the territory of maintenance. Finally, the
entire problem of female destitution was itself placed
outside the purview of the court, on the grounds that the
text of personal law did not deal with it.[2]

Perhaps if the judgement of the Supreme Court on
Mohammad Ahmed Khan's petition had ignored these
points, it might not have been so controversial. It would,
however, have been hard for them to do so, because
these points *were* being argued before them, and coun-
tered by Shah Bano's counsel, who cited two verses from
the Koran to show that the provision of maintenance was
regarded as a duty for the 'righteous'. In any case, the

five-member constitution Bench, led by Justice Chandrachud, *did* go ahead and comment on abuses on women
in the name of religion, and the advisability of a uniform
civil code.

Basically, the judgement can be summarized as follows: firstly, it upheld Shah Bano's right to maintenance
from her husband both under Section 125 and under
Muslim personal law, quoting the two verses from the
Koran which were cited by Shah Bano's counsel, Mr
Daniel Latifi.[3] Secondly, it asserted that Section 125 'cut
across the barriers of religion', that is, it transcended the
personal laws of the religious communities which any
married pair might belong to. Thirdly, it was critical of
the way women 'have been traditionally subjected to
unjust treatment', citing statements by both Manu, the
Hindu law maker, and the Prophet, as examples of
traditional injustice. And finally, it urged the Government to frame a common civil code, because the constitutional promise of a common or uniform civil code
would only be realized at the initiative of the
Government.

Neither the upholding of section 125 nor the criticisms of personal law as unjust to women were particularly new. Two earlier judgements upholding the rights

A Saheli poster on the theme of religious
fundamentalism, Delhi, 1985

The text of a Resolution adopted by women's groups in Delhi on the Muslim Women's (Right to Protection on Divorce) Bill, 1986.

This public meeting of Karmika organized on 22 March 1986 at 10 a.m. and attended by various academicians, lawyers, journalists, doctors, teachers and social workers, resolves as under:

We strongly protest against the Muslim Women's (Right to Protection on Divorce) Bill, 1986, introduced in the Lok Sabha recently. The Bill is a charter of slavery to Muslim women and highly derogatory to the dignity of all women. The Criminal Procedure Code confers a statutory right of maintenance on women in every case irrespective of creed or custom if a person of sufficient means neglects or refuses to maintain his wife. The object behind this law is to save women from being exposed to vagrancy or destitution which, as we all know, lead to other social problems. Surely no religion in the world would advocate exploitation of this deprived section and the neglect of women. The Holy Koran stipulates in Verse II.241 which also provides: *Aur talaq walon ke liye bhi munasif taur per nano-napht hai. Yeh wajib hai perhezdaron par.* Maulana Ahmed Raza Khan Sahib, the well known authority on translation of the Holy Koran has translated this verse as: 'To render divorced women appropriate reasonable maintenance. This is compulsory for the god fearing.'

It is unfortunate that people with vested interests have given this very human issue a communal and religious colouring. Ruling party MPs who had sworn in their election manifesto to protect the rights of women, have here completely gone back on their pledge. We ask: 'Are election promises mere window dressing?' Should they not apologise to the public whom they have betrayed?

The other argument of the fundamentalists that the Supreme Court has no right or authority to interpret the Holy Koran is also highly misplaced. In the codified law of Muslims, like Dissolution of Muslim Marriages Act, 1939, it has already been provided that a court may look into the relevant provisions of the Koran. This judgement of the Supreme Court in the Shah Bano case is supported by the rulings of great Muslim jurists like Imam Jafar and Imam Shafai who are accepted throughout the Muslim world as authorities.

We urge the Government to look into this issue rationally and humanely as it has far reaching implications and is even a threat to the unity of the nation. We appeal to the Honourable Prime Minister of India and the Parliament to abandon the Bill as it is against basic human rights. The Bill, if passed, will take women back by fifty years and thereby the country, for women are, after all, nearly half the population of this country, be that Muslim, Sikh, Hindu, Christian or Parsi.

---

of Muslim Women to maintenance under section 125 had been made, by the Supreme Court, in Bai Tahira *vs* Ali Hussain Fissali, 1979, and Fuzlumbi *vs* K.Khader Ali, 1980.[4] Chief justice Krishna Iyer had delivered the judgements, and in both he had urged the need for judicial reform in Muslim personal law. Yet neither of the earlier two judgements used the 'in any case' arguments of the later judgement, which might have allowed misreading: for example, having decided that Section 125 was consistent with Muslim personal law, it was unnecessary to assert that, in any case, section 125, being part of criminal law, cut across the 'barriers' of religion. Alternatively, having decided to uphold the jurisdiction of section 125, as superceding personal law, it was unnecessary to interpret the *Shariat.*

Given that the judgement ruled that Section 125 Cr. P.C. and the Shariat were mutually consistent, it was certainly odd that a common civil code was urged on grounds which appeared to contradict the ruling:

A belief seems to have gained ground that it is for the Muslim community to take a lead in the matter of reform of their personal law. *A Common Civil Code will help the cause of national integration by removing disparate loyalties to laws which have conflicting ideologies.* No community is likely to bell the cat by making *gratuitous* concessions on this issue . . . we understand the difficulties involved in bringing persons of different faiths and persuasions on a common platform. But a beginning has to be made if the constitution has to have a meaning. (Emphasis added)[5]

Put like this, it was clearly possible to infer that the judges were saying that Muslim personal law was bad, but 'the Muslim community' preferred unjust laws, so somebody (in this case the State) would have to impose justness on them. It was similarly easy to infer that imposition was to be made not for the sake of justice alone, but also for the cause of 'national integration'. And from this it was also easy to infer that national integration required Muslims to abandon 'loyalty' to Islam and Islamic personal law.

The judgement was widely criticized on a variety of grounds: overall, feminists, liberals and secularists were critical of it for having brought issues of religion and

Activists in Delhi demonstrate in the old city against the use of religion to divide women.

Activists on a peace and anti-communal march in Ayodhya, take a moment off to rest.

personal law into what was essentially a question of secular, criminal law. Further, said some feminists, instead of dealing with the general issue of personal laws and how they affected women's rights in any depth, the judgement focussed on Muslim personal law alone. Commenting on this in an article, Madhu Kishwar concluded: 'By singling out Muslim men and Islam in this way, justice Chandrachud converts what is essentially a women's rights issue into an occasion for a gratuitous attack upon the community.'[6]

Muslim religious leaders concurred in the view that the judgement represented an attack on their community. The *ulema* (scholar-priests) issued a *fatwa* (proclamation) that it was against the teachings of Islam. Wide publicity was given to the fatwa, and within a few months the whole issue took the form of a communal agitation, claiming that Islam was in danger. Muslim communalists demanded that the Supreme Court judgement be repeated and Muslim women be excluded from section 125; jumping into the fray, Hindu communalists upheld the judgement, gleefully arguing that it supported their contention that Muslims were 'barbaric' and 'anti-national'.

In August 1985, a Bill seeking to exclude Muslim women from the purview of Section 125 came up in Parliament. Sponsored by a Muslim league M.P., G.M. Banatwala, the Bill was clearly in response to the Shah Bano petition and the feminist espousal of her cause, for it was introduced while her case was being decided upon by the Supreme Court, just about a month before the judgement. The government decided to oppose the Bill, and briefed a Muslim minister, Arif Mohammad Khan, to argue against it in Parliament, on the grounds that section 125 was intended to prevent vagrancy, and as such was not interfering with the personal laws of any community. Arif Mohammad, however, diverged from his brief, delivering an impassioned plea for a humane reading of the *Shariat*.

Muslim liberals, feminists and social reformers began campaigns all over India, but especially in Maharashtra, to publicise the upholding of Section 125 and to demand improvements in the legal rights of Muslim women against polygamy, and to maintenance. At the same time outraged ulemas denounced Muhammad Arif Khan saying that as a layman he had no right to interpret the

Shariat, and joined in a massively orchestrated campaign to repeal the judgement and support Banatwala's Bill. Over one lakh demonstrated in Bombay and at least as many in Bhopal, and there were a spate of smaller demonstrations all over the country; in Hyderabad there was a bandh; in Lucknow the Muslim Personal Law Board announced that true Muslims should no longer go to the Courts for redress, but should come to the Shariat Courts which they were opening. As against this, only a few hundred demonstrated in favour of the judgement. Muslims who did so were often assaulted: the Talaq Mukti Morcha, which was launched in November in Kolhapur (Maharashtra), and which decided to march through the districts of Maharashtra publicising the judgement with a poster exhibition, was forced to call off its march because the marchers had been assaulted in so many places. They were greeted by black flags in Miraz, threatened by a mob of four hundred in Parbhani, stoned at Nanded and Jalgaon, and in Ahmednagar they were surrounded by a mob of ten thousand, brandishing black flags, who stoned them, forcing them to call off the rest of the march.

To understand why the issue became so very heated one has to look at the context in which it arose. The 1980s witnessed a steep rise in communal violence all over India, both Hindu-Mulsim and Hindu-Sikh. The November 1984 riots were particularly alarming: not only was Mrs Gandhi's assassination treated as a communal issue by the Congress-I, but no attempt at all was made either to punish the guilty, or even to investigate the charges of political and police involvement in the riots. The sense that Hindu communalism was acquiring increasing legitimacy in the eyes of the state was further strengthened by the Ram Janmabhoomi agitation which was launched in U.P.

In October 1984 the Vishwa Hindu Parishad, a relatively new Hindu communalist organization, launched a full-fledged agitation demanding that a shrine in the precincts of the Babri Masjid in Ayodhya be declared the birthplace of Ram, and a temple built on the spot. The question of worship at the shrine-cum-Masjid had been a source of conflict since the late nineteenth century and, pending a court decision on the issue, the whole place was locked up. The court case was revived by a 'Hindu' advocate, and in the meantime, the Vishwa Hindu Parishad (V.H.P.) led a 200,000 strong march to Ayodhya in 1984, to 'liberate' the shrine, and performed hundreds of fire-rituals all over the Hindi-speaking belt in 1985, to mobilize around their demand for a Ram Janmabhoomi temple to be built within the precincts of the mosque. Alarmed by the growing strength of the V.H.P.–led agitation and the threat it posed, several Muslim religious leaders and politicians formed a Babri Masjid Action committee, to defend the status quo.

The Babri Masjid issue and the Shah Bano case began to be linked as representing a Hindu communal onslaught on Indian Muslims. Syed Shahabuddin, one of the leaders of the Babri Masjid Action Committee and a member of the Janata Party, shot to prominence as a leader of the agitation against the judgement, organizing a petition against it, which was signed by over 300,000 Muslims.[7] In state elections in December 1985, Shahabuddin trounced his Congress-I opponent from the Kishenganj constituency, despite an all-out Congress-I effort to win Muslim votes by putting up the secretary of the Jamat-ul-ulema-e-Hind, and bringing two hundred ulemas to canvass for their candidate.

On February 1, 1986, the district magistrate before whom the Babri Masjid-Ram Janmabhoomi case was pending, decreed that the shrine be opened to Hindus for worship. The V.H.P. celebrated this with 'victory processions'. Muslims took out 'mourning processions' in retaliation, and soon clashes between the two groups began which escalated into riots in Delhi, Srinagar and various parts of Madhya Pradesh. Riots spilled over also

Demonstrating against the Ram Janmabhoomi agitation with the slogan 'Ram's presence is everywhere, do not instigate violence in his name,' Delhi, 1989

to Pakistan. Alarmed by their loss in Kishenganj and seeing a further loss of credibility in Muslim eyes, the Congress-I began to backtrack on their assurance of Muslim women's rights under Section 125, announcing that they were considering a review of the judgement and would introduce a Bill on the lines of Banatwala's Bill. To many this announcement appeared as an utterly cynical willingness to sacrifice the rights of Muslim women on the anvil of political expediency. Immediately, Muslim reform groups and women's organizations

tion of Indian Women and the Dahej Virodhi Chetna Manch courted arrest outside Parliament House on the same day. On the next day, February 26, Arif Muhammad Khan resigned from his post as Minister of State for Energy in protest at the change in the Government's stand on Section 125. His wife, Reshma Arif Khan, joined in campaigns against the Bill.

Opposition to the Bill took the form of public meetings, demonstrations, a concerted press campaign, and lobbying. Interestingly, however, the campaign against

Solidarity with Shah Bano, Delhi, 1985

began to lobby the government against this announcement but were unsuccessful. On the 25th of February the Muslim Women (Protection of Rights on Divorce) Bill was introduced which excluded divorced Muslim women from the purview of Section 125, stating that the obligation of their husbands to maintain them ended with a three months *iddat* period, after which their families would have to support them or, failing this, their local Waqf Board.

The introduction of the Bill caused a considerable furore. Hearing that it was due to be introduced on the 25th, about 150–200 women from the Janwadi Mahila Samiti, the Mahila Dakshata Samiti, the National Federa-

the Bill was not carried out under a single, joint action umbrella, even temporarily, as the anti-dowry and anti-rape agitations had been. Instead a series of different identities and blocs appeared, constituted separately for each form of opposition. Public meetings in Delhi, for example, were generally organized separately by different women's organizations, such as Karmika or the Mahila Dakshata Samiti. For demonstrations, on the other hand, women's groups in Delhi formed into separate blocs. The autonomous women's groups came together to organize a demonstration on March 7, demanding that the communalisation of women's issues cease, and a uniform civil code be framed. A loose

**Exercpts from an open letter
(dated February 28, 1986) to the
Prime Minister from Justice V.R. Krishna Iyer on
the question of personal laws**

Sec. 125 Cr P.C. is obviously a secular provision designed to salvage all divorced damsels in penurious distress, regardless of religion, from the throes of desparate destitution, which may drive them to prostitution and other survival alternatives. This provision is sustained by Art. 15 of the Constitution and applies to all women equally . . . . Illusory alternatives driving Muslim women to seek maintenance from their parents and from the Wakf Board (most of which have little in the kitty) are clearly and substantially discriminatory. You could as well put Hindu and Parsi and Christian women under the same handicap and drive them to their religious trusts. Why pick on Muslim women? They are the major victims, as statistics show from a study of applications for maintenance under Sec. 125 Cr. P.C.

You will easily appreciate that this provision has no relation to liability to maintenance under the personal law. The jurisdiction is different, the jurisprudence is different, the measure and procedure are different. One is rooted in family law, the other in public order and social justice. To confuse between the two is to be guilty of judicial cataract. Sec. 125 Cr. P.C. is of British vintage broadened by the benign Parliament. The 21st century is a summons to move forward progressively, not to retreat regressively, frightened by 6th century primitivism. Sec. 125 rescues needy divorcees, rendered homeless, from moral danger, resorting to means of livelihood contrary to peace, tranquillity and social health. Such a provision is founded on the secular values of our Republic and is expressly contemplated in Art. 25, which empowers the State to make provision necessitated by public order, morality and health. To contend that Sec. 125 is for or against any religion is a crass caricature of the scope and purpose of the law. To invoke 'religion in danger' to resist a provision based on the constitutional concern for public order, morality and health envisioned in Art. 25 is to draw the red herring across the trail. Three decisions of the Supreme Court, which have consistently affirmed this approach, are enough authority to negative the fundamentalist distortion. Masculine obscurantism, Muslim or Hindu, should accept the law laid down by the highest Court explaining the raison d'etre of the measure.

True, some ayatollahs of India and their political muktiars are making noises as is their wont, as if Islam would decline, if women in distress were kept contented! What a travesty of truth! Many hundreds of liberal Muslims and many organisations of Muslim and other women have, to my personal knowledge, applauded the Shahbano ruling and have been outraged by the reversal of the ruling through the legislative process. It is a grievous error to exalt the strident few reactionaries and pachydermic communalists as the sole representatives of the masses of women. Women's status is at stake; kindly discover the truth before it is too late. There is bitter disappointment among Muslims and total disenchantment among women consequent on the surrender of the Prime Minister to a handful of surrogates in Parliament whose 'sound and fury' scare him and make him deaf to the deeper feelings of the broader community.

What is more, there is a terrible danger of Hindu communalism being whipped up on this score. The temperature is hotting up. Bigots on both sides are busy. I implore you not to let down our secular stability, the political motive being transparent.

Let me tell you that the bill is a sin against the Quran and the Constitution of Wakfs. Many Islamic scholars hold that the Koranic command to husbands to pay upkeep expenses to divorcees beyond the period of *iddat* is clear. Again, Wakfs are religious and charitable trusts by pious muslims to perform specified holy acts for their spiritual benefit. It will be sacrilege to divert these funds for maintenance of other people's wives. Many Wakf Boards are themselves poor and it is an illusion to make them caretakers of jilted and jettisoned wives . . . the whole project is a legislative tamasha? Please don't stultify our great Parliament. Already the Supreme Court Judges have been insulted by Minister Ansari in Parliament.

May I conclude with a prayer to you on behalf of Indian women, human rights defenders, secularist radicals and constitutional advocates?

The bill to kill the Shabano decision of the Supreme Court is the unfortunate political product of a creative genius for multi-dimensional injustice. The bill is in an injustice to our Republic's secular principle; it is an injustice to women's basic rights and, therefore, violative of human rights; it is an injustice to the egalitarian policy in our Constitution in Arts. 14 and 21 and 25; it is a vindicative injustice to Muslim women selling the soul of the State's humanism to obscurantist fundamentalists; it is an injustice to the holy Quran which insists on payment of maintenance of divorced women in distress; it is an injustice to the

21st century because it throws us back to the 6th century to buy Islamic votes through the noisy illusion of electoral support of fundamentalists whose hold on the liberal muslim intelligentsia and the suffering masses of women is marginal; it is an ultra vires injustice to the law of Wakfs because Wakfs are not trusts to look after privatised wrongs inflicted by irresponsible talaqs; it is an injustice to family integrity because it is fraught with potential for litigation between close relatives. It is an injustice to pragmatic working of the law because, functionally speaking, the provisions lead the destitute to several cases in search of a pittance; it is an injustice to national stability, because the secular credibility of the Government will be a casualty. The dictate of the social dialectic of India today leaves no choice.

coalition across India was formed between autonomous women's groups, Socialists, Maoists and social reformers, to put together a signature petition against the Bill. CPI and CPM influenced women's organizations formed a separate coalition, organizing a rally on April 18, and jointly addressing a memorandum to M.P.s, urging them to vote against the Bill. Several different lobbying groups were formed, representing different strands of opposition to the Bill: liberal, feminist, progressive, and Muslim.

While the first three marked an evident need for separate ideological formations, the last showed the constraints which the communalisation of the issue had imposed on Muslim suporters of Shah Bano's case. The lack of any noticeable opposition to the Ram Janmabhoomi agitation from non-Muslims, especially Hindus, had left large sections of Muslims feeling more vulnerable than ever. Many Muslims who had earlier campaigned for a change in their personal law, now became ardent supporters of it. Among them was Dr Tahir Mahmood, an expert on Muslim personal law. Though he had earlier pleaded for reform of Muslim marital and divorce laws, as well as for a uniform civil code, in the revised edition of his book he withdrew his chapter on the need for a uniform civil code, and hailed the Bill as welcome. It is not surprising, then, that those Muslims who opposed the Bill felt impelled to form ranks within their own community. The Committee for the Protection of the Rights of Muslim Women, for example, which was formed solely in order to oppose the Bill, decided to limit its membership to Muslims, allowing Muslim men to join but not non-Muslim feminists.

For most of the autonomous women's groups this was a hard decision to accept, because it appeared to lend legitimacy to the idea that the rights of women *could* be defined by the religious community they belonged to, instead of arguing that religion and rights were separate and distinct. By implication, it also lent some support to two other arguments that feminists have had to contend with: one, that there is no such thing as a common category of women, because they are differentiated by caste, class and community, and therefore any definition of rights has also to be based on these differentiations:

and the other, that as different groups of women have different interests, there is no 'real' basis on which they can work together.

As the previous pages have shown, however, the situation in which the agitation against the Shah Bano judgement took place, and the form which it took, were such that lines of response—or even counter campaigns—were to a certain extent already given. At a time when Hindu communalism was on the upswing, and when there was no developed movement against communalism, the concurrence of the Shah Bano and Ram Janmabhoomi agitations did create a strong pressure on most Muslim opponents of the Bill, whether reformist, feminist or Marxist, to find a way in which they could uphold the rights granted under section 125 while making it clear that they affirmed their Muslim identity. An interesting point of comparison here is the situation of the 1930s: at a time of rising communal conflict between Hindus and Muslims, when the All India Women's Conference and other women's organizations raised demands for a unform civil code, Muslim women felt forced to choose to focus on demands for changes within their own personal law. Ironically, what they demanded was that the *Shariat* be taken as authoritative, because customary law treated women badly: 'The Muslim Women's organizations have condemned customary law as it adversely affects their rights, and have demanded that Muslim Personal Law [*Shariat*] should be made applicable to them.'[8]

In 1937, the Muslim Personal Law (*Shariat*) Application Act was passed, making the rules laid down by the *Shariat* for marriage, divorce, maintenance, inheritance and intestate succession applicable to *all* Muslim women, 'notwithstanding any custom or usage to the contrary.' Like the Widow Remarriage Act of 1856, the *Shariat* (Application) Act, while conferring better rights on some Muslim Women, curtailed the rights of others: for example, it superseded the *aliyasanthana* law followed by some of the Mapillaas of Kerala, which was based on matriliny.

Interestingly, the Muslim Women's Bill of 1986, which took away the Muslim women's right to maintenance from their husbands (to the limited extent provided for

Demonstrating against the Muslim Women's Bill, Delhi, 1986

by Section 125), also conferred a new right upon them which non-Muslim women do not have any equivalent of: the right to maintenance from the Waqf Board, that is, the body which administers communally-held lands (granted for charitable purposes, or the benefit of the community). One of the not-so-odd fallouts of the agitation against the judgement has been that after the Bill was enacted there have been a spate of lower and higher court judgements granting divorced Muslim women much higher sums of maintenance, payable by the Waqf Board, than have been granted before.

Not that this is in any way a justification of the Bill-turned-act. By removing even the minor obligation which Section 125 imposed on husbands who had abandoned or divorced their wives, the Act made it legitimate for Muslim husbands to simply leave their wives stranded. The curtailment of the jurisdiction of Section 125, moreover, not only set a precedent for doing away with any checks on mistreatment of women under personal law, it also laid the foundation for excluding specific groups or communities from culpability for acts which abet crimes relating to women. It is especially significant that it was in the course of this agitation that the demand for legalizing sati was first made.

Despite strong opposition to the Bill, it was forced through Parliament on the 6th of May 1986, after an all night debate. The Congress-I had issued a party whip instructing all its M.P.s to vote for the Bill, no matter what their opinions on the matter were. This must have been the first time that a whip had been issued on a matter concerning women.

For feminists the agitation around Muslim women's rights to maintenance consisted of a series of bitter lessons. Discovering the ease with which a 'community in danger' resorts to fundamentalist assertions of self, among which, invariably, control over women is one of the first such assertions to be made, feminists were confronted with the associated discovery of the ease with which the Indian state chose to accommodate communalism (by taking no action against the Ram Janmabhoomi agitation), and balance this by a concession to fundamentalism (allowing personal law to cut into the application of uniform laws such as Section 125). For some years prior to this agitation, feminists had revived demands for a uniform civil code to replace religion based and differentiated family laws ('personal law'), on the grounds that such laws sanctioned the oppression of women. Two initiatives against existing personal laws had received widespread support and publicity from feminists all over the country: Mary Roy's petition against Christian personal law, and Shahnaz Sheikh's petition against Muslim personal law. Filed sometime in the early eighties, in the Supreme Court, Shahnaz Sheikh's petition argued that Muslim personal law should be declared violative of Articles 13, 14 and 15 of the Indian Constitution, which guarantee equality before law and prohibit discrimination on the basis of sex, religion or race. A great deal of pressure was put on her by conservative and fundamental sections of Muslim society to withdraw this petition, but she did not do so. The petition attracted considerable press attention—so much so that some feminists feared that the petition would be adversely affected by the publicity which surrounded it. After the Shah Bano judgement the issues raised by the petition lapsed into obscurity. In effect, the agitation interrupted developing critiques of personal law and moves towards some form of uniform civil code.

At the same time the agitation posed certain issues which were to become increasingly important for feminists in the years to follow. First of all, there was the question of secularism, its definition and practice, in particular by the state, and its relation to religious freedom. By and large, opponents of the Muslim Women's Bill espoused a classic liberal democratic view of secularism as a system which separated religion from politics, which disallowed religious definitions of the rights of the individual, and which allowed freedom of religious practice only in so far as it did not cut into the rights of the indivudual. Zoya Hasan, of the Committee for the Protection of the Rights of Muslim women, for example, criticized the Bill on the grounds that it could hardly be called secular to pass a law which severely restricted the rights of the religious, while the memorandum drafted by the committee argued that 'by offering concessions to communal/sectarian groups with a view to short-term political or electoral gains', the 'secular fabric of our society' was being frayed.[9] The signature petition jointly organized by feminists, social reform and far left groups argued further, that all personal laws 'have meant inequality and subordinate status for women in relation to men', and therefore religion 'should only govern the relationship between a human being and god, and should not govern the relationship between man and man or man and woman.'[10]

As against this, the government definition of secularism appeared to be radically different. According to the Prime Minister, Rajiv Gandhi, 'secularism is the right of

Demonstrating against the Muslim Women's Bill, Delhi, 1986

every religion to coexist with another religion. We acknowledge this by allowing every religion to have its own secular laws.'[11] If this statement is not to be dismissed as mere nonsense, then the only meaning to be extracted from it is that he defined personal laws as being secular—presumably on the grounds that as religion here defined the relationships between human beings (rather than between humans and god) it was on 'secular' terrain. Religion, then, could formulate secularism.

Another implication of this statement was that all 'religions' had the right to representation within the law and, indeed, had the right to make their own laws. While to a certain extent these rights were not new, the supremacy they accorded to personal law re-affirmed the colonial codification of religion-based family laws and ran counter to the constitutional promises of offering options from personal laws and attempts to move towards uniform rights.

The second major issue which feminists were confronted with was the question of representation, or representativeness. Though the Committee for the Protection of the Rights of Muslim Women was formed partly to bypass this issue (by offering solely Muslim support for Shah Bano and Section 125), and both Mary Roy and Shahnaz Sheikh were demanding reform of personal laws which affected them directly, it was argued that none of them represented the 'real' desires of 'real' Muslim women. So much pressure was put on Shah Bano that she gave up the right she had fought for for so many years, asking the Supreme Court to record that she now stood against the petition they had upheld, and abjuring the maintenance the court had accorded her. As in the agitation against rape, the problems and needs of women were soon lost sight of in the discourse of 'community'. Even worse, in this agitation, setting a trend for others to follow, the individual woman was smothered by a newly constructed symbol of the 'real woman'. This positing of the 'real woman, in opposition to the feminist, began to be widely made for the first time in the history of the contemporary women's movement in the mid-nineteen-eighties, and it is revealing that it arose in the course of communal-fundamentalist self-assertion. In the agitation around sati which followed hard on the heels of the Muslim Women's Bill agitation, the issue of secularism, religious representation, the Indian nation-state and the symbol of 'the woman', as defined here, were expanded even further, and used as sticks to beat feminists with.

NOTES

1. One of several methods of divorce permitted by Islam, the triple *talaq* is the easiest, requiring only that one party say 'I divorce you' thrice.
2. Most of the information in this section has been compiled from press clippings from various national dailies. References are only being given for quotations, and for sources other than newspapers.
3. The same verses were also quoted in the S.C. judgement, and cited by Arif Mohammad Khan in his plea for a humane reading of the *Shariat*. They are:

Ayat 241	*English Version*
Wali'l motallaqatay	For divorced women
Mata un	Maintenance (should be provided)
Bil maroofay	On a reasonable (scale)
Haqqan	This is a duty
Alal muttaqeena	On the righteous

Ayat 242	
Kazaleka yuba iyyanullaho	Thus doth God
Lakum ayatehee la Allakum	Make clear His Signs
Taqeloon	To you: in order that you may understand

(as in AIR 1985 Supreme Court 945. Henceforth referred to as S.C. 945).

4. AIR 1979 S.C. 362 and AIR 1980 S.C. 1730.
5. S.C. 945, Para 32.
6. Madhu Kishwar, 'Pro Women or Anti–Muslim?: The Shah Bano Controversy', *Manushi*, 32 (Vol 6, No.2) Jan–Feb. 1986
7. See *India Today*, Jan 31, 1986, 'The Muslims: A Community in Turmoil'.
8. Preamble to Muslim Personal Law (Shariat) Application Act, 1937.
9. Memorandum of the Committee for the Protection of the Rights of Muslim Women, *Mainstream*, Vol XXIV No.27, March 8, 1986.
10. Extract from the opening statement of the petition.
11. Quoted in brochure for film 'In Secular India', made by *Mediastorm*.

11. The Agitation Against Sati 1987–88

सती प्रथा
पाप है पाप

Protesting against Roop Kanwar's
immolation, Delhi 1987

Young widow with her husband's
dead body, just before immolation, private
family album, Sitapur, date not known

In September 1987, an incident of sati (widow immolation) in a village in Rajasthan sparked off a campaign which gave rise to a furious debate which spanned not only the rights and wrongs of Hindu women, but questions of religious identity, communal autonomy and the role of the law and the State in a society as complex and as diverse as India's. While some of the arguments used in the debate were not new, its form and structure were illuminating, as much for what they obscured as for what they revealed of the intricate web of social change in India (including the current state of the feminist movement).

In the course of the debate a series of binary oppositions were invoked, between rural and urban, tradition and modernity, complementarity and sameness, the state and religious communities, spiritualism and materialism, and so on. The invocation of these oppositions had the effect of presenting either side (for and against sati) as homogeneous, so that the former were described as representing rural, traditional communities who were struggling to preserve themselves from the homogenizing tendencies of the Indian nation-state, while the latter were described as representing elite, urban, modern sections of society, who were pressing the state to intervene in communities they bore no relation to, and were thus supporting and encouraging the nation-state to extend its sphere of control over civil society.

Versions of this argument began to be advanced within a couple of weeks of the incident of sati, and almost immediately after the campaign against it began. While the argument itself was earlier used by the supporters of the Muslim Women's Bill in 1986–87, the way in which it appeared in the debate over sati showed how greatly the argument had developed. For example, in the earlier agitation the argument was advanced mainly by pro-Bill leaders, but in the latter it was advanced both by pro-sati leaders and by a group of 'outsiders' (in the form of a series of newspaper articles). These appeared first in the Delhi-based Hindi and English language national dailies, *Jan Satta*, ('Banwari' 29.9.87), *Indian Express* (Ashis Nandy, 5.10.87 and *Statesman* (Patrick D Harrigan, 5.11.87), and all three writers, in their various

Immolation, private family album,
Sitapur, date not known

Painted chariot celebrating widow
immolation, Rajasthan, 1987

ways, lent a kind of outsider respectability to the argument so that it also began to be advocated by considerable numbers of those very urban, modern sections of society which it sought to attack.

Perhaps the most striking point about the articles by 'Banwari', Ashis Nandy and Patrick Harrigan was that all three propounded their arguments in the form of a polemic against the Indian feminist movement, accusing Indian feminists of being agents of modernity who were attempting to impose crass market-dominated views of equality and liberty on a society which once gave the noble, the self-sacrificing and the spiritual the respect they deserve, but which is now being rapidly destroyed by the essentially selfish forces of the market. All three, moreover, defined these crass market-dominated views of equality and liberty as being drawn from the West, so Indian feminists stood accused of being Westernists, colonialists, cultural imperialists, and—indirectly—supporters of capitalist ideology.

Though Indian feminists had suffered a series of attacks in the eighties, this was to date the most major of them, for not only did it appear to be concerted, its timing was such that it appeared to lend legitimacy both to an ideology which claimed that the finest act a woman could perform was to die with her husband, and to a specific incident of sati which was beginning to seem more and more like an incident of murder. Outrageous as the accusations against themselves seemed to Indian feminists, who had shown themselves to be anti-imperialist and anti-capitalist in a number of ways—and many of whom had, ironically enough, themselves launched a critique of 'Western feminist' goals and methods many years prior to this attack—what made it worse was the fact that not one of these writers addressed themselves to the question of what had happened, or was happening, in Deorala where the sati had taken place, nor did any of them ask under what conditions Roop Kanwar had lived, or under what conditions she had died.

September 1987 was not the first time that Indian feminists encountered the problem of sati. The first encounter in Delhi was in 1983, when a campaign to further popularize the ideology of sati was launched by a Marwari-funded organization known as the Rani Sati Sarva Sangh. The RSSS, which already ran several sati temples in Rajasthan and Delhi, had got the then Government to grant them a plot of land in Delhi to build yet another sati temple, and had decided to celebrate this grant by leading a procession of men and women to the temple. Delhi feminists heard of this plan, and decided to hold a counter-demonstration along the route of the procession, which they did with signal failure, partly because they had had no time to mobilize, and thus found themselves outnumbered, and partly because this was the first time that they had had to confront a group of women in a hostile situation; this

was in itself so distressing that it took the heart out of their demonstration. Most distressing of all, however, was the way in which the processionists appropriated the language of rights, stating that they should have the right, as Hindus and as women, to commit, worship and propagate sati. At the same time, they also appropriated feminist slogans on women's militancy, for example, '*hum Bharat ki nari hain, phool nahin, chingari hain*' (we, the women of India, are not flowers but fiery sparks). The feminists who attended that demonstration experienced, therefore, the humiliating sense of loss which accompanies the discovery that your own words can so readily be snatched and turned against you to serve an antithetical cause.[1] This experience led to two different reactions: one, the determination to research into the existence of sati, sati temples and the proponents of 'sati-dharma' in India; the other, to find non-confrontational ways in which to undermine the ideology of sati. Both, however, emphasized the need to study, comprehend and deal with the traditional.

Whether for these reasons, or because no further public campaigns in support of sati occurred, the issue faded out until Roop Kanwar's death in 1987. Given that there has been, on an average, something like one sati a year in India, why did this incident arouse such frenzy when others had not? Only four months earlier, the police had prevented a woman called Banwari from committing sati, and had dispersed the twenty thousand odd people who had assembled at Bagda village in Pali district to witness the event.[2] Two years earlier, in March 1985, the police had prevented another sati in Jaipur district and had used both tear gas and lathicharges to disperse the thirty thousand odd people who had collected at the proposed site.[3] In neither incident did police intervention result in agitations against them. Yet Roop Kanwar's death, which no-one prevented, led to a massive agitation both for and against sati. It was only as a campaign around the issue developed that it became evident that this particular sati was indeed different from most of the others. In contrast to some of the other areas in which sati had been attempted, Deorala was a relatively highly developed village. The family, while not perhaps wealthy, were well-to-do. Roop Kanwar's father-in-law was headmaster of a district school, while she herself was a graduate. A Rajput family, they had links with influential Rajputs and mainstream state-level politicians.

Roop Kanwar had only been married a short while before her husband died. Her dowry included some thirty *tolas* of gold. Her husband suffered from mental disorder and they had spent only around six months together. When, after his death, it was decided that Roop Kanwar would 'become' sati, the impending event was announced in advance, because sati is always a public spectacle. Yet her family were not informed. Evidence which trickled out pointed to murder: some of her neighbours said that she had run away and tried to hide in a barn before the ceremony, but was dragged out, pumped full of drugs, dressed in her bridal finery and put on the pyre, with logs and coconuts heaped upon her. The pyre itself was lit by her brother-in-law, a minor.[4]

Hearing that the press was on its way, the organizers of her sati brought forward the 'event'. When the press arrived at Deorala, they were abused and manhandled by self-appointed protectors of the *Sati-sthal* (site of sati). In other words, it was evident that the planners of the sati saw themselves as being in a state of siege before any questions of a battle had even arisen. Could it be that they themselves chalked out the battles: were they in fact looking for a battle? Some credence was lent to this view by the response of the government.

Reports indicated that the local authorities knew of the planned sati, yet their only action was to despatch a police jeep which had overturned on its way to the site. Following this debacle, three more days elapsed before a government representative visited Deorala.[5] Even more shocking was their general attitude, consisting as it were not of the usual tactic of slothful procrastination which government uses when it wishes to avoid an issue, but of a kind of sullen paralysis in which over two weeks went by before any statement was made by government spokesmen, either in the state or at the centre. No attempts were made to arrest anybody, despite mounting evidence of coercion and mounting public pressure. The doctor who drugged Roop Kanwar meanwhile disappeared.

Immediately after the immolation, the site became a popular pilgrimage spot, and, as in Jhunjhunu, a number of stalls sprang up, selling auspicious offerings, mementoes (such as a trick photograph of Roop Kanwar sitting on the pyre with her husband's head on her lap and a blissful smile on her face, while the flames spurted about her,) and audio cassettes of devotional songs. Her father-in-law, prominent men from the village, and members of a newly formed organization, the *Sati Dharm Raksha Samiti*, (organization for the defence of the religio-ethical ideal of sati), together formed a Trust along the lines of the Rani Sati Sarva Sangha Trust, to run the site and collect donations. What passes for modern technology in our country was used by the Trust to organize worship at the site: parking lots were arranged and traffic controllers appointed; a control tower was set up near the site and a fairly elaborate system of loudspeakers was strung around the area, through which instructions from the control tower were transmitted to pilgrims, Trust functionaries, et al. The mahajans took the responsibility of organizing stalls selling food, and accommodation for the pilgrims (these are their areas of expertise). Though no information was collected as

In 1982 fundamentalist men and women in Delhi took out a procession in support of sati. This picture shows a small section of this march, with the men in the background for protection.

to how much money was made by them, or by the stall-owners, it was reported that within some three weeks the Trust itself had collected around Rs 50 lakhs.[6] Sati is big business. Despite demands from feminists and social reformers, this money was not impounded.

While certain aspects of this business side of the sati are neither new nor particularly modern, such as the site becoming a pilgrimage spot and stalls springing up all around it to sell objects to the devout, the scale of it and the technologizing of the pilgrimage event is obviously modern. Kumkum Sangari has pointed out how the new palatial sati temples replay the act of sati through models of the woman, the dead man and the burning pyre: she shows, further, that the 'worship' of sati-dharm or sati is produced and controlled through commodification, for next to the new temples there are sati-memorial stones which lie neglected and unworshipped.[7]

In other words, far from the feminists imposing market-dominated notions of equality on an anti-materialist society which celebrated self-sacrifice, the event revealed the gruesome materialism of a society which permitted the production of 'sacrifice' for profit.

Further, and in many ways more dismayingly, feminists discovered through this campaign the complex relations through which issues concerning women can be used to stake claims to power. Sudesh Vaid has shown how the 'tradition' of sati and sati-dharma was created in Shekhavati region (where Deorala is located) after Independence, largely to regain lost authority. (Interestingly, some three quarters of recorded satis since 1947 have been in this region). Originally comprising small princely states and chiefdoms, the area had supported the outlawing of sati in 1846. After Independence, with the abolition of princely states, and the further abolition of the zamindari and jagirdari systems of land relations,

Picketing pro-sati demonstration, Delhi, 1982

Demonstrating against Roop Kanwar's
immolation, Delhi, 1987

Joint Action Forum Against Sati
(15 organizations) Delhi, 1987

together with land reforms, the Kshatriyas and banias lost some of the power and privilege they had held. Anti-land reform agitations were launched first by ex-rulers and large land-owners under a newly formed organization, the Kshatriya Mahasabha. When they were successful in reinstating the Jagirdari system, small land-owners followed by launching a similar agitation and forming an organization called the Bhooswami Sangh.

Both organizations invoked a chivalric 'Rajput' tradition in which men defended the Hindu tradition on battlefields by killing and being killed, while women defended it at home by killing themselves (jauhar and sati). Rajput identity was, further, fused with a militant neo-fundamentalist Hinduism, with demonstrations of 'tens of thousands of lathi-weilding saffron-clad Rajputs'. Sati now began to be projected as exemplifying the true Rajput identity: the first post-Independence sati in this area was in 1954, and at the same time an old sati-memorial, Jhunjhunu, was rebuilt and expanded. Annual 'sati melas' now began to be held.[8]

This glorification of sati was funded and supported by mahajans, in particular, marwaris. It was they who rediscovered and rebuilt old sati shrines, and founded the Rani Sati Sarva Sangh, which now runs 105 sati temples all over India. In a sense therefore the old relations of mutual advantage between Rajputs and mahajans gained a new fillip through sati.

The parallels between the 1950s use of sati to assert an identity and the event of 1987 are fascinating. Hard on the heels of Roop Kanwar's death, a Sati Dharma Raksha Samiti was formed in Jaipur city, whose leaders were urban men, many of them professionals or businessmen from land-owning families, whose sphere of influence extended over both rural and urban areas. Together with the Deorala Trust, this Samiti announced that a *Chunri mahotsav* (veil festival) would be held some ten days after Roop Kanwar's death. A ritual cremation of the veil after the woman's death is, it seems, traditional in the area, but never before had it been called a *mahotsav* or festival.

Feminists in Jaipur petitioned the High Court to forbid the ceremony, and the High Court instructed the state government to prevent it from taking place. Though the Attorney-General announced that it would be stopped, the sole action of the state government was to stop vehicles at a certain point, but to allow people to disembark and join the procession. Five hundred policemen were posted along the route, clothed 'in civilian dress so that they would not offend the crowd'.[9] The *mahotsav* was performed, and from an act of mourning it was transformed into a show of strength, a victory celebration, with the male marchers, traditionally dressed, waving their fists aloft in triumph and shouting slogans. The site itself was transformed into a political rallying ground: a highly charged state-of-siege atmosphere was created by sword wielding youth who surrounded the sati-sthal, and instead of devotional songs they shouted slogans which were clearly modelled on mainstream political slogans. Madhu Kishwar and Ruth Vanita have shown how these slogans fell into three major groups:

(1) Slogans based on leader glorification, such as '*Sati ho to kaisi ho? Roop Kanwar jaisi ho*', which is based on '*Desh ka neta kaisa ho? Rajiv Gandhi (or x) jaisa ho*'.

(2) Victory chants, such as, '*Ek do teen char, sati mata ki jai jai kar*'.

(3) Slogans drawn from Hindu communalist movements, such as '*Desh dharam ka nata hai, sati hamari mata hai*' which is based on '*Desh dharam ka nata hai, gai hamari mata hai.*'[10]

Even though several laws exist under which the ideologues and profiteers of sati could have been punished, the state government took no action, largely because the issue had become one of Rajput community identity, and the Rajputs are an influential community. In fact, several state level politicians immediately rushed down to pay their respects at the site, among whom were the state Janata Party Chief, a Bharatiya Janata Party

'You are possessed by the truth, you are
possessed by the truth, Delhi, 1987

A group of schoolchildren at the
anti-sati march in Delhi. Many schools gave
their students a day off to participate in the march.

member of the Rajasthan Legislative Assembly and a Lok Dal member, the acting president of the Rajput Sabha, and an ex-member of the Legislative Assembly from the Congress-I.[11] So almost all the major centre to right wing political parties went to the site, not to enquire into what had happened but to stake their own claim to 'tradition', and via this to the Rajput vote. Behind this there also lurked the spectre of the 'Hindu vote', and behind both were questions of majority-minority politics, caste and communal representation.

The process through which this happened is a revealing one, for it sheds light on communal formations in India and shows how issues of gender can become central to these. At the policy-maker and intelligentsia levels the major argument of the pro-sati camp was that if the state represented the people, then the Rajputs were a people among whom sati was an ideal and a tradition and as such it should be recognized and legitimized. On the ground, however, it was argued that a refusal to legitimize sati was a deliberate attempt to marginalize the Rajputs. The opponents of sati, for example, were presented as people who were using the issue as a cover to attack the Rajputs per se. The widespread appeal of this argument became clear to feminists who were active

All India Democratic Women's Association activist, Brinda Karat at a demonstration against
Roop Kanwar's immolation, Delhi 1987

in the campaign against sati, for a majority of the Rajputs whom we met focussed on this point rather than on a defence of sati itself. Almost without exception, they asked why such an issue was being made of sati and, almost without exception, they saw the campaign as being directed against the Rajputs per se.

Both arguments were taken a step further by two other groups. The first, head priests of the major Hindu temples in such centres as Benares and Puri, issued statements that sati represented one of the most noble elements not only of Rajput culture, but of Hinduism, and claimed scriptural sanction for this view. While re-iterating the need to legitimize sati, the main thrust of their argument was that such issues came under their purview and not that of the state. At the same time they also raised the bogey of 'Hindusim in danger' from the opponents of sati.

The second group consisted of a section of extreme right Hindu nationalists, spearheaded by the Shiv Sena. The Shiv Sena was active in the pro-sati agitation, organizing demonstrations on the Hinduism-in-danger line,

and arguing that the State is particularly biased against the Hindus, for it is willing to accede to the demands of minority communities for representation, but is unwilling to do the same for the majority. (The particular point of reference here was to the Muslim Women's Bill).

In a way the definition of the democratic state in India has always been deeply ambivalent on the relationship between secularism and religious representation. What is new really is the extent to which the two are today converging, so that secularism has become synonymous with providing 'fair' representation to different religious communities, which are defined in opposition to each other. Thus the 'true' representatives of different religious communities are held to be their fundamentalist leaders, rather than, say, the reformers within their ranks. Mobilization on communal grounds is thus an extremely effective political tool, both to gain political space and State recognition, and to create political-electoral bases. An index of the mainstream communalization of politics and the constituency of women as a communal 'sign' is the rise of two centrist Janata Party

College girls marching against sati, Delhi 1987

politicians, Syed Shahabhuddin and Kalyan Singh Kalvi, both of whom shot into prominence as communal fundamentalist leaders, the former via the Muslim Women's Bill agitation, and the latter via the pro-sati agitation. Shahabuddin today heads his own political party, while Kalvi is an elected representative of the Janata Dal.

Questions of representation, politics and the state arose in a new way for feminists in 1987–88. Religious fundamentalism, as we find all over the world, not only rationalizes the sexual oppression of women, but also mobilizes them in support of their own oppression. The pro-sati agitationists mobilized considerable sections of women in their own support, both on a castiest (Rajput) and on a religious (Hindu) platform. That is to say, they mobilized women who would seem to be directly affected by their demands. This allowed them to claim that they represented the 'true' desires of Hindu women, and to accuse the feminists of being unrepresentative. So the feminists were placed in the anomalous position of appearing to speak in the interests of women whom they could not claim to represent and who defined their interests differently.

The tradition versus modernity argument entered this context in such a way as to further isolate the feminists. The bogey of modernism was so successfully created that the fact that sati was being used to create a 'tradition' went unrecognized despite feminist efforts to emphasize it. Tradition was defined so historically and so self righteously that it obscured the fact that sati was being used to reinforce caste and communal identities along 'modern' lines, with modern methods of campaigning and organizing, modern arguments, and for modern ends, such as the reformation of electoral blocs and caste and communal representation within the state.

Worst of all, by polarizing women along the rural-urban, traditional-modern axis, it disallowed a whole series of questions and insights. For example, looking more closely at the nature of women's support for the pro-sati agitation, it became clear that this was ambiguous, and at many points consisted of drawing a firm line between worship of sati and the actual practice of it.

Secondly, an examination of the women who were mobilized for the pro-sati demonstrations made it clear that they were not, in fact, the women who were most

Street play against widow immolation,
Sabala Mahila Sangh, Delhi, 1987

Critiquing the 'martial honour' ideology,
anti-sati march, Delhi 1987

directly affected by the issue. The figure of the widow was conspicuously absent. The elevation of sati into a tradition of ideal man-woman relations, in the context of widowhood, not only obscured the miserable conditions under which most Hindu widows live, it actually rationalized their slavery: for if the widowed woman is not capable of living up to the sati ideal by immolating herself, then what better fate for her than to be the servant either of her family or of the temple?

For the feminists the realization of how these polarizations between tradition and modernity, materialism and spiritualism, rural and urban, had successfully sidelined all questions of affection or compassion for women was a bitter one. Even worse, because peculiarly ironic, was the way in which these polarizations forced them into positions which appeared not only to contradict earlier stands but also to diverge sharply from the directions which they had been pursuing. One such position was the demand for state intervention, made in three ways: first, that Roop Kanwar's in-laws and the doctor who drugged her should be charged with murder; second, that all those who profited financially or politically from her death should be punished; and third, that a new law should be promulgated banning both the committal and glorification of crimes against women in the name of religion.

Feminist unease about demands of this kind has existed from the beginning of the contemporary women's movement and has been a kind of constant undercurrent in all their campaigns, most of which have, for fairly obvious reasons, tended to focus on demands of the state. Partly due to this unease, the draft Bill which was prepared by a sub-committee of the Joint Action Committee Against Sati in Delhi was never circulated to M.P.s and so never tabled in Parliament. Instead, the Government was left to introduce its own Bill (which it only did because of opposition furore), under which sati was defined as suicide and the first person to be punished was the woman herself, for attempting to commit suicide.

For most of us, at the time, the campaign around sati revealed the growing strength of the opposition to feminism, and spelt a considerable setback to the movement. Yet the challenges it posed to our self definitions yielded some insights of value: a more complex understanding of the ways in which different groups and communities saw themselves; that it is not helpful to view the state as a monolithic entity from a purely oppositional stance, especially at moments of crisis, for it is important for us to assert that we have the right to a voice in the administration of our society. Thirdly, that representation consists not merely in a show of numbers but in the seeking and encouragement of a plethora of voices, which is to some extent taking place through the feminist and associated movements. Opposition to sati, for example came from a variety of sources: both the right-wing Hindu reformist tradition and maverick left-wing Hindu reformers such as Swami Agnivesh of the Arya Samaj, opposed it. Swami Agnivesh in fact went on dharna outside Deorala, and challenged the head priests of the Puri and Benaras temples to a debate on the scriptural 'sanction' of sati. His challenge was declined. Opposition also came from sections of the Gandhians, who held a rally of about 10,000 women in Orissa, who gheraoed the head priest of the Puri temple, calling him to account for his views, which he was unable to do. And it also came from the anti-caste movement in Maharashtra, who announced their opposition to sati. Finally, within Rajasthan, considerable opposition both to sati and to state inaction of Roop Kanwar's death was voiced by huge numbers of women, largely rural, who joined demonstrations to protest against the glorification of her death.

Most of these voices and actions were not co-ordinated at the time, because feminist resources did not permit of co-ordination. But in a sense co-ordination was not really necessary, because the problem of sati, like most other problems of women, cannot be resolved simply through a campaign. Perhaps one of the most valuable insights in this regard has been the understanding that while specific and short term campaigns are necessary, if only in order to mark reactions, the roots of feminism are now spreading in a variety of ways of across the country.

NOTES

1. Recounted to me by Nandita Haksar and Sheba Chhachi, December 1983.
2. *Indian Express*, 10.5.1987.
3. *Hindustan Times*, 6.3.1985.
4. *Statesman*, 18–20.9.1987.
5. *Times of India*, 17.9.1987.
6. Ibid.
7. Kumkum Sangari, 'Perpetrating the Myth', *Seminar*, No. 342, February, 1988.
8. Sudesh Vaid, 'Politics of Widow Immolation', *Seminar* No. 342, February, 1988.
9. *Hindustan Times*, 17.9.1987.
10. Madhu Kishwar and Ruth Vanita, 'The Burning of Roop Kanwar', *Manushi*, No. 42–3, 1987. The slogans/chants listed above translate as follows: (1) 'What should a sati be like? Like Roop Kanwar; which is based on 'What should a country's leader be like? Like Rajiv Gandhi; (2) 'One, two, three, four, raise your voice in praise of sati'; 'Our land and our religion have decreed this: that sati is our mother', which is based on 'Our land and our religion have decreed this: that the cow is our mother'.
11. *Times of India*, 17.9.1987.

12. The Struggle for a Safe Environment

Discussing deforestation, Junagadh, Himachal

The Second Citizen's Report (CSE) on the state of India's Environment points out that:

probably no other group is more affected by environmental destruction than poor village women. Every dawn brings with it a new march in search of fuel, fodder and water. It does not matter if the women are old, young or pregnant: crucial household needs have to met day after weary day. As ecological conditions worsen, the long march becomes longer and even more tiresome. Caught between poverty and environmental destruction, poor rural women in India could well be reaching the limits of physical endurance.[1]

As long ago as 1952 the Indian government targetted that 33 per cent of the geographical area of India was to be brought under forest cover in order to have an ecologically balanced environment.[2] Recently, the government's Approach to the Seventh Plan reiterated this saying: 'The highest priority should be given to restore forest cover with 33 per cent of the geographical area of the country being brought under forests from the present level of 23 per cent. Measures should be intensified to restore forest cover to the full where it is at present degraded . . . .'[3] In other words, the target was never achieved.

Today, India uses only a tenth of the rainfall it receives, the water table has declined in large areas, and high profile projects such as dams, reservoirs and canal systems—on which the government has laid stress— have not been able to provide adequate irrigation or to arrest the cycle of floods and droughts that annually hits the poor in India.

The consequences have been especially grim for women. Rural women have to traverse greater distances and spend more hours collecting fuel, fodder and water: in some areas, the distance covered in search of these has quadrupled from 2 to 8 km, while the extension of hours spent in collection of basic survival necessities has both cut time available for wage labour and stretched the normal working day to 14–15 hours.

The health effects of this highly increased workload are naturally detrimental. And to these must be added illness due to inefficient stoves in closed rooms, while scarcity of fuel in conditions of poverty often forces women to cook faster—cooking less nutritious foods, or to undercook—both of which increase their ill-health, as well as that of their families.

It was against this depressing backdrop that the Chipko and Appiko movements arose. The struggle for a safe and sane environment has a history of protests in India. Among the better known of these is that of the villagers of Tilari in Tehri Garhwal in 1930, when the villagers gathered to protest the forest laws of the rulers of Tehri and, although several were killed and injured in the reprisals that followed, they did succeed in winning their traditional rights to forest produce. In the Chipko movement it was the women who came into the forefront and transformed the struggle into something that was particularly theirs, although initially the movement is said to have been initiated by men, notable among whom were two activists, Sunderlal Bahuguna and Chandi Prasad Bhatt.

The Chipko movement got its name from the word 'chipko' which, in Hindi, means to cling. This, clinging to trees, was the particular action people used to save trees, which were crucial to their lives, from being felled. Exact histories of Chipko differ. According to the CSE Report, Chipko began one morning in 1973 in the remote hill town of Gopeshwar in Chamoli district, when representatives from a sports goods factory in Allahabad arrived in Gopeshwar to cut 10 ash trees for their use. To begin with, the villagers requested them not to do this, but when the contractors persisted, the villagers came up with the idea of hugging the earmarked trees. Defeated, the contractors were forced to go back; some

weeks later the villagers marched, along with Chandi Prasad Bhatt, to Rampur Phata, another village, to foil the same contractors once again.

Women entered the movement one year later, in 1974. The villagers of Reni, some 65 kms from Joshimath town, had heard that the forest neighbouring their village was to be auctioned. Chandi Prasad Bhatt, who was at that time touring the area, came to the village and talked to the villagers about the success of Chipko in Gopeshwar. The men, however, decided that a first step was to protest to the authorities in town against the action. While they were away doing this the contractor seized his moment to start felling trees. The women of Reni, who had not formally been included in the meeting between Bhatt and the men, had nonetheless listened in because they saw this as their issue, now decided to take independent action. Led by Gaura Devi, 50 years old and widowed, they barred the path to the forest (which lies behind the village) singing

This forest is our mother's home
We will protect it with all our might

and with their united strength they foiled the contractor.

Again, in June 1975 women stopped the felling of trees in a forest near Gopeshwar village by clinging to them. They took their protest further by gheraoing (surrounding) some government staff quarters where young trees were to be cut down for kitchen fuel. The gherao was stopped only after they heard from the district magistrate that the trees would be protected.

Within a few years the Chipko movement had spread all over Chamoli district and parts of Tehri Garhwal, with women being in the forefront in many places. Indeed, after their first entry into this movement, they have never looked back and have evolved their own unique ways of registering their protest. In Henwal Ghati, for example they protested the indiscriminate tapping of pine trees by dressing the 'wounds' of the trees with mud and sacking. Each protest, whether it was to embrace trees, or to bandage them, reinforced the women's closeness to nature, their belief that natural resources were theirs to protect and conserve, not to exploit and destroy. As the movement spread, women began to realize the need to get organized and to sustain the struggle. With the help of the Dasauli Gram Swarajya Mandal, an organization headed by Chandi Prasad Bhatt, women formed Mahila Mangal Dals (women's groups) in many villages and many of them began to claim the right to decide what was done in forests and fields. In both Reni and neighbouring villages the Dals fought with the male-dominated panchayat over the protection of their crops. Here men, when they took the cattle to graze, were traditionally in the habit of going through the fields because they found these routes shorter. However, women, who tended the fields, resented cattle trampling their crop, or worse, eating it and wanted to build walls around their fields to protect them. They decided to do so and told the men. The men were furious and called a panchayat meeting. The panchayat expressed outrage at the Dal's temerity in taking such a decision and insisted that only they could decide such matters. The women, however, asserted that since they were the people who tended the fields, they were the ones who should decide. The CSE Report cites another panchayat-Dal fight:

> In one village the women fought the sarpanch over the distribution of the grass from their afforested patch. A woman from the sarpanch's family carried away grass that had not been authorised by the MMD. Usually the Dal announces a day when one person from each household can come and take grass as a simple way to ensure equitable distribution. The village women protested strongly against the sarpanch, who in turn had a case filed against them. But the district magistrate had to withdraw the case when faced with a combined protest from all the women . . . .[4]

Needless to say, these actions were not popular with the men. Gopa Joshi, a Garhwali woman, speaks of how the women of Reni are being harassed by their men. She says:

> The harassment by the village menfolk began the day when Gaura Devi led 27 village women to prevent the contractor's employees and forest department personnel, about 60 men in all, from going to the Reni forest to fell 2415 trees. While the women were blocking the narrow passage leading to the forest, the men used all sorts of threats, and later, on the pretext of being drunk, even tried to misbehave with the women. But the women refused to budge and bravely resisted all misbehaviour. Finally, one of the men spat at Gaura Devi's face. The women remained cool but firm . . . . .

Guara Devi stood by her action. First the contractor tried to bribe her into letting his men enter the

Gheraoing district government officials, Junagadh, Himachal

forest. When she refused his offer, the forest department personnel threatened to call the police and arrest her. The contractor, in league with some of the villagers, composed folk songs describing the arrest of Gaura Devi . . . . They used to sing these songs all night long and dance together . . .

Chipko women activists are being accused of getting the village blacklisted. The men say that since the village is blacklisted due to the behaviour of the women, now the young men, most of whom are in the army, will not be given employment anywhere, and also that the village will not be supplied with essential commodities like salt and kerosene . . . activists are being made out to be the villains of the piece . . .[5]

In a paper presented at a conference some time ago, Chandi Prasad Bhatt confessed that the activism of the women at Reni in 1975 came as an eye-opener to him and it was only after this that he realized how much more important ecology was to women in Garhwal than it was to men. Since then both he and Bahuguna have done considerable work with women. The Dasauli Gram Swarajya, which Bhatt heads, holds regular ecodevelopment camps where women also preside at meetings. They have been helping to get biogas plants and smokeless stoves for women—something that more and more women are asking for.

As the Chipko movement grew and developed, so did a movement for a safe environment in Uttarakhand. It was hoped that the two movements would unite the two areas which have common cultures and problems, and in some ways this has happened with the forestry movement spreading to Almora and the anti-alcohol movement (which is discussed later) spreading to Garhwal. However, while in Garhwal women's protests in the Chipko movement had been against timber contracting, in Almora they branched out into a resistance to mining. Khirakot, a small village in the Someshwar valley, lies above the Kosi river on the lower slopes of the hills. It has a population of 150 families. Above the village lies the village forest and above this the government's reserve forest. Over the years Khirakot has had to see intensive male migration. Radha Bhatt, one of the activists from this area, points out that out of some 500 men, only 25 or 30 remain in the village. The women, however, have found their own resources and ways of organizing. Several years ago a contractor from Kanpur secured a lease for soapstone mining from the government. In order to carry stone to the road, he had to pass through the outskirts of Khirakot, cutting across fields and narrow paths the villagers used whenever they went to cultivate their fields, to fetch water or fuel and fodder. Devaki Jain describes this event:

The man initially transported these loads by human labour. He found the business so remunerative that he decided to set up a power mill. The mill, in turn, had a capacity which demanded much larger volumes of stone from the quarry. This led to the use of donkeys as pack animals. Convoys of donkeys used to go from the quarry to the road, occupying the narrow footpaths used by the local population, especially the women . . .[6]

Not only did women find that the bridle paths to the reserved forests that they would normally have used were crowded with mules carrying stone and that their access to the forests was blocked, they also discovered that mine debris was cluttering their protected forests. During the rains this mine dust was carried into the fields where it settled and formed a crust that made it impossible to plough. To begin with, the women appealed to the men of the village who first talked to the contractor and, when they found he was not prepared to listen, stopped working in the mines and built walls to protect their fields. The contractor responded by filing criminal cases against them and many were intimidated and began to weaken. However the women forced them to fight the court battle, collecting money from each household to do so. Meanwhile they resorted to direct action and tried to obstruct the pack trains by narrowing the footpaths so that the donkeys could not walk on them. The miner then registered a case against the women who responded by intensifying the obstruction and physically occupying the paths. The miner once again went to the courts. The women also forced men to stop work in the mines. Said one: 'we would catch hold of the workers' implements and not let them dig.' And another: 'we asked them to kill us first, to bury us in the mountain, before they could touch the hill.' A third put it thus: 'their mining was destroying our lives, our children's futures. How could we let them mine?'

The contractor tried various ways to crush the women. He hired thugs to intimidate them, then resorted to stoning their houses. He also had a cloth shop owned by one of the women's sons burnt and when all this failed to stop the women he tried to bribe them by offering them ownership of the mines. Then, he hired outside labour but the women would not let the labourers— mainly Nepalis—work. Meanwhile the women continued to fight in court and after two years, the District Magistrate was persuaded to visit the village and taken round and shown the damage. He was so moved that he recommended that the case be cancelled and the women won their case. In late 1982, the mines were finally officially closed and:

The women of Khirakot settled down to repair the damage: they filled the ditches, built a protective

Public meeting on World Environment Day,
Saklana, Garhwal, 1986

A woman activist addressing the public
meeting on World Environment Day, 1986

Chipko activists gather together on World
Environment Day at Saklana in 1986

wall to prevent the debris from destroying their fields, and planted oak trees in the panchayat forests. But their biggest reward is similar movements emerging in other parts of the region, in Pithoragarh and in Jhiroli, sparked off by the flame of protest in Khirakot.[7]

In another instance in Khirakot women found that they themselves had contributed to the depletion of their environment as they, and neighbouring village women, had been lopping off pine trees in the village forests and this had resulted in a lack of pine needles which the women used as bedding in their cattle sheds. According to Radha Bhatt

They (the women) discussed the matter among themselves, and decided that they should protect their village forest against the lopping of branches for fuel by their own and neighbouring village women. If the pine trees grew bigger then their needles would be available close to their homes. And if the forest were managed properly, the fuel wood would also be obtainable from these trees without destroying the whole tree. They spread their ideas among the other women of the village, and they all became convinced, not by holding any formal meeting, but at the water places or along the village paths where they met one another.

Thus, after four years of continuous efforts by the collective leadership of these women, a fine pine forest can be seen above Khirakot village. The forest has already begun to provide dry pine needles for their cowsheds. This leadership is not tired, but rather increasingly enthusiastic . . . . In the first month of 1983 they involved the menfolk in their endeavours. Every family of the village agreed to pay a rupee a month as salary to a forest guard, a young man from their village. The women's group collected the money and helped the young man guard the forest.[8]

Closely linked to the Chipko movement in Garhwal and Kumaon is the anti-alcohol movement. Activists working in these areas discovered, in the course of their discussions with people, that alcoholism among men posed a major problem for the women. In some areas it resulted in severe wife battering. In others, although a large number of men had migrated to urban areas in search of work, those that remained in the villages would squander their family's earnings on liquor. Not only did this affect the men's health (much of the liquor they drank was illicit) it meant the women had less money to run the household, were often beaten and even had to resort to cutting down on their own diet in order to make do.

The problem of alcoholism among men was confirmed by the Uttarakhand Sangharsh Vahini, one of the groups responsible for spreading information about movements in this area. Formed in 1977, the Vahini has been active in the Chipko movement and its activists go from village to village to spread and collect information. In addition, they try to build networks through two papers which they bring out from Nainital: *Jangal ke Davedar* (Owners of the Forest) and *Nainital Samachar* (Nainital News). In 1983, the Vahini held a large public meeting in Almora where hill people of Garhwal and Kumaon discussed their problems. At this meeting alcoholism emerged as a major problem. This was not, however, the first time that people, especially women, had complained of the problem. According to Uma Bhatt, a sustained agitation against the sale of alcohol had taken place from 1965–71 in Uttarakhand.

Agitations against alcohol and distribution of liquor have existed since the early days of the social reform and nationalist movements. Prohibition was declared in several areas as a result of such movements in independent India. The issue of prohibition has aroused a variety of responses which we need not go into here. What is important for us, however, is to see how and why women have been involved in anti-alcohol movements and how this issue has been important in different radical movements, especially tribal and hill movements. In Jharkhand, for example, anti-alcoholism was seen as a major part of reform, since liquor consumption had played an important role in tribal acquiescence to land alienation. Generally, Hindu landlords would get tribals to sign away their land rights in return for a bottle of distilled liquor, hence activists felt that the only way to curb this was to get the tribals to forswear all forms of alcohol, even *mahua*, the local brew. In the hill areas, especially Uttarakhand, men tended to spend all their money on alcohol, leaving little or nothing for the family to subsist on.

In her article on the Uttarakhand movement Uma Bhatt says that between 1965–71 there was a widespread agitation against liquor so the government had to declare prohibition in some areas, but that they could not wipe out liquor distribution as alcohol is used in Ayurvedic tonics as 'sura.' Though officially their alcohol content is supposed to be limited to 20 per cent, surveys have shown an alcohol content up to 80 per cent in some of these tonics.

In February 1984 villagers of Basbhiva, Chaukhuya block in Almora found a man who possessed illicit liquor. Though they complained to their local officer about this, he took no action. It was later discovered that this was because he (the officer) smuggled liquor himself. The villagers responded by gheraoing him; the authorities responded in turn by threatening to kill one

Liquor contractors arrested by people at Gosainpari

of the activists. The Vahini then organized a public meeting at which it was decided to launch an anti-alcohol movement. In village after village all liquor found was thrown away, pots and shops were smashed, and in some instances liquor sellers were made to apologise in public for distribution of liquor and they had to promise never to do so again. Women were in the forefront in these campaigns and it is they who have kept the anti-alcohol movement sustained. In Himachal groups of women close down liquor shops, keep guard outside and if there is any threat to them, use drums and songs to inform their sisters who are elsewhere. Women have also used the tactic of 'shaming' the liquor sellers and drinkers, often by blackening their faces or by parading them through the streets of the town or village. For example in Dhulia in Maharashtra in the early seventies women broke wine jars, beat up individual wife beaters with broomsticks, made them promise never to beat their wives again, seized men who beat their wives or molested women, festooned them with garlands made of shoes, tied them onto donkeys' backs and paraded them around the village.

While there is a long history of rural women's environmental activism, tied to scarcity of fuel, water and fodder, the Bhopal disaster of 1984 saw the rise of a massive

Monsoon shown forces demonstrators to seek
shelter, Bhopal, 1985

Bhopal victims demonstrating outside collectorate,
demanding relief, 1985

movement of women gas victims. On the night of 2–3
December 1984, over twenty tonnes of methyl isocyanate
(MIC) exploded out of a pesticides plant in Bhopal,
owned by the U.S. multinational, Union Carbide. Several thousand were killed on that night, and thousands
have died as a result of exposure since. The official toll
today is over 4,000 dead, and around 500,000 potentially
injured. We use the term potential here because little
was known at the time about the health effects of MIC,
and most experts believe that it might take twenty years
at the very least before adequate information is available.

Known as 'killer in the night', because it escaped in
the early hours of the morning, and because it is odourless and invisible, the gas is estimated to have spread over
almost the entire old city of Bhopal, which was the most
densely populated—and poorer—part of the city. The
worst affected areas were the shanty towns and slums
adjacent to the factory, whose inhabitants worked as
cheap daily labour.

In the immediate aftermath of the disaster, the city
was chaotic. None of its facilities were equipped to
deal with an accident of such magnitude. Chaos was

compounded by the facts that no-one knew how to
treat—or even diagnose—MIC exposure. A whole range
of people poured into the city: from relief workers and
activists to Carbide officials, medical specialists, and
lawyers looking for victims to sign up for compensation
litigation.

As it became evident that the case for compensation
was going to be an enormous one, involving both the
U.S. and India, relief, medical aid, and rehabilitation
all grew to be viewed through the litigatory lens. The
central government stepped in, and said that it—and
only it—would conduct the case on behalf of the
victims. All medical information was put under the
Official Secrets Act, for fear that if the information was
freely available the other side would build up false
counter-information. Documentation of the medical
information was also put under the Official Secrets
Act. Relief and rehabilitation, however, were left to
the state government, and as this was a mammoth task,
considerable resentment was created amongst the
state bureaucracy—and this found its inevitable outlet
in penalising the gas victims.

Bhopal activists leaving police station, Bhopal, 1985

'Union Carbide, quit India, quit the world,' Bhopal, 1985

Janwadi Mahila Samiti demonstration against Union Carbide, Delhi 1985

Zahreeli Gas Kand Virodhi Sangharsh Morcha (Joint Front against Bhopal disaster) Bhopal, 1985

From the very start, it was women gas victims who were most active in campaigns for relief, medical aid and information. In the initial years, the ratio of women to men in demonstrations was something like 60:40, but as the years passed this ratio grew to 80:20, even 90:10. One of the reasons advanced was that sooner rather than later men had to find work, but women, as housewives, had more time—at any rate, their time was more flexible.

While there is some truth in this argument, it has only limited validity. A large number of the women gas victims were themselves workers; many of them became,

Bhopal Gas Peedit Mahila Udyog Sangathan (Organization of Bhopal Women Worker Victims) demonstrating against the Supreme Court's uploading of the government's settlement with carbide

after the disaster, the sole supporters of their families. Further, the organization of gas victims which emerged as chief campaigner from 1986 on was an organization of women gas victims who were employed in the sewing centres which were opened by the government as rehabilitatory training. The centres were opened in 1985, and gave training to roughly 2,000 women; one year later, the government announced that they were going to close the centres down. In protest, the women occupied the centres; the protest lasted well over a month, and out of it emerged the Bhopal Gas Peedit Mahila Udyog Sangathan (the Bhopal working women gas victims organization).

From a campaign to ensure the continuation of employment, the organization took on local campaigns for relief and rehabilitation for all gas victims, and then went on to approach the Court for relief. When in 1989, the Government of India arrived at a shameful settlement with Union Carbide under the aegis of the Supreme Court, the Sangathan launched a massive campaign against the settlement, adopting a multi-pronged strategy of demonstrations, litigation, publicity and lobbying. With the election of a new government in late 1989, they achieved the major breakthrough of winning Rs 360 lakhs as a three year relief grant from the government; getting medical information released; and gaining the support of the government in pleading that the case against Carbide be re-opened.

Sadly, the Supreme Court upheld the settlement in 1992, with the important proviso that this only applied to a settlement of the civil suit against Carbide. Damages under criminal charges remain, thus, as a possible avenue for gaining more adequate justice. The real battle, too, of how to ensure the proper distribution of compensation, has now begun.

NOTES

1. *The Second Citizens Report on the Environment*, Delhi, Centre for the Study of the Environment, 1987. Hereafter CSE Report.
2. B.B. Vohra *The Greening of India*, Delhi, Intact Environmental Series, 1985, p. 1
3. Quoted from *The Approach to the Seventh Plan* in ibid in p. 1.
4. CSE Report, op. cit. pp. 183–84.
5. Gopa Joshi, 'Slandered by the Community in Return' in Madhu Kishwar and Ruth Vanita (eds), op. cit. p. 125
6. Devaki Jain, in *Manushi*, no. 6, 1980.
7. CSE Report, op. cit. p. 178.
8. Radha Bhatt, in ibid.

Afterword: In a Small Personal Voice
(With apologies to Doris Lessing)

As I write this conclusion, large parts of the country are plunged in an agitation around the recent government's decision to implement the recommendations of the Mandal Commission Report, published over a decade ago, advocating the expansion of caste-based job reservations in the administration and public sector. The Report suggested that to the categories of castes entitled to reservation quotas, which until now came under the rubric of 'scheduled castes and tribes', be added a list of 'other backward castes' (OBCs), and special quotas be created for them. Backwardness was to be defined by social status as much as by economic condition.

That the decision was based on fairly complex political calculations is clear. To begin with the more ignoble of these, an obvious purpose was to disrupt the machinations of the ex-Deputy Prime Minister, Devi Lal, and the coterie within the Janata Dal, of which he was a part. The attempt to undermine his base by reaching out to a constituency of rich and middle peasants, however, was one element of a larger attempt to garner support for a government overwhelmed by a host of problems, ranging from communalism to secessionist movements to increasing criminalisation of both the state and civil society to economic, fiscal and resource crises.

Since the decision, the behaviour of both the government and of the agitation against the decision has been ugly. Not only has the government sanctioned police brutality, some of its members actually incited violence: both Ram Vilas Paswan and Sharad Yadav, ministers in the present government, have urged pro-reservationists to fight anti-reservationists in the streets. That this has not happened on a major scale is to the credit of the pro-reservationists. Developments in the anti-reservation agitation have been even more frightening. In the spate of immolations which are now taking place, there have been forcible immolations, that is, murder, as well. Some of the most notorious political thugs in the country have escalated violence amongst the agitators. In many parts the agitation is being used as a cover to loot shops. And from the very start many agitators have engaged in oppressive acts of casteism against members of the 'other backward castes', as well as against members of the scheduled castes.

Today it seems that the government might fall as a result of the Mandal decision and ensuing events. I must confess that this prospect saddens me. When this government came to power, less than a year ago, it appeared to herald a more democratic and representative political era. India, I thought, was not unaffected by the wave of democratisation which was sweeping so many countries, especially East Europe and the Soviet Union. At best, V.P. Singh's early actions encouraged visions of a more moral governance; at the least, I hoped that repressed and distorted movements or issues might now come to the fore and be resolved. Amongst the most important of these were renewed and increasing communal and upper-caste configurations, seeking representation within the state.

In many ways, the Mandal agitation seems to me to be an expression of trends which were brought to our attention, as feminists, with the Muslim Women's Bill and the sati campaigns. In both, anti-feminists articulated a sense of being pushed to the margins of the Indian polity; in both, they formed traditionally-defined identity blocs which, they argued, were being subordinated by modern and urban interest groups. Looking at the Mandal campaign in the context of the two earlier ones, many of the issues are common but the ways in which they are expressed and the ends which they reflect are different. The issues of identity, representation and democracy, in particular, have been central in all three. Yet the identities have differed, as have associated interpretations of representation and democracy. The identities sought in the Muslim Women's Bill agitation were communal-fundamentalist, and the definition of an Indian democratic state was one which gave such identity blocs representation, in proportion to their populations. In the agitation against sati, just over a year later, the identity at issue was casteist, fundamentalist, but a communal link was sought at the same time, through demanding the same representation as above, and citing the same definition of a democratic state. Rajput dharma was here linked with Hindu identity, and in saying 'if the "Muslims" can be accommodated by the state, why cannot the "Hindus", who are a majority?' the Hindus were presented as having a single, cohesive identity. In the Mandal Commission decision, the identity sought is neither communal nor fundamentalist: it is not based on religious definitions, not viewed through the perspective of origins; insofar as it undermines the assertion of a single cohesive Hindu identity, it is even anti-communal. Moreover, while seemingly casteist it disrupts traditional definitions of caste, by polarising the castes into two blocs—the forward, and backward (not even upper and lower). Similarly, the definition of a democratic Indian state here is one based on giving representation using developmental rather than religious criteria.

The agitation around the decision to implement the Mandal Commission recommendations is of course, different from the other two, in that it is in response to an initiative taken by the government, rather than one demanding initiatives of the government. As such, it reflects a significant shift in governmental attitudes towards the issues of communalism, fundamentalism, and the structure of a representative democratic state in India. The 1985–86 Muslim Women's Bill campaign showed us the readiness with which the Indian state accommodated communalism (it did nothing to stop the Ram Janmabhoomi agitation), and balanced this by a concession to fundamentalism (through enacting the Bill). The 1987–88 sati agitation again saw the state attempting a balancing act, but this time with less success: it tacitly okayed the caste fundamentalists and communalists by taking no action against them but did not concede their demand for legitimacy; and it ostensibly legitimised feminist demands by enacting a Bill to punish both sati and its abetters, but did nothing to punish those responsible for Roop Kanwar's immolation, nor did it take any steps for the protection and rehabilitation of widows. The Mandal Commission decision, on the other hand, clearly indicates that the government, among other things, intends to combat Hindu communalism, and is seeking to garner support in this endeavour. As in the Muslim Women's Bill, one of the points of reference for the Mandal decision is the Ram Janmabhoomi agitation. Not only has the Chief Minister of Uttar Pradesh, Mulayam Singh Yadav, appealed to the pro-reservationists to support the campaign for the defence of the Babri Masjid from the Janmabhoomi onslaught, led by the Bharatiya Janata Party (BJP) and the Vishwa Hindu Parishad (VHP), the decision itself has isolated the *Hindu Rashtravadis*, especially the BJP for they do not dare to alienate either caste bloc.

The issue of caste has long been of concern for feminists. When the contemporary feminist movement first began to make its presence felt, in the late nineteen-seventies, we used to cite Manu's couplet, '*dhol, ganwar,*

shudra, adi nari, sab hain tadan ke adhikari' (the drum, the peasant, the untouchable, and the woman, all deserve regular beating), to show that these groups had been traditionally subjected, that there were links in their subjection, and that it was necessary for them to support each other's struggles. In Maharashtra, there was already a link between the feminist and dalit movements: one of the very first women's groups to be formed, the League of Women Soldiers for Equality (see chapter V), came out of the dalit movement in Aurangabad; and in the 1987–88 sati agitation, support for the feminists came from the Maharashtrian dalits.

Historical connections between feminism and the dalit movement go back to the early nineteenth-century. Jyotiba Phule, who was one of the chief founders of the dalit movement was also one of the founders of the movement for women's rights and the reform of their conditions of existence. As we have seen from the first section of this book, the major dalit organization, the Satyashodhak Samaj, was one of the few organizations to actively campaign against child-marriage in the eighteen-nineties, at a time when many upper-caste social reformers were in retreat from the revivalist charge. And, in the nineteen-fifties, the leader of the dalit movement, Ambedkar (who was Law Minister), resigned because the uniform civil code prepared by him was successfully opposed by Hindu communalists.

At the same time, there were also historical connections between feminism and lower-caste movements for Hindu reform, such as the Arya Samaj. Dayanand Saraswati, like Phule, was an advocate of women's education; he made it clear, however, that this education, together with everything else, had to be defined and circumscribed by a reformed Hindu caste society, which would rule in India. The thrust of his efforts was towards sanskritization and conversion; from its inception the Arya Samaj has been communal, and remains so today. Indeed, Saraswati's views on women never had the breadth and compassion of Phule's: it is impossible to imagine him proposing to set up a home for women where they could come and bear illegitimate children. Over the years the Arya Samaj has taken increasingly conservative attitudes towards women's rights: today it is as strictly anti-feminist as it is communal.

Whether the reforms envisaged by the Mandal decision represent another kind of sanskritization for the lower and middle castes, via the state or whether they will give a fillip to the dalit movement instead, remains to be seen. What is clear is that, even if the government falls, the decision to give representative reservation to 'other backward castes' cannot be withdrawn.

The issues of reservation and representation have come up in both pre and post-Independence feminist movements: while the former was opposed to any statutory measures on either, the contemporary women's movement has shown more complex and ambiguous responses. The position of the pre-Independence feminists was based on the belief that an Independent Indian state would create equal opportunities for women; post-Independence feminists, on the contrary, hold that such a belief has long been exploded. The question for them, therefore, has been: through what means and which measures can better opportunities be created? For many, one of the answers has been reservation: feminists in Maharashtra, for example, demanded that the state make twenty-five per cent reservation of jobs for women statutory in all sectors of employment in the late nineteen-seventies. This demand, however, was not taken up or pressed for across the country, and appears now to have lapsed. I remember being one of the feminists who felt uneasy about the demand at that point: it seemed to me to bypass the real issues of equality of opportunity, and allow the social division of labour to go unchallenged. While these points remain valid for me, they no longer seem adequate grounds for rejecting reservation per se. Within the highly restricted scope of short-term electoral politics, reservation might be an achievable reform, and there is no doubt that it would provide immediate benefit to a large number of women. At the same time, as feminists we have always been critical of narrowly pragmatic approaches, of short-term reformism and of opportunism. The experience of reservation within state-controlled employment, especially in the administration, for scheduled castes and scheduled tribes, has shown that by itself it is an insufficient measure: to be effective it needs to be accompanied by education, training, etc. Turning to the issue of job reservation, in industry for example, there are several problems. Given that the fall in women's employment has been steady since the nineteen-thirties, and is now drastic in industries which were among the major employers of women, such as mines and textiles, it is clear that firm steps need to be taken to provide jobs for women. But what should such steps consist of? The protection of existing jobs in sick industries is again a narrow and short-term step, for it merely pushes those industries into a more acute crisis. There is, too, a trend towards the casualization of work, in a series of ways, from the putting-out system to the rise of small worksheds to the development of hi-tech outfits which minimize on labour. Schemes for diversification into socially-useful products (suggested and elaborated by workers themselves) would be a very timely intervention in this process in India. If adequately made and popularized, these could actually influence the course of our economic development. Descending from these heights, to look at the kinds of protection and resistance that are possible for women in the context of the powerlessness entailed by casualization, SEWA provides a kind of ideal, bringing together the alienated and

'self-employed' into a union. Starting with a union for street-vendors, SEWA has moved into forms of women's work which are governed by the putting-out system: while unionizing the women thus employed, they realized that one of their major problems was the provision of raw materials. The contractor expected women to buy their own raw materials: when individually bought, these cost much more than they would have done if bought in bulk; as women are paid by the piece and not by the costs of producing the piece, this cut into their already small earnings; so they formed co-operatives to buy the materials in bulk and provide them at cost-price to union members. SEWA, thus has developed one of the most useful ways of aiding women victims of casualization: through an imaginative combination of trade-union and co-operative.[1]

Going back to the issue of reservation, for feminists this issue has become crucial in terms of the ongoing debate on representation through reservation of seats for women in elective political bodies, from the village level *panchayat* upwards. Here again, I remember that in the early days of the contemporary women's movement many of us used to scoff at the idea that women's representation in such bodies would actually further feminism: our view was that such representation automatically led to de-radicalization, and that the women engaging in it would always put their own political interests above a feminist cause. Today there is not only a section of socialist-feminists arguing in favour of representative reservation for women in electoral politics, but many of the rest of us too would hesitate to dismiss their arguments out of hand. There are several reasons for this shift. Firstly, it has become increasingly evident that the contemporary Indian state is not only heterogeneous but makeshift. The loss of legitimacy it suffered from the late nineteen-sixties on grew acute in the mid-seventies, since when we have witnessed the intensifying struggles of different and opposed groups not only for representation within the state, but for supremacy over it. Communalism has been one of the strongest contenders in this battle, and from the mid-eighties on there has been a growing feeling amongst most radical movements that we must strengthen the hands of anti-communalists within the state not just by working 'with' them to whatever extent possible, but also by increasing their numbers. At the same time, what these struggles have done is to open up the sphere of electoral politics in such a way as to make it not only possible for more and more groups to enter, but almost imperative: for it is also clear that self-representation might be the only way to defend the rights of any one group. The question now being asked by many feminists is whether the movement is sufficiently advanced to avail of such reservation and the argument is, if we aren't, then we shouldn't support it.

Secondly, there has been growing interest within the feminist movement about the administration and organization of society. In part this is an extension of earlier developments: if in the early eighties feminists began to feel the need to create their own structures to aid individual women, it is not surprising that by the late eighties and early nineties this should have led to a desire to engage in and attempt to change existing administrative and political structures. Putting it another way, most movements for the rights of particular groups have sought (and when strong, won) representation in various spheres of social organization: The movement for workers' rights, for example, sought representation both through and within trade-unions; the trade-union movement has sought representation in Parliament, and has to some extent won it. As the Indian women's movement has gained in strength, it is not surprising, therefore, that they too should seek mainstream political representation. What is interesting is that this development has begun with panchayat and district level elections, not state or national ones.

Thirdly, as the movement has grown, feminist sympathies themselves have become wider and more liberal. The mutual sense of threat that pervaded relations between party-based women's organizations (especially on the left) and autonomous feminist groups has gradually lessened as the grounds of difference have shrunk. The attacks on feminism which have been made by movements attacking secularism and democracy have forged bonds between communist, socialist and autonomous women's organizations, albeit that these are weak. At the same time, with over ten years of activity below our belts, there is heightened confidence among feminists, as the following extract from a document prepared recently by the Bombay Forum Against the Oppression of Women shows:

Fears have also been expressed of other more organised parties taking over the Forum. This may be one of the 'remnants' of our political past, where often a fear psychosis of 'the other' taking over or messing up 'our organisation' was an essential element in our adherence to it. But there was also a basis to it—women from the organised political parties were a part of the Forum in the earlier period. This was one of the first experiences that many women from the Forum were having in terms of working with women from the organised left parties. We had heard of their mode of functioning, seen it partially in their participation in the Forum and there was an element of mistrust in terms of their motives in the Forum.

But this fear was not merely in the initial stages of the Forum when it was to some extent under-standable as all of us were unsure of the nature and structure of the organisation. Even after 3–4 years of our existence, this did come up once again, this time vis-a-vis a much smaller party women's group. The debate was about the structure and membership of the Forum. This small group felt that the Forum should be a federation of different groups and though any women could come to the meetings, in terms of the decisions made, every group within the forum would have only one vote. On the other hand, others in the Forum felt that we came to the Forum and related to it and to each other as individual feminists and not as members of other groups; that the Forum should be a group in its own right and not a mere federation of other groups. This attempt by the women's group was felt to be an attempt in 'taking over' the Forum. Maybe it was, from their point of view. Maybe it was not. And there will be many such grounds for this feeling. But by this time in fact the Forum was much more conscious of itself—that a 'taking over' of the Forum was an impossibility. What is there to take over? The Forum has no office, no structure. It is defined only by its activities and if anyone wants to take up those activities, so far so good! But, we suppose, it takes longer and more confidence to bury the ghosts of the past![2]

One of the themes of the annual women's liberation conference to be held at the end of this year is 'women in the political process'. The outline of issues to be addressed under this rubric includes electoral representation, obstacles faced by women engaged in mainstream politics, including women M.P.s, etc. Underlying this is an assumption that it is possible, and necessary, to relate to women 'leaders' on shared gender problems, irrespective of ideological difference. To some extent, such an assumption is based on the influence which the feminist movement has had on mainstream politics, however restricted this might have been so far. One example of this is the induction of younger women, who have been formed by the feminist years without necessarily representing a 'women's vote', or being feminist (Subhasini Ali comes immediately to mind).

Looking back over the years of the contemporary Indian feminist movement one cannot but be struck by how enormously it has spread and how rich it is. It is perhaps the only movement today which encompasses, and links such issues as work, wages, organization, environment, ecology, civil rights, sex, violence, representation, caste, class, allocation of basic resources, consumer rights, methods of production, health, religion, community, individual and social relationships, etc. An index of its influence is the extraordinarily large participation of women in most radical campaigns, particularly in urban areas, where one often finds a preponderance of women in human and social rights campaigns. If, for example, the Bhopal gas victims are finally receiving some of the care that they have needed for many years, it is solely due to the efforts of the women among them, who have not ceased to fight for their rights from the very start, forming an organization called the Bhopal Gas Peedit Mahila Udyog Sangathan in 1986, in the face of what were hugely dispiriting odds.

This link between the feminist movement and a whole host of other democratic and radical movements was present in pre-Independence India as well. Even more interesting, both pre and post-Independence feminists criticised 'Western' feminists for failing to make such links, for being introverted. One of the most fascinating of the discoveries made in the course of working on this book is of how important it has been for both pre and post-Independence feminists to maintain a distinction between themselves and 'Western' feminism, almost as if it was through this that they—and we—would prove our anti-colonial and anti-imperialist credentials. Hard on the heels of this realization followed another: that what was being said at the same time was that different societies produced different feminisms, a truism which however assumes significance in the context of feminism itself being attacked as 'Western.'

If the statement of difference from 'Western' feminism is seen, here, as being an attempt to negotiate a space for feminism within this society, it follows that the idea of feminism itself as Western was rejected by pre-Independence feminists, and continues to be rejected by post-Independence feminists. What is being claimed then is a kind of universalism, of which, Western feminism is one stream and Indian feminism another. However, nothing is as simple as that. How 'Western' or 'Indian' feminism is defined, and what the precise differences between them are, is still unclear. One of the points of definition which pre-Independence feminists used was that Western feminists were pitted against men, whereas Indian feminists were not. This was explained on the grounds that while the suffragettes had had to struggle for the vote, 'our men' (i.e. the Indian National Congress) supported the demand for female suffrage. In other words, Indian feminists were not anti-male because our men were better than Western men. In post-Independence India, few feminists have claimed that our men are better than Western men, but nonetheless 'Western' feminism has been identified as being 'separatist'. While separatist covers wider ground than anti-male (it could for example include being against any support for other liberation movements), the allegation of anti-male remains. Its importance, however, has diminished vastly over the years: where ten years ago endless time was consumed in debates over whether or not men would be appealed to to join feminist demonstrations and campaigns, today the issue almost never comes up, not because droves of men have joined us, but because it is taken for granted that it is important for women to make a show of strength.

While criticizing 'Western' feminism, contemporary Indian feminists have also made two other points: that the emphasis on personal politics has led to introversion and de-politicization; and that the concerns of the movement are too narrowly restricted to 'sexual politics'. If the echoes of much conventional Marxist criticism of feminism can be heard here, so can a fainter sound of Gandhianism. It was he, after all, who went and lectured feminists in the West in the 1930s, on how their feminism was narrow and self-centred, and how much they needed to learn from satyagraha, especially the self-sacrifice shown by Indian women.

That there are certain grains of truth in these criticisms is undeniable. The apparent dominance of postmodernist, especially Lacanian, ideas in the French feminist movement is disconcerting to us, for whom the problems of poverty and illiteracy are essential points of reference. The privileging of subjective knowledge in the English feminist movement appeared to provide an avenue for many feminists to justify ignorance, political apathy, and even violence. The feminist movement of the United States appeared to be dominated by reformist organizations such as the National Organization of Women. Yet these are all partial examples. The same criticisms that Indian feminists make have been made within, as well as without, feminist movements in all these countries. Indeed, one may well ask whether there is any such thing as a feminist movement in the West. Does the Black feminist movement in the United States qualify as a 'Western' movement or not? Similarly, how do we classify the Asian feminist movement in England? Admittedly, this is a Catch 22 situation: if we call the Black and Asian feminist movements 'Western', then we ignore many if not all of the things that 'the West' stands for, especially as defined by anti-colonial, and anti-imperialist movements. On the other hand, if we allow them to remain separate or outside 'the West', then we indirectly accept racism and the kind of lesser-citizen or second-rate status that Blacks, Asians, and other poor immigrant communities have and are struggling against.

We are today living in a period when the boundaries of the West are being redrawn. With the disintegration of the Soviet bloc, the division of Europe into East and West is coming to an end. The creation of new relationships between the more economically developed countries of Western Europe and the poorer countries of Eastern Europe is bound to be conflict-ridden. Racial and communal conflicts have rapidly spread in Germany with the pressure on employment entailed by reunification, and the consequent threat to existing West German immigrant populations in Rumania in the late eighties, with Ceasescu's brutal treatment of the large Hungarian population which lives there. The uncertainty of Germany's stand on the border with Poland might well lead to the rise of communal-nationalist conflict within Poland, which has a large German minority population.

Many of the countries which are currently in the process of democratization contain large traditional groups. The matter of representation might well become as complex as in India. In Poland, for example, it has already come up in relation to religious identity, and it is interesting that one of its first expressions has been through the assertion that the Church should determine the legal rights of women, (for example, the Solidarity-sponsored move for a ban on abortion). In Yugoslavia, communal conflict within and about the erstwhile autonomous province Kossovo focussed on women in a way that has been familiar to us for more than a hundred years: through constructing the image of the primitive and barbaric Moslem, who keeps his own women locked up and rapes 'ours' (the conflict is between Serbians and Albanians).[3]

Though the media have marginalized the peace and democracy movements which were crucial actors in the fall of their repressive regimes, we should not do so.

Major opposition to the communal conflict in Yugoslavia has come from women's groups which were part of these movements. Equally, the issue of abortion might well give rise to one of the first feminist campaigns in Poland.

In the struggle for the reconstitution of 'the West' it is these groups which have held out, and continue to hold, visions of a more democratic, less exploitative, international community. The Indian feminist movement has long experience of some of the problems which these groups are dealing with: in particular of tradition and modernity, the constitution of ethnic, religious and community identities and nationalism. We have a great deal to share, not least because our approaches both to these problems and to the issue of democracy are particular. It may be, that were we to do so, we might be able to raise the issues of racism, immigration, exploitation, cultural bias et al, which have been so important in our critique of 'the West' and 'Western feminism', in a new and more fruitful way.

The Indian feminist movement is today one of the most sophisticated in the world. It is time for us to build on that.

October 1990

NOTES

1. Renana Jhabwala: 'Self-Employed Women's Association: Organising Women by Struggle and Development', paper presented at a workshop on 'Empowering Women in the Casualised Trades', July 24–Aug 1, 1990, hosted by the World Institute for Development Economics Research, Helsinki.
2. Forum Against the Oppression of Women, Bombay: 'Sharing our problems in the FAOW — its Organisational structure and Functioning', cyclostyled paper, FAOW, Bombay.
3. Yugoslavia is of course not part of 'the West',

though there are pressures for some of its republics to seek inclusion (Slovenia, for example), just as the current Soviet leadership is seeking such inclusion, and so are some of the Baltic republics (Estonia, for example). However, the Yugoslav peace, feminist and social-democratic movements are important constituents in the east west networks that the new social movements built up from the nineteen-eighties on, and which could form a kind of internationalist pressure group.

Index

Photo Credits

Illustrations and photographs for this book have been collected sporadically, over the years, while this project has been in the making. Several people have sent in material to us, and in some instances have done so without identifying themselves or indeed the photographers. While every effort has been made to trace them and to credit every illustrator/photographer, this has not always been possible. We would, however, be happy to hear from readers if they can help us to trace a source that we have not been able to identify and will make every attempt to include it in the next edition of this book. We are grateful to the following individuals/organizations for giving us permission to use their illustrations/ photographs.

Ahmedabad Women's Action Group (AWAG) pp. 110–11, 146

Baiyeja Women's magazine p. 154

Bhopal Gas Peedit Mahila Udyog Sangathan p. 189 (right)

Sheba Chhachhi pp. 6, 109, 116, 118–21, 123–25, 129 (left), 130–35, 144 (centre and below), 147 (below), 148, 156 (above and below left), 157–59, 162, 164–66, 169–70, 172, 173 (above), 175—77, 189 (below)

Chattisgarh Mahila Jagruti Sangathan pp. 150, 152 (below)

Chhaya Datar p. 96

Eve's Weekly pp. 112 (below right), 144 (above left), 151 (below right), 152 (above)

Forum Against the Oppression of Women p. 112 (below right)

Hindustan Times pp. 129 (right), 189 (left)

Jagori/Abha Bhaiya pp 178–80

A.G. Krishna Menon p. 186

National Archives of India (NAI) pp 7, 98
National Federation of Indian Women p. 161
Nehru Memorial Museum and Library (NMML) pp. 7, 26, 34, 39, 42, 46, 48, 55–56, 58–63, 65, 75–79, 84, 86–88

Vibhuti Patel pp. 106–7, 147 (above)
Patriot p. 142
Pennuramai Iyakkam p. 156 (below right)
Peoples Association for Himalayan Action Research (PRAHAR) p 187
Private family collection p. 173 (above and below left)
Saheli 162 (below)
Maria Soderberg pp. 149, 153
Abhishek Srivastava p. 188

Vimochana p. 108

In addition, photos-illustrations on the following pages have been taken from the sources named below:

— p. 16–17, 22–23 from Mary Frances Billington *Women in India* reprinted Delhi, Amarko Book Agency, 1973;
— pp. 33–35 from A *Second Paradise*, Doubleday, 1985;
—pp. 38–39, 89 from *India's Freedom Struggle*;
— p. 43 from Pandita Ramabai Saraswati, *The High Caste Hindu Woman*;
— p. 44 from Asit Paul (ed.) *Woodcut Prints of Nineteenth Century Calcutta*, Calcutta, Seagull Books, 1983

The following documents are included courtesy of the National Archives of India

(a) Text of the Sati Regulation XVII A.D. 1829 of the Bengal Code (4 December 1929);
(b) Petition of the Hindus against the abolition of sati (19 December 1829);
(c) A bill to remove all legal obstacles to the marriage of Hindu widows;
(d) A bill to restrain the solemnisation of child marriages;
(e) Resolutions passed at the All-India anti-Hindu Code Convention held at Jaipur on the 16th, 17th and 18th December 1948.

Pictures on the following pages have not been credited as the names of the photographers were not available:
101–2, 104, 109 (above left and right), 151 (above left and right and below right), 182–83